Lecture Notes in Computer Science 4184

Commenced Publication in 1973
Founding and Former Series Editors:
Gerhard Goos, Juris Hartmanis, and Jan van Leeuwen

T0224637

Mario Bravetti   Manuel Núñez
Gianluigi Zavattaro (Eds.)

Web Services and Formal Methods

Third International Workshop, WS-FM 2006
Vienna, Austria, September 8-9, 2006
Proceedings

 Springer

Volume Editors

Mario Bravetti
Università di Bologna
Department of Computer Science
Via Sacchi 3, 47023 Cesena (FC), Italy
E-mail: bravetti@cs.unibo.it

Manuel Núñez
Facultad de Informática (UCM)
28040 Madrid, Spain
E-mail: mn@sip.ucm.es

Gianluigi Zavattaro
Università di Bologna
Dipartimento di Scienze dell' Informazione
Mura A. Zamboni, 7, 40127 Bologna, Italy
E-mail: zavattar@cs.unibo.it

Library of Congress Control Number: 2006931574

CR Subject Classification (1998): D.2.4, C.2.4, F.3, D.4, C.4, K.4.4, C.2

LNCS Sublibrary: SL 2 – Programming and Software Engineering

ISSN   0302-9743
ISBN-10   3-540-38862-1 Springer Berlin Heidelberg New York
ISBN-13   978-3-540-38862-3 Springer Berlin Heidelberg New York

Springer is a part of Springer Science+Business Media

springer.com

© Springer-Verlag Berlin Heidelberg 2006
Printed in Germany

Typesetting: Camera-ready by author, data conversion by Scientific Publishing Services, Chennai, India
Printed on acid-free paper   SPIN: 11841197   06/3142   5 4 3 2 1 0

Preface

This volume contains the proceedings of the international workshop WS-FM (Web Services and Formal Methods) held at Vienna University of Technology, Vienna, Austria, during September 8-9, 2006.

The International Workshop on Web Services and Formal Methods aims to bring together researchers working on Web services and formal methods in order to activate a fruitful collaboration in this direction of research. This, potentially, could also have a great impact on the current standardization phase of Web service technologies. The main topics of the conference include: protocols and standards for WS (SOAP, WSDL, UDDI, etc.); languages and descripion methodologies for Choreography/Orchestration/Workflow (BPML, XLANG and BizTalk, WSFL, WS-BPEL, etc.); coordination techniques for WS (transactions, agreement, coordination services, etc.); semantics-based dynamic WS discovery services (based on Semantic Web/ontology techniques or other semantic theories); security, performance evaluation and quality of service of WS; semi-structured data and XML related technologies; comparisons with different related technologies/approaches.

This third edition of the workshop (WS-FM 2006) featured 15 papers selected among 40 submissions after a rigorous review process by international reviewers and three invited talks by Wil van der Aalst (Eindhoven University of Technology, The Netherlands), Roberto Bruni (University of Pisa, Italy) and Schahram Dustdar (Vienna University of Technology, Austria). These contributions brought an additional dimension to the technical and the scientific merit of the workshop. This volume of the proceedings contains the 15 selected papers and three papers related to the invited talks.

WS-FM 2006 was held as an official event of "The Process Modelling Group" (a resarch group which promotes study and experimentation in business processes whose members mainly work in academia, for software companies or as part of standards bodies) and in conjunction with the 4th International Conference on Business Process Management (BPM 2006).

We owe special thanks to all members of the Program Committee of WS-FM 2006 and their sub-referees for their work. Finally, our thanks go to the University of Technology of Vienna for hosting the workshop and for their support in the workshop organization.

September 2006

Mario Bravetti
Manuel Núñez
Gianluigi Zavattaro

Organization

Program Committee

Co-chairs

Mario Bravetti   University of Bologna (Italy)
Gianluigi Zavattaro   University of Bologna (Italy)

Board of "The Process Modelling Group"

Wil van der Aalst   Eindhoven Univ. of Technology, The Netherlands
Rob van Glabbeek   NICTA, Sydney, Australia
Keith Harrison-Broninski   Role Modellers Ltd.
Robin Milner   Cambridge University, UK
Roger Whitehead   Office Futures

Other PC Members

Marco Aiello   University of Trento (Italy)
Farhad Arbab   CWI, The Netherlands
Matteo Baldoni   University of Turin, Italy
Jean-Pierre Banatre   University of Rennes 1 and INRIA, France
Boualem Benatallah   University of New South Wales, Australia
Karthik Bhargavan   Microsoft Research Cambridge, UK
Roberto Bruni   University of Pisa, Italy
Michael Butler   University of Southampton, UK
Fabio Casati   HP Labs, USA
Rocco De Nicola   University of Florence, Italy
Marlon Dumas   Queensland University of Technology, Australia
Schahram Dustdar   Vienna University of Technology, Austria
Gianluigi Ferrari   University of Pisa, Italy
Jose Luiz Fiadeiro   University of Leicester, UK
Stefania Gnesi   CNR Pisa, Italy
Reiko Heckel   University of Leicester, UK
Kohei Honda   Queen Mary, University of London, UK
Nickolas Kavantzas   Oracle Co., USA
Leila Kloul   Université de Versailles, France
Cosimo Laneve   University of Bologna, Italy
Mark Little   Arjuna Technologies Limited, UK
Natalia López   University Complutense of Madrid, Spain
Roberto Lucchi   University of Bologna, Italy
Jeff Magee   Imperial College London, UK

Fabio Martinelli	CNR Pisa, Italy
Manuel Mazzara	University of Bolzano, Italy
Ugo Montanari	University of Pisa, Italy
Shin Nakajima	National Institute of Informatics and JST, Japan
Manuel Nunez	University Complutense of Madrid, Spain
Fernando Pelayo	University of Castilla-La Mancha, Albacete, Spain
Marco Pistore	University of Trento, Italy
Wolfgang Reisig	Humboldt University, Berlin, Germany
Vladimiro Sassone	University of Sussex, UK
Marjan Sirjani	Tehran University, Iran
Friedrich Vogt	Technical University of Hamburg-Harburg, Germany
Martin Wirsing	Ludwig Maximilians University Munich, Germany

Additional Referees

Massimo Bartoletti	Stephanie Kemper	Marinella Petrocchi
Marzia Buscemi	Natallia Kokash	Stephan Reiff-Marganiec
Samuele Carpineti	Alessandro Lapadula	Bilel Remmache
Diego Cazorla	Luis Llana	Shamim Ripon
Corina Cirstea	Mieke Massink	Ismael Rodriguez
Sara Corfini	Ilaria Matteucci	Francesco Tiezzi
Fernando Cuartero	Hernan Melgratti	Angelo Troina
Alberto de la Encina	Sebastian Menge	Emilio Tuosto
Berndt Farwer	Mercedes G. Merayo	Divakar Yadav
Fatemeh Ghassemi	Leonardo Mezzina	Uwe Zdun
Dieter Gollmann	Luca Padovani	

Organizing Committee

Chair

Manuel Núñez	University Complutense of Madrid, Spain

Local Chair

Friedrich Neubarth	Austrian Research Institute for Artificial Intelligence

Other Members

Mario Bravetti	University of Bologna, Italy
Gregorio Díaz	Universidad Castilla-La Mancha, Spain
Alberto de la Encina	Universidad Complutense de Madrid, Spain
Roberto Lucchi	University of Bologna, Italy
Mercedes G. Merayo	Universidad Complutense de Madrid, Spain
Gianluigi Zavattaro	University of Bologna, Italy

Table of Contents

I Invited Papers

DecSerFlow: Towards a Truly Declarative Service Flow Language 1
W.M.P. van der Aalst, M. Pesic

Service QoS Composition at the Level of Part Names 24
Marco Aiello, Florian Rosenberg, Christian Platzer,
Agata Ciabattoni, Schahram Dustdar

SCC: A Service Centered Calculus 38
M. Boreale, R. Bruni, L. Caires, R. De Nicola, I. Lanese, M. Loreti,
F. Martins, U. Montanari, A. Ravara, D. Sangiorgi, V. Vasconcelos,
G. Zavattaro

II Contributed Papers

Computational Logic for Run-Time Verification of Web Services
Choreographies: Exploiting the *SOCS-SI* Tool 58
Marco Alberti, Federico Chesani, Marco Gavanelli, Evelina Lamma,
Paola Mello, Marco Montali, Sergio Storari, Paolo Torroni

Semantic Querying of Mathematical Web Service Descriptions 73
Rebhi Baraka, Wolfgang Schreiner

Verified Reference Implementations of WS-Security Protocols 88
Karthikeyan Bhargavan, Cédric Fournet, Andrew D. Gordon

From BPEL Processes to YAWL Workflows 107
Antonio Brogi, Razvan Popescu

Translating Orc Features into Petri Nets and the Join Calculus 123
Roberto Bruni, Hernán Melgratti, Emilio Tuosto

Dynamic Constraint-Based Invocation of Web Services 138
Diletta Cacciagrano, Flavio Corradini, Rosario Culmone,
Leonardo Vito

A Formal Account of Contracts for Web Services..................... 148
  S. Carpineti, G. Castagna, C. Laneve, L. Padovani

Execution Semantics for Service Choreographies 163
  Gero Decker, Johannes Maria Zaha, Marlon Dumas

Analysis and Verification of Time Requirements Applied to the Web
Services Composition 178
  Gregorio Díaz, María-Emilia Cambronero, M. Llanos Tobarra,
  Valentín Valero, Fernando Cuartero

A Formal Approach to Service Component Architecture 193
  José Luiz Fiadeiro, Antónia Lopes, Laura Bocchi

Evaluating the Scalability of a Web Service-Based Distributed
e-Learning and Course Management System 214
  Stephen Gilmore, Mirco Tribastone

Choreography Conformance Analysis: Asynchronous Communications
and Information Alignment 227
  Raman Kazhamiakin, Marco Pistore

Application of Model Checking to AXML System's Security:
A Case Study 242
  Il-Gon Kim, Debmalya Biswas

Towards a Unifying Theory for Web Services Composition 257
  Manuel Mazzara, Ivan Lanese

Towards the Formal Model and Verification of Web Service
Choreography Description Language............................... 273
  Zhao Xiangpeng, Yang Hongli, Qiu Zongyan

Author Index... 289

DecSerFlow: Towards a Truly Declarative Service Flow Language

W.M.P. van der Aalst and M. Pesic

Department of Information Systems, Eindhoven University of Technology,
P.O. Box 513, NL-5600 MB, Eindhoven, The Netherlands
w.m.p.v.d.aalst@tm.tue.nl, m.pesic@tm.tue.nl

Abstract. The need for process support in the context of web services has triggered the development of many languages, systems, and standards. Industry has been developing software solutions and proposing standards such as BPEL, while researchers have been advocating the use of formal methods such as Petri nets and π-calculus. The languages developed for *service flows*, i.e., process specification languages for web services, have adopted many concepts from classical workflow management systems. As a result, these languages are rather procedural and this does not fit well with the autonomous nature of services. Therefore, we propose *DecSerFlow* as a *Declarative Service Flow Language*. DecSerFlow can be used to specify, enact, and monitor service flows. The language is extendible (i.e., constructs can be added without changing the engine or semantical basis) and can be used to enforce or to check the conformance of service flows. Although the language has an appealing graphical representation, it is grounded in temporal logic.

Keywords: Service flows, web services, workflow management, flexibility, temporal logic.

1 Introduction

The *Business Process Execution Language for Web Services* (BPEL4WS, or BPEL for short) has become the de-facto standard for implementing processes based on web services [7]. Systems such as Oracle BPEL Process Manager, IBM WebSphere Application Server Enterprise, IBM WebSphere Studio Application Developer Integration Edition, and Microsoft BizTalk Server 2004 support BPEL, thus illustrating the practical relevance of this language. Although intended as a language for connecting web services, its application is not limited to cross-organizational processes. It is expected that in the near future a wide variety of process-aware information systems [8] will be realized using BPEL. Whilst being a powerful language, BPEL is of a *procedural nature* and not very different from classical workflow languages e.g., the languages used by systems such as Staffware, COSA, SAP Workflow, and IBM WebSphere MQ Workflow (formerly know as FlowMark). Also other languages proposed in the context of web services are of a procedural nature, e.g., the *Web Services Choreography*

M. Bravetti, M. Nuñes, and G. Zavattaro (Eds.): WS-FM 2006, LNCS 4184, pp. 1–23, 2006.

Description Language (WS-CDL) [16]. In this paper, we will not discuss these languages in detail. The interested reader is referred to [2,3,20] for a critical review of languages like BPEL. Instead, we will demonstrate that it is possible to use a more declarative style of specification by introducing *DecSerFlow*: a *Declarative Service Flow Language*.

To explain the difference between a procedural style and a declarative style of modeling, we use a simple example. Suppose that there are two activities A and B. Both *can* be executed multiple times but they *exclude* each other, i.e., after the first occurrence of A it is not allowed to do B anymore and after the first occurrence of B it is not allowed to do A. The following execution sequences are possible based on this verbal description: *[ ]* (the empty execution sequence), *[A]*, *[B]*, *[A,A]*, *[B,B]*, etc. In a *procedural* language it is difficult to specify the above process without implicitly introducing additional assumptions and constraints. In a procedural language one typically needs to make a choice with respect to whether no activities are to be executed, only A activities are to be executed, or only B activities are to be executed. Moreover, the number of times A or B needs to be executed also has to be decided. This means that one or more decision activities need to be executed before the execution of "real" activities can start. (Note that this is related to the Deferred Choice pattern described in [4].) The introduction of these decision activities typically leads to an over-specification of the process. Designers may be tempted to make this decision before the actual execution of the first A or B. This triggers the following two questions: (1) "How is this decision made?" and (2) "When is this decision made?". The designer may even remove the choice altogether and simply state that one can only do A activities. Using a more *declarative* style can avoid this over-specification. For example, in *Linear Temporal Logic* (LTL) [11,12,13] one can write $\neg(\Diamond A \wedge \Diamond B)$. This means that it cannot be the case that eventually A is executed and that eventually B is executed. This shows that a very compact LTL expression ($\neg(\Diamond A \wedge \Diamond B)$) can describe exactly what is needed without forcing the designer to specify more than strictly needed. Unfortunately, languages like LTL are difficult to use for non-experts. Therefore, we have developed a graphical language (DecSerFlow) that allows for the easy specification of processes in a declarative manner. DecSerFlow is mapped onto LTL. The innovative aspects of our approach based on DecSerFlow are:

- DecSerFlow allows for a *declarative style* of modeling which is highly relevant in the context of service flows (unlike languages like BPEL).
- Through the *graphical representation* of DecSerFlow this language is easy to use and we avoid the problems of textual languages like LTL.
- We use LTL not only for the verification of model properties: we also use the LTL formulas generated by DecSerFlow to *dynamically monitor services* and to realize an *enactment engine*.
- DecSerFlow is an extendible language (i.e., we supply an editor to extend the language with user-defined graphical constructs without the need to modify any part of the system).

– DecSerFlow can be used to specify two types of constraints: *hard* constraints and *soft* constraints. Hard constraints are enforced by the engine while soft constraints are only used to warn before the violation takes place and to monitor observed violations.

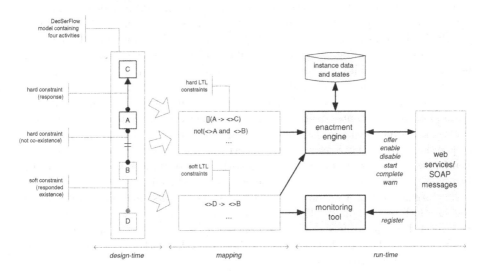

Fig. 1. Overview of the role played by DecSerFlow in supporting services flows

Figure 1 provides an overview of the way we envision DecSerFlow to be used. At design-time, a graphical model is made using the DecSerFlow notation. (Note that at design-time users can also add new modeling elements - types of constraints.) The left-hand side of Figure 1 shows a process composed of four activities, A, B, C, and D. Moreover, three constraints are shown. The connection between A and C means that any occurrence of A should eventually be followed by at least one occurrence of C (i.e., $\Box(A \rightarrow \Diamond C)$ in LTL terms). The connection between A and B means that it cannot be the case that eventually A is executed and that eventually B is executed. This is the constraint described before, i.e., $\neg(\Diamond A \land \Diamond B)$ in LTL terms. The last constraint connecting D and B is a soft constraint. This constraint states that any occurrence of D implies also the occurrence of B (before or after the occurrence of D), e.g., $[B,D,D,D,D]$, $[D,D,D,B]$, and $[B,B,B]$ are valid executions. The LTL formulation of this constraint is $\Diamond D \rightarrow \Diamond B$.

As Figure 1 shows, it is possible to automatically map the graphical model onto LTL formulas. These formulas can be used by the enactment engine to control the service flow, e.g., on the basis of hard constraints the engine can allow or prohibit certain activities and on the basis of soft constraints warnings can be issued. The soft constraints can also be used by the monitoring tool to detect and analyze violations.

Currently, we have implemented a graphical editor and the mapping of the editor to LTL. This editor supports user-defined notations as described before. We are currently investigating different ways to enact LTL formulas and in this paper we described our current efforts. Although we do not elaborate this this in this paper, our implementation will also incorporate data as is show in Figure 1. Data is used for routing purposes by making constraints data dependent, i.e., a constraint only applies if its guard evaluates to true. Moreover, in the context of the ProM (Process Mining) framework [6,18] we have developed an LTL checker [1] to compare actual behavior with specified behavior. The actual behavior can be recorded by a dedicated process engine. However, it can also be obtained by monitoring SOAP messages as described in [3].

The approach described in Figure 1 is not limited to service flows. It can be applied in any context where *autonomous* entities are executing activities. These autonomous entities can be other organizations but also people or groups of people. This is the reason that DecSerFlow has a "sister language" named *ConDec* which aims at supporting teamwork and workflow flexibility [17]. Both languages/applications share the same concepts and tools.

The remainder of this paper is organized as follows. Section 2 introduces the DecSerFlow language. Then, a non-trivial example is given in Section 3. Section 4 discusses different ways to construct an enactment (and monitoring) engine based on DecSerFlow. Finally, Section 5 concludes the paper by discussing different research directions.

2   DecSerFlow: A Declarative Service Flow Language

Languages such as *Linear Temporal Logic* (LTL) [11,12,13] allow for the a more declarative style of modeling. These languages include temporal operators such as next-time ($\bigcirc F$), eventually ($\Diamond F$), always ($\Box F$), and until ($F \sqcup G$). However, such languages are difficult to read. Therefore, we define an extendible graphical syntax for some typical constraints encountered in service flows. The combination of this graphical language and the mapping of this graphical language to LTL forms the *Declarative Service Flow (DecSerFlow) Language* . We propose DecSerFlow for the *specification of a single service, simple service compositions, and more complex choreographies*.

Developing a model in DecSerFlow starts with creating activities. The notion of an activity is like in any other workflow-like language, i.e., an activity is atomic and corresponds to a logical unit of work. However, the nature of the *relations between activities* in DecSerFlow can be quite different than in traditional procedural workflow languages (like Petri nets and BPEL). For example, places between activities in a Petri net describe causal dependencies and can be used to specify sequential, parallel, alternative, and iterative routing. Using such mechanisms it is both possible and necessary to strictly define *how* the flow will be executed. We refer to relations between activities in DecSerFlow as *constraints*. Each of the constraints represents a policy (or a business rule). At any point in time during the execution of a service, each constraint evaluates to *true* or *false*. This value can change during the execution. If a constraint has the value *true*, the referring policy is fulfilled. If a constraint has the value *false*, the policy is violated. The execution of a service is *correct* (according to the DecSerFlow model) at some point in time if all constraints (from the DecSerFlow model) evaluate to *true*. Similarly, a service has *completed correctly* if at the end of the execution all constraints evaluate to *true*. The goal of the execution of any DecSerFlow model is not to keep the values of all constraints *true* at all times during the execution. A constraint which has the value *false* during the execution is not considered an error. Consider for example the LTL expression $\Box(A \longrightarrow \Diamond B)$ where A and B are activities, i.e., each execution of A is eventually followed by B. Initially (before any activity is executed), this LTL expression evaluates to *true*. After executing A the LTL expression evaluates to *false* and this value remains *false* until B is executed. This illustrates that a constraint may be temporarily violated. However, the goal is to end the service execution in a state where all constraints evaluate to *true*.

To create constraints in DecSerFlow we use *constraint templates*. Each constraint template consists of a formula written in LTL and a graphical representation of the formula. An example is the "response constraint", which is denoted by a special arc connecting two activities A and B. The semantics of such an arc connecting A and B are given by the LTL expression $\Box(A \longrightarrow \Diamond B)$, i.e., any execution of A is eventually followed by (at least one) execution of B. We have developed a starting set of constraint templates and we will use these templates to create a DecSerFlow model. This set of templates is inspired by a collection of specification patterns for model checking and other finite-state verification tools [9]. Constraint templates define various types of dependencies between activities at an abstract level. Once defined, a template can be reused to specify constraints between activities in various DecSerFlow models. It is fairly easy to change, remove and add templates, which makes DecSerFlow an "open language" that can evolve and be extended according to the demands from different domains.[1] In the initial set of constraint templates we distinguish three groups: (1) "existence", (2) "relation", and (3) "negation" templates. Because a template assigns a graphical representation to an LTL formula, we will refer to such a template as a formula.

Before giving an overview of the initial set of formulas and their notation, we give a small example explaining the basic idea. Figure 2 shows a DecSerFlow model consisting of four activities: A, B, C, and D. Each activity is tagged with a constraint describing the number of times the activity should be executed, these are the so-called "existence formulas". The arc between A and B is an example of a "relation formula" and corresponds to the LTL expression discussed before: $\Box(A \longrightarrow \Diamond B)$. The connection between C and D denotes another "relation formula": $\Diamond D \longrightarrow \Diamond C$, i.e., if D is executed at least once, C is also executed at least once. The connection between B and C denotes a "negation formula"

---

[1] Note that we have developed a graphical editor for DecSerFlow that supports the creation of user defined templates, i.e., the user can define the graphical representation of a generic constraint and give its corresponding semantics in terms of LTL.

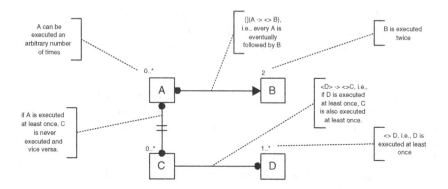

Fig. 2. A DecSerFlow model showing some example notations

(the LTL expression is not show here). Note that it is not easy to provide a classical procedural model (e.g., a Petri net) that allows for all behaviour modeled Figure 2.

Existence Formulas. Figure 3 shows the so-called "existence formulas". These formulas define the possible number of executions (cardinality) of an activity. For example, the first formula is called *existence*. The name and the formula heading are shown in the first column. From this, we can see that it takes one parameter (A), which is the name of an activity. The body of the formula is written in LTL and can be seen in the second column. In this case the LTL expression $\Diamond$ *(activity == A)* ensures that the activity given as the parameter A will execute at least once. Note that we write $\Diamond$ *(activity == A)* rather than $\Diamond$ *(A)*. The reason is that in a state we also want to access other properties, i.e., not just the activity name but also information on data, time, and resources. Therefore, we need to use a slightly more verbose notation (*activity == A*). The diagram in the third column is the graphical representation of the formula, which is assigned to the template. Parameter A is an activity and it is represented as a square with the name of the activity. The constraint is represented by a cardinality annotation above the square. In this case the cardinality is at least one, which is represented by *1..**. The first group of existence formulas are of the cardinality "N or more", denoted by *N..**. Next, the formula *absence* ensures that the activity should never execute in the service. The group of formulas with names *absence_N* uses negations of *existence_N* to specify that an activity can be executed at most *N-1* times. The last group of existence formulas defines an exact number of executions of an activity. For example, if a constraint is defined based on the formula *exactly_2*, the referring activity has to be executed exactly two times in the service.

Relation Formulas. Figure 4 shows the so-called "relations formulas". While an "existence formula" describes the cardinality of one activity, a "relation formula" defines relation(s) (dependencies) between two activities. All relation formulas

I) EXISTENCE FORMULAS

	formula	notation
1. EXISTENCE	formula existence(A: activity)	<>(activity == A);	1..* A
1.a. EXISTENCE_2	formula existence2(A: activity)	<>((activity == A ∧ _O(existence(A))));	2..* A
1.b. EXISTENCE_3	formula existence3(A: activity)	<>((activity == A ∧ _O(existence2(A))));	3..* A
1.c. EXISTENCE_N	formula existenceN(A: activity)	<>((activity == A ∧ _O(existence_N-1(A))));	N..* A
2. ABSENCE	formula absence_A(A: activity)	[](activity != A);	0 A
3.a. ABSENCE_2	formula absence2(A: activity)	!(existence2(A));	0..1 A
3.b. ABSENCE_3	formula absence3(A: activity)	!(existence3(A));	0..2 A
3.c. ABSENCE_N	formula absenceN(A: activity)	!(existenceN+1(A));	0..N A
4.a. EXACTLY_1	formula exactly1(A: activity)	(existence(A) ∧ []((activity == A -> _O(absence(A))));	1 A
4.b. EXACTLY_2	formula exactly2(A: activity)	(existence(A) ∧ (activity != A _U(activity == A ∧ _O(exactly1(A)))));	2 A
4.c. EXACTLY_N	formula exactlyN(A: activity)	(existence(A) ∧ (activity != A _U(activity == A ∧ _O(exactlyN-1(A)))));	N A

Fig. 3. Notations for the "existence formulas"

II) RELATION BETWEEN EVENTS FORMULAS

1. RESPONDED EXISTENCE formula existence_A_response_B(A: activity, B: activity)	(existence_A(A) -> existenceA(B));
2. CO-EXISTENCE formula co_existence_A_and_B(A: activity, B: activity)	(existence(A) <-> existence(B));
3. RESPONSE formula A_response_B(A: activity, B: activity)	[]((activity == A -> existence(B)));
4. PRECEDENCE formula A_precedence_B(A: activity, B: activity)	(existence_A(B) -> (!(activity == B) _U activity == A));
5. SUCCESSION formula A_succession_B(A: activity, B: activity)	(A_response_B(A,B) ∧ A_precedence_B(A,B));
6. ALTERNATE RESPONSE formula A_alternate_response_B(A: activity, B: activity)	(A_response_B(A,B) ∧ B_always_between_A(A,B)*);
7. ALTERNATE PRECEDENCE formula A_alternate_precedence_B(A: activity, B: activity)	(A_precedence_B(A,B) ∧ B_always_between_A(B,A)*);
8. ALTERNATE SUCCESSION formula A_alternate_succession_B(A: activity, B: activity)	(A_alternate_precedence_B(A,B) ∧ A_alternate_response_B(A,B));
9. CHAIN RESPONSE formula chain_A_response_B(A: activity, B: activity)	A_response_B(A,B) ∧ []((activity == A -> _O(activity == B)));
10. CHAIN PRECEDENCE formula chain_A_precedence_B(A: activity, B: activity)	(A_precedence_B(A,B) ∧ []((_O(activity == B) -> activity == A)));
11. CHAIN SUCCESSION formula chain_A_succession_B(A: activity, B: activity)	(chain_A_response_B(A,B) ∧ chain_A_precedence_B(A,B));

* subformula B_always_between_A(A: activity, B: activity)   []((activity == A -> _O(A_precedence_B(B,A))));

Fig. 4. Notations for the "relation formulas"

have two activities as parameters and two activities in the graphical representation. The line between the two activities in the graphical representation should be unique for the formula, and reflect the semantics of the relation. The *responded existence* formula specifies that if activity A is executed, activity B also has to be executed either before or after the activity A. According to the *co-existence* formula, if one of the activities A or B is executed, the other one has to be executed also.

While the previous formulas do not consider the order of activities, formulas *response, precedence* and *succession* do consider the ordering of activities. Formula *response* requires that every time activity A executes, activity B has to be executed after it. Note that this is a very relaxed relation of response, because B does not have to execute immediately after A, and another A can be executed between the first A and the subsequent B. For example, the execution sequence *[B,A,A,A,C,B]* satisfies the formula *response*. The formula *precedence* requires that activity B is preceded by activity A. i.e., it specifies that if activity B was executed, it could not have been executed until the activity A was executed. According to this formula, the execution sequence *[A,C,B,B,A]* is correct. The combination of the *response* and *precedence* formulas defines a bi-directional execution order of two activities and is called *succession*. In this formula, both *response* and *precedence* relations have to hold between the activities A and B. Thus, this formula specifies that every activity A has to be followed by an activity B and there has to be an activity A before every activity B. For example, the execution sequence *[A,C,A,B,B]* satisfies the *succession* formula.

Formulas *alternate response, alternate precedence* and *alternate succession* strengthen the *response, precedence* and *succession* formulas, respectively. If activity B is *alternate response* of the activity A, then after the execution of an activity A activity B has to be executed and between the execution of each two activities A at least one activity B has to be executed. In other words, after activity A there must be an activity B, and before that activity B there can not be another activity A. The execution sequence *[B,A,C,B,A,B]* satisfies the *alternate response*. Similarly, in the *alternate precedence* every instance of activity B has to be preceded by an instance of activity A and the next instance of activity B can not be executed before the next instance of activity A is executed. According to the *alternate precedence*, the execution sequence *[A,C,B,A,B,A]* is correct. The *alternate succession* is a combination of the *alternate response* and *alternate precedence* and the sequence *[A,C,B,A,B,A,B]* would satisfy this formula.

Even more strict ordering relations formulas are *chain response, chain precedence* and *chain succession*, which require that the executions of the two activities (A and B) are next to each other. In the *chain response* the next activity after the activity A has to be activity B and the execution *[B,A,B,C,A,B]* would be correct. The *chain precedence* formula requires that the activity A is the first preceding activity before B and, hence, the sequence *[A,B,C,A,B,A]* is correct. Since the *chain succession* formula is the combination of the *chain response* and *chain precedence* formulas, it requires that activities A and B are always executed next to each other. The execution sequence *[A,B,C,A,B,A,B]* is correct with respect to this formula.

Negation Formulas. Figure 5 shows the "negation formulas", which are the negated versions of the "relation formulas". The first two formulas negate the *responded existence* and *co-existence* formulas. The *responded absence* formula specifies that if activity A is executed activity B must never be executed (not before nor after the activity A). The *not co-existence* formula applies *responded absence* from A to B and from B to A. However, if we look at the *responded absence* formula we can see that if existence of A implies the absence of B and we first execute activity B, it will not be possible to execute activity A anymore because the formula will become permanently incorrect. This means that the formula *responded absence* is symmetric with respect to the input, i.e., we can swap the roles of A and B without changing the outcome. Therefore formula *responded absence* will be skipped and we will use only the *not co-existence* formula. The graphical representation is a modified representation of the *co-existence* formula with the negation symbol in the middle of the line. An example of a correct execution sequence for the formula *not co-existence* is *[A,C,A,A]*, while the sequence *[A,C,A,A,B]* would not be correct.

The *negation response* formula specifies that after the execution of activity A, activity B can not be executed. According to the formula *negation precedence* activity B can not be preceded by activity A. These two formulas have the same effect because if it is not possible to have activity B executed after activity A, then it is not possible to have activity A executed before activity B. Since the formula *negation succession* combines these two formulas, it also has the same effect and we will use only the *negation succession* formula. The graphical representation of this formula is a modified representation of the *succession* formula with a negation symbol in the middle of the line. The execution sequence *[B,B,C,A,C,A,A]* is an example of a correct sequence, while *[A,C,B]* would be an incorrect execution.

Formulas *negation alternate response*, *negation alternate precedence* and *negation alternate succession* are easy to understand. The formula *negation alternate response* specifies that the activity B can not be executed between the two subsequent executions of the activity A. According to this formula the execution sequence *[B,A,C,A,B]* is correct. In the case of the *negation alternate precedence* activity A can not be executed between two subsequent executions of the activity B. The execution sequence *[A,B,C,B,A]* is correct for *negation alternate precedence*. The formula *negation alternate succession* requires both *negation alternate response* and *negation alternate precedence* to be satisfied. An example of a correct execution sequence for the *negation alternate succession* formula is *[B,C,B,A,C,A]*. Graphical representations of these three formulas are similar to the representations of *alternate response*, *alternate precedence* and *alternate succession* with the negation symbol in the middle of the line.

III) NEGATION RELATION BETWEEN EVENTS FORMULAS

12.a. RESPONDED ABSENCE
formula existence_A_response_notB(A: activity, B: activity)

(existence_A(A) -> absence(B));

12.b. NOT CO_EXISTENCE
formula existence_A_response_notB(A: activity, B: activity)

(existence_A_response_notB(A,B) $\wedge$ existence_A_response_notB(B,A));

13.a. NEGATION RESPONSE
formula A_response_notB(A: activity, B: activity)

[]((activity == A -> absence(B)));

13.b. NEGATION PRECEDENCE
formula notA_precedence_B(A: activity, B: activity)

[]((existence(B) -> activity != A));

13.c. NEGATION SUCCESSION
formula notA_succession_notB(A: activity, B: activity)

(A_response_notB(A,B) $\wedge$ notA_precedence_B(A,B));

14. NEGATION ALTERNATE REPONSE
formula A_not_alternate_response_B(A: activity, B: activity)

B_never_between_A(A,B)**;

15. NEGATION ALTERNATE PRECEDENCE
formula
A_not_alternate_precedence_B(A: activity, B: activity)

B_never_between_A(B,A)**;

16. NEGATION ALTERNATE SUCCESSION
A_not_alternate_succession_B(A: activity, B: activity)

(A_not_alternate_precedence_B(A,B) $\wedge$ A_not_alternate_response_B(A,B));

17.a. NEGATION CHAIN RESPONSE
formula chain_A_response_notB(A: activity, B: activity)

[]((activity == A -> _O(activity != B)));

17.b. NEGATION CHAIN PRECEDENCE
formula chain_notA_precedence_B(A: activity, B: activity)

[]((_O(activity == B) -> activity != A));

17.c. NEGATION CHAIN SUCCESSION
formula chain_A_notsuccession_B(A: activity, B: activity)

(chain_A_response_notB(A,B) $\wedge$ chain_notA_precedence_B(A,B));

** subformula B_never_between_A(A: activity, B: activity)

[]((activity == A -> _O(<>(activity == A) -> (activity != B _U activity == A))));

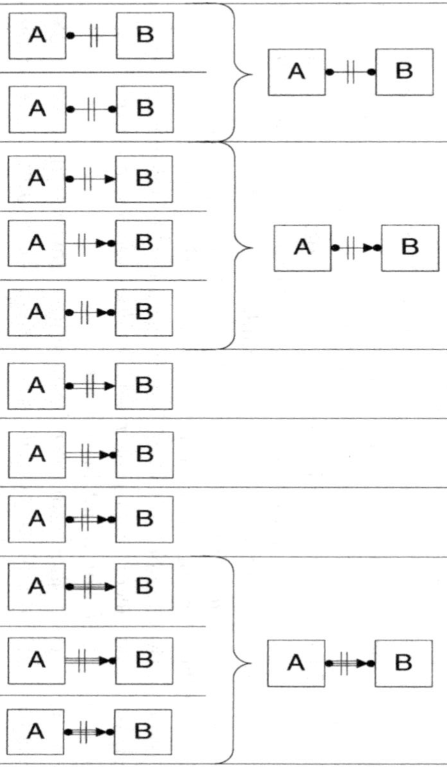

Fig. 5. Notations for the "negations formulas"

The last three formulas are negations of formulas *chain response*, *chain precedence* and *chain succession*. According to the formula *negation chain response*, activity B can not be executed directly after the activity A. Formula *negation chain precedence* specifies that activity B can never be directly preceded by activity A. These two formulas have the same effect because they forbid the activities A and B to be executed directly next to each other. Since the formula *negation chain succession* requires both *negation chain response* and *negation chain precedence* to be executed, these three formulas all have the same effect and we will use only *negation chain succession*. The graphical representation of this formula is a modified version of the representation of the *chain succession* formula with the negation symbol in the middle of the line. The execution sequence *[B,A,C,B,A]* is correct according to the *negation chain succession* formula, while the sequence *[B,A,B,A]* would not be correct.

Figures 4 and 5 only show binary relationships. However, these can easily be extended to deal with more activities. Consider for example the *response* relationship, i.e., $\Box(A \longrightarrow \Diamond B)$. We will allow multiple arcs to start from the same dot, e.g., an arc to B, C, and D. The meaning is $\Box(A \longrightarrow \Diamond(B \lor C \lor D))$, i.e., every occurrence of A is eventually followed by an occurrence of B, C, or D. Moreover, as indicated before, the set of formulas is not fixed and we also aim at supporting data. In fact, we have defined more formulas than the ones shown in figures 3, 4, and 5. For example, the *mutual substitution* relation formula specifies that at least one of two activities should occur (i.e., $\Diamond(A \lor B)$).

After this introduction to DecSerFlow we specify a concrete example. The interested reader is referred to a technical report with more information about DecSerFlow [5]. Moreover, for more information on ConDec, the sister language of DecSerFlow aiming a teamwork and workflow flexibility, we refer to [17].

3   Modelling Services With DecSerFlow: The Acme Travel Example

In this section we use the "Acme Travel Company case" to illustrate DecSerFlow. The description of the business process of the Acme Travel service is adopted from [19] is as follows:

1. Acme Travel receives an itinerary from Karla, the customer.
2. After checking the itinerary for errors, the process determines which reservations to make, sending simultaneous requests to the appropriate airline and hotel agencies to make the appropriate reservations [2].
3. If any of the reservation activities fails, the itinerary is cancelled by performing the "compensate" activity and Karla is notified of the problem.
4. Acme Travel waits for confirmation of the two reservation requests.

---

[2] The original Acme Travel service business process consists of three possible bookings: airline, hotel and vehicle. However, for the simplicity, we consider only the possibilities to book airline and hotel.

5. Upon receipt of confirmation, Acme Travel notifies Karla of the successful completion of the process and sends her the reservation confirmation numbers and the final itinerary details.
6. Once Karla is notified of either the success or failure of her requested itinerary, she may submit another travel request.

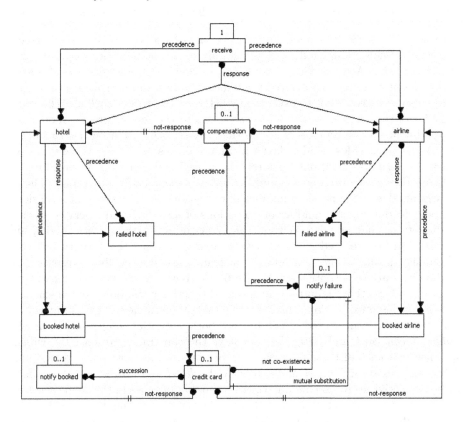

Fig. 6. DecSerFlow - Acme Travel Company

Figure 6 shows the DecSerFlow model of the Acme business process. We first define the possible activities within the service to model the business process of Acme. In this case, we define eleven activities:

receive - A request for booking is received from the customer;
airline - A request for booking is sent to an airline reservation service;
hotel - A request for booking is sent to a hotel reservation service;
booked hotel - A hotel reservation service sends a positive response for a requested booking, i.e., the hotel can be booked;
failed hotel - A hotel reservation service sends a negative response for a requested booking, i.e., the hotel cannot be booked;
booked airline - An airline reservation service sends a positive response for a requested booking, i.e., the airline can be booked;

failed airline - An airline reservation service sends a negative response for a requested booking, i.e., the airline cannot be booked;

compensation - The whole booking has failed;

notify failure - Notify the customer that the booking has failed;

credit card - Register and charge a successful booking; and

notify booked - Notify the customer that the booking was successful.

In principle, a DecSerFlow model consisting only of a set of activities is a correct model. If a DecSerFlow model consisting only of eleven activities would be implemented in the Acme service, it would be possible that the service executes any of the eleven activities, an arbitrary number of times, in an arbitrary order. It would also be possible not to execute any activity. To prevent such an "chaotic" behavior of the service, we can add *constraints* to the service process model. A constraint in service represents a rule that the service execution has to fulfill. The Acme DecSerFlow model shown in Figure 6 uses two of the three types of constraint formulas mentioned before: "existence" and "relation" constraints.

In Section 2, we presented several standard "existence" constraints. These constraints define the possible number of executions of an activity in a service. We refer to the possible number of executions of an activity in a service as the cardinality of that activity. Without any constraints in the service model, an activity can be executed an arbitrary number of times - the activity has the cardinality of (0..*). The "existence" constraints are graphically represented as cardinalities above activities (cf. Figure 6). Activity *receive* has the constraint *exactly_1* (cf. Section 2), and specifies that this activity will be executed exactly once in one instance (per one customer request) of the Acme service. Because the booking request can succeed or fail, but not both, activities *compensation, notify failure, credit card,* and *notify booking* have the constraint "absence_2", which specifies that each of these activities will be executed at most once. We do not define any "existence" constraints on activities *hotel* and *airline* and thus allow these two activities to execute an arbitrary number of times in the Acme service. If the customer does not wish to book a hotel or an airline, the Acme service will not execute the corresponding activity. In case that a booking of a hotel or an airline is requested, the booking request might be sent multiple times until the booking succeeds or fails. A booking of a hotel or an airline will be followed with a positive activity (i.e., *booked hotel* or *booked airline*) or a negative activity (i.e., *failed hotel* or *failed airline*). Therefore, activities *booked hotel, booked airline, failed hotel* and *failed airline* also can be executed an arbitrary number of times in the service.

The Acme DecSerFlow model as defined so far - only consisting of a set of activities and "existence" constraints - is a correct model. If this model would be implemented in the Acme service, the service could execute its activities in an arbitrary order, complying with the execution cardinality of each activity, as defined with "existence" constraints.

To define relations between activities in the service (and implicitly their possible order) we use the so-called "relation" constraints as defined in Section 2. Unlike "existence" constraints that were defined for single activities (unary), "relation" constraints define relations between two or more activities (e.g., a binary relationship).

After receiving the booking request from the customer, the request is checked. The customer can request to book a hotel and an airline for a destination, or only one of these. The constraint *response* from the activity *receive* is a so-called branched constraint. It has two branches: one to the activity *hotel* and the other to the activity *airline*. This branched response specifies that after the activity *receive* is executed, eventually there will be at least one execution of one of the activities *hotel* and *airline*. It is still possible that both of the activities *hotel* and *airline* execute an arbitrary number of times, as long as at least one of them executes after the activity *receive*. However, since it would not be desirable to execute any of the activities *hotel* and *airline* before the activity *receive*, we add two *precedence* constraints: (1) the *precedence* constraint between activities *receive* and *hotel* specifies that the activity *hotel* cannot execute before the activity *receive* executes, and (2) the *precedence* constraint between activities *receive* and *airline* specifies that the activity *airline* cannot execute before the activity *receive* executes. The branched constraint *response* and the two *precedence* constraints between activities *receive*, *hotel* and *airline* specify that activities *hotel* and *airline* will not execute until the activity *receive* executes, and that after the activity *receive* executes, at least one of the activities *hotel* an *airline* will execute. Activities *hotel* and *airline* can an arbitrary number of times and in an arbitrary order.

Activities *booked hotel* and *failed hotel* handle the possible responses of a hotel reservation service on the request of Acme service to book a hotel (which is sent when the activity *hotel* is executed). With the branched *response* constraint from the activity *hotel* we specify that after every execution of this activity, at least one of the activities *booked hotel* and *failed hotel* will execute. Note that, due to errors, this constraint allows for some requests for the hotel reservation to remain without response. Logically, with the two *precedence* constraints between the activity *hotel* and activities *booked hotel* and *failed hotel* we prevent that either of the activities *booked hotel* and *failed hotel* execute before the activity *hotel* executes. This is necessary, since the response from the hotel reservation service can not arrive before a reservation request is sent. The same constraints are added between activities *airline*, *booked airline* and *failed airline*, because the communication of the Acme service with the airline service is the same like the communication with the hotel reservation service.

Only after receiving at least one of the two negative responses (activities *failed hotel* and *failed airline*), the Acme service can cancel the whole booking by executing the activity *compensation*. This is specified by the branched *precedence* constraint between the activity *compensation* and activities *failed hotel* and *failed booking*. After the *compensation* activity is executed, activities *hotel* and *airline* can not execute again in the service, because the whole booking is cancelled. The two *not-response* constraints between the activity *compensation* and activities *hotel* and *airline*, make sure that after the activity *compensation* executes, none of the activities *hotel* and *airline* can execute. The *precedence* constraint between activities *notify failure* and *compensation* specifies that the activity *notify failure* cannot execute before the activity *compensate*. Note that after the activity *compensation* executes, there might still be some responses arriving from the reservation services. If an satisfactory booking response arrives after the activity *compensate* is executed, the Acme service can still decide to accept the booking. This is why the activity *notify failure* does not always necessarily execute after the activity *compensate*.

After at least one positive reservation response arrives, the Acme service can decide to accept and finalize the whole booking. This is specified with the branched *precedence* constraint between the activity *credit card* and activities *booked hotel* and *booked airline*. After the booking is charged, the new requests will not be sent to the hotel and airline reservation services, i.e., the activities *hotel* and *airline* cannot execute after the activity *credit card*. This is achieved with the two *not-response* constraints between the activity *credit card* and activities *hotel* and *airline*. Only and always after the booking is charged, the customer will be notified about the successful booking. The *succession* constraint between activities *credit card* and *notify booked* specifies that the activity *notify booked* cannot execute before the activity *credit card* and that it will have to execute after the activity *credit card*.

To conclude the booking of a customer, the Acme service will either accept or decline the requested booking. This means that in the service either one of the taks *notify failure* and *credit card* will execute. Note that even after the activity *compensation*, Acme can still receive an positive reservation response and accept the booking. The *not co-existence* constraint between activities *credit card* and *notify failure* specifies that only one of these two activities can execute in the service because it is not possible to both charge the booking and notify the customer about failure. However, eventually one of the activities *credit card* or *notify failure* will execute, as specified with the *mutual substitution* constraint between these two activities.

Note that the Acme service model in Figure 6 allows for many alternative executions of the service. For example, it is possible to handle the both late and lost reposes of reservation services. It is also possible to send requests to different reservation services regardless the order of the reception of responses. Even after the cancellation has started by executing the activity consumption, it is still possible to receive a positive response and successfully finalize the requested booking.

It is important to note that Figure 6 uses a declarative style of modelling. The DecSerFlow model allows for much more variability than a typical procedural process model (e.g., a BPEL specification). However, because the language is extendible it is possible to add constructs one can find in traditional languages, e.g., it is relatively easy to add the "place concept" from Petri nets or the "sequence concept" from BPEL. As a result, DecSerFlow can be applied using different styles ranging from highly procedural to highly declarative.

4 Enacting DecSerFlow Models of Web Services

Every DecSerFlow model consists of a set of activities and constraints. Constraints define rules that the service has to fulfill. At the end of the service execution all constraints should be fulfilled. The semantics of a constraint is defined with the LTL formula that is assigned to it. We use these LTL formulas to execute a DecSerFlow model. Every LTL formula can be translated into an Buchi automaton [10]. There are several algorithms for translating LTL expressions into Buchi automata. Different algorithms have been studied in the field of *model checking* [15]. The SPIN tool [14] is one of the most widely used tools for model checking. Using SPIN, one can develop a model of a system in Promela (PROcess MEta LAnguage) [14]. To check the model with respect to some requirements, we can write these requirements as LTL expressions. SPIN can automatically verify the correctness of the specified LTL requirements in the developed Promela model. For verification purposes, SPIN uses an algorithm for translating LTL expressions to Buchi automata [10].

A DecSerFlow model typically has multiple constraints. All of the constraints need to be taken into account at any moment of the service execution. For this purpose we can take one of the two strategies: (1) we can construct an automaton for each of the LTL expressions and then execute these automatons in parallel, or (2) construct and execute a single automaton for the whole model (i.e., construct an automaton for the conjunction of all LTL expressions).

When executing a service by executing referring Buchi automaton(s), we have to deal with two problems. First, the standard algorithms (e.g., the one presented in [10]) construct a *non-deterministic* finite automaton. A nondeterministic finite automaton is a finite state machine where for each pair (state, input symbol) there may be several possible next states. This means that for each pair (state of a DecSerFlow model, executed activity) there may be several possible next states of the DecSerFlow model. This is a problem because, given a execution history, it is not always possible to pinpoint the current state in the automaton. Second, algorithms such as the one presented in [10] construct a finite automaton for *infinite words*. Because we assume that a service will eventually finish with the execution, we have to use an automaton that can read finite words.

4.1 Executing a Non-deterministic Automaton

In this section we describe a simple algorithm that can be used to successfully execute a non-deterministic automaton in the context of the execution of a DecSerFlow model. We use a simple example of a model with three activities, as shown in Figure 7(a). This model consists of activities *curse, pray,* and *bless* and a constraint *response* between activities *curse* and *pray*. All three activities can be executed an arbitrary number of times because there are no "existence" constraints to specify cardinalities of activities. Constraint *response* between activities *curse* and *pray* specifies that, every time a person curses, (s)he should eventually pray after this.

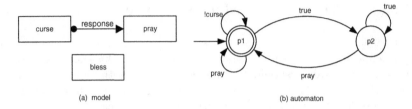

(a) model   (b) automaton

Fig. 7. A simple DecSerFlow model

For this model we construct the automaton [10], as shown in Figure 7(b). This automaton consists of two states: *p1* (accepting and initial state) and *p2*. In the beginning we assume the automaton to be in the initial state *p1*. There are three transitions possible from this state: (1) transition with the label *pray* is applied when the activity *pray* is executed, (2) transition with the label *!curse* is applied when activities *pray* or *bless* are executed, and (3) transition *true* leads to the state *p2* and is applied when any of the activities is executed. In the state *p2* two transitions are possible: (1) transition with the label *true* is applied when any of the three activities are executed and (2) transition *pray* leads to the state *p1* and is applied when the activity *pray* executes.

In a simplified case of a deterministic automaton, we would execute the model by checking at which state the automaton currently is, i.e., we would constantly store the information about the *current state* of the automaton. If the automaton is in an accepting state, the constraint(s) are fulfilled and vice versa. When executing an activity, the automaton would simply move to the next state by a transition that can be applied for that activity. When executing an activity in the case of a non-deterministic automaton, there can be *multiple* possible next states to move to. The automaton shown in Figure 7(b) is a non-deterministic automaton. Take, for example, the situation when the automaton is in the state *p1* and the activity *pray* executes. In this case (at the state *p1*), we could apply any of the transitions *pray* (the automaton remains in the state *p1*), *!curse* (the automaton remains in the state *p1*), or *true* (the automaton changes the state to *p2*) - this is a non-deterministic situation. Because we use the current state of the automaton to determine if the constraint(s) are fulfilled or not and the next possible activities, the information about the current state of the automaton is important.

A simple solution for the execution of a non-deterministic automaton is to consider a set of possible current states[3] instead of a single current state. In the situation described above (when the activity *pray* is executed in the state *p1*) we would consider the automaton to transfer to the set of possible states {p1,p2}. We take the optimistic approach and consider an automaton to be in an accepting state if any of the states in the set of current possible states is an accepting state of the automaton. Figure 8 shows the algorithm for the execution of a non-deterministic automaton. We use two data types: (1) *state* consists

---

[3] This set can have at most all states of the automaton.

of an array of incoming transitions and an array of outgoing transitions and (2) *transition* has a label (e.g., *!curse*), source state and target state. Function *nextState* generates an array of states (a set of possible next states) given the array (set) of *current* possible states and the *activity* name. This function loops through the array of *current* states. For each current state it loops through all the *outgoing* transitions. For each of the outgoing transitions it checks is the label of the transition complies with the *activity* name. If (1) the activity is accepted by the transition label and (2) the target state of the transition is not in the array of the next states, the target state of the transition is added to the array of the next states.

```
State {                  Transition{
    Transition[] in;         String label;
    Transition[] out;        State source;
}                            State target;
                         }
1   State[] nextState(State[] current, String activity){
2       State[] next;
3       for i = 0 to current.length - 1 do{       // Look at all current possible states.
4           State curr = current[i];              // For every current state
5           for j = 0 to curr.out.length - 1 {    // look at all out-transitions.
6               Transition out = curr.out[j];     // For every out-transition,
7               if (out.label parses activity)    // if the out-transition suits the activity,
8                   then if ( out.target not in  next )   // if the target state is not already in the set of new possible states
9                       then next = next + out.target; // add the target state to the set of new possible states.
10          }
11      }
12      return next;
13  }
```

Fig. 8. Execution of a non-deterministic automaton

Table 1 shows the execution of the automaton shown in Figure 7 (b). At the beginning, the set of possible states contains all initial states, which is in this case {p1}. For example, if activity *bless* is executed in the initial state, then the automaton could apply transition *!curse* (and stay in the state *p1*) or it could apply transition *true* (and move to the state *p2*). Thus, if the activity *bless* is executed when the automaton is in a state in {p1} (i.e., the initial set of possible states), the automaton can move to any state in the the set of new possible states {p1,p2}. If the automaton is, for example, in the set of possible states {p1,p2} and activity *bless* is executed, the automaton transfers to the set of possible states {p1,p2} that is formed as intersection of sets of possible states for each of the starting states *p1* ({p1,p2}) and *p2* ({p2}). Since *p1* is the accepting state of the automaton in Figure 7 (b), we consider the execution of the DecSerFlow model from Figure 7 (a) to be correct (i.e., all constraints are fulfilled) if the set of current possible states contains the state *p1*. Thus, we consider the model to be executed correctly, if the set of current possible states of the automaton is either {*p1*} or {*p1,p2*}.

Table 1. Execution of the non-deterministic automaton in Figure 7

	automaton possible states		automaton possible states
nr.	from	activity	to
1	{p1}	bless	{p1,p2}
2	{p1}	curse	{p2}
3	{p1}	pray	{p1,p2}
4	{p2}	bless	{p2}
5	{p2}	curse	{p2}
6	{p2}	pray	{p1}
7	{p1,p2}	bless	{p1,p2}
8	{p1,p2}	curse	{p2}
9	{p1,p2}	pray	{p1,p2}

4.2 Executing Finite Traces

The algorithm presented in [10] is originally dedicated for model checking of concurrent systems. Because these systems are not designed to halt during normal execution, the resulting automaton is an automaton over *infinite words (traces, runs)*. An infinite trace is accepted by the automaton [10] *iff* it visits an accepting state infinitely often. This type of acceptance cannot be applied for the case of service execution, because we require that such an execution will eventually complete.

There are two strategies that can enable checking of the acceptance of an finite trace in an automaton generated by [10]: (1) we can introduce special invisible "end" activity and constraint in a DecSerFlow model before the automaton is created or (2) we can adopt a modified version of this algorithm, which reads *finite words (traces, runs)* [11].

In the first strategy we use the original algorithm for the generation of automata, but we slightly change the DecSerFlow model before creating the automaton. To be able to check if a finite trace is accepting, we add one "invisible" activity and one "invisible" constraint to every DecSerFlow model and then construct the automaton. With this we specify that each execution of the model will eventually end. We introduce an "invisible" activity e, which represents the *ending* activity in the model. We use this activity to specify that the service will end - the *termination* constraint. This constraint has the LTL formula $\Diamond e \wedge (\Box(e \longrightarrow \bigcirc e))$, and it specifies that: (1) the service will eventually end - the "invisible" activity e will eventually be executed, and (2) after this activity, no other activity will be executed but the activity e itself, infinitely often. Take, for example, a simple DecSerFlow model with one constraint *existence(receive)*, (i.e., $\Diamond receive$), which specifies that the activity *receive* will execute at least once. To execute this model we first add the termination constraint and consider a conjunction of these two constraints: $\Diamond receive \wedge \Diamond e \wedge (\Box(e \longrightarrow \bigcirc e))$. This conjunction ensures that the trace will have the prefix required by the original DecSerFlow model and an infinite suffix containing only the "ending" activity e. The whole conjunction is then translated into an automaton using the original algorithm [10]. We check the acceptance of the finite trace (prefix) of the original DecSerFlow model by checking if the automaton is in a so-called *end* state: (1) if the automaton is in an accepting state and (2) if from this moment an accepting state can be visited infinitely often only by executing the "ending" activity e. To prevent deadlocks, the automaton is purged (before the execution) from the states from which none of the *end* states is reachable.

As the second strategy, we can use a modification of the original algorithm. The original algorithm for translating LTL formulas to Buchi automatons [10] is modified to be used for verification of *finite* executions of software programs [11]. The algorithm for translating LTL formulas into automatons over finite words introduces a change into the acceptance criteria of the original algorithm [11]. However, this algorithm assumes that any program would have to start executing, i.e., it does not consider empty traces. Therefore, an initial state is not accepting in some cases where it should be accenting for an empty trace. However, we assume that an "empty" execution of a DecSerFlow model (that does not violate any constraint) is in principle an accepting execution. Therefore, we introduce an "invisible" initial activity *init*. Using LTL we require this to be the first activity. Moreover, to any execution sequence we add a prefix containing one *init* activity, i.e., before the service can start, activity *init* is automatically executed. After this, it is possible to determine if the state where no activities have been executed (empty trace) is in an accepting state or not.

After completing the DecSerFlow editor, we are currently experimenting with different ways in which we can build useful automatons for enactment. Since we are using LTL not just for analysis but as the care technology for the engine, we also have to address issues such as performance and reliability.

5   Conclusion

This paper advocated a more declarative style of modeling in the context of web services. Therefore, we proposed a new, more declarative language: DecSerFlow. Although DecSerFlow is graphical, it is grounded in temporal logic. It can be used for the *enactment* of processes, but it is also suited for the *specification* of a single service or a complete choreography.

Besides being *declarative*, the language is also *extendible*, i.e., it is possible to add new constructs without changing the core of the language. We have developed a graphical editor to support DecSerFlow. This editor allows users to specify service flows. Moreover, the user can add user-defined constraint templates by simply selecting a graphical representation and providing parameterized semantics in terms of LTL. Currently, we are working on an engine that is able to support enactment and monitoring. If a constraint is used for enactment, it is impossible to permanently violate a constraint because the system will not allow activities that violate this constraint. If a constraint is used for monitoring, the system will allow the violation of this constraint. However, the engine will issue a warning and log the violation. The automatic construction of an automaton suitable for enactment and on-the-fly monitoring is far from trivial as shown in Section 4.

There is also a very interesting link between DecSerFlow and *process mining* [6]. In [3] we showed that it is possible to translate abstract BPEL into Petri nets and SOAP messages exchanged between services into event logs represented using our MXML format (i.e., the format used by ProM `www.processmining.org`). As a result, we could compare the modeled behavior (in terms of a Petri net) and the observed behavior (in some event log) using the conformance checker [18]. A similar approach can be followed by using the LTL checker in ProM [1]. Using the LTL checker it is possible to check LTL formulas over event logs (e.g., monitored SOAP messages). In principle it is possible to use the LTL formulas generated based on the DecSerFlow specification and load them into the LTL checker in ProM. This allows the users of ProM to specify constraints graphically rather than using the textual language that is used now.

References

1. W.M.P. van der Aalst, H.T. de Beer, and B.F. van Dongen. Process Mining and Verification of Properties: An Approach based on Temporal Logic. In R. Meersman and Z. Tari et al., editors, *On the Move to Meaningful Internet Systems 2005: CoopIS, DOA, and ODBASE: OTM Confederated International Conferences, CoopIS, DOA, and ODBASE 2005*, volume 3760 of *Lecture Notes in Computer Science*, pages 130–147. Springer-Verlag, Berlin, 2005.
2. W.M.P. van der Aalst, M. Dumas, A.H.M. ter Hofstede, N. Russell, H.M.W. Verbeek, and P. Wohed. Life After BPEL? In M. Bravetti, L. Kloul, and G. Zavattaro, editors, *WS-FM 2005*, volume 3670 of *Lecture Notes in Computer Science*, pages 35–50. Springer-Verlag, Berlin, 2005.
3. W.M.P. van der Aalst, M. Dumas, C. Ouyang, A. Rozinat, and H.M.W. Verbeek. Choreography Conformance Checking: An Approach based on BPEL and Petri Nets (extended version). BPM Center Report BPM-05-25, BPMcenter.org, 2005.
4. W.M.P. van der Aalst, A.H.M. ter Hofstede, B. Kiepuszewski, and A.P. Barros. Workflow Patterns. *Distributed and Parallel Databases*, 14(1):5–51, 2003.
5. W.M.P. van der Aalst and M. Pesic. Specifying, Discovering, and Monitoring Service Flows: Making Web Services Process-Aware. BPM Center Report BPM-06-09, BPM Center, BPMcenter.org, 2006. http://www.BPMcenter.org/reports/2006/BPM-06-09.pdf.
6. W.M.P. van der Aalst, A.J.M.M. Weijters, and L. Maruster. Workflow Mining: Discovering Process Models from Event Logs. *IEEE Transactions on Knowledge and Data Engineering*, 16(9):1128–1142, 2004.
7. T. Andrews, F. Curbera, H. Dholakia, Y. Goland, J. Klein, F. Leymann, K. Liu, D. Roller, D. Smith, S. Thatte, I. Trickovic, and S. Weerawarana. Business Process Execution Language for Web Services, Version 1.1. Standards proposal by BEA Systems, International Business Machines Corporation, and Microsoft Corporation, 2003.
8. M. Dumas, W.M.P. van der Aalst, and A.H.M. ter Hofstede. *Process-Aware Information Systems: Bridging People and Software through Process Technology*. Wiley & Sons, 2005.

9. M.B. Dwyer, G.S. Avrunin, and J.C. Corbett. Patterns in Property Specifications for Finite-State Verification. In *ICSE '99: Proceedings of the 21st international conference on Software engineering*, pages 411–420, Los Alamitos, CA, USA, 1999. IEEE Computer Society Press.

10. R. Gerth, D. Peled, M.Y. Vardi, and P. Wolper. Simple On-The-Fly Automatic Verification of Linear Temporal Logic. In *Proceedings of the Fifteenth IFIP WG6.1 International Symposium on Protocol Specification, Testing and Verification XV*, pages 3–18, London, UK, 1996. Chapman & Hall, Ltd.

11. D. Giannakopoulou and K. Havelund. Automata-Based Verification of Temporal Properties on Running Programs. In *Proceedings of the 16th IEEE International Conference on Automated Software Engineering (ASE'01)*, pages 412–416. IEEE Computer Society Press, Providence, 2001.

12. K. Havelund and G. Rosu. Monitoring Programs Using Rewriting. In *Proceedings of the 16th IEEE International Conference on Automated Software Engineering (ASE'01)*, pages 135–143. IEEE Computer Society Press, Providence, 2001.

13. K. Havelund and G. Rosu. Synthesizing Monitors for Safety Properties. In *Proceedings of the 8th International Conference on Tools and Algorithms for the Construction and Analysis of Systems (TACAS 2002)*, volume 2280 of *Lecture Notes in Computer Science*, pages 342–356. Springer-Verlag, Berlin, 2002.

14. G.J. Holzmann. *The SPIN Model Checker: Primer and Reference Manual.* Addison-Wesley, Boston, Massachusetts, USA, 2003.

15. E.M. Clarke Jr., O. Grumberg, and D.A. Peled. *Model Checking.* The MIT Press, Cambridge, Massachusetts and London, UK, 1999.

16. N. Kavantzas, D. Burdett, G. Ritzinger, T. Fletcher, and Y. Lafon. Web Services Choreography Description Language, Version 1.0. W3C Working Draft 17-12-04, 2004.

17. M. Pesic and W.M.P. van der Aalst. A Declarative Approach for Flexible Business Processes Management. In *BPM 2006 Workshops: International Workshop on Dynamic Process Management (DPM 2006)*, Lecture Notes in Computer Science. Springer-Verlag, Berlin, 2006.

18. A. Rozinat and W.M.P. van der Aalst. Conformance Testing: Measuring the Fit and Appropriateness of Event Logs and Process Models. In C. Bussler et al., editor, *BPM 2005 Workshops (Workshop on Business Process Intelligence)*, volume 3812 of *Lecture Notes in Computer Science*, pages 163–176. Springer-Verlag, Berlin, 2006.

19. J. Snell. Automating business processes and transactions in Web services: An introduction to BPELWS, WS-Coordination, and WS-Transaction. http://www-128.ibm.com/developerworks/webservices/library/ws-autobp/, June 2006.

20. P. Wohed, W.M.P. van der Aalst, M. Dumas, and A.H.M. ter Hofstede. Analysis of Web Services Composition Languages: The Case of BPEL4WS. In I.Y. Song, S.W. Liddle, T.W. Ling, and P. Scheuermann, editors, *22nd International Conference on Conceptual Modeling (ER 2003)*, volume 2813 of *Lecture Notes in Computer Science*, pages 200–215. Springer-Verlag, Berlin, 2003.

Service QoS Composition at the Level
of Part Names

Marco Aiello[1], Florian Rosenberg[1], Christian Platzer[1],
Agata Ciabattoni[1,2], and Schahram Dustdar[1]

[1] VitaLab, Distributed Systems Group, Information Systems Institute
Vienna University of Technology
1040 Vienna, Argentinierstrasse 8/184-1
Austria
{aiellom, florian, christian, dustdar}@infosys.tuwien.ac.at
[2] Institut für Diskrete Mathematik und Geometrie
Vienna University of Technology
1040 Vienna, Wiedner Hauptstrasse 8-10
Austria
agata@logic.at

Abstract. The cornerstone for the success of Service-Oriented Computing lies in its promise to allow fast and easy composition of services to create added-value applications. Compositions need to be described in terms of their desired functional properties, but the non-functional properties are of paramount importance as well. Inspired by the Web service challenge we propose a new model for describing the Quality of Service (QoS) of a composition which considers the information flow and describes basic service qualities at the granularity level of service part names, that is, operations comprised in service invocation/response messages. In this initial investigation, we overview a number of formal methods techniques that allow to reason with QoS composition based on the proposed model, and propose an algorithm for determining the QoS of a composition given the QoS associated with the individual services.

Keywords: Service-Oriented Computing, Web Services, Service Composition, Quality of Service.

1 Introduction

Service-Oriented Computing (SOC) is an emerging computing paradigm for building distributed information systems in which the concepts of distribution, openness, asynchronous messaging and loose coupling take a leading role. In this context, applications are built out of individual services that expose functionalities by publishing their interfaces into appropriate repositories, abstracting entirely from the underlying implementation. Published interfaces may be searched by other services or users and subsequently be invoked. The interest

M. Bravetti, M. Nuñes, and G. Zavattaro (Eds.): WS-FM 2006, LNCS 4184, pp. 24–37, 2006.

in Service-Oriented Computing is a consequence of the shift from a vision of a Web based on the presentation of information to a vision of the Web as computational infrastructure, where systems and services can interact in order to fulfill user's requests. Web services (WS), the best-known example, are the realization of service-oriented systems based on open standards and infrastructures, extending the XML syntax [4].

Web service technology is being increasingly adopted. Particularly successful are the protocols for the transport of messages (SOAP)[1] and for the description of basic service operations (the Web service Description Language WSDL).[2] The latter protocol describes messages to be exchanged with a remote Web service. Exchanged messages are a set of *part names*, that is, operation name and input and output types. The description of functional Web service properties is thus covered by the WSDL standard. But functional properties are not enough. In fact, non-functional properties of any information systems are as important as the functional ones. Having to wait too long for the output of a system can make it as useless as not having the system at all. This is even more true when considering loosely coupled distributed systems such as those designed following the SOC paradigm.

Quality of Service is the set of properties of a service which have to do with 'how' a service is delivered rather than 'what' is delivered. There is no shared agreement on what QoS is and what is not, but generally properties such as response time, latency, availability, and costs are regarded as QoS. Classifications of QoS features in the context of Web services have been proposed by several authors [13,10,17]. For instance, Ran [15] proposed a QoS model and a UDDI extension for associating QoS to a specific Web service. An approach for defining QoS requirements is QML [9]: a language for QoS description using XML. QoS aspects are qualified by characteristics as direction and value type. A set of measures for reliability and performance are proposed. Atzeni and Lioy [5] overview security system assessment methods and metrics. A number of approaches to QoS description of services rely on extensions of WSDL, e.g., [10,18]. The main idea is simple: provide syntax to define terms which refer to non-functional properties of operations. Given such description, one can then build a framework for the dynamic selection of Web services based on QoS requirements. In [20,1], the description of elementary service qualities as a quality vector each component of which is a quality parameter for the service is proposed. In [11] Lin, Xie, Guo and Wang use fuzzy logic techniques to handle QoS requirements. The description of QoS of services can also be the object of the negotiation of services in long running-transactions or repeated interactions. QoS become then the object of Service-Level Agreement, see e.g. [12]. We investigated the use of formal methods to describe service level agreements in [2].

In this paper we focus on the composition of services especially considering Quality of Service aspects. A service composition is a set of services together with rules specifying how the various service work together to perform a common

---

task. There are various issues related to QoS composition. One could have a design of a composition with information regarding QoS of individual elements and wish to know the resulting QoS of the composition. One could have an abstract composition and might need to decide which services to select when implementing the composition in order to fulfill some QoS desiderata, e.g., [14]. In [20,19], the authors propose a QoS model and a middleware approach for dynamic QoS-driven service composition. They investigate a global planning approach to determine optimal service execution plans for composite service based on QoS criteria. Another interesting question is that of determining the QoS of a composition given basic QoS information of single service operations. In [6], a method is proposed to assess the QoS of a workflow, given the QoS of the individual tasks of the workflow. The methodology consists of a set of rewrite rules for the workflow aiming at arriving at the description of the QoS of the whole workflow.

In this paper, we consider the problem of QoS composition from a different perspective. Instead of resorting to a state based representation giving emphasis to tasks and the flow of control, as e.g. in [6], we take a stateless representation of composition, with individual services as elementary components, and WSDL message part names to represent the data flow. This choice is motivated by the Web service challenge (see http://www.comp.hkbu.edu.hk/~ctr/wschallenge/ and http://insel.flp.cs.tu-berlin.de/wsc06/) that consists in finding a composition of services which satisfies a given query. The granularity level of the query is at the level of message part names and the composition is modeled as a multigraph of services with part names as edges. In the present work, we generalize the simple model of the Web service challenge to include Quality of Service attributes, but also to allow defining different patterns in the composition by introducing input service expressions, built using logical operators. The resulting model turns out to be a compact form in which services have a central role and one can appreciate the message exchanged among services.

The rest of the paper is organized as follows. In Section 2, we introduce a simple running example of an application to know the temperature at a given location based on several services. In Section 3, we introduce the QoS model. Formal methods to reason about the QoS of the composition are discussed in Section 4, where we also give an algorithm for establishing the QoS of a composition. Concluding remarks and open research issues are summarized in Section 5.

2   A Service Composition Example

Suppose one wants to build an application for knowing the temperature at a given location. The application should be built using existing services. The non-functional requirements of the application consider the response time and cost of each run of the system. A design of the application is having a program invoking three services: Google to find out the longitude and latitude of the desired location,[3] a weather service to find the temperature,[4] and a temperature converter for having the temperature in either Fahrenheit or Celsius.[5] In addition, some processing will be done internally, e.g., extracting the coordinate information from Google result snippets. The example services should be considered only as motivation for the present work, for the ease of presentation we take the liberty of simplifying part names and messages of the services. We also assume that part names of services match, e.g., the output name of Google matches the input part name of Weather.org, even though this is not true in practice. Matching can be achieved resorting to semantic web, or more generally, ontology techniques (see for instance [1]) or by syntactic matching (see for instance [8]).

The input of the application is a text string identifying the location and a date. The output is a temperature in Celsius. Next, we consider how this simple example is formally modeled taking into account both the functional and the non-functional properties of the services, of the composition and the query.

3 Service Model

Web services standards originated from the industrial need for loosely coupled interprocess communication, there is very little formality beyond the mere XML schema definitions. Here we provide a formalization which allows us to represent both the functional and non-functional properties of services, of service compositions and of queries. Let us begin by the domain of our information system.

Definition 1 (functional service model). *A functional service model is a tuple $\langle S, P, M, in, out \rangle$ defined in the following way:*

- *S is a set of services,*
- *P is a set of part names,*
- *$M \in \mathcal{P}(P)$ is a set of messages consisting of part names*
- *in is a function $S \to \mathcal{P}(P)$, the set of input part names of a service,*
- *out is a function $S \to \mathcal{P}(P)$, the set of output part names of a service.*

By this definition, a *service* is thus a collection of input and output part names grouped into messages. In the present treatment, we do not consider part types and we use the message information to classify part names into input and output for the various services.

Example 1. Considering the weather example of Section 2, S consists of the services $\{Google, Weather.org, ITempConverter\}$, P consists of many part names, such as the following ones:

Google:
```
<xsd:element name="searchQuery" type="xsd:string"/>
<xsd:element name="searchTime" type="xsd:double"/>
```

---

[3] http://www.Google.com/apis/

[4] http://www.weather.gov/forecasts/xml/DWMLgen/wsdl/ndfdXML.wsdl

[5] http://developerdays.com/cgi-bin/tempconverter.exe/soap/ITempConverter

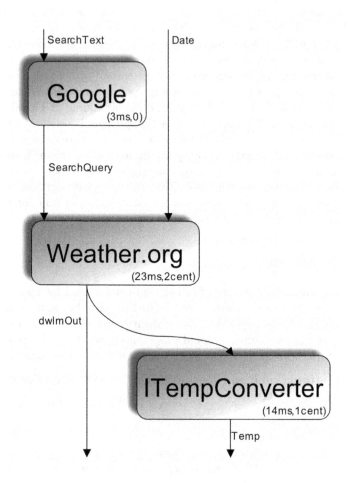

Fig. 1. The weather example modeled

```
Weather.org:
  <xsd:element name="temp" type="xsd:boolean"/>
  <part name="dwmlOut" type="xsd:string" />

ITempConverter:
  <part name="temp" type="xs:int"/>
```

an example of a message in M is given by the message of Google consisting of an input and an output message

```
<operation name="doGoogleSearch">
  <input message="typens:doGoogleSearch"/>
  <output message="typens:doGoogleSearchResponse"/>
</operation>
```

Finally, an example of an output function for the Google Web service is, omitting the XML syntactic sugar, $out(\text{Google})=\{\text{searchQuery}, \text{searchTime}\}$.

Let us now consider the non-functional properties by introducing our QoS model.

Definition 2 (QoS service model). *A* Quality of Service model *is an ordered set of groupoids* $\langle (G_i, \check{\star}_i \hat{\star}_i)_{i=1,\ldots,n} \rangle$*, where each groupoid i consist of a set G_i with two operations $\hat{\star}_i$ and $\check{\star}_i$. A* QoS element *with respect to a QoS model is a vector* $\langle q_1 \ldots q_n \rangle$ *were $q_i \in G_i$, for each $i = 1, \ldots, n$. We denote by $\check{\star}(q_a, q_b)$ and $\hat{\star}(q_a, q_b)$ the componentwise operations $(q_{a_1} \check{\star}_1 q_{b_1} \ldots q_{a_n} \check{\star}_n q_{b_n})$ and $(q_{a_1} \hat{\star}_1 q_{b_1} \ldots q_{a_n} \hat{\star}_n q_{b_n})$ among two services a and b with QoS elements $q_a = \langle q_{a_1} \ldots q_{a_n} \rangle$ and $q_b = \langle q_{b_1} \ldots q_{b_n} \rangle$.*

Notice that each groupoid models a QoS requirement and the groupoid operations, interpreting the operators in Definition 4, will be used to compute the QoS of a given composition.

Example 2. The weather example presented in Section 2 considers two QoS requirements. One tied to execution time and one to costs. Therefore, the QoS service model consists of two groupoids, e.g., the real numbers with the addition and the average for considering time and the integers with addition and max for the cost. Then we have that any part name associated with Google has a quality cost which is zero, while an execution time which is in the range of the few seconds. The latter can be modeled in various ways. One can take the average of the execution times experienced in the past, one can consider the value returned by Google itself as output in searchTime for a given request. One may even look at a finer granularity of the execution time as we do in [16]. The choice is not relevant for the present treatment.

Having defined what a service is from a functional and a from a non-functional point of view, let us consider collections of services populating the same network which can be invoked as parts of a same composition process. Such a composition can be the result of a design process or of a search to satisfy a service query. Let us define the latter concept formally.

Definition 3 (service query). *A* service query *over a set of services S is an expression of the form i^*, o^+ where $i \in P$ are the optional input query part names, $o \in P$ are the query output part names, and $^*,^+$ are the usual Kleene string operators.*

Example 3. The service query **SearchText Date , Temp** means that the requester provides a text and a date, and desires to get a temperature.

Definition 4 (input service expressions). *An* input service expression *associated to a service S_1 is a string built over the input part names of S_1 (called atoms) using the binary, associative, and commutative operators $\bar{\wedge}$ and $\bar{\vee}$ and the auxiliary symbols $(,)$.*

Example 4. An input service expression associated to a "transform address into zip code" service which has in ={address, city, zip_code}, out ={zip_code,time} is (address∧̄city)∇̄zip_code whose intended semantics is that either a zip code or an address **and** a city are provided.

We are now in the position of defining a service composition.

Definition 5 (service composition). *A* service composition *over a service collection* $C = \langle S, P, M, in, out \rangle$ *and QoS model* $\langle (G_i, \star_i \hat{\star}_i)_{i=1,...,n} \rangle$, *is a labeled multigraph* $\langle V, E, ExpI, Q_V \rangle$ *with the following properties:*

1. *each element* $v \in V$, *is either in* S *or* $\exists\, v' \in V \cap S$ *such that the services* v *and* v' *differ only for their names.*
2. $E \subseteq V \times V \times P$, *and* $e = \langle v_1, v_2, p \rangle \in E$ *if* $out(v_1) = in(v_2) = p \in P$
3. *ExpI is a function associating to each element* $v \in V$ *an input service expression associated to* v.
4. Q_V *is a function associating to each element* $v \in V$ *a QoS element.*

Condition 1. in the above definition says that multiple occurrences of a service in the multigraph are identified using different node names. Condition 2. says that there is an edge in the graph connecting two services only if a part name is output and input of the two services, respectively. Condition 3. and 4. specify the labels assigned to each node v: an input expression ($ExpI(v)$) and an element of QoS ($Q_V(v)$) that is, the quality of the individual service.

Example 5. Following the above definition, the composition presented in Section 2 is then modeled as shown in Figure 1. Where the query is `SearchText Date, Temp`. Consider the service Weather.org: its associated input expression can be SearchQuery∧̄Date "meaning" that both a SearchQuery and a Date must be provided while (23ms,2cent) stands for its QoS values of time and cost.

4   Model Inspection, Checking, Construction

Having a formal model of services and their compositions from a functional and non-functional point of view enables the use of a number of formal methods techniques to reason about services. The main methods to be used range from the simple model inspection to determine the QoS of a given composition, to the model checking of a composition, up to the more complex task of model construction. Figure 2 summarizes the most interesting methods and the tasks they address. In the present treatment we take a closer look at the first one, that is, the model inspection for determining the QoS of a given composition.

In [3], we provided algorithms for dealing with the model construction problem where we do not consider input expressions for QoS. The same problem is solved using a partial order planner in [7].

method	input	task	output
model inspection	a composition and a query	know the QoS for the query	an element of the QoS model
model checking	a composition, a query, and a QoS property	find if the query satisfies the QoS	yes/no
(directed) model checking	a composition, a query, and a QoS property	find, if it exists, the proof which is optimal w.r.t. QoS	optimal proof
model construction	a query, a functional and QoS service models	create a composition	the composition, if it exists, satisfying the query

Fig. 2. Methods to reason about QoS service composition

4.1   Modeling at the Level of Part Names

Given a composition of services (that is, a multigraph like the one in Figure 1 together with input, and QoS values) and a query stating which part names are available and which are the desired ones, we want to arrive at the determination of the QoS of the composition for the given query. But first we need to lift the Q_V function, that associates qualities of services with services (nodes v in the labeled multigraph) in the composition, to input service expressions. We do so using the following recursive definition.

Definition 6. *(input expression QoS) Given a service composition $\langle V, E, ExpI, Q_V \rangle$, let $v \in V$ and $e, e_1, e_2 \in ExpI(v)$, then the input expression QoS function Q over an input service expression e is defined in the following way:*

- *if e is an atom, $Q(e) = Q_V(w)$, where $\langle w, v, e \rangle$ is in E;*
- *$Q(e_1 \bar{\wedge} e_2) = \hat{\star}(Q(e_1), Q(e_2))$ where e_1, e_2 are input expressions and $\star$ are the first operators of the respective QoS groupoids;*
- *$Q(e_1 \bar{\vee} e_2) = \check{\star}(Q(e_1), Q(e_2))$ where e_1, e_2 are input expressions and $\check{\star}$ are the second operators of the respective QoS groupoids.*

We remark that the $\hat{\star}$ and $\check{\star}$ operators are chosen when designing the composition.

Example 6. If we are interested in QoS time, then it could be modeled by a groupoid whose universe is the set of real numbers and whose operations $\hat{\star}$ and $\check{\star}$

could be the addition and the max function. The operations's choice depends on the considered web service composition and on the goal of the QoS model as defined by the composition designer or user. E.g., addition and max allow both sequential and parallel arcs to be modeled in the service composition graph. On the other hand, when parallel arcs do not occur in the service composition graph and we are interested in the average QoS of the composition, then the function max could be replaced by the function average.

Notice that in our model, the information on how services relate/interact are contained both in the arcs and in the input service expressions associated to nodes of the labeled multigraphs. This renders the modeling of composition provided a more compact and flexible form for representing Web service compositions than, e.g., workflows. For instance, the sequential composition at the task level of Fig. 3 (assume the operations between S_1 and S_2 consist of the three part names p_a, p_b and p_c and the considered QoS is time) can be represented by the labeled composition multigraph of Fig. 4. in which $ExpI(S_2) = p_a \bar{\wedge} p_b \bar{\wedge} p_c$ and the operator $\bar{\wedge}$

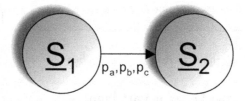

Fig. 3. Sequential flow

is interpreted as real numbers addition. Taking however $ExpI(S_2) = p_a \bar{\vee} p_b \bar{\vee} p_c$, where $\bar{\vee}$ is interpreted as the maximum between real numbers, the composition multigraph of Fig. 4 . would then correspond to the parallel composition at the task level of Fig. 5.

Therefore, by changing the input service expressions associated to S_2 (while the interpretations of $\bar{\wedge}$ and $\bar{\vee}$ remain the same), the composition multigraph of Fig. 4 would correspond to 2^3 different workflows.

Of course, there are other differences among the modeling we propose at the part name level and workflows beside the compact representation of the former with respect to the latter. The most notable differences include: stateless vs. statefull representation and data centered representation vs. control flow representation, respectively.

4.2   Model Inspection

In the following we assume there are no loops and that the compositions are correctly designed with respect to the queries. Relaxing the former assumption requires appropriate algorithms in the spirit of [6], while relaxing the latter assumption brings us to the terrain of model checking, rather than model inspection.

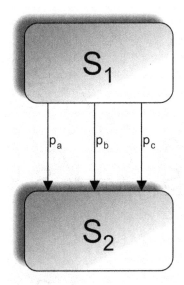

Fig. 4. Composition at the part name level

Algorithm 1. Model Inspection(composition $\langle V, E, ExpI, Q_V \rangle$, query i, o)

$V = V \bigcup \{\text{query } Qu_I, Qu_O \text{ nodes created using } i, o\}$
active parts $= i$
QoS associated with Qu_I set to the default value
loop
    consider a node $v \in V$ such that $in(v) \in$active parts
    active parts $=$ active parts $\bigcup out(v)$
    $Q(v) = \hat{\star}(Q(v), Q(ExpI(v)))$ according to Definition 6
    if $v = Qu_O$ **return** $Q(Qu_O)$
end loop

The algorithm (Algorithm 1) for model inspection works by traversing the composition graph and computing the QoS of the composition. The algorithm takes a composition graph and a query. It uses the query for determining the set of initial active parts and builds two extra nodes to represent the query input Q_I and output Q_O. Active parts are the messages which are available for the composition. The vector QoS keeps the value of the QoS during the computation and is initially set to the default values (for instance cost is set to 0). The loop of the algorithm takes nondeterministically a node for which all input parts are active. Given the assumption of correct design there is always such a node, or we have reached the end of the computation. Then the output part of the considered node are added to the set of active parts. We are now in the position of computing the new QoS for the considered node. The computation of the service QoS in the

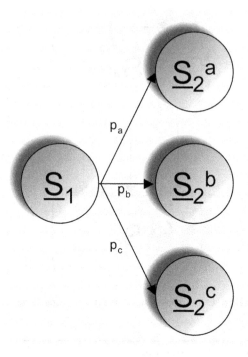

Fig. 5. Parallel flow

given composition is performed by computing the QoS of its input expression and 'adding' $\hat{\star}$ the QoS of the service. Of the two groupoid operation sets $\hat{\star}$ and $\check{\star}$, the former is in the algorithm as this is the one which should model the logical and, i.e., the addition of the quality of service computed so far and the quality of service of the specific service. Given the absence of loops we notice that the non-deterministic choice of a node does not affect the correctness of the algorithm. Finally, if the node considered was the final node of the composition we exit the loop returning the computed QoS.

4.3   A Run on the Weather Example

Let us consider again the weather example of Section 2, shown in Figure 1, and apply Algorithm 1. We start by setting the active parts to the query SearchText and Date, adding the node Q_I to which we associate the default quality of service of $(0,0)$: no time and no costs. We also add the node Q_O to represent the end of the query which has as input parts the queried Temp, its input expression is simply $Temp$. Then the loop begins.

At the first iteration we can only consider the Google service. In fact, its input part names are all active, on the other hand Weather.org has one input part name active (Date) but not the other one (SearchQuery). We then add the output part (SearchQuery) of Google to the active part names and update its quality of service. The quality of service associated with this service was (3,0)—it takes Google 3 milliseconds and it is for free—which is combined with the evaluation of the input expression of SearchText which is (0,0). In this case, the quality of service does not change.

At the following iteration we can choose the Weather.org service. We add its output part to the active part names and then we compute the quality of service for its two inputs. We have (3,0) and (0,0), respectively. Supposing that the input expression is SearchQuery∧Date, that $\hat{\star}$ is modeled as real numbers addition and integer addition, and that its QoS is (23,2), then we update the QoS of Weather org with (26,2). At the final iteration iTempConverter is chosen yielding a final QoS associated with it of (40,3). We then conclude that the QoS of the composition is 40 milliseconds and 3 cents. Again these could be minimum, maximal, average values or something else, depending on the choice made in the composition design.

5   Concluding Remarks

We have presented preliminary work aimed at modeling Web service compositions from a functional and non-functional point of view at the granularity level of the part names. Following this modeling, we overview a number of formal methods techniques that allow to reason with QoS composition based on the proposed model, and propose an algorithm for determining the QoS of a given composition given the QoS associated with the individual services.

In this initial work, we made a number of simplifying assumptions which we will remove in future work. In particular, we have not considered loops in the compositions while these could be present and need to be modeled. We have not presented output expressions (the natural counterpart of input expressions for services), and we have not considered limitations on the use of part names (for instance, one could impose that a part name is used only once by any service). Furthermore, we have only provided an algorithm for the case of model inspection, leaving open the challenge of finding algorithms for model checking and model constructions.

Acknowledgments

We thank Ganna Frankova for comments on a previous version of this paper and discussion on related work.

References

1. R. Aggarwal, K. Verma, J. Miller, and W. Milnor. Constraint Driven Web Service Composition in METEOR-S. In *Proceedings of the 2004 IEEE International Conference on Services Computing*, Shanghai, China, September 2004.

2. M. Aiello, G. Frankova, and D. Malfatti. What's in an agreement? A formal analysis and an extension of WS-Agreement. In *Int. Conf. on Service-Oriented Computing (ICSOC 2005)*, 2005.

3. M. Aiello, C. Platzer, F. Rosenberg, H. Tran, M. Vasko, and S. Dustdar. Web service indexing for efficient retrieval and composition. In *In Joint 8th IEEE Conference on E-Commerce Technology (CEC'06) and the 3rd IEEE Conference on Enterprise Computing, E-Commerce and E-Services*. IEEE Computer, 2006. To appear.

4. G. Alonso, F. Casati, H Kuno, and V. Machiraju. *Web Services*. Springer-Verlag, 2004.

5. A. Atzeni and A. Lioy. Why to Adopt a Security Metric? A Brief Survey. In *Proceedings of the First Workshop on Quality of Protection*, Milan, Italy, September 2005.

6. J. Cardoso, A. Sheth, J. Miller, J. Arnold, and K. Kochut. Quality of service for workflows and web service processes. *Journal of Web Semantics*, 1(3):281–308, 2004.

7. J. Dorn, P. Hrastnik, and A. Rainer. Web service discovery and composition for virtual enterprises. *International Journal of Web Services Research*, 2006. To appear.

8. I. Elgedawy, Z. Tari, and M. Winikoff. Exact functional context matching for web services. In M. Aiello, M. Aoyama, F. Curbera, and M. P. Papazoglou, editors, *Int. Conf. on Service-Oriented Computing (ICSOC 2004)*, pages 143–152. ACM, 2004.

9. S. Frølund and J. Koistinen. Quality-of-Service Specification in Distributed Object Systems. *Distributed Systems Engineering*, 5(4):179–202, December 1998.

10. D. Gouscos, M. Kalikakis, and P. Georgiadis. An approach to modeling web service QoS and provision price. In *1st Web Services Quality Workshop (WQW2003) at WISE*, 2003.

11. M. Lin, J. Xie, H. Guo, and H. Wang. Solving QoS-Driven Web Service Dynamic Composition as Fuzzy Constraint Satisfaction. In *Proceedings of the IEEE International Conference on e-Technology, e-Commerce and e-Service*, Hong Kong, China, March-April 2005.

12. H. Ludwig. Web services QoS: External SLAs and internal policies or: How do we deliver what we promise? In *1st Web Services Quality Workshop (WQW2003) at WISE*, 2003.

13. D.A. Menasce. QoS issues in Web services. *IEEE Internet Computing*, 6(6):72–75, November/December 2002.

14. D.A. Menasce. Composing Web Services: A QoS View. *IEEE Internet Computing*, 8(6):88–90, November/December 2004.

15. S. Ran. A model for web services discovery with QoS. *SIGecom Exchanges*, 4(1): 1–10, 2003.

16. F. Rosenberg, C. Platzer, and S. Dustdar. Bootstrapping performance and dependability attributes of web services. In *Proceedings of the IEEE International Conference on Web Services (ICWS'06)*. IEEE Computer, 2006. To appear.

17. M. Tian, A. Gramm, T. Naumowicz, H. Ritter, and J. Schiller. A concept for QoS integration in web services. In *1st Web Services Quality Workshop (WQW2003) at WISE*, 2003.

18. M. Tian, A. Gramm, H. Ritter, and J. Schiller. Efficient Selection and Monitoring of QoS-aware Web Services with the WS-QoS Framework. In *Proceedings of the IEEE/WIC/ACM International Conference on Web Intelligence*, Beijing, China, September 2004.

19. L. Zeng, B. Benatallah, Ngu; A.H.H., M. Dumas, J. Kalagnanam, and H. Chang. Qos-aware middleware for web services composition. *IEEE Transactions on Software Engineering*, 30(5):311–327, May 2004.
20. L. Zeng, B. Benatallah, M. Dumas, J. Kalagnanam, and Q.Z. Sheng. Quality driven web services composition. In *Proceedings of the 12th International Conference on World Wide Web (WWW'03)*, pages 411–421, New York, NY, USA, 2003. ACM Press.

SCC: A Service Centered Calculus*

M. Boreale, R. Bruni, L. Caires, R. De Nicola,
I. Lanese, M. Loreti, F. Martins, U. Montanari,
A. Ravara, D. Sangiorgi, V. Vasconcelos, and G. Zavattaro

EU Integrated Project SENSORIA
sensoria-core@di.unipi.it

Abstract. We seek for a small set of primitives that might serve as a
basis for formalising and programming service oriented applications over
global computers. As an outcome of this study we introduce here SCC,
a process calculus that features explicit notions of service definition, service invocation and session handling. Our proposal has been influenced
by Orc, a programming model for structured orchestration of services,
but the SCC's session handling mechanism allows for the definition of
structured interaction protocols, more complex than the basic *request-
response* provided by Orc. We present syntax and operational semantics
of SCC and a number of simple but nontrivial programming examples
that demonstrate flexibility of the chosen set of primitives. A few encodings are also provided to relate our proposal with existing ones.

1 Introduction

The SENSORIA project [17], funded by the European Union, aims at developing a novel, comprehensive approach to the engineering of software systems for
service-oriented overlay computers. Specifically, SENSORIA focuses on methods
and tools for the development of global services that are context adaptive, per-
sonalisable, possibly with different constraints on resources and performance,
and to be deployed on significantly different global computers. SENSORIA seeks
for full integration of foundational theories, techniques and methods in a prag-
matic software engineering approach.

A crucial role in the project will be played by formalisms for service description that lay the mathematical basis for analysing and experimenting with
components interactions, for combining services and formalising crucial aspects
of service level agreements.

Industrial consortia are developing orchestration languages, targeting the
standardization of Web services and XML-centric technologies. However, existing standards lack clear semantic foundations. We aim at developing a general
theory of services that should lead to calculi based on process algebras but enriched with primitives for manipulating semi-structured data (such as pattern
matching or unification). The theory should encompass techniques for deriving

---

* Research supported by the Project FET-GC II IST-2005-16004 SENSORIA.

M. Bravetti, M. Nuñes, and G. Zavattaro (Eds.): WS-FM 2006, LNCS 4184, pp. 38–57, 2006.

contracts, tools for querying and discovery of service specifications, transactional mechanisms to aggregate unreliable services. The calculi will be equipped with rigorous semantic foundations and analytical tools to prove correctness of system specifications and enable formal verification of properties.

Herewith we present a name passing process calculus with explicit notions of *service definition, service invocation* and *bi-directional sessioning*. During the first year of the project a few other work-in-progress proposals emerged [8,10,14,4], and their comparison, refinement and integration will constitute a prominent research activity for the prosecution of the project. Our proposal has been influenced by Cook and Misra's Orc [16], a basic programming model for structured orchestration of services, for which we show a rather natural encoding. In particular, Orc is particularly appealing because of its simplicity and yet great generality: its three basic composition operators can be used to model the most common workflow patterns, identified by van der Aalst et al. in [18].

Our calculus, called SCC (for Service Centered Calculus), has novel features for programming and composing services, while taking into account their dynamic behaviour. In particular, SCC supports explicit modeling of sessions both on client- and on service-side, including protocols executed by each side during an interaction and mechanisms for session naming and scoping, the latter inspired by the π-calculus. Sessions allow us to describe and reason about interaction modalities more structured than the simple *one-way* and *request-response* modalities provided by Orc and typical of a producer / consumer pattern. Moreover, in SCC sessions can be closed thus providing a mechanism for process interruption and service cancellation and update which has no counterpart in most process calculi.

Summarising, SCC combines the service oriented flavour of Orc with the name passing communication mechanism of the π-calculus. One may argue that we could, in our analysis of service oriented computing, exploit directly π-calculus instead of introducing yet another process calculus. It can be easily seen, from the encoding of a fragment of our calculus in the π-calculus reported in Figure 5, that all the information pertaining to sessioning and client-service protocols get mixed up (if not lost) with the other communication primitives, making it difficult to reason on the resulting process. The motivation behind the introduction of a new calculus is that a small set of well-disciplined primitives will favor and make more scalable the development of typing systems and proof techniques centered around the notions of service and session, for ensuring, e.g., compatibility of client and service behaviour, or the absence of deadlock in service composition.

Within SCC, services are seen as sort of interacting functions (and even stream processing functions) that can be invoked by clients. Service definitions take the form $s \Rightarrow (x)P$, where s is the service name, x is a formal parameter, and P is the actual implementation of the service. For instance, $\mathtt{succ} \Rightarrow (x)x + 1$ models a service that, received an integer returns its successor. Service invocations are written as $s\{(x)P\} \Leftarrow Q$: each new value v produced by the client Q will trigger a new invocation of service s; for each invocation, an instance of the process P, with x bound to the actual invocation value v, implements the client-side protocol for interacting with the new instance of s. As an example, a client for the simple service described above will be written in SCC as $\mathsf{succ}\{(x)(y)\mathsf{return}\,y\} \Leftarrow 5$: after the invocation x is bound to the argument 5, the client waits for a value from the server and the received value is substituted for y and hence returned as the result of the service invocation.

A service invocation causes activation of a new session. A pair of dual fresh names, r and $\bar{r}$, identifies the two sides of the session. Client and service protocols are instantiated each at the proper side of the session. For instance, interaction of the client and of the service described above triggers the session

$$(\nu r)(r \rhd 5+1 \,|\, \bar{r} \rhd (y)\mathsf{return}\,y)$$

(in this case, the client side makes no use of the formal parameter). The value 6 is computed on the service-side and then received at the client side, that reduces first to $\bar{r} \rhd \mathsf{return}\,6$ and then to $6 \,|\, \bar{r} \rhd \mathbf{0}$ (where $\mathbf{0}$ denotes the nil process).

More generally, within sessions communication is bi-directional, in the sense that the interacting protocols can exchange data in both directions. Values returned outside the session to the enclosing environment can be used for invoking other services. For instance, what follows is a client that invokes the service succ and then prints the obtained result:

$$\mathsf{print}\{(z)\mathbf{0}\} \Leftarrow (\,\mathsf{succ}\{(x)(y)\mathsf{return}\,y\} \Leftarrow 5\,).$$

(in this case, the service print is invoked with vacuous protocol $(z)\mathbf{0}$).

A protocol, both on client-side and on service-side, can be interrupted (e.g. due to the occurrence of an unexpected event), and interruption can be notified to the environment. More generally, the keyword close can be used to terminate a protocol on one side and to notify the termination status to a suitable handler at the partner site. For example, the above client is extended below for exploiting a suitable service $\mathtt{fault}$ that can handle printer failures:

$$\mathsf{print}\{(z)\mathbf{0}\} \Leftarrow_{\mathtt{fault}} (\,\mathsf{succ}\{(x)(y)\mathsf{return}\,y\} \Leftarrow 5\,).$$

The formal presentation of SCC involves some key notational and technical solutions that must be well motivated and explained. For this reason, our choice is to give a gentle, step-by-step presentation of the various ingredients.

Synopsis. The paper is organized as follows. Syntax and reduction semantics of the close-free fragment of SCC are presented in Section 2, together with a few motivating examples and encodings. The full calculus is discussed in Section 3. In Section 4 we show how to encode Orc programs into SCC. Some concluding remarks are in Section 5.

2 Persistent Sessions: The **Close-Free** Fragment of **SCC**

We start by presenting the close-free fragment of SCC, based on three main concepts: (i) service definition, (ii) service invocation, and (iii) bi-directional

$$
\begin{array}{lll}
P, Q & ::= \mathbf{0} & \text{Nil} \\
& | \ a.P & \text{Concretion} \\
& | \ (x)P & \text{Abstraction} \\
& | \ \text{return } a.P & \text{Return Value} \\
& | \ a \Rightarrow (x)P & \text{Service Definition} \\
& | \ a\{(x)P\} \Leftarrow Q & \text{Service Invocation} \\
& | \ a \rhd P & \text{Session} \\
& | \ P|Q & \text{Parallel Composition} \\
& | \ (\nu a)P & \text{New Name}
\end{array}
$$

Fig. 1. Syntax of processes

$$
\begin{array}{lll}
(P|Q)|R \equiv P|(Q|R) & P|\mathbf{0} \equiv P & P|Q \equiv Q|P \\
(\nu x)(\nu y)P \equiv (\nu y)(\nu x)P & (\nu x)\mathbf{0} \equiv \mathbf{0} & a \rhd \mathbf{0} \equiv \mathbf{0} \\
P|(\nu x)Q \equiv (\nu x)(P|Q) \text{ if } x \notin \text{fn}(P) & a \rhd (\nu x)P \equiv (\nu x)(a \rhd P) \text{ if } x \neq a, \bar{a} \\
\multicolumn{3}{c}{a\{(x)P\} \Leftarrow (\nu y)Q \equiv (\nu y)(a\{(x)P\} \Leftarrow Q) \text{ if } y \notin \text{fn}((x)P) \cup \{a, \bar{a}\}}
\end{array}
$$

Fig. 2. Structural congruence

sessioning. We call it PSC for *persistent session calculus*: sessions can be established and garbage collected when the protocol has run entirely, but can neither be aborted nor closed by one of the parties.

Syntax. We presuppose a countable set $\mathcal{N}$ of names $a, b, c, ..., r, s, ..., x, y, ...$ A bijection $^-$ on $\mathcal{N}$ is presupposed s.t. $\bar{\bar{a}} = a$ for each name a. Note that contrary to common use of the notation, a for input and $\bar{a}$ denoting output, in SCC a and $\bar{a}$ denote dual session names, that can be used for communicating in both directions. The syntax of PSC is in Figure 1, with the operators listed in decreasing order of precedence. Free occurrences of x in P (including $\bar{x}$) are bound in $(\nu x)P$ and $(x)P$. Capture-avoiding substitution of the free occurrences of x with v (and of $\bar{x}$ with $\bar{v}$) in P is denoted by $P[v/x]$. Moreover, we identify processes up to alpha-equivalence and we omit trailing $\mathbf{0}$.

Structural Congruence. Structural congruence $\equiv$ is defined as the least congruence relation induced by the rules in Figure 2. We include the expected structural laws for parallel composition and restriction, and one rule for garbage collection of completed sessions ($a \rhd \mathbf{0} \equiv \mathbf{0}$). Note that scope extrusion for restriction comes in three different forms.

Well-Formedness. Assuming by alpha conversion that all bound names in a process P are different from each other and from the free names, the process P is *well-formed* if each session name a occurs only once (occurrences that can be deleted using structural congruence do not count), but it is allowed to have both sessions $a \rhd Q$ and $\bar{a} \rhd Q'$. In the remainder of this paper, all processes are well-formed. It is straightforward to check that the semantic rules preserve well-formedness. Note that, for the economy of this paper, it is not stricly

$$\begin{aligned}
&\mathbb{C}[\![\, s \Rightarrow (x)P \,]\!] \mid \\
&\mathbb{D}[\![\, s\{(y)P'\} \Leftarrow (Q|u.R) \,]\!]
\end{aligned} \quad \rightarrow \quad (\nu r) \left(\begin{aligned} &\mathbb{C}[\![\, r \triangleright P[u\!/x] \mid s \Rightarrow (x)P \,]\!] \mid \\ &\mathbb{D}[\![\, \bar{r} \triangleright P'[u\!/y] \mid s\{(y)P'\} \Leftarrow (Q|R) \,]\!] \end{aligned} \right)$$

if r is fresh and u, s not bound by $\mathbb{C}, \mathbb{D}$

$$\mathbb{C}[\![\, r \triangleright (P|u.Q) \,]\!] \mid \mathbb{D}[\![\, \bar{r} \triangleright (R|(z)S) \,]\!] \quad \rightarrow \quad \mathbb{C}[\![\, r \triangleright (P|Q) \,]\!] \mid \mathbb{D}[\![\, \bar{r} \triangleright (R|S[u\!/z]) \,]\!]$$

if u, r not bound by $\mathbb{C}, \mathbb{D}$

$$r \triangleright (P|\mathsf{return}\, u.Q) \quad \rightarrow \quad u \mid r \triangleright (P|Q)$$

$$\mathbb{C}[\![P]\!] \quad \rightarrow \quad \mathbb{C}[\![P']\!] \quad \text{if } P \equiv Q,\ Q \rightarrow Q',\ Q' \equiv P'$$

where $\mathbb{C}, \mathbb{D} ::= [\cdot] \mid \mathbb{C}|P \mid a\{(x)P\} \Leftarrow \mathbb{C} \mid a \triangleright \mathbb{C} \mid (\nu a)\mathbb{C}$

Fig. 3. Reduction semantics

necessary to introduce dual names, but we prefer to keep this distinction to make evident that once the protocol is started there might still be some reasons for distinguishing the two side ends (e.g., when typing is considered).

Operational Semantics. Restriction and parallel composition have the standard meaning. Informally, the meaning of the other primitives listed in Figure 1 can be explained as follows. Service definitions take the form $s \Rightarrow (x)P$, where s is the name of the service and $(x)P$ is the body of the service: a (service-side) interaction protocol with formal parameter x. Service definitions are persistent, i.e., each new invocation is served by a fresh instance of the protocol (process calculists may think of an implicit replication prefixing each service definition). A service invocation $s\{(x)P'\} \Leftarrow Q$ invokes s for any concretion (value) u produced by the execution of Q. The process $(x)P'$ is the client-side protocol for interacting with (the instance of) s. For example if after some steps Q reduces to $Q'|u$, then a fresh session can be established, that takes the form

$$(\nu r)(r \triangleright P[u\!/x] \mid \bar{r} \triangleright P'[u\!/x])$$

and that runs in parallel with $s\{(x)P'\} \Leftarrow Q'$ and $s \Rightarrow (x)P$. The session r has two sides: one for the client and one for the service. Note that value u serves as the actual parameter of both P and P'. Within the session r, the protocols $P[u\!/x]$ and $P'[u\!/x]$ can communicate whenever a concretion a is available on one side and an abstraction $(z)R'$ is ready on the other side, i.e., abstractions and concretions model input and output, respectively. For example, $r \triangleright (a|R) \mid \bar{r} \triangleright (z)R'$ would reduce to $r \triangleright R \mid \bar{r} \triangleright R'[a\!/z]$. The primitive $\mathsf{return}\, a$ can then be used to return a value outside the current session (just one level up, not to the top level). Sessions, service definitions and service invocations can be nested at arbitrary depth, but in any interaction just the innermost service or session name counts.

Formally, the reduction semantics is defined in Figure 3. The reduction rules are defined using the active contexts $\mathbb{C}, \mathbb{D}$ that specify where the processes that interact can be located. An active context is simply a process with a hole in an active position, i.e., a place where a process can execute. With $\mathbb{C}[\![P]\!]$ we denote the process obtained by filling the hole in $\mathbb{C}$ with P. In PSC only two kinds of interactions are permitted: service invocation and session communication modeled by the first two rules, respectively. A third rule models returned values, that are made available outside the session. Finally, the last rule simply closes the reduction semantics with respect to structural congruence and active contexts.

2.1 Toy Examples

We present in this section a few simple examples. Some of them are also used to introduce some shorthand notation for syntax of frequent use.

Precisely, the notations that we introduce are:

$$s \Leftarrow P \text{ Example 1}$$
$$(-)P \text{ Example 2}$$
$$a\{\} \Leftarrow P \text{ Example 3}$$

Also, we presuppose a distinct name $\bullet$ to be used as a unit value.

The examples are chosen so to evaluate the expressiveness and usability of PSC as a language for service orchestration, challenging its ability of encoding some frequently used service composition patterns. A library of basic patterns, called the *workflow patterns*, has been identified by van der Aalst et al. in [18]. It will be shown in Section 4 that full SCC can encode Orc [16], a script language for service orchestration able to model the workflow patterns [9].

Example 1 (Functional flavour). A simple example of service invocation is

$$s\{(x)(y)\mathsf{return}\, y\} \Leftarrow v$$

where the service s is invoked with just one value v. The client-side protocol $(x)(y)\mathsf{return}\, y$ has the following meaning: the name x is bound to the invocation value v at invocation time, thus the actual protocol run after service invocation is $((y)\mathsf{return}\, y)[v/x] = (y)\mathsf{return}\, y$ that simply waits for a value as the result of the service invocation and then publishes it locally (outside the private session started upon invocation).

This example reports a typical pattern of service invocation for which we introduce the specific notation $s \Leftarrow P$ which stands for $s\{(x)(y)\mathsf{return}\, y\} \Leftarrow P$. In order to show the advantages of this abbreviation, consider e.g. the functional composition of services: a service f is invoked first (with argument v) and the returned value (if any) is then given as an argument to another service g. With the shorthand notation, then the process can be written as

$$g \Leftarrow (f \Leftarrow v)$$

or simply $g \Leftarrow f \Leftarrow v$, stipulating that $\Leftarrow$ is right-associative. For example, $\mathsf{succ} \Leftarrow \mathsf{succ} \Leftarrow 5$ will return 7. Without abbreviations, one should write something like $\mathsf{succ}\{(z)(w)\mathsf{return}\, w\} \Leftarrow (\mathsf{succ}\{(x)(y)\mathsf{return}\, y\} \Leftarrow v)$.

Example 2 (Pairing service). Starting from this example, to shorten the notation, we use tuples of values $\langle v_1, \ldots, v_n \rangle$ and polyadic abstractions $(a_1, \ldots, a_n)P$. As an example of service definition consider the following *pairing* service

$$pair \Rightarrow (z)(x)(y)\langle x, y \rangle$$

Note that the invocation value z is not used, and the two values to be paired are passed to the protocol executed on service-side from the protocol run on client-side (after service invocation) and bound to x and y respectively. Binding occurrences of names that are not subsequently used (like z above) are abbreviated with $-$. Hence the pairing service can be written as $pair \Rightarrow (-)(x)(y)\langle x, y \rangle$.

A sample usage of the *pairing* service is

$$pair\{(-)(\, P \,|\, Q \,|\, (p)\textsf{return}\, p \,)\} \Leftarrow \bullet$$

where P and Q give results to be paired. The pair produced by the service is bound to p and returned as the result. This example also shows that client-side and service-side protocols can exchange values bi-directionally.

Though for the sake of simplicity, this example (and other examples discussed later) might suggest that an instantiation value for starting the session is not always necessary, we have wired its presence in the syntax as a guidance to a uniform style of service programming: in practice it is often the case that sessions can be established only upon authentication checks or that different kinds of sessions are selected based on the kind of the request (e.g. for balancing the load of different servers).

Another point to notice is that inside a session it is possible not only to exchange data with the partner and return values to the environment, but also to input data from outside source (in the example above, this can be achieved by using service invocations within P and Q).

Example 3 (Blind invocation). Sometimes no reply is expected from a service, thus the client employs a vacuous protocol, in which case we just write

$$a\{\} \Leftarrow P$$

for $a\{(-)\mathbf{0}\} \Leftarrow P$. As an example combining the notational conventions seen so far, assume that there are the following available services: service *emailMe* that expects a value *msg* and then sends the message *msg* to your email address; services *ANSA*, *BBC* and *CNN* that return the latest news. Then the process

$$emailMe\{\} \Leftarrow pair\{(-)(ANSA \Leftarrow \bullet \,|\, BBC \Leftarrow \bullet \,|\, CNN \Leftarrow \bullet \,|\, (p)\textsf{return}\, p)\} \Leftarrow \bullet$$

will send you only the first two news items collected from *ANSA*, *BBC* and *CNN*.

Example 4 (Recursion). Service invocations can be nested recursively inside a service definition. For example

$$clock \Rightarrow (-)(\textsf{return}\, \texttt{tick} \,|\, clock\{\} \Leftarrow \bullet)$$

defines a service that, when invoked with $clock\{\} \Leftarrow \bullet$, produces an infinite number of tick values on the service-side. To produce the tick values on a specific location different from the service-side, the service to be invoked can be written as

$$remoteClock \Rightarrow (s)\big(s\{\} \Leftarrow \text{tick} \mid remoteClock\{\} \Leftarrow s\big)$$

and a local publishing service

$$pub \Rightarrow (s)\text{return } s$$

should be located where the tick is to be produced. The name pub should be passed to $remoteClock$ as argument: $remoteClock\{\} \Leftarrow pub$. This is also an example of service-name passing. The service pub (or alike) can be useful in many applications, because it allows to publish values in the location where it is placed. In fact, in PSC *sessions cannot be closed* and therefore recursive invocations on the client-side are nested at increasing depth (while the return instruction can move values only one level up).

Similarly to the last example, a recursive process that receives the name of a service s and a value x and then repeatedly invokes s (the first time on x, then on the last value computed by previous invocations) is shown below:

$$rec \Rightarrow (s,x)\big(s\{(-)(y)(\text{return } y \mid rec\{\} \Leftarrow \langle s,y \rangle)\} \Leftarrow x\big).$$

Again, if the computed values have to be published on the client-side, then the service can carry the name of the publishing service p located on the client-side as an additional parameter:

$$remoteRec \Rightarrow (s,x,p)\big(s\{(-)(y)(p\{\} \Leftarrow y \mid remoteRec\{\} \Leftarrow \langle s,y,p \rangle)\} \Leftarrow x\big).$$

As an example of invocation of the service $remoteRec$, consider the client

$$remoteRec\{\} \Leftarrow \langle \text{succ}, 0, pub \rangle \mid pub \Rightarrow (x)\text{return } x$$

that returns (at the client-side) the stream of positive integers.

Example 5 (Pipeline and forwarder). The process seen at the end of the previous example produces an unbound stream of values. More generally, it should be possible to deploy some sort of pipeline between two services p and q in such a way that q is invoked for each value produced by p. If P is a process that produces a stream of values then the composition $q \Leftarrow P$ already achieves the aim. Thus to compose p and q in a pipeline it suffices to design a client-side protocol for collecting all the values returned by p. If the calculus included a π-calculus like replicator $!P$ or even just abstraction guarded like $!(x)P$, then the protocol could be written just as

$$pipe = (-)!(x)\text{return } x.$$

Another possibility is to extend the return prefix so to return an arbitrary process, with syntax return $P.Q$ and semantics:

$$r \rhd (R|\text{return } P.Q) \;\rightarrow\; P \mid r \rhd (R|Q).$$

Replication can then be coded as follows:

$$!P = (\nu\,rec)\big(\ rec \Rightarrow (-)(\,\text{return } P\,|\,rec\{\} \Leftarrow \bullet\,)\,|\,rec\{\} \Leftarrow \bullet\ \big).$$

In absence of replicator, one might think to exploit recursion to deploy local receivers of the form (x)return x, but unfortunately the implicit nesting of sessions would cause all such receivers to collect values only from different sessions than the original one.

Without extending the syntax of the calculus, a solution is to exploit a publishing service like *pub* above, which must be passed to p (and properly used therein). For instance, if *EATCS* and *EAPLS* return streams of conference announcements on the received service name, then the process

$$emailMe\{\} \Leftarrow \big(pub \Rightarrow (s)\text{return } s\ |\ EATCS\{\} \Leftarrow pub\ |\ EAPLS\{\} \Leftarrow pub\big)$$

will send you all the announcements collected from *EATCS* and *EAPLS*, one by one. More concisely, this can be equivalently written as

$$EATCS\{\} \Leftarrow emailMe\ |\ EAPLS\{\} \Leftarrow emailMe.$$

Example 6 (Structured protocols). As an example that requires a more elaborated client-side protocol than those examined so far, let us consider the room reservation service

$$bookRoom \Rightarrow (d)\left(\begin{array}{l} avail \Leftarrow d\ |\\ (cs)(\nu\,code)code.(cc)epay\{(-)cc.(i)\text{return } i\} \Leftarrow price \Leftarrow cs \end{array}\right)$$

that must be invoked with the dates d for the reservation, then proposes to the client the set of available rooms for that dates (obtained by invoking the local service *avail* with d), then waits for the client selection cs and sends a fresh reservation code to the client, then waits for the credit card number cc and debits the price of the selection to the credit card by exploiting a suitable electronic payment service *epay*, and finally, if everything is ok, communicates to the client the confirmation id i obtained from *epay*. Note that we suppose a service *price* that computes the price of the chosen room.

The corresponding client can can be written as:

$$bookRoom\{(-)(r)(select \Leftarrow r\ |\ (c)myCCnum.(cid)\text{return } \langle c, cid\rangle)\} \Leftarrow \texttt{dates}$$

It invokes the room reservation service, then waits for the available rooms r, then selects a suitable room (assume the local service *select* is exploited e.g. for interacting with the user) and communicates the choice to the service-side protocol, then waits for the reservation code c before sending the credit card number, and finally waits for the payment confirmation id cid, which is returned outside the session together with the reservation code c.

Example 7 (Encoding of the lazy λ-calculus). As a last example, we analyse the expressive power of the PSC in a more traditional manner by discussing the encoding of a typical computational model such as the lazy λ-calculus [3,1]. We

$$[\![x]\!]_p = x\{\} \Leftarrow p$$
$$[\![\lambda x.M]\!]_p = p \Rightarrow (x)(q)[\![M]\!]_q$$
$$[\![M\,N]\!]_p = (\nu m)(\nu n)\,(\,[\![M]\!]_m \mid n \Rightarrow (s)[\![N]\!]_s \mid m\{(-)p\} \Leftarrow n\,)$$

Fig. 4. Encoding of the lazy λ-calculus

recall that the λ expressions $M, N, \ldots$ can be either a variable x, the abstraction $\lambda x.M$ or the application $M\,N$, and that the β-reduction rules for the lazy semantics are:

$$(\lambda x.M)N \rightarrow M[^N\!/x] \qquad \frac{M \rightarrow M'}{M\,N \rightarrow M'\,N}$$

The translation is much in the spirit of Milner's encoding of λ-calculus in π-calculus [15]: agents can represent both "functions" and "arguments" which are composed in parallel and interact to β-reduce. Likewise [15], during communication we just transmit *access points* to terms instead of terms themselves.

The encoding is in Figure 4. We use a translation $[\![M]\!]_p$, with p representing the port to be used for interaction between M and the environment. From the point of view of syntax, the main differences w.r.t. the π-calculus encoding are: (i) service definitions replace input and replicated input prefixes; (ii) service invocations (with empty protocol) replace output particles. From the point of view of semantics, the more important differences are: (i) each service invocation opens a new session where the computation can progress (remind that sessions cannot be closed in PSC); (ii) all service definitions will remain available even when no further invocation will be possible!

If on one hand, the encoding witnesses the expressive power of PSC, on the other hand, it also motivates the introduction of some mechanism for closing sessions, like the one available in the full calculus.

2.2   Encoding of PSC into π-Calculus

In this subsection we aim to show that PSC can be seen as a disciplined fragment of the π-calculus, where processes can communicate only according to the interaction mechanisms provided by the service oriented metaphor. This strong relationship between PSC and the π-calculus does not hold any longer for the full SCC due to the session interruption mechanism (discussed in the next section) that has no direct couterpart in the π-calculus.

In Figure 5 we define the translation $[\![-]\!]_{in,out,ret}$ from PSC to π-calculus (all the operators not treated in Figure 5 are mapped homomorphically). The encoding is parametric on three names used to receive values from (in), send values to (out), and return values to the enclosing session (ret). These channels mimic the structure of sessions, which is lost in the π-calculus, and must be different w.r.t. service names. To avoid confusion with the use of overline in the π-calculus, in this mapping we use $\tilde{a}$ instead of $\bar{a}$ in the syntax of PSC. Moreover, we assume that the two operators are unrelated, namely, for any name a we have that $\tilde{a}$ and $\bar{a}$ are two distinct names.

$$[\![a\{(x)P\} \Leftarrow Q]\!]_{in,out,ret} = (\nu z)\big(\ [\![Q]\!]_{in,z,ret} \mid !z(x).(\nu r, \tilde{r})\overline{a}\langle r, \tilde{r}, x\rangle.[\![P]\!]_{r,\tilde{r},out}\ \big)$$
$$[\![a \Rightarrow (x)P]\!]_{in,out,ret} = !a(r, \tilde{r}, x).([\![P]\!]_{\tilde{r},r,out})$$
$$[\![a \triangleright P]\!]_{in,out,ret} = [\![P]\!]_{a,\tilde{a},out}$$
$$[\![a.P]\!]_{in,out,ret} = \overline{out}\ a.[\![P]\!]_{in,out,ret}$$
$$[\![(x)P]\!]_{in,out,ret} = in(x).[\![P]\!]_{in,out,ret}$$
$$[\![\mathsf{return}\ a.P]\!]_{in,out,ret} = \overline{ret}\ a \mid [\![P]\!]_{in,out,ret}$$

Fig. 5. Encoding PSC into π-calculus

The most interesting part is the translation of service invocation. Outputs on channel z where process Q produces the parameters for service invocation are intercepted, and each value v triggers an output on the service name a. The output extrudes two new names r and $\tilde{r}$ to be used for communication between the two sessions to be created, it also carries the parameter v (substituted for x) of the invocation. Note that the client protocol uses the channels r and $\tilde{r}$ above for communication and out for returning values. On the service-side, an instance of service protocol is started, using the same channels but swapped (so that input of client is connected to output of service and vice versa).

3   The Full Service Centered Calculus

Even though PSC is expressive enough to model service definitions and invocations, it does not provide operators for explicit closing of sessions. Namely, once the two protocols $\tilde{r} \triangleright P_1$ at client-side and $r \triangleright P_2$ at service-side are instantiated (as the effect of a service invocation), the session $\tilde{r}$ (resp. r) is garbage collected by the structural congruence only if the protocol P_1 (resp. P_2) reduces to $\mathbf{0}$. However, many sessions can never reduce to $\mathbf{0}$, e.g., those containing service definitions. Also, one may want to explicit program session termination, for instance in order to implement cancellation workflow patterns [18], or to manage abnormal events, or to use timeouts.

The full SCC comprises a mechanism for closing sessions that can be roughly described as follows. Let us consider the session r running the protocol P; we associate to this session a service name k which identifies a *termination handler* service, the first time the protocol P invokes such a service, the session r is closed. The notation that we consider is

$$r \triangleright_k P$$

where the name of the termination handler service appears in subscript position. In case P contains an invocation to k, like $k\{(x)P'\} \Leftarrow (Q|v.R)$, the overall session r may be closed, formally

$$r \triangleright_k \big(k\{(x)P'\} \Leftarrow (Q|v.R) \mid S\big) \qquad \text{may evolve to} \qquad k\{\} \Leftarrow v$$

where only the invocation to the termination handler service is kept and the session r (thus also the processes Q, R and S) is removed.

The termination handler service is associated to sessions on their instantiation. The intuition that we follow is that the termination of the session on one side, should be communicated to the opposite side. To achieve this, the clients indicate the name of the termination handler service for the session on the service-side, while services manage the termination handler service for the session on the client-side. Nevertheless, an asymmetric approach among the client- and the service-side is adopted, that reflects the asymmetry in the modeling of clients and services that we have already discussed in the previous section.

The syntax of clients becomes $a\{(x)P\} \Leftarrow_k Q$ where, besides the explicit indication of the service a to be invoked, we add the name k of the termination handler service to be associated to the session instantiated on the service-side. We usually omit the subscript k when it is not relevant. On the other hand, services are now specified with the process $a \Rightarrow (x)P : (y)T$ where, besides the service protocol $(x)P$, an additional protocol $(y)T$ is specified which represents the body of a termination handler service that will be instantiated on service invocation; this fresh service will be included in the corresponding session on the client-side.

Finally, the full calculus has a special name close that can be used in the specification of session protocols; this name is replaced by the name of the corresponding termination handler on session instantiation.

Remark 1. A first alternative would be to use close as a primitive for terminating instantaneously *both* the client-side and service-side sessions. This strategy conflicts with parties being in charge for the closing of their own sessions. A second alternative would be to use close as a synchronization primitive, so that the client-side and service-side sessions are terminated when close is encountered on one side and $\overline{\text{close}}$ on the other side. This strategy conflicts with parties being able to decide autonomously when to end their own sessions. The use of termination handler services looks a reasonable compromise: each party can exit a session autonomously but it is obliged to inform the other party.

Example 8. In order to become more familiar with the new service invocation mechanism that includes also the termination handler services, let us consider the following process composed (from left to right) by a termination handler service k, a client willing to invoke service a with value v, and the definition of the service a:

$$(k \Rightarrow (x)S : (-)\mathbf{0}) \mid (a\{(x)P\} \Leftarrow_k (v|Q)) \mid (a \Rightarrow (x)P' : (y)T)$$

This process can start a new session. This happens as soon as the value v is passed to the corresponding service a. The new session is assigned a fresh session name r, identifying the service- and the client-sides with r and $\overline{r}$, respectively. As discussed in the previous section, the protocols $(x)P$ and $(x)P'$ specified by the client and the service, will be installed on the respective sides upon session creation. Moreover, a fresh service name k' is associated to the newly installed termination handler service specified on the service-side. Notice that the new service k' has an associated empty second protocol $(-)\mathbf{0}$. Thus, the freshly activated processes will look like:

$$(\nu r, k')\big(\overline{r} \triangleright_{k'} P[v/x][k'/\mathsf{close}] \mid r \triangleright_k (P'[v/x][k/\mathsf{close}] \mid k' \Rightarrow (y)T[k/\mathsf{close}] : (-)\mathbf{0})\big)$$

The process $P[v/x][k'/\mathsf{close}]$ is the instance of the client session protocol that will exchange values with the instance $P'[v/x][k/\mathsf{close}]$ of the service protocol. Note that the session on the client-side has associated the name k', while the session on the service-side has associated the name k. Moreover, note that the termination handler service on service side is included inside the instantiated session and the name close occurring in its protocol is replaced by k, the name that permits to close the overall session on the service-side.

Example 9 (Closure protocol). A typical usage of termination handler services is to program them to close the current session. This can be achieved on the service-side with the service definition

$$s \Rightarrow (x)P' : (y)\mathsf{close}\,\{\} \Leftarrow y$$

and on the client-side with the process

$$(\nu\,end)s\{(y)\big(P \mid \mathsf{close}\,\{\} \Leftarrow (end \Rightarrow (x)\mathsf{return}\,x : (-)\mathbf{0})\big)\} \Leftarrow_{end} v$$

Indeed, after invocation of service s with value v, the instantiated sessions will be of the form

$$r \triangleright_{end} \big(P'[v/x][end/\mathsf{close}] \mid k' \Rightarrow (y)\,(end\{\} \Leftarrow y) : (-)\mathbf{0}\big)$$
$$\overline{r} \triangleright_{k'} \big(P[v/y][k'/\mathsf{close}] \mid k'\{\} \Leftarrow (end \Rightarrow (x)\mathsf{return}\,x : (-)\mathbf{0})\big)$$

Note that in case one of the two session closes, the corresponding notification will cause the closure of the session on the opposite side.

We are now ready to formally define the syntax and semantics of the full SCC. To be complete, we report also some auxiliary definitions already discussed for PSC.

Syntax. We presuppose a countable set $\mathcal{N}$ of names $a, b, c, ..., r, s, ..., x, y, ...$ A distinct name close belongs to this set. A bijection $\overline{}$ on $\mathcal{N}$ is presupposed s.t. $\overline{\overline{a}} = a$ for each name a.

The syntax of processes $P, Q, ...$ is given in Figure 6 with the operators listed in decreasing order of precedence. All operators have been discussed either in the previous section or in the initial part of this section.

Abstraction $(x)P$ and restriction $(\nu x)P$ act as binders for the name x (and also $\overline{x}$) with scope P. Given a process $a \Rightarrow (x)P : (y)T$, the name close is bound in P and T; given a process $a\{(x)P\} \Leftarrow_k Q$, the name close is bound in P. Notions of free names $\mathrm{fn}(\cdot)$ and alpha-equivalence arise as expected. We identify processes up to alpha-equivalence.

$$P, Q, T, \ldots ::= \mathbf{0} \qquad\qquad\qquad \text{Nil}$$

$\mid a.P$	Concretion
$\mid (x)P$	Abstraction
$\mid \mathsf{return}\, a.P$	Return Value
$\mid a \Rightarrow (x)P : (y)T$	Service Definition
$\mid a\{(x)P\} \Leftarrow_k Q$	Service Invocation
$\mid a \triangleright_k P$	Session
$\mid P\mid Q$	Parallel Composition
$\mid (\nu a)P$	New Name

Fig. 6. Syntax of processes

Notational Conventions. We omit trailing $\mathbf{0}$. Also, in service invocation we write $a\{\} \Leftarrow_k Q$ for $a\{(x)\mathbf{0}\} \Leftarrow_k Q$. In service definition we write $a \Rightarrow (x)P$ for $a \Rightarrow (x)P : (y)\mathbf{0}$. We also omit k in $a\{(x)P\} \Leftarrow_k Q$ and $a \Leftarrow_k Q$ when it is not relevant. Under these conventions and exploiting operator precedences, the process in the Example 8 would be written

$$k \Rightarrow (x)S \mid a\{(x)P\} \Leftarrow_k (v\mid Q) \mid a \Rightarrow (x)P' : (y)T$$

and the instantiated session is

$$(\nu r)(\nu k')\big(\bar{r} \triangleright_{k'} P[v/x][k'/\mathsf{close}] \mid r \triangleright_k (P'[v/x][k/\mathsf{close}] : k' \Rightarrow (y)T[k/\mathsf{close}])\big)$$

Operational Semantics. As for PSC, the operational semantics is defined in terms of a structural congruence and a reduction relation. The rules for structural congruence are as in Figure 2 where occurrences of the symbols $\triangleright$ and $\Leftarrow$ are replaced by $\triangleright_k$ and $\Leftarrow_k$, respectively.

The rules for the reduction semantics of the full calculus are reported in Figure 7.

An auxiliary function tn is defined on active contexts that keeps track of the termination names associated to sessions in which the hole of the context is enclosed. This function is used to check whether a service invocation should be interpreted as a closing signal for some of the enclosing sessions. For instance, in the first rule (which is an adaptation of the corresponding first rule in Figure 3) the function tn is used to check whether the invocation of the service s must be interpreted as a termination signal or not. The second is a novel rule; in the case the name s of the service to be invoked is a termination name for an enclosing session, the closest of these sessions is closed. The remaining rules are trivial adaptations of the corresponding last three rules of Figure 3.

Example 10 (Service update). Another example where session closing is needed is service update. Consider, for instance, the service

$$soccer WorldChampion \Rightarrow (-)\texttt{brasil}$$

that returns the name of the last winner of the soccer world championship. The service must be updated as soon as a new team becomes the new world champion.

$$\begin{aligned}
&\mathbb{C}[\![\, s \Rightarrow (x)P : (z)T \,]\!] \mid \\
&\mathbb{D}[\![\, s\{(y)P'\} \Leftarrow_k (Q|u.R) \,]\!]
\end{aligned}
\;\rightarrow\; (\nu r)(\nu k')
\left(
\begin{array}{l}
\mathbb{C}[\![\, s \Rightarrow (x)P : (z)T \mid \\
\quad r \rhd_k (k' \Rightarrow (z)T[k\!/\mathsf{close}\,] \mid \\
\qquad P[u\!/x][k\!/\mathsf{close}\,]) \,]\!] \\
\mid \mathbb{D}[\![\, \overline{r} \rhd_{k'} P'[u\!/y][k'\!/\mathsf{close}\,] \mid \\
\quad s\{(y)P'\} \Leftarrow_k (Q|R) \,]\!]
\end{array}
\right)$$

if $s \notin tn(\mathbb{D})$, r, k' are fresh and u, s, k not bound by $\mathbb{C},\mathbb{D}$

$r \rhd_s \mathbb{D}[\![\, s\{(y)P\} \Leftarrow_k (Q|u.R) \,]\!] \;\rightarrow\; s\{\} \Leftarrow_k u$

if $s \notin tn(\mathbb{D})$ and u, k not bound by $\mathbb{D}$

$\mathbb{C}[\![\, r \rhd_k (P|u.Q) \,]\!] \mid \mathbb{D}[\![\, \overline{r} \rhd_{k'} (R|(z)S) \,]\!] \;\rightarrow\; \mathbb{C}[\![\, r \rhd_k (P|Q) \,]\!] \mid \mathbb{D}[\![\, \overline{r} \rhd_{k'} (S[u\!/z] \mid R) \,]\!]$

if u, r not bound by $\mathbb{C},\mathbb{D}$

$r \rhd_k (P|\mathsf{return}\, u.Q) \;\rightarrow\; u \mid r \rhd_k (P|Q)$

$\mathbb{C}[\![\, P \,]\!] \;\rightarrow\; \mathbb{C}[\![\, P' \,]\!]$ if $P \equiv Q$, $Q \rightarrow Q'$, $Q' \equiv P'$

where $\mathbb{C}, \mathbb{D} ::= [\cdot] \mid \mathbb{C}|P \mid a\{(x)P\} \Leftarrow_k \mathbb{C} \mid a \rhd_k \mathbb{C} \mid (\nu a)\mathbb{C}$

and $tn([\cdot]) = \emptyset$ $tn(\mathbb{C}|P) = tn(a\{(x)P\} \Leftarrow_k \mathbb{C}) = tn(\mathbb{C})$
$tn(a \rhd_k \mathbb{C}) = tn(\mathbb{C}) \cup \{s\}$ $tn((\nu a)\mathbb{C}) = tn(\mathbb{C}) \setminus \{a\}$

Fig. 7. Reduction semantics

In PSC there is no way to cancel a definition and replace it with a new one. By contrast, in the full calculus, we can exploit session closing in order to remove services and the termination handler service can be used to instantiate a new version of the same service. Consider, for instance,

$$r \rhd_{new} \left(\begin{array}{l} soccerWorldChampion \Rightarrow (-)\mathsf{brasil} \mid \\ new\{\} \Leftarrow_{new} (update \Rightarrow (y)\mathsf{return}\, y) \end{array} \right) \mid$$

$$new \Rightarrow (z) \left(\begin{array}{l} soccerWorldChampion \Rightarrow (-)z \mid \\ new\{\} \Leftarrow_{new} (update \Rightarrow (y)\mathsf{return}\, y) \end{array} \right)$$

The service *update*, when invoked with a new name z, permits to cancel the currently available service *soccerWorldChampion* and replace it with a new instance that returns the name z. Notice that the service *update* is located within the same session r of the service *soccerWorldChampion*; this ensures that when it invokes the termination handler service *new* the initial instance of the service *soccerWorldChampion* is removed.

Example 11 (A blog service). We consider a service that implements a *blog*, i.e. a web page used by a web client to log personal annotations. A blog provides two services *get* and *set*, the former to read the current contents of the blog and the latter to modify them. The close-free fragment is not expressive enough to faithfully model such a service because it does not support service update, here needed to update the blog contents.

We use the service *newBlog* as a factory of blogs; this receives three names, the initial content v, the name for the new *get* service, and the name for the new *set* service. Upon invocation, the factory forwards the three received values to the *blog* service which is the responsible for the actual instantiation of the *get* and *set* services:

$$newBlog \Rightarrow (v, get, set)(blog\{\} \Leftarrow_{newBlog} \langle v, get, set \rangle) \mid$$
$$blog \Rightarrow (v, get, set)(\ get \Rightarrow (-)v \mid$$
$$close\{\} \Leftarrow (set \Rightarrow (v')\mathsf{return} \ \langle v', get, set \rangle) \ )$$

Note that the update of the blog contents is achieved by invoking the service close which is bound to *newBlog*; this invocation cancels the currently available *get* and *set* services and delegates to *newBlog* the creation of their new instances passing also the new contents v'.

As an example of a client of the blog service, we consider a process that installs a wiki page with initial contents v, then it adds some new contents v'.

$$newBlog\{\} \Leftarrow \langle v, get, set \rangle \mid$$
$$set\{\} \Leftarrow (concat\{(-)v'.get \Leftarrow \bullet | (x)\mathsf{return} \ x\} \Leftarrow \bullet)$$

The service *concat* simply computes the new contents appending v' to v, that are received in this order after service invocation:

$$concat \Rightarrow (-)(v')(v).v \circ v'$$

Here $\circ$ denotes juxtaposition of blog contents.

4   Encoding Orc in SCC

Orc [16,9] is one of the emerging basic programming models for service orchestration. In this section we show that SCC is expressive enough to model in a natural manner the Orc language.

We start by a brief overview of Orc. Orc is centered on the idea of service orchestration, and it assumes that basic services, able to perform computations, are available on primitive *sites*. Orc concentrates on invoking and orchestrating those services to reach some goal. Services may *publish* streams of values.

Orc uses the following syntax categories: site names, ranged by $a, b, c, ...$, variables, ranged by $x, y, ...$, values (including site names), ranged by $u, v, ...$. Actual parameters, ranged by $p, q, ...$, can be either values or variables. We use $P, Q, ...$ to range over expressions (since they correspond to processes in SCC) and $E, F, ...$ to range over expression names.

An Orc expression can be either a site call, an expression call or a composition of expressions according to one of the three basic orchestration patterns.

Site call: a site call can have either the form $a(p)$ or $x(p)$. In the first case the site name is known statically, in the other case it is computed dynamically. In both the cases p is the parameter of the call. If p is a variable, then it must be instantiated before the call is made. A site call may publish a value (but it is not obliged to do so).

Expression call: an expression call has the form $E(p)$, and it executes the expression defined by $E(x) \triangleq P$ after having replaced x by p. Here p is passed by reference. Note that expression definitions can be recursive.

Symmetric parallel composition: the composition $P|Q$ executes both P and Q concurrently, assuming that there is no interaction between them. It publishes the interleaving of the two streams of values published by P and Q, in temporal order.

Sequential composition: the composition $P > x > Q$ executes P, and, for each value v returned by P, it executes an instance of Q with v assigned to x. It publishes the interleaving (in temporal order) of the streams of values published by the different instances of Q.

Asymmetric parallel composition: the composition Q **where** $x :\in P$ starts in parallel both P and the parts of Q that do not need x. When P publishes the first value, let say v, it is killed and v is assigned to x. The composition publishes the stream obtained from Q (instantiated with v).

An Orc program is composed by an expression and a set of expression definitions. The encoding of an Orc program in SCC is the parallel composition of the expression and of the expression definitions.

We define now the different cases of the encoding $[\![\text{-}]\!]$. A value is trivially encoded as itself, i.e., $[\![u]\!] = u$. For variables (and thus for actual parameters) we need two different encodings, depending on whether they are passed by name or evaluated. We distinguish the two encodings by different subscripts:

$$[\![x]\!]_n = x \qquad [\![x]\!]_v = x \Leftarrow \bullet$$

The evaluation of a variable x is encoded as a request for the current value to the variable manager of x. Variable managers are created by both sequential composition and asymmetric parallel composition.

In general, both site calls and expression calls are encoded as service invocations returning the published results. Expressions too return their published results. Thus the encoding of an expression definition is simply:

$$[\![E(x) \triangleq P]\!] = E \Rightarrow (x)[\![P]\!]$$

The encoding of Orc expressions is detailed in Figure 8 and explained below:

$[\![a(p)]\!]$: a call to a statically-known site a with argument p is encoded as a service invocation of service a with arguments from $[\![p]\!]_v$;

$[\![x(p)]\!]$: in case the name of the site is stored in a variable x, we first ask the variable manager for x to get its current value v, and then make the site invocation through the auxiliary service $forw$; the result from the site v is received in an inner session, in order to pass the value at top level we use another auxiliary service pub;

$[\![E(p)]\!]$: an expression call is simply a service call; just notice that variables are passed by name;

$[\![P|Q]\!]$: obvious;

$$[\![a(p)]\!] = a \Leftarrow [\![p]\!]_v$$
$$[\![x(p)]\!] = (\nu forw, pub)(\ forw\{\} \Leftarrow [\![x]\!]_v \ |$$
$$forw \Rightarrow (a)pub\{\} \Leftarrow [\![a(p)]\!] \ |$$
$$pub \Rightarrow (y)\mathsf{return}\, y\ )$$
$$[\![E(p)]\!] = E \Leftarrow [\![p]\!]_n$$
$$[\![P|Q]\!] = [\![P]\!]\,|\,[\![Q]\!]$$
$$[\![P > x > Q]\!] = (\nu z, pub)(\ z\{\} \Leftarrow [\![P]\!] \ |$$
$$z \Rightarrow (y)(\nu x)(x \Rightarrow (-)y \ | \ pub\{\} \Leftarrow [\![Q]\!]) \ |$$
$$pub \Rightarrow (y)\mathsf{return}\, y\ )$$
$$[\![Q \textbf{ where}\, x :\in P]\!] = (\nu x, z, s)(\ [\![Q]\!] \ | \ (z \Rightarrow (y)(x \Rightarrow (-)y)) \ |$$
$$(s\{\} \Leftarrow_z \bullet) \ | \ s \Rightarrow (-)(\mathsf{close}\,\{\} \Leftarrow [\![P]\!])\ )$$

Fig. 8. Encoding of Orc expressions in SCC

$[\![P > x > Q]\!]$: a private service z is created, where $[\![P]\!]$ will send all computed values; at each invocation service z will activate fresh instances of $[\![Q]\!]$ in parallel with fresh variable managers for x that will serve value requests in $[\![Q]\!]$; in this case too, a service pub is used to pass the results at top level;

$[\![Q \textbf{ where}\, x :\in P]\!]$: both P and Q are executed (the parts of Q requiring the value of x are stopped since there is no manager for x available yet), but P is executed inside a session: the first value v published by P is used to terminate the session. Also, the termination handler will take the value and create a variable manager for x with this value.

Our encoding allows to simulate Orc orchestration policies inside SCC as far as the asynchronous semantics [16] is concerned (the synchronous semantics is mainly used to deal with timing issues, thus it is left for future extensions of SCC with time). We give here a simple example, inspired by [16], to show how the encoding actually works.

Example 12 (Emailing news in Orc). Let us consider the Orc expression

$$CNN(d)|BBC(d) > x > emailMe(x)$$

which invokes the news services of both *CNN* and *BBC* asking for news of day d. For each reply it sends to me an email with the received news. Thus this expression can send from zero up to two emails.

The encoding is as follows:

$$(\nu z, pub)(z\{\} \Leftarrow (CNN \Leftarrow d|BBC \Leftarrow d) \ |$$
$$z \Rightarrow (y)(\nu x)(x \Rightarrow (-)y \ | \ pub\{\} \Leftarrow emailMe \Leftarrow x \Leftarrow \bullet) \ |$$
$$pub \Rightarrow (y)\mathsf{return}\, y\ )$$

We have supposed here to have *CNN*, *BBC* and *emailMe* available as services.

When the expression is executed, both *CNN* and *BBC* are invoked. For each returned value y, z is invoked with that value, a new variable manager is created for it and the email protocol is called with the value taken from the variable, i.e., y. If some acknowledgment is returned by *emailMe*, then it is returned using the auxiliary service *pub*.

5   Conclusions and Future Work

We have presented SCC, a core calculus for service-oriented applications. SCC draws inspiration from different sources, primarily the π-calculus and Cook and Misra's service orchestration language [16], but enhances them with a mechanism for handling sessions. Sessions permit to model interaction modalities between clients and services which are more structured than the simple *one-way* and *request-response* modalities. Moreover, sessions can be explicitly closed, thus providing for a mechanism of process interruption.

Some features that naturally fall within the scope of service oriented computing have been left out of (well-formed processes in) the present version of the calculus. While distribution of processes over sites is certainly a needed issue in our agenda, the development of a type system is a major goal for future work. Specifically, it seems natural to associate service names with types describing the expected behaviour of clients and services, possibly along the lines of the session type systems in [12] or [11]. We believe that this type system would show the benefits of the concept of session even more clearly. Moreover, typing could be used in a prescriptive way to refine and redesign certain aspects and primitives of our calculus, whenever necessary for rendering their use more natural and smooth. The impact of adding a mechanism of *delegation* deserves further investigation. In fact, delegation could be simply achieved by enabling session-name passing, forbidden in the present version; consequences of this choice at the level of semantics and (prospect) type systems are at the moment not clear, though. For example, while many-party sessions have not been considered here, they could be modeled by passing the name of the current session as an argument to a third invoked service. We also plan to investigate the use of the session-closing mechanism for programming long-running transactions and related compensation policies in the context of web applications, in the vein e.g. of [7,13], and its relationship with the cCSP and the sagas-calculi discussed in [6]. Finally, integration of XML documents querying, in the vein of e.g. [2,5], and related typing issues, deserve further consideration.

Acknoweldgements. We warmfully thank Hernán Melgratti, Diego Latella, Mieke Massink, Flemming Nielson for many interesting comments on preliminary versions of this paper. The names SCC and PSC have been chosen as an homage the pioneering process algebras designed by Robin Milner and Tony Hoare.

References

1. S. Abramsky. The lazy lambda calculus. In *Research Topics in Functional Programming*, pages 65–116. Addison-Welsey, 1990.
2. L. Acciai and M. Boreale. Xpi: a typed process calculus for xml messaging. In *Proc. of FMOODS'05*, volume 3535 of *Lect. Notes in Comput. Sci.*, pages 47–66. Springer, 2005.
3. H. Barendregt. *The lambda calculus, its syntax and semantics.* North-Holland, 1984.
4. M. Bartoletti, P. Degano, and G. Ferrari. Types and effects for secure service orchestration. In *Proc. of CSFW'06*, 2006. To appear.
5. A. L. Brown, C. Laneve, and L. G. Meredith. Piduce: A process calculus with native xml datatypes. In *Proc. of EPEW'05/WS-FM'05*, volume 3670 of *Lect. Notes in Comput. Sci.*, pages 18–34. Springer, 2005.
6. R. Bruni, M. Butler, C. Ferreira, T. Hoare, H. Melgratti, and U. Montanari. Comparing two approaches to compensable flow composition. In *Proc. of CONCUR'05*, volume 3653 of *Lect. Notes in Comput. Sci.*, pages 383–397. Springer, 2005.
7. R. Bruni, H. Melgratti, and U. Montanari. Nested commits for mobile calculi: extending join. In *Proc. of IFIP TCS'04*, pages 367–379. Kluwer Academics, 2004.
8. N. Busi, R. Gorrieri, C. Guidi, R. Lucchi, and G. Zavattaro. Choreography and orchestration conformance for system design. In *Proc. of COORDINATION'06*, volume 4038 of *Lect. Notes in Comput. Sci.*, pages 63–81. Springer, 2006.
9. W. R. Cook, S. Patwardhan, and J. Misra. Workflow patterns in orc. In *Proc. of COORDINATION'06*, volume 4038 of *Lect. Notes in Comput. Sci.*, pages 82–96. Springer, 2006.
10. G. Ferrari, R. Guanciale, and D. Strollo. Jscl: a middleware for service coordination. In *Proc. of FORTE'06*, Lect. Notes in Comput. Sci. Springer, 2006. To appear.
11. S. J. Gay and M. J. Hole. Types and subtypes for client-server interactions. In *Proc. of ESOP'99*, volume 1576 of *Lect. Notes in Comput. Sci.*, pages 74–90. Springer, 1999.
12. K. Honda, V. T. Vasconcelos, and M. Kubo. Language primitives and type discipline for structured communication-based programming. In *Proc. of ESOP'98*, volume 1381 of *Lect. Notes in Comput. Sci.*, pages 122–138. Springer, 1998.
13. C. Laneve and G. Zavattaro. Foundations of web transactions. In *Proc. of FOSSACS'05*, volume 3441 of *Lect. Notes in Comput. Sci.*, pages 282–298. Springer, 2005.
14. A. Lapadula, R. Pugliese, and F. Tiezzi. A calculus for orchestration of web services. Technical report, University of Florence, 2006.
15. R. Milner. Functions as processes. *Math. Struct. in Comput. Sci.*, 2(2):119–141, 1992.
16. J. Misra and W. R. Cook. Computation orchestration: A basis for wide-area computing. *Journal of Software and Systems Modeling*, 2006. To appear. A preliminary version of this paper appeared in the Lecture Notes for NATO summer school, held at Marktoberdorf in August 2004.
17. Sensoria Project. Public web site. `http://sensoria.fast.de/`.
18. W. M. P. van der Aalst, A. H. M. ter Hofstede, B. Kiepuszewski, and A. P. Barros. Workflow patterns. *Distributed and Parallel Databases*, 14(1):5–51, 2003.

Computational Logic for Run-Time Verification of Web Services Choreographies: Exploiting the *SOCS-SI* Tool

Marco Alberti[2], Federico Chesani[1], Marco Gavanelli[2], Evelina Lamma[2],
Paola Mello[1], Marco Montali[1], Sergio Storari[2], and Paolo Torroni[1]

[1] DEIS - Dipartimento di Elettronica, Informatica e Sistemistica
Facoltà di Ingegneria, Università di Bologna
viale Risorgimento, 2
40136 – Bologna, Italy
{fchesani, pmello, mmontali, ptorroni}@deis.unibo.it
[2] DI - Dipartimento di Ingegneria
Facoltà di Ingegneria, Università di Ferrara
Via Saragat, 1
44100 – Ferrara, Italy
{marco.gavanelli, marco.alberti, lme, strsrg}@unife.it

Abstract. In this work, we investigate the feasibility of using a framework based on computational logic, and mainly defined in the context of Multi-Agent Systems for Global Computing (SOCS UE Project), for modeling choreographies of Web Services with respect to the conversational aspect.

One of the fundamental motivations of using computational logic, beside its declarative and highly expressive nature, is given by its operational counterpart, that can provide a proof-theoretic framework able to verify the consistency of services designed in a cooperative and incremental manner.

In particular, in this paper we show that suitable "Social Integrity Constraints", introduced in the SOCS social model, can be used for specifying global protocols at the choreography level. In this way, we can use a suitable tool, derived from the proof-procedure defined in the context of the SOCS project, to check at run-time whether a set of existing services behave in a conformant manner w.r.t. the defined choreography.

1 Introduction

Service Oriented Architectures (SOA) have recently emerged as a new paradigm for structuring inter-/intra- business information processes. While SOA is indeed a set of principles, methodologies and architectural patterns, a more practical instance of SOA can be identified in the Web Services technology, where the business functionalities are encapsulated in software components, and can be invoked through a stack of Internet Standards.

The standardization process of the Web Service technology is at a good maturation point: in particular, the W3C Consortium has proposed standards for developing basic services and for interconnecting them on a point-to-point basis. These standards have been widely accepted; vendors like Microsoft and IBM are supporting the technology within their development tools; private firms are already developing solutions

M. Bravetti, M. Nuñes, and G. Zavattaro (Eds.): WS-FM 2006, LNCS 4184, pp. 58–72, 2006.

for their business customer, based on the web services paradigm. However, the needs for more sophisticated standards for service composition have not yet fully satisfied. Several attempts have been made (WSFL, XLang, BPML, WSCL, WSCI), leading to two dominant initiatives: BPEL [1] and WS-CDL [2].

Both these initiatives however have missed to tackle some important issues. We agree with the view [3,4] that both BPEL and WS-CDL languages lack of declarativeness, and more dangerous, they both lack an underlying formal model and semantics. Hence, issues like *run-time conformance testing, composition verification, verification of properties* are not fully addressed by the current proposals. Also semantics issues, needed in order to verify more complex properties (besides properties like livelock, deadlock, leak freedom, etc.), have been left behind.

Some of these issues have been already subject of research: generally, a mapping between choreographed/orchestrated models to specific formalisms is proposed, and then single issues are solved in the transformed model. E.g., the *composition verification* is addressed in [5,6]; *process mining* and *a-posteriori conformance testing* are addressed in [7]; livelock, deadlock, etc. properties are tackled in [8,9].

In this paper, we focus on a particular issue: the *conformance testing* (also called *run-time behaviour conformance* in [3]). Once a global protocol (or choreography) has been defined, a question arises: how is it possible to check if the actors play in a conformant manner w.r.t the defined choreography? Any solution should take into account answering the question by analyzing only the external, observable behaviour of the peers, without assuming any hypothesis or knowledge on their internals (in order to not undermine the heterogeneity).

Taking inspiration by the many analogies between the Web Services research field and the Multi Agent System (MAS) field [5], we exploit a framework, namely $\mathcal{S}$CIFF, for verifying at run-time (or a-posteriori using an *event log*) if the peers behave in a conformant manner w.r.t. a given choreography. Within the $\mathcal{S}$CIFF framework, a language suitable for specifying global choreographies is provided: a formal semantics is provided too, based on abductive logic programming [10]. We defined the $\mathcal{S}$CIFF framework in the SOCS european project [11], where we addressed the issue of providing a formal language to define multi agent protocols. Its operational counterpart is an abductive proof procedure, called $\mathcal{S}$CIFF, exploited to check the compliance of agents to protocols. Moreover, a tool (namely *SOCS-SI* [12]) has been developed for automatically analyzing and verifying peers interactions, w.r.t. a protocol expressed in the language above.

In this paper we show that suitable "Social Integrity Constraints", introduced in the SOCS social model, can be used for specifying global protocols at the choreography level. In this way, we can use a suitable tool, derived from the proof-procedure defined in the context of the SOCS project, to check at run-time whether a set of existing services behave in a conformant manner w.r.t. the defined choreography.

The paper is organized as follows: in Section 2 we introduce the $\mathcal{S}$CIFF framework and provide its declarative semantics. Then, in Section 3 we sketch how a simple choreography can be modeled within the framework. In Section 4 we show how the *run-time conformance testing* issue can be addressed in our framework, grounding our proposal to a practical example. Discussion and conclusions follow in Section 5.

2   The SCIFF Framework

In this section, we present the SCIFF framework, describing how the conversational part of a choreography as well as its static knowledge can be suitably expressed within the framework. Moreover, we provide a formal definition of *fulfillment* (i.e., a run-time behaviour of some peers respects a given choreography) and *violation* (i.e., when the peers does not behave in a conformant manner).

2.1   Events, Happened Events and Expected Events

The definition of *Event* greatly varies, depending on the application domain. For example, in the Web Service domain, an event could be the fact that a certain web method has been invoked; in a Semantic Web scenario instead, an event could be the fact that some information available on a site has been updated. Moreover, within the same application domain there could be several different notions of events, depending on the assumed perspective, the granularity, etc.

The SCIFF language abstracts completely from the problem of deciding "what is an event", and rather lets the developers decide which are the important events for modeling the domain, at the desired level. Each event that can be described by a *Term*, can be used in SCIFF. For example, in a peer-to-peer communication system, an event could be the fact that someone communicates something to someone else (i.e., a *communicative* action has been performed):

$$tell(alice, bob, msgContent)$$

Another event could be the fact that a web service has updated some information stored into an external database, or that a bank clerk, upon the request of a customer, has provided him/her some money (like in Eq. 2). Of course, in order to perform some reasoning about such events, accessibility to such information is a mandatory requirement.

In the SCIFF framework, similarly to what has been done in [13], we distinguish between the description of the *event*, and the fact that the event has happened. Typically, an event happens at a certain time instant; moreover the same event could happen many times [1]. Happened events are represented as an atom $\mathbf{H}(Event, Time)$, where $Event$ is a *Term*, and $Time$ is an integer, representing the discrete time point in which the event happened.

One innovative contribution of the SCIFF framework is the introduction of *expectations* about events. Indeed, beside the explicit representation of "what" happened and "when", it is possible to explicitly represent also "what" is expected, and "when" it is expected. The notion of *expectation* plays a key role when defining global interaction protocols, choreographies, and more in general any dynamically evolving process: it is quite natural, in fact, to think of such processes in terms of rules of the form *"if A happened, then B should be expected to happen"*. Expectations about events come with form

$$\mathbf{E}(Event, Time)$$

---

[1] In our approach the happening of identical events at the same time instant are considered as if only one event happens; if the same event happens more than once, but at different time instants, then they are indeed considered as different happenings.

where $Event$ and $Time$ can be a variable, or they could be grounded to a particular term/value. Constraints, like $Time > 10$, can be specified over the variables: in the given example, the expectation is about an event to happen at a time greater than 10 (hence the event is expected to happen *after* the time instant 10).

Given the notions of *happened event* and of *expected event*, two fundamental issues arise: first, how it is possible to specify the link between these two notions. Second, how it is possible to verify if all the expectations have been effectively satisfied. The first issue is fundamental in order to easy the definition of a choreography, and it will be addressed in the rest of this section. The second issue, instead, is inherently related to the problem of establishing if a web service is indeed behaving in a compliant manner w.r.t. a given choreography: the solution proposed by the $\mathcal{S}$CIFF framework is presented in Section 4.1.

2.2 Choreography Integrity Constraints

Choreography Integrity Constraints $\mathcal{IC}_{chor}$ are forward rules, of the form

$$Body \rightarrow Head$$

whose *Body* can contain literals and (happened and expected) events, and whose *Head* can contain (disjunctions of) conjunctions of expectations. In Eq. (1) we report the formal definition of the grammar, where $Atom$ and $Term$ have the usual meaning in Logic Programming [14] and $Constraint$ is interpreted as in Constraint Logic Programming [15].

$$
\begin{aligned}
\mathcal{IC}_{chor} &::= [IC]^\star \\
IC &::= Body \rightarrow Head \\
Body &::= (HapEvent|Expect)\,[\wedge BodyLit]^\star \\
BodyLit &::= HapEvent|Expect|Literal|Constraint \\
Head &::= Disjunct\,[\ \vee Disjunct\,]^\star|false \qquad\qquad (1)\\
Disjunct &::= Expect\,[\ \wedge (Expect|Literal|Constraint)]^\star \\
Expect &::= \mathbf{E}(Term\,[,T]) \\
HapEvent &::= \mathbf{H}(Term\,[,T]) \\
Literal &::= Atom\ |\ \neg Atom
\end{aligned}
$$

The syntax of $\mathcal{IC}_{chor}$ is a simplified version of that one defined for the SOCS Integrity Constraints [16]. In particular, in the context of choreographies, we do not consider negative expectations (informally, expectations about prohibited events) and explicit negation. In fact, we assume that choreographies completely specify all the events that must happen (by means of expectations), and that not expected events are indeed forbidden. This assumption is formally specified by the definition of violation of a choreography, that we provide later in the paper (see Def. 2).

CLP constraints [15] can be used to impose relations or restrictions on any of the variables that occur in an expectation, like imposing conditions on the role of the participants, or on the time instants the events are expected to happen. For example, time conditions might define orderings between the messages, or enforce deadlines.

$\mathcal{IC}_{chor}$ allows the user to define how an interaction should evolve, given some previous situation, that can be represented in terms of happened events. Rules like:

> *"if a customer requests the withdrawal of X euros from the bank account, the bank should give the requested money within 24 hours from the request, or should explicitly notify the user of the impossibility"*

can be translated straightforward, e.g. in the corresponding $\mathcal{IC}_{chor}$:

$$\mathbf{H}(request(User, Bank, withdraw(X)), T_r)$$
$$\rightarrow \mathbf{E}(give(Bank, User, money(X)), T_a) \wedge T_a < T_r + 24 \qquad (2)$$
$$\vee \mathbf{E}(tell(Bank, User, not\_possible, reason(\ldots)), T_p)$$

2.3   The Choreography Knowledge Base

The *Integrity Constraints* are a suitable tool for effectively defining the desired behaviour of the participants to an interaction, as well as the evolution of the interaction itself. However, they mostly capture the "dynamic" aspects of the interactions, while more static information is not so easily tackled by these rules. For example, a common situation is the one where, before giving the money requested, the bank could check if the customer's deposit contains enough money to cover the withdrawal. Or, if the customer indeed has a bank account with that bank, and hence if he/she is entailed to ask for a withdrawal.

Such type of knowledge is independent of the single instance of interaction, but is often referred during the interaction. The $\mathcal{SCIFF}$ framework allows to define such knowledge in the *Choreography Knowledge Base* KB_{chor}. The KB_{chor} specifies declaratively pieces of knowledge of the choreography, such as roles descriptions, list of participants, etc. KB_{chor} is expressed in the form of clauses (a logic program); the clauses may contain in their body expectations about the behaviour of participants, defined literals, and constraints, while their heads are atoms. The syntax is reported in Equation (3).

$$
\begin{aligned}
KB_{chor} &::= [Clause]^* \\
Clause &::= Atom \leftarrow Cond \\
Cond &::= ExtLiteral \,[\, \wedge \, ExtLiteral \,]^* \\
ExtLiteral &::= Literal | Expectation | Constraint \\
Expectation &::= \mathbf{E}(Term \,[, T]) \\
Literal &::= Atom \mid \neg Atom \mid true
\end{aligned}
\qquad (3)
$$

Moreover, in our vision, a choreography can be *goal directed*, i.e. a specific goal $\mathcal{G}_{chor}$ can be specified. E.g., a choreography used in an electronic auction system could have the goal of selling all the goods in the store. Another goal could be instead to sell at least n items at a price higher than a given threshold. Hence, the same auction mechanism described by the same rules (integrity constraints), can be used seamlessly for achieving different goals. Such goals can be defined like the clauses of the KB_{chor}, as specified in Eq. 3. Typically, a goal is defined as expectations about the outcomes of the choreography, i.e. in terms of messages (and their contents) that should be exchanged. If no particular goal is required to be achieved, $\mathcal{G}_{chor}$ is bound to *true*.

2.4   Declarative Semantics of the $\mathcal{S}$CIFF Framework

In the $\mathcal{S}$CIFF framework, a choreography is interpreted in terms of an Abductive Logic Program (ALP). In general, an ALP [10] is a triple $\langle P, A, IC \rangle$, where P is a logic program, A is a set of predicates named *abducibles*, and IC is a set of integrity constraints. Roughly speaking, the role of P is to define predicates, the role of A is to fill-in the parts of P which are unknown, and the role if IC is to control the ways elements of A are hypothesised, or "abduced". Reasoning in abductive logic programming is usually goal-directed (being G a goal), and it accounts to finding a set of abduced hypotheses Δ built from predicates in A such that $P \cup \Delta \models G$ and $P \cup \Delta \models IC$. In the past, a number of proof-procedures have been proposed to compute Δ (see Kakas and Mancarella [17], Fung and Kowalski [18], Denecker and De Schreye [19], etc.).

The idea we exploited in the $\mathcal{S}$CIFF framework is to adopt abduction to dynamically *generate* the expectations and to perform the *conformance check*. Expectations are defined as abducibles, and are hypothesised by the abductive proof procedure, i.e. the proof procedure makes hypotheses about the behaviour of the peers. A confirmation step, where these hypotheses must be confirmed by happened events, is then performed: if no set of hypotheses can be fulfilled, a violation is detected. In this paper, we also require that all the happened events are indeed expected.

A choreography specification $\mathcal{C}$ is defined by the triple:

$$\mathcal{C} \equiv \langle KB_{chor}, \mathcal{E}_{chor}, \mathcal{IC}_{chor} \rangle$$

where:

– KB_{chor} is the *Knowledge Base*,
– $\mathcal{E}_{chor}$ is the set of *abducible predicates* (i.e. expectations), and
– $\mathcal{IC}_{chor}$ is the set of *Choreography Integrity Constraints*.

A *choreography instance* $\mathcal{C}_{HAP}$ is a choreography specification grounded on a set **HAP** of happened events. We give semantics to a choreography instance by defining those sets **PEND** (Δ in the abductive framework) of expectations which, together with the choreography's knowledge base and the happened events **HAP**, imply an instance of the goal (Eq. 4) - if any - and *satisfy* the integrity constraints (Eq. 5).

$$KB_{chor} \cup \mathbf{HAP} \cup \mathbf{PEND} \models \mathcal{G}_{chor} \tag{4}$$
$$KB_{chor} \cup \mathbf{HAP} \cup \mathbf{PEND} \models \mathcal{IC}_{chor} \tag{5}$$

At this point it is possible to define the concepts of *fulfillment* and *violation* of a set **PEND** of expectations. Fulfillment requires all the **E** expectations to have a matching happened event, and that all the happened event were indeed expected:

Definition 1. (Fulfillment) *Given a choreography instance* $\mathcal{C}_{\mathbf{HAP}}$, *a set of expectations* **PEND** *is fulfilled if and only if for all (ground) terms p:*

$$\mathbf{HAP} \cup \mathbf{PEND} \cup \{\mathbf{E}(p) \leftrightarrow \mathbf{H}(p)\} \not\models false \tag{6}$$

Symmetrically, we define violation as follows:

Definition 2. (Violation) *Given a choreography instance* $\mathcal{C}_{\mathbf{HAP}}$, *a set of expectations* **PEND** *is violated if and only if there exists a (ground) term p such that:*

$$\mathbf{HAP} \cup \mathbf{PEND} \cup \{\mathbf{E}(p) \leftrightarrow \mathbf{H}(p)\} \models false \qquad (7)$$

Notice that, w.r.t. the original $\mathcal{S}$CIFF framework defined for the MAS scenario, the definitions of *fulfillment* and *violation* are slightly different. In fact in the Web Services scenario we consider as a violation all the events that happen without being expected. Notice that two different kinds of violation are detected by $\mathcal{S}$CIFF: i) an expected event does not have a corresponding happened event, and therefore the expectation is not fulfilled; ii) an event happens without an explicit corresponding expectation.

The operational counterpart of this declarative semantics is the $\mathcal{S}$CIFF proof procedure described in Section 4. $\mathcal{S}$CIFF has been proven sound and complete in relevant cases [20].

3   Specifying a Choreography in the $\mathcal{S}$CIFF Framework

In this section we develop a simple example in the $\mathcal{S}$CIFF framework. To our purposes, let us consider a revised version of the choreography proposed in [3]. The choreography (shown in Figure 1) models a 3-party interaction, in which a supplier coordinates with its warehouse in order to sell and ship electronic devices. Due to some laws, the supplier should trade only with customers who do not belong to a publicly known list of banned countries.

The choreography starts when a *Customer* communicates a purchase order to the *Supplier*. *Supplier* reacts to this request asking the *Warehouse* about the availability of the ordered item. Once *Supplier* has received the response, it decides to cancel or confirm the order, basing this choice upon *Item*'s availability and *Customer*'s country. In the former case, the choreography terminates, whereas in the latter one a concurrent phase is performed: *Customer* sends an order payment, while *Warehouse* handles the item's shipment. When both the payment and the shipment confirmation are received by *Supplier*, it delivers a final receipt to the *Customer*. The specification of this choreography is given in Spec. 3.1 [2]. The events are represented in the form $msgType(sender, receiver, content_1, \ldots, content_n)$, where the $msgType$, $sender$, $receiver$ and $content_i$ retain their intuitive meaning.

(IC_1) specifies that, when *Customer* sends to *Supplier* the purchase order, including the requested *Item* and his/her *Country*, *Supplier* should request *Item*'s availability to *Warehouse*. *Warehouse* should respond within 10 minutes to *Supplier*'s request giving the corresponding quantity *Qty* (IC_2). The deadline is imposed as a CLP constraint over the variable T_{qty}, that represents the time in which the response is sent.

---

[2] For the sake of clarity, we omit roles specification, which may be simply expressed in the KB_{chor}. Moreover, although it is possible to introduce expectations also in the body of the $\mathcal{IC}_{chor}$, here we show an example where the bodies of the rules contain only happened events.

Specification 3.1 $\mathcal{IC}_{chor}$ specification of the example in figure 1

$$\mathbf{H}(purchase\_order(Customer, Supplier, Item, Country), T_{po})$$
$$\rightarrow\mathbf{E}(check\_availability(Supplier, Warehouse, Item), T_{ca}) \wedge T_{ca} > T_{po} \qquad (IC_1)$$

$$\mathbf{H}(check\_availability(Supplier, Warehouse, Item), T_{ca})$$
$$\rightarrow\mathbf{E}(inform(Warehouse, Supplier, Item, Qty), T_{qty}) \qquad (IC_2)$$
$$\wedge\, T_{qty} > T_{ca} \wedge T_{qty} < T_{ca} + 10$$

$$\mathbf{H}(purchase\_order(Customer, Supplier, Item, Country), T_{po})$$
$$\wedge\, \mathbf{H}(inform(Warehouse, Supplier, Item, Qty), T_{qty})$$
$$\rightarrow\mathbf{E}(accept\_order(Supplier, Customer, Item), T_{ao})$$
$$\wedge\, ok(Qty, Country) \wedge T_{ao} > T_{po} \wedge T_{ao} > T_{qty} \qquad (IC_3)$$
$$\vee\mathbf{E}(reject\_order(Supplier, Customer, Item), T_{ro})$$
$$\wedge\, \neg ok(Qty, Country) \wedge T_{ro} > T_{po} \wedge T_{ro} > T_{qty}$$

$$\mathbf{H}(accept\_order(Supplier, Customer, Item), T_{ao})$$
$$\rightarrow\mathbf{E}(shipment\_order(Supplier, Warehouse, Item, Customer), T_{so}) \qquad (IC_4)$$
$$\wedge\, \mathbf{E}(payment(Customer, Supplier, Item), T_p) \wedge T_{so} > T_{ao} \wedge T_p > T_{ao}$$

$$\mathbf{H}(shipment\_order(Supplier, Warehouse, Item, Customer), T_{so})$$
$$\rightarrow\mathbf{E}(request\_details(Warehouse, Customer), T_{rd}) \wedge T_{rd} > T_{so} \qquad (IC_5)$$

$$\mathbf{H}(request\_details(Warehouse, Customer), T_{rd})$$
$$\rightarrow\mathbf{E}(inform(Customer, Warehouse, Details), T_{det}) \wedge T_{det} > T_{rd} \qquad (IC_6)$$

$$\mathbf{H}(shipment\_order(Supplier, Warehouse, Item, Customer), T_{so})$$
$$\wedge\, \mathbf{H}(inform(Customer, Warehouse, Details), T_{det}) \qquad (IC_7)$$
$$\rightarrow\mathbf{E}(confirm\_shipment(Warehouse, Supplier, Item), T_{cs}) \wedge T_{cs} > T_{so} \wedge T_{cs} > T_{det}$$

$$\mathbf{H}(payment(Customer, Supplier, Item), T_p)$$
$$\wedge\, \mathbf{H}(confirm\_shipment(Warehouse, Supplier, Item), T_{cs}) \qquad (IC_8)$$
$$\rightarrow\mathbf{E}(delivery(Supplier, Customer, Item, Receipt), T_{del}) \wedge T_{del} > T_{cs} \wedge T_{del} > T_p$$

Specification 3.2 KB_{chor} with some banned countries

```
ok( Qty, Country):-
     Qty>0,
     not banned_country( Country).

banned_country( shackLand).
banned_country( badLand).
```

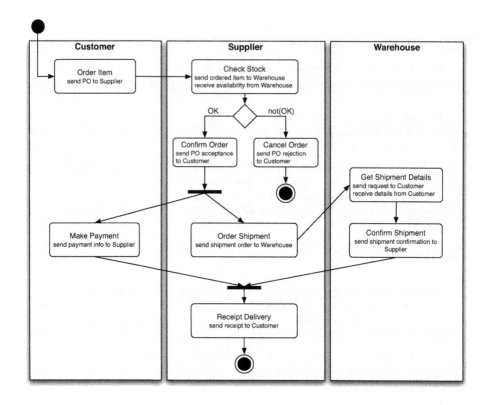

Fig. 1. A simple choreography example

After having received the requested quantity, $Supplier$ decides whether to accept or reject $Customer$'s order (IC_3). As we have pointed out, the decision depends upon the quantity and the $Country$ the $Customer$ belongs to; $Supplier$ may accept the order only when Qty is positive and customer's $Country$ is not in the list of banned countries. This last condition has been expressed using a predicate defined in the KB_{chor}, showed in Spec. 3.2. If $Supplier$ has accepted the purchase order, then $Customer$ is expected to pay for the requested $Item$ and, at the same time, $Supplier$ will send a shipment order to $Warehouse$, communicating the involved $Item$ and $Customer$'s identity (IC_4). $Warehouse$ will use $Customer$'s identity in order to communicate with him/her and asking for shipment details (IC_5). [3]

When $Customer$ receives the request for details, then he/she is expected to respond giving his/her own $Details$ (IC_6). After having received them, $Warehouse$ should sends to $Supplier$ a shipment confirmation (IC_7). Finally, (IC_8) states that when both the payment and the shipment confirmation actually happen $Supplier$ is expected to deliver a $Receipt$ to $Customer$.

---

[3] This could be viewed, at a higher level, as a channel passing mechanism, since $Customer$ is used as a content part of the first message, and as receiver of the second one.

4 Run-Time Conformance Verification of Web Services Interactions

In Section 2 we have introduced some key concepts of our approach, in particular *happened events* and *expectations*, and a declarative semantics, together with the notion of *fulfillment* and *violation* of a choreography specification. In this section we show how, by exploiting these concepts, it is possible to perform the run-time conformance check, by the operational counterpart of the declarative semantics, represented by the $\mathcal{S}$CIFF proof procedure. We also show how $\mathcal{S}$CIFF operates on a concrete interaction example.

4.1 Detecting Fulfilment and Violation: The $\mathcal{S}$CIFF Proof Procedure and the *SOCS-SI* Tool

We developed the $\mathcal{S}$CIFF proof procedure for the automatic verification of compliance of interactions w.r.t. a given choreography. Then, we developed a Java-based application, *SOCS-SI*, that receives as input the specification of a choreography and the happening events, and provides as output the answer about the conformance issue. *SOCS-SI* uses the $\mathcal{S}$CIFF proof procedure as inference engine, and provides a Graphical User Interface for accessing the results of the conformance task.

Fig. 2. The *SOCS-SI* tool

The $\mathcal{S}$CIFF proof procedure considers the **H** events as predicates defined by a set of incoming atoms, and is devoted to generate expectations corresponding to a given set of happened events and to check that expectations indeed match with those events. The proof procedure is based on a rewriting system transforming one node to another (or to others) as specified by rewriting steps called *transitions*. A node can be either the special node *false*, or defined by the following tuple

$$T \equiv \langle R, CS, PSIC, \mathbf{PEND}, \mathbf{HAP}, \mathbf{FULF}, \mathbf{VIOL} \rangle$$

where

- R is the resolvent (initially set to the goal G);
- CS is the constraint store (à la CLP [15]);
- $PSIC$ is a set of implications, derived from the $\mathcal{IC}_{chor}$;
- **PEND** is the set of (pending) expectations (i.e., expectations have not been fulfilled (yet), nor they have been violated=;
- **HAP** is the history of happened events;
- **FULF** and **VIOL** are the sets of fulfilled and violated expectations, respectively.

We cannot report here all the transitions, due to lack of space; the interested reader can refer to [21]. As an example, the *fulfilment* transition is devoted to prove that an expectation $\mathbf{E}(X, T_x)$ has been fulfilled by an event $\mathbf{H}(Y, T_y)$. Two nodes are generated: in the first, X and T_x are unified respectively with Y and T_y, and the expectation is fulfilled (i.e., it is moved to the set **FULF**); in the second a new constraint that imposes disunification between (X, T_x) and (Y, T_y) is added to the constraint store CS. At the end of the computation, a *closure* transition is applied, and all the expectations remaining in the set **PEND** are considered as violated. The $\mathcal{S}$CIFF proof procedure can be downloaded at http://lia.deis.unibo.it/research/sciff/.

The *SOCS-SI* software tool is a Java-based application, that provides to the user a GUI to access the outcomes of the $\mathcal{S}$CIFF proof procedure. It has been developed to accept events that happen dynamically, from various events source. It accepts, as event source, also a log file containing the log of the relevant events. In this way, it is possible to perform the conformance verification i) at run-time, by checking immediately the incoming happened events (possibly raising violations as soon as possible), and ii) a posteriori, analyzing log files. When performing run-time verification, if time events (i.e., events that represent the current time instant) are provided (possibly by an external source, e.g. a clock), *SOCS-SI* is able to use such information to detect deadline expirations with a discrete approximation to the nearest greater time instant. A snapshot of *SOCS-SI* GUI is shown in Figure 2. *SOCS-SI* can be downloaded at http://www.lia.deis.unibo.it/research/socs_si/socs_si.shtml.

4.2   Example of Run-Time Conformance Verification

In our scenario, the criminal *bankJob* beagle wants to buy a device from the online shop *devOnline*, whose warehouse is *devWare*. *devOnline* is quite greedy, and therefore trades with everyone, without checking if the customer comes from one of the banned countries. As a consequence, even if *bankJob* comes from *shackLand*, one of the banned countries, *devOnline* sells him the requested device, thus violating the choreography. Table 1 contains the log of the scenario from the viewpoint of *devOnline*; note that messages are expressed in high level way, abstracting from the SOAP exchange format.

When the first event (labeled m_1 in Table 1) happens, (IC_1) is triggered, and an expectation about *devOnline*'s behaviour is consequently generated:

$$\mathbf{PEND} = \{\ \mathbf{E}(check\_availability(devOnline, Warehouse, device), T_{ca}) \wedge T_{ca} > 2\}$$

Table 1. Log of messages exchanged by *devOnline* in our scenario

Id	message	sender	receiver	content	time
m_1	purchase_order	bankJob	devOnline	[device,shackLand]	2
m_2	check_availability	devOnline	devWare	[device]	3
m_3	inform	devWare	devOnline	[device,3]	10
m_4	accept_order	devOnline	bankJob	[device]	12
m_5	shipment_order	devOnline	devWare	[device,bankJob]	13
m_6	confirm_shipment	devWare	devOnline	[device]	16
m_7	payment	bankJob	devOnline	[device]	19
m_8	delivery	devOnline	bankJob	[device,receipt]	21

The happening of m_2 fullfills the pending expectation and matches with the body of (IC_2), generating a new one:

FULF = { $\mathbf{E}(check\_availability(devOnline, devWare, device), 3)$}

PEND = { $\mathbf{E}(inform(devWare, devOnline, device, Qty), T_{Qty})$

$\wedge T_{qty} > 3 \wedge T_{qty} < 13$}

The happening of m_3 fulfills the current pending expectation respecting the deadline. Moreover, it triggers (IC_3), and two different hypotheses are considered (acceptance and rejection of the order). However, since the predicate ok(3, shackLand) is evaluated by $\mathcal{S}$CIFF to false, only the expectation about the order rejection is considered:

FULF = { $\mathbf{E}(check\_availability(devOnline, devWare, device), 3)$,

$\mathbf{E}(inform(devWare, devOnline, device, 3), 10)$}

PEND = { $\mathbf{E}(reject\_order(devOnline, bankJob, device), T_{ro})$

$\wedge T_{ro} > 3 \wedge T_{ro} > 10$}

As a consequence, when *devOnline* accepts the purchase order of *bankJob* sending the message m_4, the $\mathcal{S}$CIFF proof procedure detects a violation, since m_4 is not explicitly expected.

5   Discussion and Conclusion

In this paper, we have addressed the run-time conformance verification issue w.r.t. web services interaction. We propose to use the $\mathcal{S}$CIFF framework and the *SOCS-SI* tool, and to adapt them to the Web Services peculiar features. Indeed, the presented proposal is part of a bigger and complex framework, sketched in Figure 3. We envisage two major research directions:

1. a *translation issue*, where a choreography specification is automatically translated to its corresponding $\mathcal{IC}_{chor}$ and KB_{chor}, together with its $\mathcal{G}_{chor}$;
2. a *verification issue*, that consists in three different types of verification (each one addressed by its own proof-theoretic verification tool).

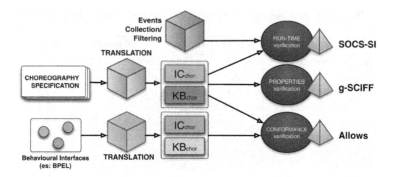

Fig. 3. Global view of our ongoing research

With respect to the translation issue, currently the link between known and widely accepted formalisms, such as BPEL and WS-CDL, and our model, is missing. We are aware that this part is of a fundamental importance, in order to effectively support our framework. Therefore, we are currently studying a translation algorithm capable to automatically convert a WS-BPEL/WS-CDL specification to our formalism. We are also working on the automatic translation of graphical specifications, like for example BPMN [22]. A first algorithm, that translates a simple graphical workflow language, has been presented in [23].

With respect to the verification issue, we envisage three possible types of verification. The first type has been addressed in this work, and is tackled by the *SOCS-SI* tool and the *SCIFF* proof-procedure. Noticeably, *SCIFF* operates indifferently off-line on a complete log or at run-time on events as soon as they happen. Therefore, the same tool is able to perform the conformance verification at run-time or a-posteriori. To support this type of verification, however, a low-level mechanism for capturing the interaction events is needed. We do not address this issue, but we recognize it is an important one, to the end of developing a real system.

The second type of verification is about the proof of "high level" properties: in fact, besides control-flow properties (like deadlock, liveness, etc.), it is interesting to check if a group of peers, whose interaction follows a given choreography, can benefit of particular properties. E.g., in a e-commerce scenario, a buyer is guaranteed to receive the good he paid for, and the seller is guaranteed to be paid. Assuming the peers behave correctly (w.r.t. the choreography), the fact that a property holds or not is a consequence of how the choreography has been specified. To this end, we have developed the g-*SCIFF*, an extension of the *SCIFF* proof procedure, and we applied it to verify some properties of a security protocol [24]. Other approaches tackle this issue by means of model checking techniques: e.g., in [25], the authors use model checking techniques to formally verify that requirements are met by web service systems, and to tackle the property verification issue. High level properties are expressed by means of *Linear Temporal Logic* formulas, and then verified using model checkers like SPIN or NuSMV.

The third type of verification aims to check if a web service, described by its behavioural interface, can play a given role within a choreography. This issue is known as "A-Priori Conformance Verification", and it has been tackled by many works in the research literature ([5,6], to cite some). We have addressed this problem in [26], combining $\mathcal{S}$CIFF and g-$\mathcal{S}$CIFF: the interested reader can refer to such paper for a comparison of the mentioned approaches.

We would like to clearly state that this is an ongoing work, and that it is far from being concluded. Several aspects have not yet been exhaustively researched: beside the automatic translation from other formalisms to our model, we need to test our approach on significant choreography specifications (currently, we have performed some tests on global interaction protocols for multi agent systems [27]).

However, we claim that our proposal indeed offers some noticeable advantages. First, the proposed specification language is declarative, intuitive and of highly expressive nature; $\mathcal{IC}_{chor}$ are human readable and clearly represent how the choreography should be followed by the interacting services. Moreover, a single specification language can be used to perform several different types of verification. Second, we claim the importance of modeling messages data and content as well as control flow among them. This kind of "content awareness" is required to model constraints about the content of messages and to formalize decisions or, more generally, pieces of knowledge of the choreography. Moreover, deadline specification is easily performed by means of CLP constraints, and business rules can be seamlessly expressed in the choreography knowledge base. Since the knowledge base is defined as an abductive logic program, powerful forms of reasoning, such as planning and diagnosis, can be easily integrated into the framework.

Acknowledgements. This work has been partially funded by the MIUR Projects PRIN 2005: *"Linguaggi per la specifica e la verifica di protocolli di interazione fra agenti"* and *"Vincoli e preferenze come formalismo unificante per l'analisi di sistemi informatici e la soluzione di problemi reali"*.

References

1. Andrews, T., Curbera, F., Dholakia, H., Goland, Y., Klein, J., Leymann, F., Liu, K., Roller, D., Smith, D., Thatte, S., Trickovic, I., Weerawarana, S.: Business Process Execution Language for Web Services version 1.1. (2003) Available at http://www-128.ibm.com/developerworks/library/specification/ws-bpel/.
2. W3C: (Web services choreography description language version 1.0) Home Page: http://www.w3.org/TR/ws-cdl-10/.
3. Barros, A., Dumas, M., Oaks, P.: A critical overview of the web services choreography description language (WS-CDL). BPTrends (2005)
4. van der Aalst, W., Dumas, M., ter Hofstede, A., Russell, N., Verbeek, H.M.W., Wohed, P.: Life after BPEL? In Bravetti, M., Kloul, L., Zavattaro, G., eds.: EPEW/WS-FM. Volume 3670 of LNCS., Springer (2005) 35–50
5. Baldoni, M., Baroglio, C., Martelli, A., Patti, V., Schifanella, C.: Verifying the conformance of web services to global interaction protocols: A first step. In Bravetti, M., Kloul, L., Zavattaro, G., eds.: EPEW/WS-FM. Volume 3670 of LNCS., Springer (2005)
6. Kazhamiakin, R., Pistore, M.: A parametric communication model for the verification of bpel4ws compositions. In: EPEW/WS-FM. (2005) 318–332
7. van der Aalst, W.: Business alignment: Using process mining as a tool for delta analysis and conformance testing. Requirements Engineering Journal **to appear** (2005)

8. Ouyang, C., van der Aalst, W., Breutel, S., Dumas, M., ter Hofstede, A., , Verbeek, H.: Formal semantics and analysis of control flow in ws-bpel. Technical Report BPM-05-15, BPMcenter.org (2005)

9. Rozinat, A., van der Aalst, W.M.P.: Conformance testing: Measuring the fit and appropriateness of event logs and process models. In Bussler, C., Haller, A., eds.: Business Process Management Workshops. Volume 3812. (2005) 163–176

10. Kakas, A.C., Kowalski, R.A., Toni, F.: Abductive Logic Programming. Journal of Logic and Computation 2(6) (1993) 719–770

11. (Societies Of ComputeeS (SOCS): a computational logic model for the description, analysis and verification of global and open societies of heterogeneous computees. IST-2001-32530) Home Page: http://lia.deis.unibo.it/Research/SOCS/.

12. Alberti, M., Chesani, F., Gavanelli, M., Lamma, E., Mello, P., Torroni, P.: Compliance verification of agent interaction: a logic-based software tool. Applied Artificial Intelligence 20(2-4) (2006) 133–157

13. Bry, F., Eckert, M., Patranjan, P.: Reactivity on the web: Paradigms and applications of the language xchange. Journal of Web Engineering 5(1) (2006) 3–24

14. Lloyd, J.W.: Foundations of Logic Programming. 2nd edn. Springer-Verlag (1987)

15. Jaffar, J., Maher, M.: Constraint logic programming: a survey. Journal of Logic Programming 19-20 (1994) 503–582

16. Alberti, M., Chesani, F., Gavanelli, M., Lamma, E., Mello, P., Torroni, P.: The SOCS computational logic approach for the specification and verification of agent societies. In Priami, C., Quaglia, P., eds.: Global Computing: IST/FET Intl. Workshop, GC 2004 Rovereto, Italy, March 9-12. Volume 3267 of LNAI. Springer-Verlag (2005) 324–339

17. Kakas, A.C., Mancarella, P.: On the relation between Truth Maintenance and Abduction. In Fukumura, T., ed.: Proc. PRICAI-90, Nagoya, Japan, (Ohmsha Ltd.) 438–443

18. Fung, T.H., Kowalski, R.A.: The IFF proof procedure for abductive logic programming. Journal of Logic Programming 33(2) (1997) 151–165

19. Denecker, M., Schreye, D.D.: SLDNFA: an abductive procedure for abductive logic programs. Journal of Logic Programming 34(2) (1998) 111–167

20. Gavanelli, M., Lamma, E., Mello, P.: Proof of properties of the SCIFF proof-procedure. Technical Report CS-2005-01, Computer science group, Dept. of Engineering, Ferrara University (2005) http://www.ing.unife.it/informatica/tr/.

21. Alberti, M., Gavanelli, M., Lamma, E., Mello, P., Torroni, P.: The sciff abductive proof-procedure. In: Proc. of the 9th National Congress on Artificial Intelligence, AI*IA 2005. Volume 3673 of LNAI., Springer-Verlag (2005) 135–147

22. Initiative, B.P.M.: (Business process modeling notation)

23. Chesani, F., Ciampolini, A., Mello, P., Montali, M., Storari, S.: Testing guidelines conformance by translating a graphical language to computational logic, Workshop on AI techniques in healthcare. In conjunction with ECAI (2006) To appear.

24. Alberti, M., Chesani, F., Gavanelli, M., Lamma, E., Mello, P., Torroni, P.: Security protocols verification in abductive logic programming: a case study. In Dikenelli, O., Gleizes, M., Ricci, A., eds.: Proc. of ESAW'05, Ege University (2005) 283–295

25. Kazhamiakin, R., Pistore, M., Roveri, M.: Formal verification of requirements using spin: A case study on web services. In: Proc. of the Software Engineering and Formal Methods (SEFM'04), Washington, DC, USA, IEEE Computer Society (2004) 406–415

26. Alberti, M., Chesani, F., Gavanelli, M., Lamma, E., Mello, P., Montali, M.: An abductive framework for a-priori verification of web services. In Maher, M., ed.: Principles and Practice of Declarative Programming (PPDP'06), ACM Press (2006) to appear.

27. (The socs protocols repository) Available at http://edu59.deis.unibo.it:8079/SOCSProtocolsRepository/jsp/index.jsp.

Semantic Querying of Mathematical Web Service Descriptions

Rebhi Baraka* and Wolfgang Schreiner

Research Institute for Symbolic Computation (RISC)
Johannes Kepler University, Linz, Austria
{rbaraka, schreine}@risc.uni-linz.ac.at

Abstract. This paper describes a semantic extension to the Mathematical Services Query Language (MSQL). MSQL is a language for querying registry-published mathematical Web service descriptions expressed in the Mathematical Services Description Language (MSDL). The semantic extension allows queries in MSQL to be based on the underlying semantics of service descriptions; the MSQL engine processes these queries with the help of an automated reasoner.

1 Introduction

Semantic-based discovery of Web services is one of the crucial issues that are currently receiving considerable attention in the field of the Semantic Web. In the case of mathematical Web services, this issue is more subtle due to the fact that they operate within semantically rich domains on objects that need proper encoding and specification.

A *mathematical Web service* is a Web service that offers the solution to a mathematical problem (based on e.g. a computer algebra system or on an automated theorem prover). In the MathBroker project [12], we have developed a framework for mathematical services based on standards such as XML, SOAP, WSDL, and OpenMath. We have developed the XML-based Mathematical Services Description Language (MSDL) [8] to adequately describe mathematical services and their constituent entities. The description of a mathematical service in MSDL may contain information related to the type of the problem, the algorithm(s) used to solve the problem, related problems, machines executing the problem, etc. A skeleton of a service description in MSDL is shown in Figure 1.

To facilitate the process of publishing and discovering mathematical services, we have developed an ebXML-based mathematical registry [3] where MSDL descriptions of services are published such that clients can discover them by browsing or querying the registry (and consequently receive corresponding WSDL descriptions). Since the querying facilities of the registry do not support content-based querying, we have developed the content-based Mathematical Services

---

* This work was sponsored by the FWF Project P17643-NO4 "MathBroker II: Brokering Distributed Mathematical Services".

```
<monet:definitions>
  <mathb:machine_hardware name="perseus">
    ...
  </mathb:machine_hardware>
  <monet:problem name="integration">
    ...
  </monet:problem>
  <monet:algorithm name="RischAlg">
    ...
  </monet:algorithm>
  <monet:implementation name="RImpl">
    ...
   <monet:hardware href=".../perseus"/>
   <monet:algorithm href=".../RischAlg"/>
  </monet:implementation>
  <monet:service name="RRISC">
    ...
   <monet:problem href=".../integration"/>
   <monet:implementation href=".../RImpl"/>
  </monet:service>
</monet:definitions>
```

Fig. 1. A Skeleton of a Service Description

Query Language (MSQL) [1,4] which is able to perform queries at the syntactical structure of a MSDL service description. However, mathematical objects respectively their MSDL descriptions are semantically rich and MSQL does not capture these semantic structures and their relations. This limits the effectiveness of service discovery since it is not based on the semantic information contained in MSDL descriptions. In this paper we present an extension to MSQL that addresses the semantic information contained in service descriptions. This extension adds a number of constructs to the language in order to express predicate logic formulas and adds a semantic evaluator to the MSQL engine to process these formulas with the help of an automated reasoner. The rest of this paper briefly describes the syntactic structure of MSQL (Section 2), the semantic extension to MSQL (Section 3), the MSQL engine architecture and implementation (Section 4), and finally reviews related work (Section 5).

2   The MSQL Syntactic Structure

The Mathematical Services Query Language is a language designed and implemented to query registry-published services based on the contents of their MSDL descriptions. It provides the functionality to interface to a registry and retrieve service descriptions on which queries are performed. Its implementation is based on a formally defined semantics [1].

A query in MSQL conforms to the following syntax:

```
SELECT EVERY|SOME <entity>
FROM <classificationConcept>
WHERE <expression>
ORDERBY <expression> ASCENDING|DESCENDING
```

The query has four main clauses:

- The *SELECT* clause selects EVERY or SOME description of the type specified by *entity* from a given classification scheme in the registry. The *entity* types defined by MSDL are *problem, algorithm, implementation, realization* (*including a WSDL service description*), and *machine*.
- The *FROM* clause determines the classification scheme from which the specified description is to be selected. Every service respectively its description in the registry is classified according to predefined classification schemes in the registry. The *FROM* clause limits the range of descriptions to be retrieved for querying to those classified under *ClassificationConcept*.
- The *WHERE* clause applies its *expression* parts to each candidate document retrieved from the registry. The expression of the *WHERE* clause is a logical condition: if it is evaluated to *true*, the document is considered as (part of) the result of the query.
- The *ORDERBY* clause sorts the resulting documents in *ASCENDING* or *DESCENDING* order based on the comparison criteria resulting from the evaluation of its *expression* on each document.

MSQL is designed such that it has a minimal set of expressions that are sufficient to construct logical statements on the contents of the target MSDL descriptions and that it is able to address the structure of such descriptions. MSQL expressions include: path expressions that can access every part of an MSDL document; expressions involving logical, arithmetic, and comparative operators; conditional expressions; quantified expressions; functions; and variable bindings. The following is a sample MSQL query that illustrates the usage of some of these expressions.

Example 1. *Find every service in "/GAMS/Symbolic Computation" such that, if it has an implementation, it runs on a machine called "perseus", otherwise its interface is on this machine.*

```
SELECT EVERY service
FROM /GAMS/Symbolic Computation
WHERE
  if not (/service[empty(//implementation)])
  then
    let $d := doc(//implementation/@href) in
      $d/hardware[contains(@name, "perseus")]
  else
    //service-interface-description[contains(@href, "perseus")]
ORDERBY /service/@name descending
```

This query asks for every service description classified under "/GAMS/Symbolic Computation" that satisfies the WHERE expression. The resulting documents are to be sorted in descending order according to their names. The conditional expression (if .. then .. else) is used to decide if the current service document node has an implementation. If this is the case, it takes from the service document the URI of such implementation document, retrieves it from the registry (`let $d := doc(//implementation/@href)`), and checks if this implementation is related to the machine `perseus`. If this is not the case, it checks in the `else` branch, if the service has its interface on the said machine. The `let` clause is used to assign a document to the variable d which is then used as part of the path expression. The `doc` function returns the root node of the document whose name appears as its argument. Its argument is a URI that is used as the address of the required document in the registry. The `contains` function returns *true* if its first argument value contains as part of it its second argument value.

Although MSQL provides the functionality to express and perform queries on the syntactic structure of MSDL descriptions, it does not provide the functionality to express and perform queries on their semantic content. In the next section, we present an extension to MSQL that addresses this limitation.

3   A Semantic Extension to MSQL

The Mathematical Services Description Language (MSDL) is capable of representing not only syntactic structures, but also semantic information. This information is expressed in OpenMath [6], an XML-based standard format for representing mathematical objects in a semantics-preserving way. To illustrate this approach, we first present a sample description to show the underlying semantics of MSDL and then show how a query that operates on this semantics can be constructed .

Consider a description of the mathematical problem of indefinite integration (Figure 2). It consists of the following pieces of semantic information:

- Input: $f : \mathbb{R} \to \mathbb{R}$ (lines 3 to 13) which expresses the type $\mathbb{R} \to \mathbb{R}$ of the input and gives it the local name f.
- Output: $i : \mathbb{R} \to \mathbb{R}$ which expresses the type $\mathbb{R} \to \mathbb{R}$ of the output and gives it the local name i.
- Post-condition: $i = indefint(f)$ (lines 17 to 28) which states that the output i equals the indefinite integral of the input f.

The semantic information expressed in this problem description can be used as a basis for discovering suitable services published in the mathematical registry. Suppose a client wants to solve a problem with the following specification:

- Input: $a : \mathbb{R} \to \mathbb{R}$
- Output: $b : \mathbb{R} \to \mathbb{R}$
- Post-condition: $diff(b) = a$ (which states that the differentiated output equals the input).

```
1   <problem name="indefinite-integration">
2   <body>
3    <input name="f">
4     <signature>
5      <OMOBJ>
6       <OMA>
7        <OMS cd="sts" name="mapsto"/>
8        <OMS cd="setname1" name="R"/>
9        <OMS cd="setname1" name="R"/>
10       </OMA>
11      </OMOBJ>
12     </signature>
13    </input>
14    <output name="i">
15     ...
16    </output>
17    <post-condition>
18     <OMOBJ>
19      <OMA>
20       <OMS cd="relation1" name="eq"/>
21       <OMV name="i"/>
22       <OMA>
23        <OMS cd="calculus1" name="indefint"/>
24        <OMV name="f"/>
25       </OMA>
26      </OMA>
27     </OMOBJ>
28    </post-condition>
29   </body>
30  </problem>
```

Fig. 2. An MSDL Problem Description

The client would thus like to find some service which solves a problem p such that

$$type(input_p) = \mathbb{R} \to \mathbb{R} \ \wedge \qquad (1)$$

$$type(output_p) = \mathbb{R} \to \mathbb{R} \ \wedge \qquad (2)$$

$$\forall a \in \mathbb{R} \to \mathbb{R}, \, b \in \mathbb{R} \to \mathbb{R} \ (post_p(a,b) \Rightarrow diff(b) = a) \qquad (3)$$

where formulas (1) and (2) state that the types of the input and output shall be $\mathbb{R} \to \mathbb{R}$ and the universally quantified subformula (3) states that the post-condition $post_p$ of the problem p implies that the differentiation of the output b equals the input a. The truth of this statement depends on knowledge available about the operation $diff$, e.g. a knowledge base may contain the formula $diff(indefint(a)) = a$ which semantically relates the operators $diff$ and $indefint$.

To express such a formula in MSQL, we extended the grammar of MSQL as shown in Figure 3 by adding two clauses:

```
       <msqlQuery> ::= 'SELECT' ( 'EVERY' | 'SOME' ) <entity>
                       ( 'FROM' <classification> )?
                       ( 'WHERE' <msqlExpr> )?
                       ( 'ORDERBY' <msqlExpr )?;
                       ...
        <msqlExpr> ::= ... | <typematch> | <semanticExpr>;
       <typematch> ::= 'typematch' (omObjExpr, omObjExpr);
    <semanticExpr> ::= 'satisfy' ( <omObjExpr> );
       <omObjExpr> ::= <omApplication> | <omAttribution> | <omBinding>
                       | <omInt> | <omVar> | <omString> | <omSymbol>
                       | <var>;
    <omApplication> ::= 'oma' '(' <omObjExpr> (, <omObjExpr> )* (
                       <varReplacement> )? ')';
    <omAttribution> ::= 'omattr' '(' <omObjExpr>, ( <omObjExpr>
                       <omObjExpr> )(, ( <omObjExpr> <omObjExpr> ))*
                       ( <varReplacement> )? ')' ;
       <omBinding> ::= 'ombind' '(' <omObjExpr> '[' <omBoundVariable>
                       (, omBoundVariable )* ']' <omObjExpr>
                       ( <varReplacement> )? ')';
 <omBoundVariable> ::= 'omvar' ':' ( <var> | <omVar> ) '@' '('<omObjExpr>,
                       <omObjExpr> ( <varReplacement> )? ')';
  <varReplacement> ::= '[' <omObjExpr> '/' <var> (, <omObjExpr> '/'
                       <var> )* ']';
           <omInt> ::= 'omi' ':' <number>;
           <omVar> ::= 'omv' ':' ( <letter> | <var> );
        <omString> ::= 'omstr' ':' <letter> ;
        <omSymbol> ::= 'oms' ':' <letter> ':' <letter>;
             <var> ::= '$' <letter>;
                       ...
```

Fig. 3. The MSQL Semantic Extension Grammar

- The clause 'typematch(a,b)' states that type *a* matches (i.e. equals or is a special version of) type *b*.
- The clause 'satisfy e' states that the semantic interpretation of the predicate logic formula *e* (encoded as an OpenMath expression) yields *true*.

The `<semanticExpr>` rule and its subrules define the grammar of predicate logic formulas based on the classification of OpenMath objects into *basic* objects and *compound* objects [6]. *Basic* objects include *Integers*, *Strings*, *Variables*, and *Symbols*. *Compound* objects include *Application*, *Attribution*, and *Binding*. The syntax is defined such that expressions are written in a prefix notation which is internally transformed to OpenMath syntax. For instance the `<omBinding>` subrule (see also Example 2) expresses an OpenMath *Binding* object which is constructed from an OpenMath object (the binder), and from zero or more variables (the bound variables) followed by another OpenMath object (the body). The MSQL expression

```
oma(oms:relation1:eq, oma(oms:calculus1:diff, omv:b), omv:a)
```

is thus transformed to the OpenMath XML object

```
<OMA>
 <OMS name="eq" cd="relation1"/>
  <OMA>
    <OMS name="diff" cd="calculus1"/>
    <OMV name="b"/>
  </OMA>
  <OMV name="a"/>
</OMA>
```

Example 2. Our request to *find some service with problem* p *such that the type checks (1) and (2) and the subformula (3) are satisfied* can be expressed by the following MSQL query:

```
SELECT SOME service
FROM /GAMS/Symbolic Computation
WHERE let $p:= doc(//problem/@href) in
           $a:= $p//input/@name,
           $b:= $p//output/@name,
           $ta:= $p//input/signature/OMOBJ,
           $tb:= $p//output/signature/OMOBJ,
        $post:= $p//post-condition/OMOBJ in
  (typematch(oma(oms:sts:mapsto(oms:setname1:R,
                       oms:setname1:R)), $ta)) and
  (typematch($tb, oma(oms:sts:mapsto(oms:setname1:R,
                       oms:setname1:R)))) and
  (satisfy(ombind(oms:quant1:forall
    [omvar:$a@(oms:sts:type, $ta),
     omvar:$b@(oms:sts:type, $tb)]
    oma(oms:logic1:implies, $post,
        oma(oms:relation1:eq,
           oma(oms:calculus1:diff, omv:$b), omv:$a)))))
```

Variable $p represents the problem description of the service retrieved from the registry by the *doc* function according to the problem *href* provided as part of the service description. Variables $a and $b represent the names of the input and the output of the problem. Variables $ta and $tb represent the types of the input and the output of the problem. Variable $post represents the post-condition of the problem.

The two typematch expressions correspond to formulas (1) and (2). They check if type $R \rightarrow R$ matches the type $ta of the input and if the type $tb of the output matches type $R \rightarrow R$.

The satisfy expression corresponds to the universally quantified subformula (3).

In the next section, we explain how the query is handled by the MSQL engine.

4   The MSQL Architecture and Implementation

MSQL including its semantic extension has been implemented as MSQL engine [1,4] and has been incorporated into the MathBroker framework [12] for service publication and discovery.

4.1   Architecture

Figure 4 illustrates the architecture of the MSQL engine which consists of the following components:

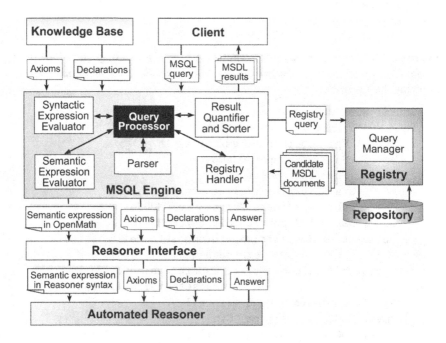

Fig. 4. The MSQL Engine Architecture

- The **MSQL Engine** which has the MSQL query functionality. It consists of the following components:
  - The **Query Processor** which receives the query from the client, decomposes it into processable parts, and hands each part to the corresponding component.
  - The **Parser** receives the query from the processor and parses it according to the MSQL syntax. If the query does not comply with the syntax, an error message is returned to the processor which forwards the message to the client.
  - The **Registry Handler** receives from the processor the *entity* and *classificationConcept* parts of the query. It composes a registry query to retrieve *EVERY/SOME* description document of the given *entity* type classified under the given *classificationConcept*.

- The **Syntactic Expression Evaluator** receives from the Query Processor the syntactic expression part of the query and evaluates it against each description document retrieved from the registry. It returns to Query Processor those documents for which the expression evaluates to *true*.
- The **Semantic Expression Evaluator** receives from the Query Processor the semantic expression part of the query and evaluates it against each description document retrieved from the registry. It returns to the Query Processor those documents for which the expression evaluates to *true*. Unlike the Syntactic Expression Evaluator, the Semantic Expression Evaluator does not perform the whole evaluation by itself. It rather takes the semantic expression, converts it into OpenMath format (see Figure 5), retrieves from the Knowledge Base the axiom(s) and type declaration(s) needed to reason about the semantic expression and sends all of them to the Reasoner Interface. As required by the Reasoner Interface, the axioms are represented in OpenMath format and the declarations are represented in OMDoc [16] format.
- The **Result Quantifier and Sorter** receives from the Query Processor SOME/EVERY document filtered by the two evaluators, orders (if needed) the documents according to the ORDERBY expression, and returns them as the query result to the Client.

- The **Registry** which stores a collection of published MSDL documents of different *entity* types and classifies them according to some registry-predefined classification schemes. Query requests to the registry are handled by the Query Manager of the registry.
- The **Reasoner Interface** receives from the Semantic Expression Evaluator the semantic expression part of the query in OpenMath, the axiom(s) in OpenMath, and the declaration(s) in OMDoc and converts each one to the format required by the Automated Reasoner and hands them to the reasoner. It gets the answer from the reasoner and sends it to the Semantic Expression Evaluator. The Reasoner Interface used is a component of the RISC ProofNavigator [19].
- The **Automated Reasoner** reasons about semantic expressions based on the axiom(s) and declaration(s) given and returns the answer to the Reasoner Interface. The Automated Reasoner currently used is the Cooperating Validity Checker Lite (CVCL) [5].
- The **Knowledge Base** holds declarations of OpenMath symbols that may be used in semantic queries together with axioms that describe the semantics of that symbols.

4.2 Performing the Semantic Query

Based on this architecture, we summarize the actions taken to perform the query in Example 2:

- The MSQL Engine receives the query from the Client and hands it to the Query Processor

- The Query Processor asks the Parser to parse the query according to the MSQL syntax. If the query does not comply with the MSQL syntax, an error message is returned to the user.
- The Query Processor decomposes the query to processable parts. It hands the registry-related part (the *entity service* and the *classificationConcept* "*/GAMS/Symbolic Computation*") to the registry handler.
- The Registry Handler forms a registry query based on the *entity* and the *classificationConcept*, connects to the Registry and hands the registry query to the Query Manager of the Registry which performs the query and returns a set of candidate *service* documents to the Registry Handler.
- The Query Processor asks the Syntactic Expression Evaluator to evaluate the syntactic expression part on the current *service* document. The Syntactic Expression part consists of a *let* expression which has six assignment subexpressions. The evaluations of these subexpressions assign values to variables \$a, \$b, \$ta, \$tb, and \$post representing input, output, input type, output type, and post-condition respectively. These variables are used in the semantic expression of the query.
- The Query Processor asks the Semantic Expression Evaluator to evaluate the semantics expression against the (same) current *service* document. The Semantic Evaluator performs the following steps:
  - It performs the type checking required by the two typematch expressions. If the result of the check is *true* it proceeds to the next step. Otherwise it returns *false* and the Query Processor proceeds to perform the query on the next candidate document.
  - It converts the `satisfy` expression to OpenMath format. The OpenMath representation of the satisfy expression is shown in Figure 5. The conversion also takes care of variable substitution (e.g., variable \$a is substituted by the input name f).
  - It retrieves from the Knowledge Base the declarations of the symbols *diff* and *indefint* represented in OMDoc. The two symbols occur in the OpenMath representation of the `satisfy` formula after variable substitution. The declaration of the *diff* symbol is shown in Figure 6. The *indefint* symbol has a similar declaration.
  - It retrieves from the Knowledge Base the axiom $diff(indefint(a)) = a$. This axiom is represented by the following quantified formula in OpenMath format (similar to the OpenMath format of the *satisfy* expression)

$$\forall f \in \mathbb{R} \rightarrow \mathbb{R}\ (indefint(diff(f)) = f)$$

  - It hands the satisfy expression (in OpenMath), the declarations (in OMDoc), and the axiom (in OpenMath) to the Reasoner Interface which converts each of them to the syntax required by the reasoner. The reasoner decides about the truth value of the expression based on the given axiom and declarations and returns the answer to the RISC ProofNavigator which in turn returns the answer to the Semantic Expression Evaluator.

```
1  <OMOBJ>
2  <OMBIND>
3   <OMS name="forall" cd="quant1"/>
4   <OMBVAR>
5    <OMATTR>
6      <OMATP>
7        <OMS name="type" cd="sts"/>
8        <OMA>
9         <OMS name="mapsto" cd="sts"/>
10        <OMS name="R" cd="setname1"/>
11        <OMS name="R" cd="setname1"/>
12       </OMA>
13      </OMATP>
14      <OMV name="f"/>
15     </OMATTR>
16     <OMATTR>
17       ...
18      <OMV name="i"/>
19     </OMATTR>
20    </OMBVAR>
21    <OMA>
22     <OMS name="implies" cd="logic1"/>
23     <OMA>
24      <OMS name="eq" cd="relation1"/>
25      <OMV name="i"/>
26      <OMA>
27       <OMV name="indefint" cd="calculus1"/>
28       <OMV name="f"/>
29      </OMA>
30     </OMA>
31     <OMA>
32      <OMS name="eq" cd="relation1"/>
33      <OMA>
34       <OMV name="diff" cd="calculus1"/>
35       <OMV name="i"/>
36      </OMA>
37      <OMV name="f"/>
38     </OMA>
39    </OMA>
40   </OMBIND>
41  </OMOBJ>
```

Lines 5 to 15 represent the conversion of the binder expression

```
omvar:$a@(oms:sts:type, $ta)
```

with the variables $a and $b substituted by their values. It represents the declaration

$$f : \mathbb{R} \to \mathbb{R}$$

Lines 21 to 39 represent the conversion of the *satisfy* subexpression

```
oma(oms:logic1:implies, $post,
    oma(oms:relation1:eq,
        oma(oms:calculus1:diff,
            omv:$b), omv:$a))
```

with the variables $post, $a, and $b appropriately substituted by their values. It represents the implication

$$i = indefint(f) \Rightarrow diff(i) = f.$$

Fig. 5. OpenMath Representation of the *satisfy* Expression in Example 2

– If the evaluation of the semantic expression yields *true*, the Query Processor returns the current *service* document to the Result Quantifier and Sorter which returns it to the Client as the ultimate result (because of the SOME clause) of the query. If the evaluation is *false* the Query Processor proceeds to process the query on the next candidate *service* document. If the evaluation is *false* for all candidate documents, then no document is returned as a result of the query.

4.3   A Prototype Implementation

A prototype of the architecture has been implemented in Java making use of the registry [3] for publishing service descriptions, a component of the RISC ProofNavigator [19] as the Reasoner Interface, and the Cooperating Validity Checker Lite (CVCL) [5] as the Automated Reasoner.

The implementation of the MSQL engine is based on a formal definition [1] using denotational semantics [18]. The implementation consists of a set of

```
<omdoc:omgroup>
 <omdoc:symbol kind="object" name="calculus1_diff">
  <omdoc:type system="simply_typed"
  xml:id="calculus1_diff_type">
  <om:OMA>
    <om:OMS cd="sts" name="mapsto"/>
    <om:OMA>
      <om:OMS cd="sts" name="mapsto"/>
      <om:OMS cd="setname1" name="R"/>
      <om:OMS cd="setname1" name="R"/>
    </om:OMA>
    <om:OMA>
      <om:OMS cd="sts" name="mapsto"/>
      <om:OMS cd="setname1" name="R"/>
      <om:OMS cd="setname1" name="R"/>
    </om:OMA>
  </om:OMA>
  </omdoc:type>
 </omdoc:symbol>
</omdoc:omgroup>
```

Fig. 6. The declaration of variable *diff* in OMDoc Format

evaluation classes each of which corresponds to one component of the MSQL engine with a set of methods each of which corresponds to one equation in the denotational semantics. The signature of a method corresponds to the signature of the semantic function. For example, the equation

$$\mathbf{E}[\![V]\!] \ d \ n \ r = lookup(d, \ [\![V]\!])$$

with the semantic function

$$\mathbf{E} : Expression \times Declaration \times Node \times Registry \rightarrow Value$$

is implemented by the Java method with the signature

```
evaluateVariableExpr(ChildAST expression, Declaration declaration,
                     Node node, Registry registry)
```

The prototype implementation of the MSQL engine including its API can be found in [2].

5   Related Work

The semantic-based discovery of Web services has recently received growing interest. The METEOR-S Web Service Discovery Infrastructure (MWSDI) [20] aims to provide efficient publication and discovery mechanisms in a federation of registries. It uses an ontology-based approach to organize registries, enabling semantic classification of services based on domains. Registries support semantic publication of services which is used during the discovery process.

The Ontology Web Language for Services (OWL-S) [17] allows Semantic Web tools to process Web services in order to enable software agents to automatically discover, invoke, compose, and monitor Web services. In [11], OWL-S is used in conjunction with WSDL to add semantic descriptions to a Web service. When a registry is used for the publication and discovery of a service, OWL-S is used in this respect to add capability matching to the registry.

The Web Service Modeling Ontology (WSMO) [21] is a formal language for semantically describing Web services to facilitate the automation of discovering, composing, and invoking such services. WSMO uses a formal logic for describing its own elements such as ontologies, descriptions, goals, and mediators.

Few approaches have focused on the semantic description and discovery of mathematical Web services. In the MONET project [14], ontologies [7] are used to model service descriptions as well as queries on these descriptions. These ontologies are ontological conversions of MSDL descriptions written in OWL [13] and are used by a component within the MONET architecture called *Instance Store* [10] which uses the Description Logic reasoner RACER [9] for matching queries to appropriate services. The reasoning process in the case of MONET is based on a restricted form of first order logic which is more tractable for automated reasoning but strictly less expressive. In our semantic queries, we use full predicate logic which is a highly expressive language.

A matching-based discovery approach [15] to registry-published mathematical services performs matchmaking between representations of tasks (client requests) and capabilities (service descriptions). The approach applies a normalization process on a task. It then compares the normalized task with a registered capability calculating a similarity value that is used in the matchmaking process. Task normalization amounts to carrying out a sequence of transformations on the task description rewriting all logical parts in disjunctive normal form, flattening arguments of n-associative operations, and consistent variable renaming.

The similarity value is calculated based on the matching of the capability precondition (or the task postcondition) and the capability postcondition (or the task precondition). Matchmaking is performed by: registering capabilities in the database, taking a description of a task normalizes it, and returns an ordered list of the capabilities from the registry database based on their calculated similarity.

The matching process used in the discovery is ultimately based on the syntactic similarity traced between tasks and capabilities. In our case, the decision is based on logical implications between statements extracted from descriptions, which is strictly more general.

6   Conclusion and Future Work

The semantic extension of MSQL supports semantic-based discovery of registry published mathematical services. Semantic queries formed in predicate logic

capture the underlying semantical structures of mathematical service specifications. The MSQL engine performs semantic-based queries with the help of an
automated reasoner which takes predicate logic formulas, decides their validity,
and returns the answer to the engine.

The syntax of MSQL and the presented query examples reveal an apparent
difficulty in forming queries on target documents. Such a difficulty is alleviated
partly by the fact that MSQL has a relatively small number of constructs for
forming queries and by the fact that its queries operate on documents that
possess common structures imposed by a schema. Thus, a user-friendly tool for
forming queries on target MSDL documents should be developed.

A future extension to the presented framework may involve service compositions: when a client submits a service request, a broker agent determines suitable
service compositions satisfying the client request and returns the description of
a composition rather than that of a single service. To find the suitable candidate
services, the agent might form MSQL queries based on information contained
in the client request, send them to the MSQL engine, and make composition
decisions based on the results returned by the MSQL engine.

References

1. Rebhi Baraka. Mathematical Services Query Language: Design, Formalization, and Implementation. Technical report, Research Institute for Symbolic Computation (RISC), Johannes Kepler University, Linz, Austria, September 2005. See ftp://ftp.risc.uni-linz.ac.at/pub/techreports/.
2. Rebhi Baraka. Mathematical Services Query Language (MSQL) API. Research Institute for Symbolic Computation (RISC), Johannes Kepler University, Linz, Austria, September 2005. See http://poseidon.risc.uni-linz.ac.at:8080/results/msql/doc/index.html.
3. Rebhi Baraka, Olga Caprotti, and Wolfgang Schreiner. A Web Registry for Publishing and Discovering Mathematical Services. In *Proc. of IEEE Conf. on e-Technology, e-Commerce, and e-Service*, Hong Kong Baptist University, Hong Kong, March 29 – April 1, 2005. IEEE Computer Society, Los Alamitos, CA.
4. Rebhi Baraka and Wolfgang Schreiner. Querying Registry-Published Mathematical Web Services. In *Proc. of the IEEE 20th Int. Conf. on Advanced Information Networking and Applications (AINA 2006)*, Vienna, Austria April 18 – April 20, 2006. IEEE Computer Society.
5. Clark W. Barrett and Sergey Berezin. CVC Lite: A New Implementation of the Cooperating Validity Checker Category B. In *Proc. of 16th Int. Conf. on Computer Aided Verification*, Boston, MA, USA, July 13-17, 2004. Springer.
6. Stephen Buswell, Olgo Caprotti, David Carlisle, Mike Dewar, Marc Gaëtano, and Michael Kohlhase. The OpenMath Standard (v 2.0). The OpenMath Society, June 2004. See http://www.openmath.org/cocoon/openmath/index.html.
7. Olga Caprotti, Mike Dewar, and Daniele Turi. Mathematical Service Matching Using Description Logic and OWL. In *Proc. of the 3rd Int. Conf. on Mathematical Knowledge Management (MKM 2004)*, Bialowieza, Poland, September 19-21.
8. Olga Caprotti and Wolfgang Schreiner. Towards a Mathematical Service Description Language. In *International Congress of Mathematical Software ICMS 2002*, Bejing, China, August 17–19, 2002. World Scientific Publishing, Singapore.

9. Volker Haarslev and Ralf Moller. Description of the RACER system and its applications. In *Automated reasoning: 1st Int. Joint Conf., IJCAR 2001*, Siena, Itally, June 18–23, 2001. volume 2083 of Lecture Notes in Artificial Intelligence, New York, NY, USA, 2001. Springer Verlag Inc.

10. Instance Store - Database Support for Reasoning over Individuals. The University of Manchester, 2002. See http://instancestore.man.ac.uk/instancestore.pdf.

11. David L. Martin, Massimo Paolucci, Sheila A. McIlraith, Mark H. Burstein, Drew V. McDermott, Deborah L. McGuinness, Bijan Parsia, Terry R. Payne, Marta Sabou, Monika Solanki, Naveen Srinivasan, and Katia P. Sycara. Bringing Semantics to Web Services: The OWL-S Approach. In Jorge Cardoso and Amit P. Sheth, editors, *SWSWPC*, volume 3387 of *Lecture Notes in Computer Science*, pages 26–42. Springer, 2004.

12. MathBroker II: Brokering Distributed Mathematical Services. Research Institute for Symbolic Computation (RISC), Johannes Kepler University, Linz, Austria, April 2006. See http://www.risc.uni-linz.ac.at/research/parallel/projects/mathbroker2/.

13. Deborah L. McGuinness and Frank van Harmelen. OWL Web Ontology Language Overview. W3C Recommendation, February 2004. See http://www.w3.org/TR/owl-features/.

14. MONET — Mathematics on the Web. The MONET Consortium, April 2004. http://monet.nag.co.uk.

15. William Naylor and Julian Padget. Semantic Matching for Mathematical Services. In *Proc. of the 4th Int. conf. on Mathematical Knowledge Management*, Bremen, Germany, 15 – 17 July, 2005. Springer.

16. OMDoc: A Standard for Open Mathematical Documents. MathWeb.org, September 2005. See http://www.mathweb.org/omdoc/.

17. OWL-S: Semantic Markup for Web Services. W3C Member Submission, November 2004. See http://www.w3.org/Submission/OWL-S/.

18. David A. Schmidt. Denotational Semantics – A Methodology for Language Development. Allyn and Bacon, Boston, 1986.

19. Wolfgang Schreiner. The RISC ProofNavigator. Research Institute for Symbolic Computation (RISC), Johannes Kepler University, Linz, Austria, March 2006. See http://www.risc.uni-linz.ac.at/research/formal/software/ProofNavigator/.

20. Kunal Verma, Kaarthik Sivashanmugam, Amit Sheth, Abhijit Patil, Swapna Oundhakar, and John Miller. METEOR-S WSDI: A Scalable P2P Infrastructure of Registries for Semantic Publication and Discovery of Web Services. *Journal of Information Technology and Management*, 6(1):17–39, 2005.

21. Web Service Modeling Ontology (WSMO). W3C Member Submission, June 2005. See http://www.w3.org/Submission/WSMO/.

Verified Reference Implementations
of WS-Security Protocols

Karthikeyan Bhargavan, Cédric Fournet, and Andrew D. Gordon

Microsoft Research

Abstract. We describe a new reference implementation of the web services security specifications. The implementation is structured as a library in the functional programming language F#. Applications written using this library can interoperate with other compliant web services, such as those written using Microsoft WSE and WCF frameworks. Moreover, the security of such applications can be automatically verified by translating them to the applied pi calculus and using an automated theorem prover. We illustrate the use of our reference implementation through examples drawn from the sample applications included with WSE and WCF. We formally verify their security properties. We also experimentally evaluate their interoperability and performance.

1 Introduction

XML web services offer a standards-based framework for deploying secure networked applications. Using SOAP [16] to serialize data, WS-Addressing [10] to identify endpoints, WS-Security [24] to protect messages, and HTTP or TCP as transport, programmers can deploy clients and servers that can operate across different platforms.

To this end, the WS-Security standard defines a security header for SOAP messages that may include signatures, ciphertexts, key identifiers, and tokens identifying particular principals. Environments such as Apache WSS4J [3], IBM WebSphere [17], and Microsoft Web Services Enhancements (WSE) [20] and Windows Communication Foundation (WCF) [21], provide tools and libraries for building web services that are secured via the mechanisms of WS-Security and related specifications.

In general, even if an attacker is unable to compromise the underlying cryptographic algorithms used in a protocol, there may be successful attacks based on intercepting, rewriting, and sending messages, as noted by Needham and Schroeder [25] and later formalized by Dolev and Yao [11]. Due to the flexibility of composable specifications and the semi-structured nature of the XML message format, WS-Security protocols are actually more prone to message rewriting attacks than protocols based on binary formats. In particular, studies of the usage of WS-Security reveal a wide range of vulnerabilities to message rewriting attacks [5,6,4,18,19]. Hence, it is essential to verify the security of WS-Security protocol implementations before deployment.

Almost all verification tools for cryptographic protocols analyze abstract models rather than implementations. For instance, the ProVerif [9,8] theorem prover takes a protocol model written in a variant of the pi calculus [23,2] plus target authentication and secrecy goals, and attempts to prove that the model satisfies these goals. So, to verify

M. Bravetti, M. Nuñes, and G. Zavattaro (Eds.): WS-FM 2006, LNCS 4184, pp. 88–106, 2006.

the security of a web services protocol implementation, one may write a detailed formal model for the protocol by studying the standards, by carefully observing the messages it sends, or by reading its source code. Using such models, previous analyses establish correctness theorems [14,5,4,18,19] and report attacks [5,6] on many WS-Security protocols. Still, writing formal models remains difficult and time-consuming; hence, this approach is typically applied only to common protocols. Even for these protocols, a precise and detailed formal model is lengthy, and its fidelity to the implementation is difficult to maintain.

In earlier work [7], we present an automated verification method for security protocol implementations written in F# [26], a dialect of ML. Our tool, named fs2pv, relies on the ProVerif theorem prover to verify that an F# program meets its security goals in the presence of an active attacker. The capabilities of the active attacker can be flexibly defined as a programming interface that lists all the values and functions of the protocol that the attacker may access. Our earlier work demonstrates the effectiveness of these tools on several protocol implementations, including protocol implementations based on WS-Security, and establishes a general theorem stating the correctness of our method.

The present paper complements and extends this work by elaborating the details of our verifiable programming style for WS-Security. We propose to build reference implementations for WS-Security protocols in F#. We develop a verified library that partially implements WS-Security and its related specifications. With this library, we can quickly implement, test, and verify new protocol implementations. Our reference implementations are readable, succinct, and verified.

The contributions of this paper are as follows:

1. A description of the design and architecture of a reusable library for building web services and verifying their security. Our library supports a significant subset of the specifications for web services security and can interoperate with other web services implementations.
2. A detailed case study of the implementation and verification of a WS-Security security protocol. To the best of our knowledge, the thousand line pi calculus process we verify is the largest model of a cryptographic protocol to be extracted from code. We provide interoperability results and performance comparisons; as a benchmark, our implementations pass interoperability tests with at least two production implementations, Microsoft WSE and WCF. We also give formal security guarantees for this protocol, established by running verification tools and instantiating general theorems that justify our method.

Our earlier paper discusses related work, including tools that derive implementation code from models. We are aware of only one other tool that extracts models from cryptographic protocol implementations, Goubault-Larrecq and Parrenne's Csur [15]. Their tool extracts Horn clauses from C code; it has been applied successfully to the Needham-Schroeder protocol.

The structure of the rest of the paper is as follows. Section 2 recalls the verification method developed in our previous work. Section 3 details the implementation and verification of a WS-Security X.509 mutual authentication protocol. Section 4 presents ver-

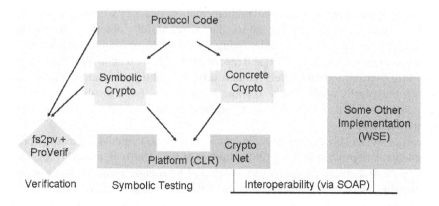

ification results for some WS-Security protocol implementations. Section 5 describes
the structure of our WS-Security library. Section 6 concludes.

2   Verifying Security Protocol Implementations in F# (Review)

The F# programming language [26] is a dialect of ML that executes on the Common
Language Runtime (CLR). The figure above shows the structure of our formal method
for verifying protocol models that are derived from the F# code of security protocols.
This section outlines our method; the description draws in part on material included in
our earlier paper [7].

Our tool fs2pv captures the semantics of an expressive subset of F# by translating
F# implementation code to the dialect of the applied pi calculus [2] analyzed by the
ProVerif theorem prover [8]. The core of our translation is Milner's interpretation of
functions as pi calculus processes [22]. Still, we implement many optimizations to take
advantage of features of ProVerif and to facilitate automated verification. Our translation, and the analysis performed by ProVerif, rely on a symbolic, algebraic representation of cryptography, as first proposed by Dolev and Yao [11]. We conjecture that
our method could be adapted to other source languages whose semantics can be directly represented in the pi calculus, and that other tools could be used to analyze the
translated pi calculus processes.

Dual Implementations for Trusted Libraries.   Each of our protocol implementations is
a composition of typed F# modules. Each module exports types, values, and functions,
and may depend on other modules. We write standard F# interface files to describe the
types and the typed values and functions provided by a module.

Ideally, we would construct our pi calculus model of a protocol entirely from the
actual source code of its modules. For a few, trusted libraries, however, we instead
write a dual, symbolic implementation. We assume (but do not formally verify) that
the symbolic implementation of a library is an appropriate abstraction of its concrete
implementation. These symbolic abstractions correspond to Dolev and Yao's algebraic
treatment of cryptography and networking. For example, our protocols depend on an
interface crypto.fsi, shown in Table 1, to perform cryptographic algorithms used for

Table 1. The Attacker's Interface to the Trusted Libraries

```
type keybytes                                           crypto.fsi (excerpt)
val rsa_encrypt: keybytes → bytes → bytes
val rsa_decrypt: keybytes → bytes → bytes
val sha1: bytes → bytes
val rsa_sign: keybytes → bytes → bytes
val rsa_verify: keybytes → bytes → bytes → unit


                                                         prins.fsi (excerpt)
type principalX =
        {subject:str;
         cert: bytes;
         pubkey: keybytes;
         privkey: keybytes;}
val genX509: str → unit
val getX509Cert: str → bytes
val leakX509: str → principalX


                                                         net.fsi
val request: (str → str → item → item)
val accept: (str → item)
val respond: (item → unit)
```

web services security. The concrete library implements the abstract type bytes as actual byte arrays, and the various functions as actual cryptographic algorithms, as provided by CLR libraries. The symbolic library implements bytes as an algebraic data type; a function such as rsa_encrypt becomes a constructor of this datatype, while the function rsa_decrypt is defined by pattern-matching on the datatype. We also define dual implementations for an interface prins.fsi, that provides access to the operating system security context, and an interface net.fsi, that provides networking capabilities.

We write S for the *symbolic implementation* of a protocol in F#: the composition of all the modules of a protocol, but with the symbolic code instead of the concrete code for those trusted libraries with dual implementations. This is the code that fs2pv translates to the pi calculus. Our method does not verify the concrete code of the library modules with dual implementations, it is not included in S; it is trusted, not verified.

As well as verifying S, we can build a symbolic version of the protocol implementation by compiling S. Running this symbolic implementation generates readable messages, containing symbolic representations of cryptographic materials, useful for prototyping and debugging.

The Attacker Interface. The aim of the analysis is to prove security properties such as message authentication and secrecy in the face of an attacker able to monitor, rewrite, and substitute messages sent between the machines playing a role in a protocol.

We envisage the attacker as a top-level F# module that can call some but not all of the modules making up a protocol implementation. The *attacker interface*, I_{pub}, models the capabilities of the attacker; it is expressed as the concatenation of the interfaces for the modules that are deemed accessible by the attacker. (The list of these modules is an input of our verification tool; their selection is an important step of our method, and should reflect the informal threat model for the protocol.) This attacker interface typically includes the three interfaces in Table 1—to allow the attacker communication and cryptographic facilities—plus functions representing protocol roles—to allow the attacker to start arbitrary numbers of initiators and responders, for example. We write $S :: I_{pub}$ to mean that the symbolic implementation S correctly exports (at least) the types, values, and functions in I_{pub}. We can check $S :: I_{pub}$ with the F# typechecker.

Queries for Authentication and Secrecy. We express authentication properties as correspondences between protocol events, in the style of Woo and Lam [27]. For instance, suppose a principal A begins a protocol with some parameters P; before sending the first message, it logs an event Begin(P). Then, if a principal B ends the protocol, logging the event End(P′), an authentication goal would be that A and B agree on these parameters (P = P′). In particular, P may include the name of principal A (to ensure sender authentication), the contents of the message (to ensure message authentication), and the content of related messages (to ensure correlation and session integrity).

Similarly, we express syntactic secrecy properties as correspondences: whenever the attacker obtains a value s marked as secret, the attacker can trigger the logging of the event NotSecret(s); hence, s remains secret only if this event is not reachable.

In ProVerif syntax, these correspondences are represented by *queries*:

query ev:End(P) $\implies$ ev:Begin(P).
query ev:NotSecret(s) $\implies$ ev:Unreachable().

The first query says that in any run of the program, if event End(P) occurs, then event Begin(P) must have occurred before. The second query says that NotSecret(s) is unreachable. (We arrange that ev:Unreachable() occurs in no run of the program.) In general, queries may include conjunctions (&) and disjunctions (|) of events on the right hand side of the implication.

We say that S is *robustly safe* for q and I_{pub} to mean that, for every attacker module O that is well-typed against I_{pub}, the query q holds in all runs of the symbolic implementation S composed with the top-level module O. The attacker interface I_{pub} typically excludes the function for logging events, so the attacker O cannot log events itself. The formal details are elsewhere [7].

Automated Verification of Authentication and Secrecy. For any symbolic implementation S with attacker interface I_{pub}, our verification method consists of the following steps. First, we identify the attacker interface I_{pub} and represent our authentication and secrecy goals as ProVerif queries. Second, we run fs2pv to generate a ProVerif script, written $[\![S :: I_{pub}]\!]$. Third, we run ProVerif to check the script for each query q.

The following theorem states the correctness of our method. It follows as a corollary of the correctness of ProVerif [1] and the correctness of fs2pv [7]. The proof of the latter involves defining a direct semantics for the F# programs S accepted by fs2pv, and proving a correspondence between the direct semantics of each S and its pi calculus translation $[\![S :: I_{pub}]\!]$.

Theorem 1. *Suppose that* $S :: I_{pub}$ *and that* $[\![S :: I_{pub}]\!]$ *is the* ProVerif *script generated by* fs2pv *from* S *and* I_{pub}. *If* ProVerif *terminates having proved that* $[\![S :: I_{pub}]\!]$ *satisfies the query q, then* S *is robustly safe for q and* I_{pub}.

3 X.509 Mutual Authentication

As our main case study, we consider a mutual authentication protocol based on X.509 public key certificates. Both WSE and WCF already implement this protocol as part of their sample code.

We begin with an informal narration of the protocol, then provide a complete implementation in F#. The code is quite short, as it mostly relies on our WS-Security libraries. We describe executions of the protocol, both symbolically (to produce readable message traces) and concretely (to evaluate its performance). We also report on interoperability testing with the WSE and WCF implementations. Finally, we present verification results for this implementation.

Protocol Narration. The protocol has two roles, a client and a server. Every session of the protocol involves a principal A acting as client and a principal B acting as server. Each principal is associated with an RSA key-pair, consisting of a private key and a corresponding public key; A's key-pair is written (sk_A, pk_A), and B's key-pair is written (sk_B, pk_B). We assume that the principals have already exchanged their public key certificates. Hence, the principals can identify one another using their public keys.

The goal of the protocol is to exchange two XML messages: a request and a response, such that both the client and server can authenticate the two-message session and keep the messages secret, even in the presence of an active attacker. To accomplish this goal, we rely on XML digital signatures and XML Encryption. The abstract message sequence of the protocol can be written as follows (where | denotes concatenation):

$$A \rightarrow B : TS \mid$$
$$\text{RSA-SHA1}\{sk_A\}[request \mid TS] \mid$$
$$\text{RSA-Encrypt}\{pk_B\}[symkey_1] \mid$$
$$\text{AES-Encrypt}\{symkey_1\}[request]$$
$$B \rightarrow A : \text{RSA-SHA1}\{sk_B\}[response \mid \text{RSA-SHA1}\{sk_A\}[request \mid TS]] \mid$$
$$\text{RSA-Encrypt}\{pk_B\}[symkey_2] \mid$$
$$\text{AES-Encrypt}\{symkey_2\}[response]$$

The client acting for principal A sends a message *request* at time *TS* to the server acting for B. To support message authentication, the client jointly signs *request* and *TS* using the signature algorithm RSA-SHA1 keyed with A's private key sk_A. To protect the secrecy of the message, the client uses AES-Encrypt to encrypt it under a fresh symmetric key $symkey_1$. The symmetric key is in turn encrypted using RSA-Encrypt under pk_B. (This standard, two-step encryption is motivated by the relative costs of symmetric and asymmetric encryptions for large messages.)

The server repeatedly processes request messages. After accepting a request, the server returns a *response* to the client. Like the request, the response is signed (using sk_B) then encrypted (using a fresh $symkey_2$ encrypted under pk_A). To correlate requests and responses, the server jointly signs the response and the signature value of the request. (Otherwise, since clients and servers may run several sessions in parallel, an attacker may confuse the client by swapping two responses.) This correlation mechanism is called *signature confirmation*.

The security goals of the protocol are:

Request Authentication: B accepts a *request* from A with timestamp *TS* only if A sent such a *request* with timestamp *TS*.

Response Authentication and Correlation: A accepts a *response* to its *request* only if B sent *response* on receiving A's *request*.

Secrecy: The message payloads *request* and *response* are kept secret from all principals other than A and B.

Implementation. Our protocol implementation is listed as X509MutualAuth.fs. The module consists of four functions: mkEnvelope and isEnvelope generate and check the protocol messages, while client and server implement the two protocol roles.

To parse and generate standards-compliant SOAP envelopes, and to sign and encrypt XML elements, we rely on functions of the web services security library. As an example, consider the mkEnvelope function. Depending on its arguments, mkEnvelope constructs either a request message or a response message. To construct a request, it takes a message body containing the *request*, the X.509 entry snd for the sending principal A, the X.509 certificate rcvcert for the receiving principal B, and an empty list corr. (When constructing a response, snd is the X.509 entry for B, rcvcert is the X.509 certificate for A, and corr contains the signature value of the request.) The code for mkEnvelope successively calls the following library functions, defined in modules wssecurity.fs and soap.fs:

- mkTimestamp and genTimestamp create a new timestamp and serialize it to XML;
- mkX509Signature generates the XML digital signature for the message;
- mkX509Encdatakey generates the two encrypted components;
- mkX509SecurityHeader generates the security header;
- genEnvelope generates the whole SOAP envelope for the message.

Finally, the function returns the envelope (for sending) paired with its signature value (kept for correlating the response).

Unlike mkEnvelope and isEnvelope, the client and server functions are part of the attacker interface; both these functions are included in the interface X509MutualAuth.fsi for the protocol module X509MutualAuth.fs. Hence, an attacker can call these functions to initiate sessions and instantiate roles.

The four arguments to client are the name of the client and server principals (clPrin, srvPrin), and the HTTP URI and SOAP action (servUri, servAction) that identify the server location. The client first calls the request function from the service.fs module (described in the next subsection) to compute the XML request payload (req). It then instantiates both principals; it gets the X.509 entry (cl) for clPrin from a private database;

```
                                                          X509MutualAuth.fs
(* Opening Library Modules *)
open Data (* Standard datatypes: str, bytes, item *)
open Events (* Protocol Events *)


(* Constructing Messages *)
let mkEnvelope (body:item) (snd:Prins.principalX) (rcvcert:bytes)
               (corr:item list) : item*bytes =
  let ts = Wssecurity.genTimestamp(Wssecurity.mkTimestamp()) in
  let (dsig,sv) = Wssecurity.mkX509Signature snd (body::ts::corr) in
  let (ed,ek) = Wssecurity.mkX509Encdatakey rcvcert body in
  let sec = Wssecurity.mkX509SecurityHeader (Prins.cert snd) ek ts dsig in
  let envXml = Soap.genEnvelope {Soap.header=[sec]; Soap.body=ed} in
  (envXml,sv)


(* Checking Messages *)
let isEnvelope (envXml:item) (sndcert:bytes) (rcv:Prins.principalX)
               (corr:item list) : item*bytes =
  let env = Soap.parseEnvelope envXml in
  let ([sec],ed) = (env.header,env.body) in
  let (ts,ek,dsig) = Wssecurity.isX509SecurityHeader sec in
  let body = Wssecurity.isX509Encdatakey rcv ek ed in
  let sv = Wssecurity.isX509Signature dsig sndcert (body::ts::corr) in
  (body,sv)


(* Client Role *)
let client (clPrin: str) (srvPrin:str) (servUri:str) (servAction:str) =
  let req = Service.request() in
  let cl = Prins.getX509 clPrin in
  let srvCert = Prins.getX509Cert srvPrin in
  let (reqXml,sv) = mkEnvelope req cl srvCert [] in
  log (ClientSend(clPrin,srvPrin,req));
  let respXml = Net.request servUri servAction reqXml in
  let sc = Wssecurity.genSigConf sv in
  let (resp,_) = isEnvelope respXml srvCert cl [sc] in
  log (ClientCorr(clPrin,srvPrin,req,resp))


(* Server Role *)
let server (clPrin:str) (srvPrin:str) (servUri:str) =
  let clCert = Prins.getX509Cert clPrin in
  let srv = Prins.getX509 srvPrin in
  let reqXml = Net.accept servUri in
  let (req,sv) = isEnvelope reqXml clCert srv [] in
  log (ServerRecv(clPrin,srvPrin,req));
  let resp = Service.response(req) in
  let sc = Wssecurity.genSigConf sv in
  let (respXml,_) = mkEnvelope resp srv clCert [sc] in
  log (ServerCorr(clPrin,srvPrin,req,resp));
  Net.respond respXml
```

the entry consists of an X.509 certificate and its associated private key; it then extracts the certificate (srvCert) for the server principal srvPrin. Next, it prepares the request message (reqXml), using mkEnvelope, logs an event ClientSend(clPrin,srvPrin,req) to indicate that it is sending the first message, and makes an HTTP request to the server, using Net.request. The client remembers the signature value (sv) of the request for correlating the response. When the client receives a response (respXml), it uses isEnvelope to check that the response message is valid and that it includes a signature confirmation (sc) echoing sv. It then logs the event ClientCorr(clPrin,srvPrin,req,resp) indicating that a valid response has been received and correlated with the request.

The server proceeds symmetrically: it uses the client certificate and the server X.509 entry to check requests and issue responses. After accepting a request, the server logs an event ServerRecv(clPrin,srvPrin,req); it then calls Service.response(req) to compute the response resp, and logs the event ServerCorr(clPrin,srvPrin,req,resp) before issuing the response.

Protocol Execution. To run the protocol, we write a main module X509Main.fs, listed below. (This module is not used for verification; formally, it is just a simple instance of the attackers considered in our theorems.)

```
let clntPrin = S "client.com"
let srvPrin = S "localhost"
do match Sys.argv.(1) with
  | "client" → client clntPrin srvPrin Service.uri Service.action;
  | "server" → server clntPrin srvPrin Service.uri;
  | "local"  → Pi.fork (fun () → server clntPrin srvPrin Service.uri);
               client clntPrin srvPrin Service.uri Service.action
```

This module first instantiates the client and server principals (identified by their X.509 common names "client.com" and "localhost"), and then runs either the client, or the server, or both, depending on the command-line argument. The X509Main.fs module is used only for executing the protocol; they are not used for verification.

We also write a module service.fs to encode an exemplary addition service. The module consists of two functions: Service.request extracts two numbers from the command line and returns them in a request body; Service.response computes the sum of the two numbers in a request and returns it in a response body.

For verification, we write a dual, symbolic implementation of this module that generalizes the two functions by allowing the attacker to choose some payloads: the symbolic version of Service.request (Service.response) returns a request (response) body that it either received from the attacker or it computed from a secret value. Hence, our security goals require request and response authentication even when the attacker is allowed to choose arbitrary payloads, and require secrecy of the secret payloads.

Symbolic runs. To run the protocol symbolically, we compile the X509MutualAuth.fs and X509Main.fs modules with the web services library and the symbolic version of the modules crypto.fs, net.fs, prins.fs, and service.fs to generate an executable run.exe. We can then execute the command run local 100 15.99, for example. Our implementation pretty-prints the communicated messages, using an abbreviated XML-like format with embedded symbolic expressions. The first message has 304 symbols while the second has 531. Both messages are listed and described in the appendix.

Concrete Runs and Performance. To run the protocol concretely, we compile X509MutualAuth.fs, X509Main.fs, and the web services library with the concrete versions of crypto.fs, net.fs, prins.fs, and service.fs to generate a new run.exe. We can then execute the command run server on one machine, and execute run client 100 15.99 on another. The resulting 4-kilobyte messages are instances of the symbolic messages, where each symbol expression is replaced by a concrete, string-encoded value.

To test our concrete implementation for interoperability, we run our client with servers implemented with WSE and WCF. The response message generated by the WCF server does not include the X.509 certificate of the server, since the client is expected to have it already. We easily modify our client to ignore this difference and it successfully executes the protocol with WCF. The WSE server, however, does not support the <SignatureConfirmation> mechanism. Moreover, the key-sizes and encryption algorithms supported by WSE are different from and more limited than WCF. After disabling correlation and using WSE's key sizes and algorithms, our client successfully executes the protocol with the WSE server.

Each session of our implementation takes 1.2 seconds to complete the protocol. We expect that this is comparable to the performance of the WSE and WCF implementations because all three implementations use the same .NET cryptography libraries, XML parsers, and X.509 certificate stores. Indeed, in the default configuration, both WSE and WCF take around one second per session for our protocol. A direct comparison of the performance of the three protocol implementations has little significance, because WCF, and to a lesser extent WSE, is a full web services implementation running within a web server, whereas ours is a partial implementation focusing on security. The WSE implementation consists of around 185 lines of C# code, while the WCF implementation consists of around 70 lines of C# code and 160 lines of security-related XML configuration. In contrast, our implementation consists of 104 lines of F# code that can be executed concretely or symbolically, as well as automatically verified.

Security Goals and Theorem. We use the fs2pv/ProVerif tool chain to verify our protocol implementation against its security goals. Recall the three security goals for our protocol. Let G be these security goals expressed as ProVerif queries:

query ev:ServerRecv(u,s,x) $\implies$ ev:ClientSend(u,_,x) | ev:Leak(u).
query ev:ClientCorr(u,s,x,y) $\implies$ ev:ServerCorr(u,s,x,y) | ev:Leak(s).
query ev:NotSecret(v) $\implies$
        (ev:ClientSend(u,s,DataTxt(DataBase64(DataFresh(v)))) & ev:Leak(s))
    | (ev:ServerCorr(u,s,r,DataTxt(DataBase64(DataFresh(v)))) & ev:Leak(u)).

The first query formalizes request authentication: it says that, if the server principal s accepts a request x from a client principal u (ServerRecv(u,s,x)), then u has sent the request x (ClientSend(u,_,x)) or else u has been compromised. The second query formalizes response authentication and correlation: if the client principal u accepts a response y for request x from server principal s (ClientCorr(u,s,x,y)), then s must have sent the response y to u for request x (ServerCorr(u,s,x,y)).

The third query expresses the secrecy of the request and response. It says that the only secrets v available to the attacker (NotSecret(v)) are those that have been sent within requests or responses to compromised servers or clients, respectively.

Let S be the F# system consisting of the X509MutualAuth.fs module, the web services library, and the symbolic implementations for the modules crypto.fs, net.fs, prins.fs, and service.fs. Let I_{pub} be the attacker interface from Table 1 extended with the protocol interface X509MutualAuth.fsi. We use fs2pv to compile S to a script consisting of 988 lines of pi calculus code. Then we run ProVerif to verify all three queries in G above. By Theorem 1, we obtain:

Theorem 2. *For each $q \in G$, the system S is robustly safe for q and I_{pub}.*

Hence, we verify the security of our protocol implementation and all the functions it uses from the web services library against a powerful attacker model. The only modules we trust to be correct, and do not verify, are crypto.fs, net.fs, prins.fs, and service.fs.

Vulnerabilities and Attacks. Theorem 2 applies to our protocol implementation before modifying it for interoperation with WCF or WSE. The modification for WCF makes no difference to protocol correctness: we automatically establish Theorem 2 for the modified implementation.

The modification for WSE, however, weakens the protocol: the second query (response authentication) fails and ProVerif reports an attack. Indeed, since the modified protocol does not use signature confirmation, an attacker can forward to the client a response generated by the server in reply to another request by the same client. As a result, requests and responses are not securely correlated—this is a known issue in WS-Security 1.0, which led to the design of signature confirmation in WS-Security 1.1. More precisely, we can still capture a weaker notion of response authentication that holds for WSE, using the following, weaker variant of the second query:

query ev:ClientCorr(u,s,x,y) $\Longrightarrow$ ev:ServerCorr(_,s,_,y) | ev:Leak(s).

We then verify that all variants of our protocol implementation satisfy this query.

The X.509 mutual authentication protocol presented in this section meets our specific set of authentication and secrecy goals, but is not unconditionally secure. We discuss two of its limitations.

– The protocol fails to guarantee certain other security properties. For instance, it fails to protect (stronger variants of) secrecy of *request* or *response* against guessing attacks, when these messages have low entropy. If such protection is required, we can either encrypt the signature in addition to the message content, or we can add a nonce to the message content.
– The protocol also fails to prevent certain replay attacks on the server. If the client produces a new timestamp for each request and if the server maintains a cache of these timestamps, then replays can be detected and discarded. Indeed, our formal model generates fresh timestamps for each message. Alternatively, we can include a unique message identifier in each request.

We also coded stronger variants of the protocol that meet at least the requirements of Theorem 2 and also address these limitations, and verified their implementation using additional queries. We omit the details for simplicity.

4   Other Protocols and Verification Results

In addition to the X.509 Mutual Authentication protocol, we have implemented several other sample WSE and WCF protocols in F# and verified them. Table 2 reports our experimental results. For each protocol, Table 2 states the program size for the implementation (in lines of F# code, excluding interfaces and code for shared libraries), the number of messages exchanged, and the size of each message, measured both in bytes for concrete runs and in number of constructors for symbolic runs. Concerning verification, it gives the number of queries and the kinds of security properties they express. A secrecy query requires that the message body be protected. An authentication query requires that a message, its sender, or the whole session be authentic. All queries are verified assuming that the attacker controls some corrupted principals, and thereby has access to their keys and passwords. Finally, the table gives the total running time for ProVerif to verify all queries for the protocol.

Table 2. Verification results for example protocols

Protocol	Implementation				Security Goals and Verification			
	LoC	msgs	bytes	symbols	queries	secrecy	authentication	time
Password-based auth	85	1	3835	394	5	no	msg, sender	5.3 s
X.509 auth	85	1	4650	389	5	no	msg, sender	2.6 s
Pwd-X.509 mutual auth	149	2	6206; 3187	486; 542	15	no	session	44m
X.509 mutual auth	117	2	4533; 4836	304; 531	18	msg	session	51m

Table 3. Comparative sizes of implementation modules

Trusted Library			Verified Web Services Library	Protocol Module
Modules	Concrete LoC	Symbolic LoC	Modules	LoC	LoC
4	793 + CLR	575	5	1648	85-149

Table 3 lists the sizes (in lines of F# code) of the modules in the protocol implementation, classified as trusted library code, verified web services code, and protocol code. The concrete implementations of the trusted library modules rely on CLR libraries, such as System.Cryptography for cryptographic functions; so, their size cannot be precisely determined.

5   Implementing the Verified WS-Security Library

Programming a security protocol based on WS-Security is an exercise in modularity. The messages of the protocol include elements, such as timestamps, addresses, encrypted keys, and signatures, that are defined by different specifications. Many of these elements eventually rely on low-level cryptographic computations. To assemble the complete SOAP message, each element must be encoded in some XML format.

To support this kind of programming, we structure our WS-Security library as follows. For each specification, we define an F# module Spec.fs and an interface Spec.fsi. Within a module, each high-level message component is defined as a datatype T. Operations to generate and check elements of type T (typically using cryptographic functions) are written as functions mkT and isT. Finally, for each datatype T, the module defines functions genT and parseT to translate elements of T to and from XML items. In this way, users of the library can ignore the XML representation and instead program with the more abstract representation T and its corresponding functions.

For instance, the soap.fs module partially implements the SOAP standard [16]. It has the following interface:

```
type envelope = { header: item list; body: item }
val parseEnvelope: item → envelope
val genEnvelope: envelope → item
```

A SOAP envelope is abstractly represented as a record that contains a list of headers and a body. The functions parseEnvelope and genEnvelope translate such records to and from XML items. Since there is no cryptography involved in constructing an envelope, there are no other functions in the interface.

Similarly, the wsaddressing.fs module implements the headers defined in the WS-Addressing specification [10]; it has a record type that abstractly represents optional headers and it has functions to translate records to and from SOAP header elements.

The full WS-Security library consists of five F# modules, including soap.fs and wsaddressing.fs, with a total of 1648 lines of code. We believe that these modules are usable not only by programmers aiming to write verifiable web services security protocols, but also by protocol designers looking for precise executable specifications for the web services standards. In the rest of this section, we look in more detail at the modules that implement the security mechanisms of WS-Security.

XML Signature. The XML Signature standard "specifies XML syntax and processing rules for creating and representing digital signatures." [13] An XML signature, as defined in the standard, cryptographically attests to the integrity and authenticity of a set of XML items. An example is the <Signature> element in the protocol messages in the appendix. It includes metadata describing the computation of the signature value: each signed element is first transformed using the specified canonicalization method (xml−exc−c14n), then hashed using the specified digest method (SHA1); the digests and metadata are finally signed using the specified signature method (RSA−SHA1). The recipient of such a signature recomputes the digests and checks the received signature value before accepting the signed elements as authentic.

In our library, the xmldsig.fs module implements XML signatures. The datatype for an XML signature is a record dsig that includes the relevant contents of the <Signature> element as well as additional values needed for computing and checking the signature:

```
type dsig = {
    siginfo: item;
    sigval: bytes;
    keyinfo: item;
```

```
signkey: keybytes option;
verifkey: keybytes option;
targets: item list }
```

The field siginfo corresponds to the <SignedInfo> element containing the metadata and all the digests; sigval contains the signature value; keyinfo identifies the signing key. The module contains auxiliary functions for generating siginfo from the list of signed elements (targets). To compute the sigval, we use a signing key (signkey); to check a received sigval, we use the corresponding verification key (verifkey).

The module provides functions for constructing and checking signatures using both symmetric and asymmetric signing algorithms, such as HMAC−SHA1 and RSA−SHA1:

val mkSignature: item list → item → keybytes → str → dsig
val isSignature: item list → keybytes → dsig → bytes

The function call, mkSignature targets keyinfo signkey alg, constructs a dsig element for the elements listed in targets, using signature key signkey and signing algorithm alg. Conversely, isSignature targets verifkey dsig uses verifkey to check that dsig is a valid XML signature computed from targets. The full module consists of 307 lines of code.

There are several challenges in implementing XML Signature. First, our functions must correctly implement the low-level details of the signature. This includes not only the details of the XML format such as namespaces and attributes, but also the use of the canonicalization, digest, and signature algorithms. In xmldsig.fs, the functions parseSignature and genSignature translate records of type dsig to and from XML. We test these functions by inspecting the message traces as well as by extensive interoperability testing with other implementations. Our datatype and functions hide these details from the programmer, so all programs using these functions are guaranteed to generate standards-conformant XML signatures.

Second, the standard offers several options for each step of signature computation and an implementation is expected to support a subset. In our implementaion, we choose one canonicalization and one digest algorithm, but allow two signature algorithms and several ways of referring to signing keys. These choices do not affect the module interface: the types and functions remain the same. Hence, we can easily add implementations for additional algorithms as the need arises and rely on the F# module and type system to integrate them.

XML Encryption. The XML Encryption standard "specifies a process for encrypting data and representing the result in XML" [12]. When parts of a message are to be encrypted using a symmetric key, the encrypted data mechanism can be used; when only an asymmetric key is available for encryption, one first generates a fresh symmetric key, uses it to encrypt data, and then protects the symmetric key using the encrypted key mechanism. Both these mechanisms are depicted in the protocol messages in the appendix; the <EncryptedData> element contains a cipher value computed by applying a symmetric encryption algorithm (AES−128) to the message body using a key encrypted within an <EncryptedKey> element using an asymmetric algorithm (RSA−1.5).

The xmlenc.fs module implements XML encryption, in a similar style to xmldsig.fs. It defines two record types encdata and encrkey representing encrypted data and encrypted keys. It provides functions to construct (encrypt) and decrypt records of these types and functions to translate them to and from XML. It also provides functions to combine common encryption tasks; for instance, the function call, mkEncDatakey ek str plain, generates a fresh symmetric key, uses it to encrypt the plain-text plain as an encrypted data block, uses the public-key ek to in turn encrypt the symmetric key, and returns both the encrypted data and the encrypted key.

The module xmlenc.fs is implemented in 419 lines of code. It implements two symmetric algorithms for encrypting data, AES$-$128 and AES$-$256, and two asymmetric algorithms for encrypting keys, RSA$-$1.5 and RSA$-$OAEP. Our choices are motivated by the default settings in WSE and WCF; WSE supports AES$-$128 and RSA$-$1.5, while WCF uses AES$-$256 and RSA$-$OAEP.

WS-Security. The wssecurity.fs module implements the content of the security header, as specified in the WS-Security standard [24]. The security header contains several optional elements, such as a message timestamp, tokens identifying principals, XML signatures, and encrypted keys. The record representing this header is as follows:

```
type security = {
    timestamp: ts;
    utoks: utok list;
    xtoks: xtok list;
    ekeys: encrkey list;
    dsigs: dsig list }
```

It consists of a timestamp (ts), generated using the mkTimeStamp function, username tokens (utoks) identifying users and passwords, X.509 tokens (xtoks) containing public-key certificates, encrypted keys (ekeys), and XML signatures (dsigs).

The module offers functions for constructing different kinds of tokens and for generating signatures and encrypted blocks using them. For instance, the function call, mkX509Signature prin targets, generates an X.509 token corresponding to principal prin and uses its private key to compute an XML signature for the element list targets. The module also provides functions for translating security headers to and from XML. For instance, the function genX509SecurityHeader takes a certificate, an encrypted key, a timestamp, and a signature and generates the corresponding XML security header; parseX509SecurityHeader does the reverse.

The wssecurity.fs module consists of 538 lines of F# code. It does not yet support several token types defined in WS-Security, such as Kerberos and SAML tokens.

6   Conclusions

This paper demonstrates a new programming method for developing verified WS-Security protocol implementations. Our implementations rely on a reusable library that implements a significant subset of the web services security specifications. We demonstrate the effectiveness of our method on a detailed example of a WS-Security mutual authentication protocol. We verify a series of security properties, and discover some vulnerabilities. Verification depends on our custom optimizing compiler from a subset of F# into the pi calculus, and on ProVerif, a resolution-based prover for the pi calculus.

Although the bulk of our code is verified, we assume the correctness of a few core libraries, such as those implementing cryptographic algorithms and networking. The combination of our compiler and ProVerif is effective, but in case of failure the user does need to interpret rather low-level error messages in source language terms.

In future, we aim to improve the usability of our tools, and to extend our work to more complicated protocols and protocol compositions.

Acknowledgements. Stephen Tse, co-author of our previous paper [7], participated in the design of fs2pv, and completed its original implementation, during his internship at Microsoft Research.

References

1. M. Abadi and B. Blanchet. Analyzing security protocols with secrecy types and logic programs. *J. ACM*, 52(1):102–146, 2005.
2. M. Abadi and C. Fournet. Mobile values, new names, and secure communication. In *28th ACM Symposium on Principles of Programming Languages (POPL'01)*, pages 104–115, 2001.
3. Apache Software Foundation. *Apache WSS4J*, 2006. At http://ws.apache.org/wss4j/.
4. K. Bhargavan, R. Corin, C. Fournet, and A. D. Gordon. Secure sessions for web services. In *2004 ACM Workshop on Secure Web Services*, pages 11–22, October 2004.
5. K. Bhargavan, C. Fournet, and A. D. Gordon. A semantics for web services authentication. *Theoretical Computer Science*, 340(1):102–153, June 2005.
6. K. Bhargavan, C. Fournet, A. D. Gordon, and R. Pucella. TulaFale: A security tool for web services. In *International Symposium on Formal Methods for Components and Objects (FMCO'03)*, volume 3188 of *LNCS*, pages 197–222. Springer, 2004.
7. K. Bhargavan, C. Fournet, A. D. Gordon, and S. Tse. Verified interoperable implementations of security protocols. In *19th IEEE Computer Security Foundations Workshop (CSFW'06)*, 2006. To appear.
8. B. Blanchet. An efficient cryptographic protocol verifier based on Prolog rules. In *14th IEEE Computer Security Foundations Workshop (CSFW'01)*, pages 82–96, 2001.
9. B. Blanchet, M. Abadi, and C. Fournet. Automated verification of selected equivalences for security protocols. In *20th IEEE Symposium on Logic in Computer Science (LICS'05)*, pages 331–340, 2005.
10. D. Box, F. Curbera, et al. *Web Services Addressing (WS-Addressing)*, August 2004. W3C Member Submission.
11. D. Dolev and A. C. Yao. On the security of public key protocols. *IEEE Transactions on Information Theory*, IT–29(2):198–208, 1983.
12. D. Eastlake, J. Reagle, et al. *XML Encryption Syntax and Processing*, 2002. W3C Recommendation.
13. D. Eastlake, J. Reagle, D. Solo, et al. *XML-Signature Syntax and Processing*, 2002. W3C Recommendation.
14. A. D. Gordon and R. Pucella. Validating a web service security abstraction by typing. In *2002 ACM workshop on XML Security*, pages 18–29, 2002.
15. J. Goubault-Larrecq and F. Parrennes. Cryptographic protocol analysis on real C code. In *6th International Conference on Verification, Model Checking and Abstract Interpretation (VMCAI'05)*, volume 3385 of *LNCS*, pages 363–379. Springer, 2005.
16. M. Gudgin et al. *SOAP Version 1.2*, 2003. W3C Recommendation.

17. IBM Corporation. *IBM WebSphere Application Server*, 2006. At http://www.ibm. com/software/websphere/.
18. E. Kleiner and A. W. Roscoe. Web services security: A preliminary study using Casper and FDR. In *Automated Reasoning for Security Protocol Analysis (ARSPA 04)*, 2004.
19. E. Kleiner and A. W. Roscoe. On the relationship between web services security and traditional protocols. In *Mathematical Foundations of Programming Semantics (MFPS XXI)*, 2005.
20. Microsoft Corporation. *Web Services Enhancements (WSE) 2.0*, 2004. At http://msdn. microsoft.com/webservices/building/wse/default.aspx.
21. Microsoft Corporation. *Windows Communication Foundation (WCF)*, 2006. At http:// windowscommunication.net.
22. R. Milner. Functions as processes. *Mathematical Structures in Computer Science*, 2(2):119–141, 1992.
23. R. Milner. *Communicating and Mobile Systems: the π-Calculus*. CUP, 1999.
24. A. Nadalin, C. Kaler, P. Hallam-Baker, and R. Monzillo. *OASIS Web Services Security: SOAP Message Security 1.0 (WS-Security 2004)*, March 2004. OASIS Standard 200401.
25. R. M. Needham and M. D. Schroeder. Using encryption for authentication in large networks of computers. *Communications of the ACM*, 21(12):993–999, 1978.
26. D. Syme. *F#*, 2005. At http://research.microsoft.com/fsharp/fsharp.aspx.
27. T. Y. C. Woo and S. S. Lam. A semantic model for authentication protocols. In *IEEE Computer Society Symposium on Research in Security and Privacy*, pages 178–194, 1993.

Appendix

This appendix presents and describes the protocol messages for the X.509 mutual authentication protocol of Section 3.

Symbolic Messages. The listing X509MutualAuthMsg1.xml shows the first message as printed out by a symbolic run of the protocol; X509MutualAuthMsg2.xml shows the second message.

In X509MutualAuthMsg1.xml, ts1 is the symbolic timestamp, and req is the serialized request. The message has a security header that contains ts1, an encrypted symmetric key key1, and an XML digital signature for req and ts1. The key key1 is encrypted using the public key certificate for the server; in this message the certificate is issued by Root and has a serial number guid4 and public key PK(rsa_secret3). The XML signature value sv1 is computed as the RSA−SHA1 signature of the element si, which in turn contains the SHA1 hashes of req and ts1. Finally, the body of the message is the request req encrypted under the symmetric key key5.

The second message can be read similarly; the main difference is that the signature includes a new <SignatureConfirmation> element containing the signature value sv1 from the first message.

Concrete Messages. The XML messages printed our in concrete runs of the protocol are instances of the symbolic messages, where each symbol expression is replaced by a concrete, string-encoded value.

For instance, the timestamp ts1 is now the concrete XML element

```
<Timestamp Id="Timestamp" xmlns="http://...wss−wssecurity−utility−1.0.xsd">
  <Created>2006−04−27T09:12:17Z</Created>
```

<Expires>2006−04−27T09:13:17Z</Expires>
</Timestamp>

and the signature value sv1 is now the 172-character base64-encoded string

4Bpd7K+2n6eW+brpEwYO9hdwHrcNPOAoK+Bqn4........KCstFrZQ24=

X509MutualAuthMsg1.xml

```
        <Envelope>
         <Header>
          <Security>
ts1  =   <Timestamp Id='Timestamp'>
            <Created>Now1</>
            <Expires>PlusOneMinute</></>
            <BinarySecurityToken EncodingType='Base64Binary' ValueType='X509v3'
                         Id='X509Token-client.com'>
             X509(Root,client . com,sha1RSA,PK(rsa_secret1))</>
            <EncryptedKey Id='Encrkey'>
             <EncryptionMethod Algorithm='rsa-1_5' />
             <KeyInfo>
              <SecurityTokenReference>
               <X509Data>
                <X509IssuerSerial>
                 <X509IssuerName>Root</>
                 <X509SerialNumber>guid4</></></></></>
             <CipherData>
              <CipherValue>RSA−Enc{PK(rsa_secret3)}[key5]</></>
             <ReferenceList>
              <DataReference URI='guid6' /></></>
            <Signature>
si1  =    <SignedInfo>
             <CanonicalizationMethod Algorithm='xml-exc-c14n#' />
             <SignatureMethod Algorithm='rsa-sha1' />
             <Reference URI='Body'>
              <Transforms>
               <Transform Algorithm='xml-exc-c14n#' /></>
              <DigestMethod Algorithm='sha1' />
              <DigestValue>SHA1(
               <Body Id='Body'>req</>)</></>
             <Reference URI='Timestamp'>
              <Transforms>
               <Transform Algorithm='xml-exc-c14n#' /></>
              <DigestMethod Algorithm='sha1' />
              <DigestValue>SHA1(ts)</></></>
            <SignatureValue>
sv1  =       RSA−SHA1{rsa_secret1}[si]
            </>
            <KeyInfo>
             <SecurityTokenReference>
              <Reference URI='X509Token-client.com' ValueType='X509v3' />
             </></></></>
          <Body Id='Body'>
           <EncryptedData Id='guid6' Type='Content'>
            <EncryptionMethod Algorithm='aes128-cbc' />
            <CipherData>
             <CipherValue>AES−Enc{key5}[
req  =        <Add>
               <n1>100</>
               <n2>15.99</></></>]</></></></></>
```

```
                                                              X509MutualAuthMsg2.xml
      <Envelope>
        <Header>
         <Security>
ts2 =  <Timestamp Id='Timestamp'>
           <Created>Now2</>
           <Expires>PlusOneMinute</></>
           <BinarySecurityToken EncodingType='Base64Binary' ValueType='X509v3'
                                 Id='X509Token-localhost'>
             X509(Root,localhost , sha1RSA,PK(rsa_secret3)) </>
           <EncryptedKey Id='Encrkey'>
           <EncryptionMethod Algorithm='rsa-1_5' />
           <KeyInfo>
             <SecurityTokenReference>
              <X509Data>
               <X509IssuerSerial>
                 <X509IssuerName>Root</>
                 <X509SerialNumber>guid2</></></></></>
           <CipherData>
             <CipherValue>RSA-Enc{PK(rsa_secret1)}[key7]</></>
           <ReferenceList>
             <DataReference URI='guid8' /></></>
         <Signature>
si2 =    <SignedInfo>
             <CanonicalizationMethod Algorithm='xml-exc-c14n#' />
             <SignatureMethod Algorithm='rsa-sha1' />
             <Reference URI='Body'>
              <Transforms>
                <Transform Algorithm='xml-exc-c14n#' /></>
              <DigestMethod Algorithm='sha1' />
              <DigestValue>SHA1(
                <Body Id='Body'>resp</>)</></>
             <Reference URI='Timestamp'>
              <Transforms>
                <Transform Algorithm='xml-exc-c14n#' /></>
              <DigestMethod Algorithm='sha1' />
              <DigestValue>SHA1(ts)</></>
             <Reference URI='SigConf'>
              <Transforms>
                <Transform Algorithm='xml-exc-c14n#' /></>
              <DigestMethod Algorithm='sha1' />
              <DigestValue>SHA1(
                <SignatureConfirmation Value='sv1' Id='SigConf' />
                )</></></>
         <SignatureValue>
sv2 =       RSA-SHA1{rsa_secret3}[si2]
           </>
           <KeyInfo>
             <SecurityTokenReference>
              <Reference URI='X509Token-localhost' ValueType='X509v3' />
             </></></></>
        <Body Id='Body'>
         <EncryptedData Id='guid8' Type='Content'>
           <EncryptionMethod Algorithm='aes128-cbc' />
           <CipherData>
             <CipherValue>AES-Enc{key7}[
resp =       <AddResponse>
               <n>115.99</></></>]</></></></></>
```

From BPEL Processes to YAWL Workflows[*]

Antonio Brogi and Razvan Popescu

Computer Science Department, University of Pisa, Italy

Abstract. BPEL is currently the most widespread language for composing Web services, but it lacks formal semantics. YAWL is a workflow language with a well defined formal semantics that implements the most common workflow patterns. In this paper we provide a methodology for translating BPEL processes into YAWL workflows, thus paving the way for the formal analysis, aggregation and adaptation of BPEL processes. The approach we propose defines a YAWL pattern for each BPEL activity. The translation of a BPEL process reduces then to suitably instantiating and interconnecting the patterns of its activities.

1 Introduction

The service-oriented computing paradigm [9] uses services as building blocks for developing future heterogeneous, distributed applications. Two main reasons for composing (Web) services are the need for rapid application development, and the need to answer complex queries that cannot be satisfied by one service alone.

WSDL [12] is the current standard for describing Web service interfaces, yet it provides only a syntactic description of the supported operations. This severely affects the process of (semi-)automated service composition as composed services may lock during their interaction.

BPEL [2] has emerged as a language for expressing Web service compositions. A BPEL process provides the behaviour of a Web service in terms of coordinating one or more WSDL services. A downside of BPEL is that clients of the business process are in charge of manually selecting the services to be composed, and of building the composite service. Furthermore, BPEL lacks a formal semantics and hence it does not provide suitable means for the analysis of service compositions.

YAWL [10] is a new proposal of a workflow/business processing system that supports a concise and powerful workflow language and handles complex data transformations and Web service integrations. As it implements the most common workflow patterns, YAWL can be used as a *lingua franca* for expressing the behaviour of Web services (described using BPEL or OWL-S [8], for example). Despite its graphical nature, YAWL has a well defined formal semantics. It is a state-based language and the semantics of a workflow specification is defined as a transition system. Furthermore, being based on Petri nets, it provides a firm basis for the formal analysis of real-world services.

Our long-term goal is to provide a methodology for the (semi-)automated aggregation and adaptation of Web services into new heterogeneous applications.

[*] This work has been partially supported by F.I.R.B. project TOCAI.IT.

M. Bravetti, M. Nuñes, and G. Zavattaro (Eds.): WS-FM 2006, LNCS 4184, pp. 107–122, 2006.
© Springer-Verlag Berlin Heidelberg 2006

To cope with the previous issues we argue for the use of *service contracts* [4] consisting of (a) a (WSDL) signature, (b) an (OWL) ontological description, and (c) a (YAWL) behaviour (or protocol). The signature and the ontological information serve for enhancing the service discovery process and for overcoming signature mismatches. The protocol information can be employed for generating the behaviour of the aggregated service and for verifying properties of the aggregate (such as lock freedom), as well as for coping with behavioural mismatches.

In [4] we described a core aggregation process for composing YAWL services. The core aggregation process inputs a set of service contracts to be aggregated and it outputs the contract of the aggregated service. The control-flow of the aggregate is built, on the one hand, from the initial control-flow of the participant services, and on the other hand, from data-flow dependencies obtained by semantically matching service parameters. This paper complements [4] by devising a methodology for translating BPEL processes into YAWL workflows. As a result, BPEL services can be translated into YAWL workflows, then aggregated, and finally deployed as a new BPEL service. It is worth stressing the importance of the last two features. As we will see, handling synchronisation links, scope activities, events, faults, and compensations, sensibly complicates the translation. Probably because of their complexity, these mechanisms have not usually been considered by the formalisations of BPEL that have been proposed so far (e.g., [6,1]). On the other hand, since these features are indeed exploited in real BPEL descriptions, and do contribute to the expressiveness of "real" BPEL, we argue that they cannot be ignored.

The translation approach we describe here defines a YAWL pattern for each BPEL activity, as well as for a whole BPEL process. The role of an activity pattern is twofold – to provide a unique representation of the activity, and to provide an execution context for it. Given a BPEL process, the approach automatically generates its YAWL translation by:

1. Instantiating the pattern of each activity defined in the BPEL process, and
2. Suitably connecting the obtained patterns into the final workflow.

The main features of the translation methodology can be summarised as follows:

- It is a pattern-based, compositional approach,
- It copes with all types of BPEL activities, and
- It handles events, faults and (explicit) compensation.

2   A Brief Introduction to BPEL and YAWL

The next two Subsections give a very high-level view of both languages. Some other details on the two languages will be discussed in the next Section, while describing the translation methodology. For a complete description of the two languages, please see [2] for BPEL, and [10] for YAWL.

2.1 BPEL: Business Process Execution Language

BPEL is a language for expressing the behaviour of a business process. It enables the specification of control and data logic around a set of Web service interactions. A BPEL process exposes a WSDL interface to its clients.

A BPEL process can be either abstract or executable. An abstract process hides implementation details (i.e., private information), while an executable process provides the full interaction behaviour.

BPEL defines the notion of *partner link* to model the interaction between a business process and its partners. A partner link refers to at most two WSDL *port types*, one of the interface to the business process (viz., operations offered by the process to the partner), and the other of the interface of a partner (viz., operations offered by the partner to the business process).

BPEL is a hybrid language that combines features from both the block-structured language XLANG and from the graph-based language WSFL. The former contributed with basic activities (e.g., for sending and receiving messages, for waiting for a period of time, and so on) as well as with structured ones (e.g., sequential or parallel execution of activities, activity scoping, and so on) for combining activities into complex ones. The latter brought the definition of links to synchronise activities executed in parallel. Other features of BPEL are instance management through correlation sets, event and fault handling, as well as compensation capabilities.

The BPEL basic activities are: *receive/reply* through which a BPEL process inputs/sends a message from/to a partner service, *invoke* through which a BPEL process asynchronously/synchronously invokes an operation of a partner service, *wait* for delaying the execution of the process, *throw* for signalling faults, *terminate* for explicitly terminating the execution of the process, a dummy *empty* for doing a "no-op", *assign* for copying values between variables, and *compensate* for invoking a compensation handler.

The structured activities are: *sequence, switch,* and *while* for sequential, conditional and repeated activity execution, *flow* for parallel activity execution, *pick* for managing the non-deterministic choice of the activity to be executed, and *scope* for providing an execution context for an activity.

2.2 YAWL: Yet Another Workflow Language

YAWL is a new proposal of a workflow/business processing system, which supports a concise and powerful workflow language and handles complex data transformations and Web service integration. YAWL defines twenty most used workflow patterns divided in six groups – basic control-flow, advanced branching and synchronisation, structural, multiple instances, state-based, and cancellation. A thorough description of these patterns may be found in [11].

YAWL extends Petri Nets by introducing some workflow patterns (for multiple instances, complex synchronisations, and cancellation) that are not easy to express using (high-level) Petri Nets. Being built on Petri Nets, YAWL is an easy to understand and to use formalism, which features an intuitive (graphical) representation of services. Moreover, it can benefit from the abundance of Petri net analysis techniques. With respect to the other workflow languages (mostly proposed by industry), YAWL relies on a well-defined formal semantics based on transition systems. Moreover, not being a commercial language, YAWL supporting tools (editor, engine) are freely available.

From a control-flow perspective, a YAWL file describes a *workflow specification* that consists of a tree-like structure of *extended workflow nets* (or EWF-nets for short). An EWF-net is a graph where nodes are *tasks* or *conditions*, and edges define the control-flow relation. Each EWF-net has a single *input condition* and a single *output condition*.

Tasks employ one *join* and one *split* construct, which may be one of the following: AND, OR, XOR, or EMPTY. Intuitively, the join of a task T specifies "how many" tasks before T are to be terminated in order to execute T, while the split construct specifies "how many" tasks following T are to be executed.

It is worth noting that YAWL tasks may be interpreted as Petri net *transitions*, and YAWL conditions can be represented as Petri net *places*. The control-flow for tasks with XOR/OR splits is managed through *predicates* in the form of logical expressions. When a task finishes its execution, it places tokens in its output places, depending on its split type. Dually, a task is enabled for execution depending on its join and on the tokens available in its input places.

Another feature of YAWL is the use of *cancellation sets* consisting of conditions and tasks. When a task is executed all tokens from its cancellation set (if any) are removed.

From a data-flow perspective, YAWL uses XMLSchema, XPath and XQuery for dealing with data. Variables are defined at both EWF-net and task levels, and bindings between them are realised through XQuery expressions.

3   From BPEL to YAWL

The objective of this paper is to present a methodology for translating BPEL processes into YAWL workflows. First, we define a YAWL pattern for each BPEL activity, as well as for the entire business process. Then, the workflow corresponding to a BPEL process is obtained by suitably instantiating and interconnecting the workflows of all its activities.

Subsections 3.1 and 3.2 introduce the *basic pattern template* and the *structured pattern template*, which are used to define the patterns of the basic and structured activities, respectively. Subsection 3.3 defines the *process pattern* and describes the process of obtaining the final workflow.

In the following we shall use the term *pattern template* to refer to the pattern of a generic BPEL activity (viz., either basic or structured). The role of a pattern template is twofold: It provides the necessary elements for uniquely identifying an activity/process, as well as an execution context for the translated activity/process.

3.1   The Basic Pattern Template

BPEL uses structured activities to specify the order in which activities have to be executed. For example, the second activity in a sequence can be executed only

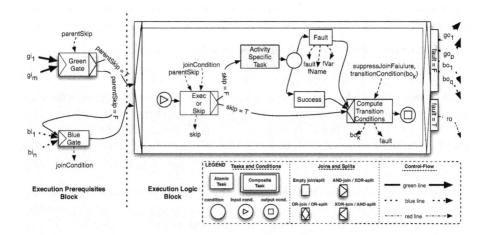

Fig. 1. The *basic pattern template*

when the first has finished its execution. Moreover, the *flow* construct allows for synchronisation links to be defined among activities. When an activity is structurally enabled, BPEL waits for the statuses of all its incoming links (if any) to be determined. At that point BPEL computes the *joinCondition* (a logical expression), which guards the execution of the activity. A *true* value leads to the execution of the activity, while a *false* value leads to either raising a *joinFailure* fault, or to skipping the entire activity. It is important to note that a structured activity that is skipped leads to skipping all the activities nested within it. Skipping an activity leads to propagating negative (viz., false) statuses on its output links. This process is called *dead-path-elimination*.

We model the structural relations among BPEL activities through what we call *green lines*. A pattern has one or more green inputs, which are used to enable it from the structural point of view. Dually, it has one or more green outputs, to be sent upon completion of the pattern, which will be used to enable other patterns. For example, the patterns translating child activities of a BPEL *sequence* have to be linked through green lines. On the other hand, we model the synchronisation links among BPEL activities using *blue lines*. A pattern has one blue input for each synchronisation link that targets the activity it translates. Analogously, it has one blue output for each link that emerges from the activity it translates. For example, inside a BPEL *flow*, a synchronisation link from activity A to activity B is translated into a blue line from the pattern translating A to the pattern translating B. Finally, in order to cope with faults we use *red lines*. Patterns that treat errors have red inputs, while patterns that generate errors have red outputs. For example, the translation of the BPEL *throw* activity has to have a red line as output, while the translation of the BPEL *fault handler* should input a red line.

The *basic pattern template* is illustrated in Figure 1. It consists of an *Execution Prerequisites Block* and of an *Execution Logic Block*. Green input lines of a pattern are denoted by *gi*, and green outputs by *go*. Similarly, *bi* and *bo* denote blue inputs and ouputs, and *ri* and *ro* red ones.

The Execution Prerequisites Block (EPB).   The EPB is in charge of enabling the pattern. In order to execute, a pattern has to be enabled both from the structural and from the synchronisation point of view.

The *GreenGate* task of the EPB is in charge of waiting for the green tokens. It also inputs a *parentSkip* boolean variable from its parent[1] activity, whose value indicates whether the latter is skipped or not. Indeed, since each structured activity could be skipped if it is the target of a synchronisation link, it outputs a *parentSkip* variable to all the patterns corresponding to its nested (child) activities.

If *parentSkip* holds *true* then the pattern must be skipped, as one of its ancestors was skipped. In this case *GreenGate* will immediately enable the *Execution Logic Block*, without having to wait for the statuses of its incoming links to be computed. If instead *parentSkip* holds *false* then the pattern is ready to be executed from the structural viewpoint. In this case, the execution of the EPB continues with the *BlueGate* task, which waits for all blue tokens and then it computes the value of the *joinCondition* by taking into account the statuses of its incoming links stored into *bi* boolean variables. Then, the *BlueGate* enables the *Execution Logic Block*.

The Execution Logic Block (ELB).   The ELB has three possible behaviours: It can execute successfully, it can be silently skipped, or it can raise a fault. The third behaviour corresponds to a false *joinCondition* (see next) or to an erroneous execution of the activity.

The *ExecOrSkip* task of ELB computes the skipping condition (into the *skip* boolean variable) as a logical disjunction between the *parentSkip* and the negation of the *joinCondition* variables. Indeed, an activity is skipped either since one of its ancestors was skipped (*parentSkip=true*), or since its *joinCondition* is false. If *skip* evelutes to *false* then the *ActivitySpecificTask* is executed, otherwise the *ComputeTransitionConditions* task is executed.

The *ActivitySpecificTask* is the key task of the pattern. It uniquely identifies the translated activity and it provides the computations needed by the activity. Instantiating the basic pattern template for a particular activity consists of equipping the *ActivitySpecificTask* with a name identifying the activity, and with the inputs and outputs defined by the activity. For example, the *Wait* pattern has an *ActivitySpecificTask* called *Wait* that inputs the duration of the *wait*.

The execution of the *ActivitySpecificTask* is simlutated through the deferred choice consisting of the *Fault* and *Success* tasks, together with their input place. The environment (viz., the "client" of the workflow) will determine whether *Fault* or *Success* will be executed. The execution of the *Fault* task corresponds to an erroneous execution of the activity (e.g., a *receive* activity has received an incorrect message). The *Fault* task outputs the name and data associated with

---

[1] When an activity *A* is directly nested within a structured activity *S*, we also say that *S* is the *parent* of *A* and that *A* is a *child* of *S*.

the fault, and it sets the boolean *fault* flag to *true*. Dually, *Success* corresponds to a successful execution of the activity. It is important to note that the deferred choice must be defined only for activities whose execution may be erroneous (e.g., *receive*, *invoke*, and so on). Otherwise, the *ActivitySpecificTask* is directly connected to the *ComputeTransitionConditions* task.

BPEL uses the *suppressJoinFailure* attribute to determine the process behaviour when the *joinCondition* is *false*. If the *suppressJoinFailure* attribute corresponding to an activity (defined by it or by one of its ancestors) is set to *NO*, the BPEL engine raises a *joinFailure* fault. Otherwise, it employs the dead-path-elimination by propagating negative statuses on all its output links. The *ComputeTransitionConditions* task concludes the execution of the ELB and of the pattern. On the one hand, it computes the status of each output (synchronisation) link, as defined by the *transitionCondition* attribute of the respective BPEL link. Link statuses are stored into *bo* variables, which have to be mapped onto *bi* variables of other patterns when constructing the workflow of the business process. On the other hand, it signals a *joinFailure* by setting the *fault* flag to *true* in case of a *false joinCondition* if the corresponding *suppressJoinFailure* attribute is set to *NO*.

Upon completion, the ELB outputs green and blue tokens if and only if the pattern was successfully executed. Dually, it outputs a red token if and only if a fault was raised.

BPEL Basic Activities.   Space limitations do not allow us to present the patterns of all the basic BPEL activities. We shall resume to presenting some general guidelines for customising and instantiating the basic pattern template.

In order to obtain the pattern of a basic activity, one has to (1) customise the *ActivitySpecificTask*, and (2) remove the deferred choice controlling the success of the activity if the activity cannot have an erroneous execution, as well as (3) set the (maximum) number of inputs and outputs of the pattern. The customisation of the *ActivitySpecificTask* regards the name of the task, which has to identify the pattern, as well as the inputs and the outputs of the task, which are obtained from the inputs and the outputs of the BPEL activity. Note that a pattern has at least one green input and one green output.

The *Invoke*, *Receive* and *Reply* patterns all have one green input. *Invoke* and *Reply* patterns have only one green output (for the pattern of the following activity, if any), while *Receive* can have at most two green outputs (the second to enable the pattern for event handling of the entire business process, if the *createInstance* attribute of the BPEL *receive* is set to *yes*).

The patterns *Throw*, *Wait*, *Terminate* and *Empty* have one green input and one green output, and they do not need the deferred choice block, as their execution cannot be erroneous. The *ActivitySpecificTask* will be hence directly connected to the *ComputeTransitionConditions* task. Note that a fault raised by a *Throw* pattern is not considered as an erroneous execution of the *throw* activity. Some other particularities are that the *ActivitySpecificTask* of the *Wait* pattern invokes the YAWL TimeService in order to delay the execution of the workflow, while the successful execution of a *Terminate* pattern leads to the cancellation of all tokens inside the pattern translating the process activity. (Further details on the latter will be given later on when describing the *process* pattern.)

The *assign* and the *compensate* activities are treated as structured patterns, as we will see in the next Subsection.

3.2   The Structured Pattern Template

A BPEL structured activity defines one or more activities to be executed in a certain order. In order to cope with this, we define the *structured pattern template* as a tuple consisting of a *Begin* pattern, an *End* pattern, as well as of a *PatternTemplate* for each child activity.

The purpose of the *Begin* and *End* patterns is to provide an identification for the activity being translated. More importantly, the execution of *Begin* logically corresponds to the initiation of the structured activity (as a whole), whereas the execution of *End* logically marks the termination of the structured activity.

Both *Begin* and *End* patterns are generated from the *basic pattern template*, and they are quite similar to the *Empty* pattern. On the one hand, *Begin* is in charge of enabling the structured pattern both from the structural and synchronisation viewpoints. Hence, *Begin* has to input the green and the blue lines and to raise a *joinFailure* in case of a *false joinCondition* if the corresponding *suppressJoinFailure* attribute is set to *NO*. Furthermore, it provides a green output for each *PatternTemplate* corresponding to a child activity that can be executed first. On the other hand, *End* has to wait for the green tokens from all *PatternTemplates* of the child activities that have to be executed last. Moreover, *End* is the source of the blue outputs corresponding to synchronisation links having as source the structured activity. In general, *End* cannot lead to any fault being raised, and hence it does not have a red output.

A structured activity introduces a new nesting level and consequently *Begin* has to output a *parentSkip* variable to the patterns of all the (child) activities nested inside the structured one, as well as to *End*. In this way we achieve the dead-path-elimination inside structured patterns.

Now, the patterns of all structured activities are obtained by adjusting the *Begin* and *End* patterns and by suitably interconnecting them with the *PatternTemplates*. Basically, both processes depend on the way in which the structured activity enables for execution its child activities. In the following we shall write *Begin(X)* and *End(X)* to refer to the *Begin* and *End* patterns of a structured activity *X*.

BPEL Structured Activities.   Space limitations do not allow us a detailed description of all the structured patterns. However, we shall try to describe the most relevant features of each pattern.

The *Sequence, Switch, Flow* and *Pick* patterns all share the same structure:

$$Sequence \rightarrow Begin(Sequence)\ PatternTemplate^+\ End(Sequence)$$
$$Switch \rightarrow Begin(Switch)\ PatternTemplate^+\ End(Switch)$$
$$Flow \rightarrow Begin(Flow)\ PatternTemplate^+\ End(Flow)$$
$$Pick \rightarrow Begin(Pick)\ PatternTemplate^+\ End(Pick)$$

The *Sequence* pattern consists of a *Begin* and an *End* pattern, together with at least one *PatternTemplate*. *Begin(Sequence)* must enable the execution of only the first *PatternTemplate* in the sequence, each *PatternTemplate* enables the next one in the sequence, and *End[Sequence]* must wait for the last *PatternTemplate* to finish its execution.

The *Switch* pattern includes one *PatternTemplate* for each conditional branch, and each *PatternTemplate* must verify the guard condition of the corresponding branch. A *false* guard leads to skipping the corresponding branch and hence to dead-path-elimination inside the corresponding pattern. The *PatternTemplates* are linked in the order in which the conditional branches occur in the *switch* activity. If no *otherwise* branch is defined, a default one with an *empty* activity guarded by an (always) *true* condition is considered.

A *flow* activity concurrently executes a bag of activities among which synchronisation links can be defined. *Begin(Flow)* has to enable the patterns of all its child activities, and hence it has one green output for each *PatternTemplate*. Dually, the execution of *End(Flow)* is delayed until all *PatternTemplates* finish their execution.

A *pick* basically waits for a message or an alarm event to take place. Its pattern is slightly more complicated due to the fact that the first event that is triggered causes all other events to be cancelled. *Begin(Pick)* mainly differs from *Begin(Flow)* in that its *ActivitySpecificTask* is a composite task in charge of branch selection. Moreover, each *PatternTemplate* of the pick has a guard condition that checks whether its branch id matches the id of the branch selected in *Begin(Pick)*. Although only one branch will be actually executed, *Begin(Pick)* sends green tokens to all *PatternTemplates* in order to perform the dead-path-elimination on the branches that were not selected. *End(Pick)*, similarly to *End(Flow)*, waits for the green tokens from all branch patterns.

The *While* pattern

$$While \rightarrow Begin(While)\ PatternTemplate\ End(While)$$

differs from the *Sequence* pattern as *Begin(While)* has two green input lines and a guard condition. A green input token comes either from the pattern structurally preceding the while, or from *End(While)* in order to loop. Dually, *End(While)* outputs a green token either for the pattern structurally following the while, or for *Begin(While)*. The guard condition is checked again by *End(While)* in order to avoid skipping the whole while in case of a *false* guard at the end of a cycle.

Although *assign* is a basic activity, it is translated with a structured pattern since it can contain several *copy* tags, each of which requiring a data exchange which may lead to a fault being raised. The *Assign* pattern:

$$Assign \rightarrow Begin(Assign)\ Copy^+\ End(Assign)$$

has the same structure of the *Sequence* pattern, but it includes *Copy* patterns rather than arbitrary *PatternTemplates*. A *Copy* pattern is obtained from the *basic pattern template* by replacing the *ActivitySpecificTask* with a task named *Copy*, which inputs the "source" variable and which outputs the "target" variable. In this way, the assignment is achieved through the data mappings of the

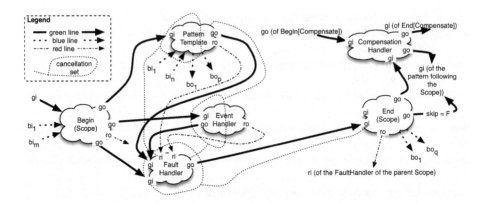

Fig. 2. High level view of the *Scope* pattern

Copy patterns. Furthermore, the *Copy* pattern does not have blue inputs and outputs.

A BPEL *scope* provides a specific context for an activity. It contains a (possibly default) *fault handler*, a (possibly default) *compensation handler*, as well as an optional *event handler*. The *fault handler* consists of one or more *catch* clauses for grabbing faults raised inside the scope. A *catch* is a container of an activity, guarded by a fault name and an optional fault variable. A *catchAll* has an always true guard and no fault name or variable. The *compensation handler* provides a (compensating) activity that can be invoked either explicitly (through a *compensate*), or implicitly (in case of a fault). The *compensation handler* is activated only when the scope finished its execution successfully. (In this paper we deal with explicit compensation only, due to the troublesome default compensation mechanism, e.g., compensating a *scope* inside a *while*). Last but not least, an *event handler* defines message and alarm events that can be triggered repeatedly and concurrently during the lifetime of the scope. The *Scope* pattern has the structure:

$$Scope \;\rightarrow\; Begin(Scope)\; PatternTemplate\; FaultHandler$$
$$[CompensationHandler]\; [EventHandler]\; End(Scope)$$

and the structural dependencies among the various patterns involved are illustrated in Figure 2. *Begin(Scope)* sends green tokens to the *PatternTemplate*, to the *EventHandler*, and to the *FaultHandler*. The *FaultHandler* will further receive either one green token from the *PatternTemplate* and one green token from the *EventHandler* (if any), or one red token from the *PatternTemplate* or from the *EventHandler*. In the former case, the entire *FaultHandler* will be skipped either because the *PatternTemplate* was completed successfully, or because the entire scope has to be skipped. The latter case corresponds to a fault being raised (and uncaught) inside the *PatternTemplate*, or inside the *EventHandler*. In case that the fault cannot be processed, the *FaultHandler* will send a green token to *End(Scope)*, which has to send a red token further to the *FaultHandler* of the parent scope pattern (if any). Note that only the *FaultHandler* will forward a (green) token to *End(Scope)*. *End(Scope)* is in charge of enabling the *Compensa-tionHandler* if the *PatternTemplate* was successful. It is important to note that *End(Scope)* has to save a copy of all the scope variables as required by the *Com-pensationHandler*. If the scope is skipped, *End(Scope)* has to clear the green tokens received by the *FaultHandler* from the *PatternTemplate* and from the *EventHandler* as they are redundant. Furthermore, in this case it is unnecessary to perform the dead-path-elimination inside the *EventHandler* as links cannot cross its boundary. However, we do have to perform the dead-path-elimination inside the *FaultHandler*.

The *FaultHandler* pattern has a similar structure to the *Sequence* pattern:

$$Begin(FaultHandler)\ PatternTemplate^*\ End(FaultHandler)$$

except that each *PatternTemplate* corresponds here to a *catch* activity and hence it has a guard condition checking the fault name and data. Furthermore, *Be-gin(FaultHandler)* uses a *RedGate* (instead of a *BlueGate*) that waits for red tokens to be sent (viz., faults to be raised) from inside the *PatternTemplate* (or from inside the *EventHandler*) of its scope. In order to interrupt the normal execution of the scope in case of a fault being raised, the *RedGate* uses a cancel-lation set that includes all patterns of the scope's *PatternTemplate* and *Even-tHandler* except *CompensationHandler* patterns corresponding to scopes nested in its scope. If the BPEL process does not define a *fault handler*, the translator generates a default *FaultHandler* pattern consisting of *Begin(FaultHandler)* and *End(FaultHandler)* only. In this way, the faults received by this default *Fault-Handler* will be forwarded (through *EndScope*) to the *FaultHandler* of the parent scope (or of the entire process). In the pattern of the *EventHandler*:

$$Begin(EventHandler)\ PatternTemplate^+\ End(EventHandler)$$

the *PatternTemplates* execute concurrently, and each one is placed in a loop with a guard that checks the end of the *PatternTemplate* pattern translating the activity inside the scope. Note that the scope's *PatternTemplate* is in charge of clearing all tokens of the *PatternTemplates* that implement alarms upon its completion. Finally, the *CompensationHandler* pattern is:

$$Begin(CompensationHandler)\ PatternTemplate^*\ End(CompensationHandler)$$

If the scope completes successfully, the *Begin(CompensationHandler)* is acti-vated and waits for a green token from a *Compensate* pattern. Upon completion, the *End(CompensationHandler)* returns the green token to the *Compensate*. If a BPEL scope does not define a *compensation handler* yet there is a *compen-sate* activity targeting the respective scope, the translator generates a default *CompensationHandler* consisting only of *Begin(CompensationHandler)* directly linked to *End(CompensationHandler)*.

Finally, the BPEL *compensate* is translated with the pattern:

$$Begin(Compensate)\ End(Compensate)$$

since *compensate* terminates only when the invoked *CompensationHandler* fin-ishes its execution. Recall that we consider only simple explicit compensation, that is *compensate* activities specifying the name of the scope to be compensated, without considering scopes nested inside *while* activities. *Begin(Compensate)* sends a green token directly to *End(Compensate)* if the *compensate* is skipped, or if the scope to be compensated did not finish its execution. Otherwise, the green token is sent to the *Begin(CompensationHandler)* of the scope to be compensated. Dually, *End(Compensate)* receives a green token either directly from *Begin(Compensate)*, or from the *End(CompensationHandler)* of the scope to be compensated. Then, it forwards it to the pattern structurally following the *compensate*. Further details on the *Scope* pattern will be commented in the Section dedicated to discussing an use case.

3.3 BPEL Processes

A BPEL *process* encapsulates the process activity and it can further define a *fault handler*, a *compensation handler*, as well as an *event handler*.

The *Process* pattern:

Begin(Process) FaultHandler [EventHandler] PatternTemplate End(Process) resembles the *Scope* pattern, altohough there are several differences between the two. For example, *Begin(Process)* and *End(Process)* have to be connected to the *input condition* and to the *output condition*, respectively, of the workflow.

Begin(Process) enables the *PatternTemplate*, the *FaultHandler*, as well as the *EventHandler* (if any). If the BPEL process does not define a *FaultHandler*, or if it does but it does not contain a *catchAll* clause, one (default) *FaultHandler* with a default *catchAll* (viz., an *Empty* pattern) must be defined in the *Process* pattern. This is needed to catch all uncaught faults being raised within the process. Note that the reception of a fault by the process *FaultHandler* leads to an abnormal process termination, even if the fault is processed. Furthermore, faults being raised (and uncaught) inside the process *FaultHandler* lead to the immediate execution of the *End(Process)* pattern, as in the case of a *Terminate* (see next). Differently from the *Scope*, there are no green tokens being sent from the *PatternTemplate* and from the *EventHandler* to the *FaultHandler*. This is due to the fact that the *FaultHandler* cannot be skipped because neither the *Process* can be skipped nor the dead-path-elimination must be employed inside its *FaultHandler* pattern. The *PatternTemplate* and *EventHandler* forward each one green token to *End(Process)*.

The *EventHandler* is active for the entire process lifetime and the *PatternTemplate* of the process is in charge of clearing its tokens upon its completion, similarly to a *Scope*. In order to minimise the number of cancellation sets defined in the workflow, all *Terminate* patterns forward the green token to *End(Process)*, which is in charge of immediately terminating the entire business process. It does so by clearing all the tokens of the *PatternTemplate* corresponding to the activity defined by the process. Hence, *End(Process)* is enabled if it receives either one green token from the process *PatternTemplate* and another from the *EventHandler* (if any), or one green token from a *Terminate*, or from the process *FaultHandler*.

The *compensation handler* can only be invoked by platform-specific means. Consequently, we do not consider a *compensation handler* for the entire business process. Furthermore, the process *compensation handler* would block the workflow waiting for a green token.

A BPEL process is translated into a YAWL workflow by instantiating the *Process* pattern. This leads to recursively instantiating the *Begin(Process)*, *Fault-Handler*, *EventHandler* (if any), and *End(Process)* patterns, as well as the *Pattern Template* corresponding to the process activity. Note that the instantiation of a pattern takes into account the context in which the activity is placed inside the BPEL process. Namely, instantiating a pattern means adjusting the (number of) input and output lines, setting and mapping the inputs and outputs of the tasks in the pattern, as well as suitably interconnecting its child patterns. The instantiating process bottoms-out at *basic pattern templates*.

4   A Use Case

Consider a simple BPEL process that computes the greatest common divisor (GCD) of two numbers. Basically, the GCD is computed by repeatedly raising an exception if one of the two numbers is bigger than the other and by decreasing its value in the corresponding catch. Due to space limitations we present hereafter a simplification of the BPEL process. Figure 3 gives the high-level view of the YAWL workflow obtained from the GCD process. The interested reader is kindly asked to download the archive containing the full BPEL process as well as the YAWL workflow of the example from the following address: `http://www.di.unipi.it/~popescu/GCD_Example.zip`.

```
<process name="S" suppressJoinFailure="yes">
    <faultHandler><catch fault="negNum"><reply fault="negNum"/></catch></faultHandler>
    <flow>
        <receive(a,b) createInstance="yes">
            <source link="RCV2THR" transitionCondition="a<=0 or b<=0"/>
            <source link="RCV2WHL" transitionCondition="a>0 and b>0"/></receive>
        <throw fault="negNum"><target link="RCV2THR"/></throw>
        <while condition="a!=b"><source link="WHL2SEQ"/><target link="RCV2WHL"/>
            <scope>
                <faultHandler><catch fault="dec_a"><assign a:=a-b/></catch>
                    <catch fault="dec_b"><assign b:=b-a/></catch></faultHandler>
                <switch>
                    <case condition="a>b"><throw fault="dec_a"/></case>
                    <otherwise><throw fault="dec_b"/></otherwise></switch></scope></while>
        <sequence><target link="WHL2SEQ"/><assign c:=a/><reply(c)/></sequence>
    </flow></process>
```

Consider an execution scenario in which the two input variables a and b take the values of 2 and 4, respectively. The workflow executes first *Begin(Process)* (that outputs two green tokens) followed by *Begin(Flow)* (that outputs four green tokens) and by *Receive* (that outputs one green token). As both numbers are strictly positive, *Receive* sends a blue token to *Begin(While)* and another blue (skipping) token to *Throw*. Because the *suppressJoinFailure* (set for the entire process only) has a *yes* value, skipping the *Throw* does not raise a *joinFailure*, but forwards the green token to *End(Flow)*. The execution continues with *Begin(While)* and then with *Begin(Scope)* (as $a \mathrel{!{=}} b$) that forwards a green token to *Begin(Switch)* and another to the *Begin(FaultHandler)* of the scope. The first

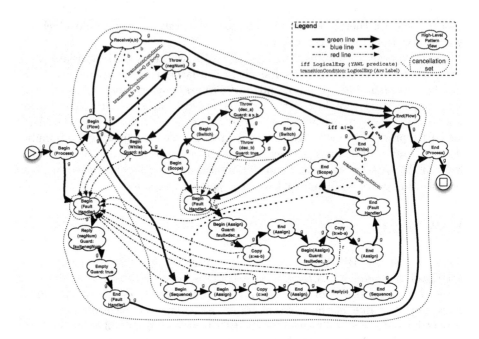

Fig. 3. YAWL workflow obtained from the GCD process

Throw in the *switch* is skipped as $a<b$, yet the second one (of the *otherwise* branch) is executed, and a *dec_b* fault is raised. As a result, only a red token is sent further to the *Begin(FaultHandler)* of the scope (that clears all tokens of the *Switch*). The first *Assign* is skipped (as *fault= "dec_b"*), while the second *Assign* decreases the value of b by a. The green token will reach next *End(FaultHandler)* and then *End(Scope)* that forwards the green token to *End(While)* (as the fault was processed). Because $a=b=2$, *End(While)* sends a green token to *End(Flow)* and a blue token to *Begin(Sequence)*. The execution of the *Assign* inside the *Sequence* leads to copying the value of a into c and to replying with the latter to the client. Finally, *End(Sequence)* outputs a green token that enables *End(Flow)*, which has now gathered all its input (green) tokens. *End(Flow)* forwards a green token to *End(Process)* that first clears all input tokens of the *Begin(FaultHandler)* of the process, and then it sends the green token to the output condition, marking in this way the end of the workflow.

5   Concluding Remarks

We have outlined a methodology for translating BPEL processes into YAWL workflows. Its main strengths are that (1) it defines YAWL patterns for all BPEL activities, (2) it provides a compositional approach to construct structured patterns from suitably interconnecting other patterns, and (3) it handles events, faults and (explicit) compensation.

Fisteus et al. [1] describe VERBUS, a FSM-based framework for the formal verification of BPEL processes, but they do not treat synchronisation links, complex fault handling, as well as event and compensation handling. Koshkina and van Breugel [6] introduce the BPE-calculus in order to formalise the control-flow of BPEL and build upon it a tool for the analysis (e.g., deadlock freedom) of business processes. Still, they do not tackle fault and compensation handling. Hinz et al. [5] give a PN semantics to BPEL processes by defining a pattern for each BPEL activity. However, they abstract from data and leave out transition guards. Consequently, control-flow decisions based on the evaluation of data are replaced by non-deterministic choices. Our approach does not suffer from this limitation as both BPEL and YAWL use XMLSchema and XPath for data manipulation, and hence the data translation between the two is straightforward. Ouyang et al. [7] formalise BPEL in terms of PNs with the purpose of analysing its control-flow. Although they handle both synchronisation links and exceptional behaviour, their focus is on the analysis, and not on the composition of business processes.

We believe that the translation described in this paper constitutes an important brick for the development of formal analysis and transformations of BPEL processes. It also directly contributes to our long-term goal of aggregating and adapting heterogeneous Web services [4,3]. In this perspective, our next step will be the integration of our Java prototype implementation of the BPEL2YAWL translator with the Java implementation of the core aggregation mechanism of [4], in order to yield a single tool supporting the disciplined, semi-automated aggregation of BPEL services. A further line for future work is the development of other translators to convert other types of Web service descriptions (e.g., OWL-S) into YAWL.

References

1. J. Arias-Fisteus, L. S. Fernández, and C. D. Kloos. Formal Verification of BPEL4WS Business Collaborations. In K. Bauknecht, M. Bichler, and B. Pröll, editors, *EC-Web*, volume 3182 of *LNCS*, pages 76–85. Springer, 2004.
2. BPEL4WS Coalition. Business Process Execution Language for Web Services (BPEL4WS) Version 1.1. (`ftp://www6.software.ibm.com/software/developer/library/ws-bpel.pdf`).
3. A. Brogi and R. Popescu. Service Adaptation through Trace Inspection. In S. Gagnon, H. Ludwig, M. Pistore, and W. Sadiq, editors, *Proceedings of SOBPI'05*, pages 44–58, 2005. (`http://elab.njit.edu/sobpi/sobpi05-proceedings.pdf`).
4. A. Brogi and R. Popescu. Towards Semi-automated Workflow-Based Aggregation of Web Services. In B. Benatallah, F. Casati, and P. Traverso, editors, *ICSOC'05*, volume 3826 of *LNCS*, pages 214–227. Springer, 2005.
5. S. Hinz, K. Schmidt, and C. Stahl. Transforming BPEL to Petri Nets. In W. van der Aalst, B. Benatallah, F. Casati, and F. Curbera, editors, *Proceedings of the Third International Conference on Business Process Management (BPM 2005)*, volume 3649 of *LNCS*, pages 220–235, Nancy, France, Sept. 2005. Springer-Verlag.
6. M. Koshkina and F. van Breugel. Verification of business processes for Web services. Technical Report CS-2003-11, York University, October 2003. (`http://www.cs.yorku.ca/techreports/2003/CS-2003-11.ps`).

7. C. Ouyang, E. Verbeek, W. M. van der Aalst, S. Breutel, M. Dumas, and A. H. ter Hofstede. Formal Semantics and Analysis of Control Flow in WS-BPEL. Technical Report 2174, Queensland University of Technology, February 2006. Available from: http://eprints.qut.edu.au/archive/00002174/01/BPM-05-15.pdf.
8. OWL-S Coalition. OWL-S: Semantic Markup for Web Services Version 1.1. (http://www.daml.org/services/owl-s/1.1/overview/).
9. M. P. Papazoglou and D. Georgakopoulos. Service-Oriented Computing. *Communication of the ACM*, 46(10):24–28, 2003.
10. W. M. P. van der Aalst and A. H. M. ter Hofstede. YAWL: Yet Another Workflow Language. *Inf. Syst.*, 30(4):245–275, 2005.
11. W. M. P. van der Aalst, A. H. M. ter Hofstede, B. Kiepuszewski, and A. P. Barros. Workflow Patterns. *Distrib. Parallel Databases*, 14(1):5–51, 2003.
12. WSDL Coalition. Web Service Description Language (WSDL) version 1.1. (http://www.w3.org/TR/wsdl).

Translating Orc Features into Petri Nets
and the Join Calculus⋆

Roberto Bruni[1], Hernán Melgratti[2], and Emilio Tuosto[3]

[1] Computer Science Department, University of Pisa, Italy
[2] IMT, Lucca Institute for Advanced Studies, Italia
[3] Department of Computer Science, University of Leicester, UK
bruni@di.unipi.it, hernan.melgratti@imtlucca.it, et52@mcs.le.ac.uk

Abstract. Cook and Misra's Orc is an elegant language for orchestrating distributed services, able to cover e.g. van der Aalst's workflow patterns. We aim to understand the key novel features of Orc by comparing it with variations of Petri nets. The comparison shows that Orc hides powerful mechanisms for name handling (creation and passing) and for atomic distributed termination. Petri nets with static topology can encode Orc under severe restrictions while the full language (up to a more realistic cancellation strategy) can be encoded in Join (that can be seen as a higher-order extension of Petri nets). As an overall result, we promote Join calculus as an elegant language embedding orchestration and computation.

1 Introduction

Service Oriented Computing and its most successful current realisation based on Web Services are challenging science and technology in laying foundations, techniques and engineered development for supporting just-in-time assembly of complex business processes according to the publish-find-bind paradigm. Main issues are concerned with, e.g., security, behavioural description of services with the integration of functional and non-functional requirements, trade-off between network awareness and network transparency, dynamic binding and reconfiguration, model-driven development.

A common theme to all these aspects is service composition. The difference w.r.t. classic program or process composition here is that beside answering the question on "how to compose services", one has to provide languages and logic for "describing composite services" and "use composition as a specification requirement for querying service repositories". Descriptions should be accurate enough to guarantee that dynamically found and bound composite services behave well.

The terms *orchestration* and *choreography* were coined to describe two different flavors of service compositions: orchestration is about describing and executing a single view point model, while choreography is about specifying and guiding a global model. Though the difference between the two terms can be sometimes abused or blurred, substantially orchestration has a more centralised flavor, as opposed to the more distributed vision of choreography. The typical example is that of a ballet: the choreographer fixes

⋆ Research supported by the EU FET-GC2 IST-2004-16004 Integrated Project SENSORIA and by the Italian FIRB Project TOCAI.IT.

M. Bravetti, M. Nuñes, and G. Zavattaro (Eds.): WS-FM 2006, LNCS 4184, pp. 123–137, 2006.

the overall scheme for the movements of all dancers, but then each dancer orchestrates her/his own movements. Roughly, from a formal modelling viewpoint, orchestration is mainly concerned with the regulation of control and data flow between services, while choreography is concerned with interaction protocols between single and composite services. In this paper we focus on orchestration, but with an eye left to choreography.

Cook and Misra's Orc [20,19] is a basic programming model for structured orchestration of services, whose primitives meet simplicity with yet great generality. The basic computational entities orchestrated by Orc expressions are *sites*: upon invocation, a site can publish at most one response value. A site call can be an RMI, a call to a monitor procedure, to a function or to a web service. A site computation might itself start other orchestrations, store effects locally and make (or not) such effects visible to clients.

Orc has three composition principles. The first one is the ordinary parallel composition $f|g$ (e.g., the parallel composition of two site calls can produce zero, one or many values). The other two, sequencing and asymmetric parallel composition, take inspiration from universal and existential quantification, respectively. In the sequential expression $f > x > g$, a fresh copy $g[v/x]$ of g is executed for *any* value v returned by f, i.e., a sort of pipeline is established between f and g. The evaluation of the asymmetric parallel expression f **where** $x :\in g$ is lazy: f and g start in parallel, but all sub-expressions of f that depend on the value of x must wait for g to publish *one* value. When g produces a value it is assigned to x and that side of the orchestration is cancelled.

As a workflow language, Orc can encode all most common workflow patterns [11]. Contrary to many other process algebras, Orc neatly separates orchestration from computation: Orc expressions should be considered as scripts to be invoked, e.g., within imperative programming languages using assignments such as $z :\in e$, where z is a variable and the Orc expression e can involve wide-area computation over multiple servers. The assignment symbol $:\in$ (due to Hoare) makes it explicit that e can return zero or more results, one of which is assigned to z.

This papers tries to characterise the distinguishing features of Orc by carrying a comparison with two other main paradigms, namely Petri nets and Join calculus as suitable representatives of workflow and messaging models, respectively. (The basics of Orc, Petri nets and Join are recalled in § 2.) Petri nets are a foundational model of concurrency, hence their choice as a reference model for carrying the comparison is well justified. The choice of Join instead of, e.g., the maybe more popular pi-calculus, might appear less obvious, so it is worth giving some explanation.

First, the multiple input prefix of Join looks more suitable than the single prefix of pi-calculus to smoothly model many orchestration patterns. For example, consider the process that must wait for messages on both x and y or in either one of the two. This is coded in Join as $x\langle u\rangle|tok\langle\rangle \triangleright P_1 \wedge y\langle v\rangle|tok\langle\rangle \triangleright P_2 \wedge x\langle u\rangle|y\langle v\rangle|tok\langle\rangle \triangleright P_3$ and by assuring there is a unique message $tok\langle\rangle$, whereas the pi-calculus expression $x(u).P_1 + y(v).P_2 + x(u).y(v).P_3$ used, e.g., in [23] is a less faithful encoding, because: (i) in the third sub-expression multiple inputs must be arbitrarily sequentialised and (ii) the third alternative can be selected even if a message arrives on x but none arrives on y, causing a deadlock. Of course one can still use the more precise translation $x(u).(P_1 + y(v).P_3) + y(v).(x(u).P_3 + P_2)$ but it is immediately seen that combinatorial explosion would make the encoding unreadable when larger groups of actions and more complex patterns are considered. Second, Join adheres to a locality principle ensuring that extruded names cannot be used in input by the process that received them (they can only output values on such ports). This feature is crucial for deploying distributed implementations [10,7] and it is not enforced in the full pi-calculus. Third, but not last, in [9], Join has been envisaged as some kind of higher-order version of Petri nets making it easier to reconcile all views analysed here.

Our contribution shows that:

- In absence of mobility, P/T nets can encode Orc expressions when mono-sessions are considered.
- Serialised multi-sessions require reset nets [6,12] (as shown in § 3).
- The Join calculus encodes Orc primitives in a rather natural way (as shown in § 4, the only verbosity is due to the encoding of variables, which is also very simple).

The last item shows that Orc primitives can be seen as syntactic sugar for Join processes. Therefore, as an overall result, we would like to promote Join as an elegant language integrating workflow orchestration, messaging, and computation (see § 5).

2 Background

2.1 Orc

This section briefly recaps Orc, borrowing definitions from [20] (apart from minor syntactical differences). Orc relies on the notion of a *site*, an abstraction amenable for being invoked and for publishing values. Each site invocation to s elicits at most one value published by s. Sites can be composed (by means of sequential and symmetric/asymmetric parallel composition) to form expressions. The difference between sites and expressions is that the latter can publish more than one value for each evaluation.

The syntax of Orc is given by the following grammar

$$D ::= E(x_1,\ldots,x_n) \triangleq f$$
$$e,f,g ::= 0 \mid M\langle p_1,\ldots,p_n\rangle \mid E\langle p_1,\ldots,p_n\rangle \mid f > x > g \mid f|g \mid f \text{ where } x :\in g$$

where $x_1,\ldots,x_n$ are variables, M stands for site names and E for expression names. We consider a set of constants $\mathcal{C}$ ranged over by c and the special site $let(x_1,\ldots,x_n)$ that publishes the tuple $\langle c_1,\ldots,c_n\rangle$. A value is either a variable, a site name or a constant (values are ranged over by $p_1,p_2,\ldots$).

The expressions g **where** $x :\in f$ and $f > x > g$ bind the occurrences of x in g (in g **where** $x :\in f$, the expression g is said to be in the scope of $x :\in f$). The occurrences of variables not bound are free and the set of free variables of an expression f is denoted by $fn(f)$. In the following, all definitions $E(x_1,\ldots,x_n) \triangleq f$ are well-formed, i.e., $fn(f) \subseteq \{x_1,\ldots,x_n\}$ and $x_1,\ldots,x_n$ are pairwise distinct. We write $\vec{x}$ for $x_1,\ldots,x_n$ and $f[c/x]$ for the expression obtained by replacing the free occurrences of x in f with c.

The operational semantics of Orc is formalised in Figure 1 as a labelled transition system with four kinds of labels: (1) a site call event $M(\vec{c},k)$, representing a call to site M with arguments $\vec{c}$ waiting for response on the dedicated handler k; (2) a response

$$\frac{}{let(c) \xrightarrow{!c} 0}\ (\text{LET}) \qquad \frac{k \text{ globally fresh}}{M\langle \bar{c}\rangle \xrightarrow{M\langle \bar{c},k\rangle} ?k}\ (\text{SITECALL}) \qquad \frac{}{?k \xrightarrow{k?c} let(c)}\ (\text{SITERET}) \qquad \frac{E(\bar{x}) \triangleq f}{E\langle \bar{p}\rangle \xrightarrow{\tau} f[\bar{p}/\bar{x}]}\ (\text{DEF})$$

$$\frac{f \xrightarrow{!c} f'}{f > x > g \xrightarrow{\tau} (f' > x > g) | g[c/x]}\ (\text{SEQPIPE}) \qquad\qquad \frac{f \xrightarrow{l} f' \quad l \neq !c}{f > x > g \xrightarrow{l} f' > x > g}\ (\text{SEQ})$$

$$\frac{g \xrightarrow{l} g'}{g|f \xrightarrow{l} g'|f}\ (\text{SYML}) \qquad \frac{f \xrightarrow{l} f'}{g|f \xrightarrow{l} g|f'}\ (\text{SYMR}) \qquad \frac{g \xrightarrow{l} g'}{g \text{ where } x :\in f \xrightarrow{l} g' \text{ where } x :\in f}\ (\text{ASYML})$$

$$\frac{f \xrightarrow{l} f' \quad l \neq !c}{g \text{ where } x :\in f \xrightarrow{l} g \text{ where } x :\in f'}\ (\text{ASYMR}) \qquad\qquad \frac{f \xrightarrow{!c} f'}{g \text{ where } x :\in f \xrightarrow{\tau} g[c/x]}\ (\text{ASYMPRUNE})$$

Fig. 1. Operational semantics of Orc

event $k?c$, sending the response c to the call handler k (there is at most one such event for each k); (3) a publish event $!c$; (4) an internal event τ.

A declaration D specifies an expression name E, the formal parameters $x_1, \ldots, x_n$ and the body f, like for usual function or procedure declarations. The body f of an expression declaration can be the expression 0 (i.e., a site which never publishes any value), the invocation of a site $M\langle p_1, \ldots, p_n\rangle$, or an expression call $E\langle p_1, \ldots, p_n\rangle$. Calls to sites are strict (actual parameters are evaluated before the call) while expression calls are non-strict. Expressions f and g can be sequentially composed with $f > x > g$ which first evaluates f and then, for each value v published by f, evaluates a new copy of g where x is replaced with v (if f never publishes any value, no fresh g will ever be evaluated). Expressions can be composed with the symmetric and asymmetric parallel operators. The former is written $f|g$; it evaluates f and g in parallel and publishes the values that f and g publish (we remark that there is no interaction between f and g and that usual monoidal laws for | with 0 as neutral element hold). The latter, called *where-expression*, is written g **where** $x :\in f$. The evaluation of g **where** $x :\in f$ proceeds by evaluating f and g in parallel. Expression f is meant to publish a value to be assigned to x and all the parts of g depending on x must wait until such a value is available. Evaluation of f stops as soon as any value, say v, is published. Then, v is assigned to x so that all the parts in g depending of x can execute, but the residual of f is cancelled.

Example 2.1. We borrow from [20] some of interesting examples of Orc declarations.

- Assume that *CNN* and *BBC* are two sites that return recent news when invoked while site *Email*(a, m) sends an email containing message m to the address a. (Notice that an invocation to *Email* changes the receiver's mailbox).
- Declaration *Notify*$(a) \triangleq (CNN|BBC) > x > Email(x, a)$ specifies a service for notifying last news from *CNN* and *BBC*. By rule SEQPIPE, the news from both *CNN* and *BBC* are notified in two different emails.
- Another interesting example is *MailOnce*$(a) \triangleq Email(x, a)$ **where** $x :\in (CNN|BBC)$ specifying service *MailOnce*(a) that notifies address a with only one of the news selected either from *CNN* or from *BBC*.

An Orc program represents an orchestrator O executed in a host sequential program; O is a pair $\langle \mathcal{D}, z :\in E(\vec{p}) \rangle$ where $\mathcal{D}$ is a set of definitions, z a variable of the host program, $E\langle \vec{c} \rangle$ is an Orc expression call where (*i*) E is an expression name defined in $\mathcal{D}$ and (*ii*) $\vec{c}$ are the actual parameters. The notation $z :\in E\langle \vec{c} \rangle$ specifies that even if $E\langle \vec{c} \rangle$ might publish any number of values, z will be bound to just one of them. The types of values published by $E\langle \vec{c} \rangle$ are left unspecified, however it is assumed that they can be dealt with in the hosting program (see § 2.2 of [20]).

2.2 Petri Nets

Petri nets, introduced in [21], have become a reference model for studying concurrent systems, mainly due to their simplicity and the intrinsic concurrent nature of their behaviour. They rely on solid theoretical basis that allows for the formalisation of causality, concurrency, and non-determinism (in terms of non-sequential processes or unfolding constructions). Petri nets are built up from *places* (denoting resources types), which are repositories of *tokens* (representing instances of resources), and *transitions*, which fetch and produce tokens. We assume an infinite set $\mathcal{P}$ of resource names is fixed.

Definition 2.1 (Net). *A net N is a 4-tuple $N = (S_N, T_N, \delta_{0N}, \delta_{1N})$ where $S_N \subseteq \mathcal{P}$ is the (nonempty) set of places, $\mathsf{a}, \mathsf{a}', \ldots$, T_N is the set of transitions, $\mathsf{t}, \mathsf{t}', \ldots$ (with $S_N \cap T_N = \emptyset$), and the functions $\delta_{0N}, \delta_{1N} : T_N \to \wp_f(S_N)$ assign finite sets of places, called respectively source and target, to each transition.*

Place / Transition nets (P/T nets) are the most widespread model of nets. The places of a P/T net can hold zero, one or more tokens and arcs are weighted. Hence, the state of the P/T net is described in terms of *markings*, i.e., multisets of tokens available in the places of the net. Given a set S, a *multiset* over S is a function $m : S \to \mathbb{N}$ (where $\mathbb{N}$ is the set of natural numbers). The set of all finite multisets over S is denoted by $\mathcal{M}_S$ and the empty multiset by $\emptyset$.

Definition 2.2 (P/T net). *A marked place / transition Petri net (P/T net) is a tuple $N = (S_N, T_N, \delta_{0N}, \delta_{1N}, m_{0N})$ where $S_N \subseteq \mathcal{P}$ is a set of places, T_N is a set of transitions, the functions $\delta_{0N}, \delta_{1N} : T_N \to \mathcal{M}_{S_N}$ assign respectively, source and target to each transition, and $m_{0N} \in \mathcal{M}_{S_N}$ is the initial marking.*

Given a transition $t \in T$, ${}^\bullet t = \delta_0(t)$ is its *preset* and $t^\bullet = \delta_1(t)$ is its *postset*. Let N be a net and u a marking of N; then a transition $t \in T_N$ is *enabled at u* iff ${}^\bullet t(\mathsf{a}) \leq u(\mathsf{a}), \forall \mathsf{a} \in S_N$. We say a marking u evolves to u' under the *firing* of the transition t written $u[t\rangle u'$, iff t is enabled at u and $u'(\mathsf{a}) = u(\mathsf{a}) - {}^\bullet t(\mathsf{a}) + t^\bullet(\mathsf{a}), \forall \mathsf{a} \in S$. A *firing sequence* from u_0 to u_n is a sequence of markings and firings s.t. $u_0[t_1\rangle u_1 \ldots u_{n_1}[t_n\rangle u_n$.

Reset nets [6] extend P/T nets with special *reset arcs*. A reset arc associating a transition t with a place a causes the place a to reset when t is fired.

Definition 2.3 (Reset net). *A reset net is a tuple $N = (S_N, T_N, \delta_{0N}, \delta_{1N}, m_{0N}, R_N)$, where $(S_N, T_N, \delta_{0N}, \delta_{1N}, m_{0N})$ is a P/T net and $R_N : T_N \to \wp_f(S_N)$ defines reset arcs.*

The condition for the enabling of a reset transition is the same as for ordinary P/T nets, while their firings are defined as follows: u evolves to u' under the *firing* of the reset transition t, written $u[t\rangle u'$, if and only if t is enabled at u and $\forall \mathsf{a} \in S_N : u'(\mathsf{a}) = u(\mathsf{a}) - {}^\bullet t(\mathsf{a}) + t^\bullet(\mathsf{a})$ if $\mathsf{a} \notin R_N(t)$, and $u'(\mathsf{a}) = 0$ otherwise.

$$(\text{OPEN}) \quad A,B ::= 0 \mid x\langle \vec{y}\rangle \mid \mathbf{def}_S \ D \ \mathbf{in} \ A \mid A|B \qquad D,E ::= J \triangleright P \mid D \wedge E \quad (\text{DEF})$$

$$(\text{PROC}) \quad P,Q ::= 0 \mid x\langle \vec{y}\rangle \mid \mathbf{def} \ D \ \mathbf{in} \ P \mid P|Q \qquad J,K ::= x\langle \vec{y}\rangle \mid J|K \quad (\text{PAT})$$

(a) Syntax

$$rn(x\langle \vec{y}\rangle) = \{\vec{y}\} \qquad\qquad dn(x\langle \vec{y}\rangle) = \{x\}$$
$$rn(J|K) = rn(J) \uplus rn(K) \qquad\qquad dn(J|K) = dn(J) \uplus dn(K)$$

$$fn(J \triangleright P) = dn(J) \cup (fn(P) \backslash rn(J)) \qquad dn(J \triangleright P) = dn(J)$$
$$fn(D \wedge E) = fn(D) \cup fn(E) \qquad\qquad dn(D \wedge E) = dn(D) \cup dn(E)$$

$$fn(0) = \emptyset \qquad\qquad xn(0) = \emptyset$$
$$fn(x\langle \vec{y}\rangle) = \{x\} \cup \{\vec{y}\} \qquad\qquad xn(x\langle \vec{y}\rangle) = \emptyset$$
$$fn(\mathbf{def}_S \ D \ \mathbf{in} \ A) = (fn(D) \cup fn(P)) \backslash dn(D) \qquad xn(\mathbf{def}_S \ D \ \mathbf{in} \ A) = S \uplus xn(A)$$
$$fn(A|B) = (fn(A) \backslash xn(B)) \cup (fn(B) \backslash xn(A)) \qquad xn(A|B) = xn(A) \uplus xn(B)$$

(b) Free, Defined, Bound and Received names

(STR-NULL)	$\Vdash_S 0$	$\leftrightharpoons$	$\Vdash_S$	
(STR-JOIN)	$\Vdash_S P \mid Q$	$\leftrightharpoons$	$\Vdash_S P,Q$	
(STR-AND)	$D \wedge E \Vdash_S$	$\leftrightharpoons$	$D,E \Vdash_S$	
(STR-DEF)	$\Vdash_S \mathbf{def}_{S'} \ D \ \mathbf{in} \ P$	$\leftrightharpoons$	$D\sigma \Vdash_{S \uplus S'} P\sigma$	σ a globally fresh renaming of $dn(D)\backslash S'$
(RED)	$J \triangleright P \Vdash_S J\sigma$	$\xrightarrow{\tau}$	$J \triangleright P \Vdash_S P\sigma$	
(EXT)	$\Vdash_S x\langle \vec{u}\rangle$	$\xrightarrow{S' x\langle \vec{u}\rangle}$	$\Vdash_{S \uplus S'}$	x is free, and S' are the local names in $\vec{u}$ not in S
(INT)	$\Vdash_{\{x\} \uplus S}$	$\xrightarrow{x\langle \vec{u}\rangle}$	$\Vdash_{\{x\} \uplus S} x\langle \vec{u}\rangle$	$\vec{u}$ contains free, extruded and fresh names

(c) Semantics

Fig. 2. Open-join Calculus

2.3 Join Calculus

This section summarises the basics of the Open-join [15], a conservative extension of Join [14] equipped with the notion of weak bisimulation used in § 4. We rely on an infinite set of names $x, y, u, v, \ldots$ each carrying fixed length tuple of names (denoted as $\vec{u}$). A sorting discipline that avoids arity mismatch is implicitly assumed and only well-sorted terms are considered. Open processes A, processes P, definitions D and patterns J are defined in Figure 2(a). A Join process is either the inert process 0, the asynchronous emission $x\langle \vec{y}\rangle$ of message on port x that carries a tuple of names $\vec{y}$, the process $\mathbf{def} \ D \ \mathbf{in} \ P$ equipped with local ports defined by D, or a parallel composition of processes $P|Q$. An open process A is like a Join process, except that it has open definitions at top-level. The open definition $\mathbf{def}_S \ D \ \mathbf{in} \ P$ exhibits a subset S of names defined by D that are visible from the environment: the *extruded names*. Open processes are identified with ordinary Join processes when the set S of extruded names is empty. A *definition* is a conjunction of elementary reactions $J \triangleright P$ that associate *join-patterns* J with *guarded processes* P.

The sets of defined names dn, received names rn, free names fn and extruded names xn are shown in Figure 2(b) ($\uplus$ denotes the disjoint union of sets). Note that the extruded names of two parallel processes are required to be disjoint because they are introduced by different definitions. Similarly, the extruded names S of $\mathbf{def}_S\ D\ \mathbf{in}\ A$ are disjoint from the extruded names of A. As usual, patterns are required to be disjoint.

The semantics of the Open-join calculus relies on the *open reflexive chemical abstract machine* model (*Open* RCHAM) [15]. A solution of an Open RCHAM is a triple $(\mathcal{R}, \mathcal{S}, \mathcal{A})$, written $\mathcal{R} \Vdash_S \mathcal{A}$, where $\mathcal{A}$ is a multiset of open processes with disjoint sets of extruded names, $\mathcal{R}$ is a multiset of active definitions s.t. $dn(\mathcal{R}) \cap xn(\mathcal{A}) = \emptyset$, and $\mathcal{S} \subseteq dn(\mathcal{R})$ is a set of extruded names (*fn*, *dn* and *xn* lift to multisets in the obvious way). Moves are distinguished between *structural* $\rightleftharpoons$ (or heating/cooling), which stand for the syntactical rearrangement of terms, and reductions $\rightarrow$, which are the basic computational steps. The multiset rewriting rules for Open-join are shown in Figure 2(c). Rule STR-NULL states that 0 can be added or removed from any solution. Rules STR-JOIN and STR-AND stand for the associativity and commutativity of $|$ and $\wedge$, because $\_\,,\_$ is such. STR-DEF denotes the activation of a local definition, which implements a static scoping discipline by properly renaming defined ports by *globally fresh* names.

Reduction rules are labelled either by (i) internal reduction τ, (ii) output messages $Sx\langle\vec{u}\rangle$ on the free port x that extrude the set S of local names, or (iii) $x\langle\vec{u}\rangle$ denoting the intrusion of a message on the already extruded local name x. Rule RED describes the use of an active reaction rule $(J \triangleright P)$ to consume messages forming an instance of J (for a suitable substitution σ, with $dom(\sigma) = rn(J)$), and to produce a new instance $P\sigma$ of its guarded process P. Rule (EXT) consumes messages sent on free names; these messages may extrude some names S' for the first time, thus increasing the set of extruded names. Rule (INT) stands for the intrusion of a message on a defined-extruded name. We remark that rules are local and describe only the portion of the solution that actually reacts. Hence, any rule can be applied in a larger context.

3 Orc vs Petri Nets

In this section we sketch an intuitive explanation of Orc basic orchestration primitives in terms of Petri nets. At first glance, the composition patterns available in Orc can seem easily representable using (workflow) Petri nets. Assume that each Orc expression f is represented by a suitable net N_f with two distinguished places in_f (for getting tokens in input that activate the net) and out_f for publishing tokens. A pipeline between the nets N_f and N_g can be obtained by adding just one transition from out_f to in_g. Similarly, the parallel composition of N_f and N_g can be obtained by adding places $in_{f|g}$ and $out_{f|g}$ with three transitions: (i) from $in_{f|g}$ to in_f and in_g, (ii) from out_f to $out_{f|g}$, and (iii) from out_g to $out_{f|g}$. Finally asymmetric parallel composition can be obtained by adding a place $wh_{f,g}$ with just one token in it and no incoming arc, together with a transition from out_f and $wh_{f,g}$ to in_g (so that such transition can be fired at most once).

However it is easy to realise that the modelling is not as simple as above. Take Example 2.1, where two instances of $Email(\_, a)$ can concurrently run when $Notify(a)$ is invoked. If site invocation is modelled by passing the control-flow token to the net representing $Email$, then the tokens of two different sessions can be mixed! Apart from the cumbersome solution of representing sessions identifiers within tokens, there are two possible solutions to the multi-session problem (i.e., the possibility of re-using parts of the net when for different invocations). The first is to replicate the net corresponding to

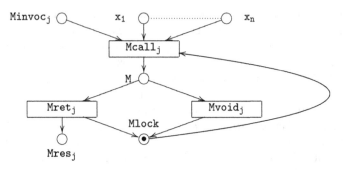

Fig. 3. Net for the invocation of a site M

the body of an expression for each invocation, while the second is using dynamic nets, where fresh ports of the net can be released during the execution. The first alternative is considered here, while § 4 provides an encoding of Orc in Join, as a linguistic counterpart of dynamic nets [9]. Another problem is that expressions can carry arguments, so that more than one input place can be needed (e.g., one for each variable).

In this section we shall focus on Orc^-, a simplified fragment of Orc, where recursion is avoided and values are not considered. Avoiding recursion is necessary in order to have finite nets, indeed each invocation will result in a new instance of the body of the defined expression. Petri nets can encode Orc^- expressions in absence of mobility and when each expression is evaluated at most once (i.e., when mono-session are considered). Multi-sessions require reset arcs and can only be dealt with by serialising the accesses to the re-used part of the net. We prefer to keep the presentation of the Petri net semantics at an informal level. A more technical presentation is postponed to § 4, where the concurrent multi-session problem is tackled by establishing a strong formal correspondence between observational semantics of Orc and its encoding in Join.

Since recursion is banned from Orc^- programs, invocations to site (resp. expressions) can be enumerated and we write $M_j\langle x_1,\ldots,x_n\rangle$ (resp. $E_j\langle x_1,\ldots,x_n\rangle$) to denote the j-th invocation to site M (resp. expression E). The main difference w.r.t. Orc, is that Orc^- uses names (i.e., variables) only for passing signals. For instance, the sequential operator of Orc^- is simplified as $f >> g$. This implies that variables are only required for site invocations and asymmetric parallel composition, say _ **where** $z :\in g$. In the former case, variables are used to render the strict policy of site invocation in the Petri net encoding. In the latter case, z will be used as the output place for the net representing g.

Let $\langle \mathcal{D}, z :\in E(\vec{p})\rangle$ be an Orc^- program. The encoding of an Orc^- expression f into Petri nets is denoted as $[\![f]\!]_{\mathcal{D}}^{f_i,f_o}$ where f_i and f_o are distinguished places (entry and exit points of f). The idea is that f_i is the place for the activation of f and f_o is the place for returning the control. Data dependencies/flows due to asymmetric parallelism are rendered by places associated with variable names, which may coincide with output places of other parts of the net (to store results).

We first consider the translation $[\![M_j\langle x_1,\ldots,x_n\rangle]\!]_{\mathcal{D}}^{\mathtt{Minvoc_j,Mres_j}}$ of the j-th invocation to site M (see Figure 3). The places M and Mlock are shared by all the invocations and Mlock is meant as a lock mechanism for serialising multiple concurrent invocations to M. Indeed, $\mathtt{Mcall_j}$ is enabled only if Mlock contains a token as it initially does. The

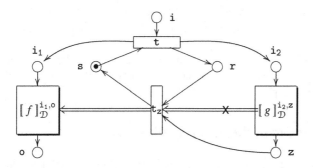

Fig. 4. A schema of net for $[\![\, f \textbf{ where } z :\in g \,]\!]_{\mathcal{D}}^{i,o}$

invocation takes place when $\texttt{Minvoc}_j$ and all places $x_1, \ldots, x_n$ contain a token (i.e., the actual parameters have been evaluated). Moreover, both $\texttt{Mret}_j$ and $\texttt{Mvoid}_j$ put a token into $\texttt{Mlock}$ once they are fired so that the next invocation can proceed. Remarkably, $\texttt{Mret}_j$ and $\texttt{Mvoid}_j$ are mutually exclusive: $\texttt{Mret}_j$ models the case in which M returns a value, while $\texttt{Mvoid}_j$ the case in which no value is returned to the invoker.

If $E\langle z_1, \ldots, z_n \rangle \underline{\Delta} f \in \mathcal{D}$, the j-th invocation of E, say $E_j\langle x_1, \ldots, x_n \rangle$, is translated as $[\![\, E_j\langle x_1, \ldots, x_n \rangle \,]\!]_{\mathcal{D}}^{i,o} = [\![\, f[x_1/z_1, \ldots, x_n/z_n] \,]\!]_{\mathcal{D}}^{i,o}$. For the remaining constructs of Orc^-, the simplest case is $[\![\, 0 \,]\!]_{\mathcal{D}}^{i,o}$ which is the net with a single transition whose preset is the place i and whose postset is empty. For the sequential operator, $[\![\, f \gg g \,]\!]_{\mathcal{D}}^{i,o} = [\![\, f \,]\!]_{\mathcal{D}}^{i,o'} \cup [\![\, g \,]\!]_{\mathcal{D}}^{o',o}$ where o' is a fresh place and where given two nets N_1 and N_2, we write $N_1 \cup N_2$ for the net whose set of places (resp. transitions) is the union of the places (resp. transitions) of N_1 and N_2 and, for each transition $\texttt{t}$ in N_1 and N_2, the preset (resp. postset) of $\texttt{t}$ is the union of the presets (resp. postset) of $\texttt{t}$ in N_1 and N_2. For the parallel operator, given two fresh places i_1 and i_2, $[\![\, f | g \,]\!]_{\mathcal{D}}^{i,o} = [\![\, f \,]\!]_{\mathcal{D}}^{i_1,o} \cup [\![\, g \,]\!]_{\mathcal{D}}^{i_2,o} \cup N$ where N is the net made by a single transition with preset i and postset $\{i_1, i_2\}$.

Where-expressions, say $f \textbf{ where } z :\in g$, require some subtlety, because their evaluation requires that g terminates when a value for z is available. In our encoding, this is modelled by resetting all the places of g.

$$[\![\, f \textbf{ where } z :\in g \,]\!]_{\mathcal{D}}^{i,o} = [\![\, f \,]\!]_{\mathcal{D}}^{i_1,o} \cup [\![\, g \,]\!]_{\mathcal{D}}^{i_2,z} \cup R \qquad (1)$$

where i_1, i_2 are two new places and R is a net for connecting $[\![\, f \,]\!]_{\mathcal{D}}^{i_1,o}$ and $[\![\, g \,]\!]_{\mathcal{D}}^{i_2,z}$ and for resetting the places of $[\![\, g \,]\!]_{\mathcal{D}}^{i_2,z}$. More precisely, R contains

1. the place i together with two fresh places s and r and a token in s;
2. a fresh transition t such that ${}^\bullet t = \{i, s\}$ and $t^\bullet = \{i_1, i_2, r\}$;
3. a fresh transition t_z such that ${}^\bullet t_z = \{z, r\}$ and $t_z{}^\bullet$ includes s and the set of all the places in $[\![\, f \,]\!]_{\mathcal{D}}^{i_1,o}$ corresponding to the occurrences of z in f, moreover, for each place p in $[\![\, g \,]\!]_{\mathcal{D}}^{i_2,z}$ (including i_2 and z), there is a reset arc from p to t_z.

A pictorial representation of $[\![\, f \textbf{ where } z :\in g \,]\!]_{\mathcal{D}}^{i,o}$ is given in Figure 4 where the bold boxes represent the nets for f and g; the double arrow is the set of arcs described in 3 and the crossed double arrow is the set or reset arcs described in 3. Places s and r

serialise the activation of f and g. When a token is available on z, then t_z can be fired: it distributes the token to all the occurrences of z in f, resets g and enables further activation of the net by restoring the token in s.

Reset arcs are not needed if just mono-sessions are considered. As an alternative to reset arcs, inhibitor arcs [13] could have been used. However, the net R in (1) would have been more complex.

4   Encoding Orc in the Join Calculus

When encoding Orc⁻ either into reset or inhibitor nets, different evaluations of certain expressions are computed sequentially (e.g., site calls, where-expressions). Since in general it is possible to write expressions involving an unbounded number of concurrently executing sessions, it is evident that any static net topology will either introduce some serialisation or mix tokens from different sessions.

In this section, we propose an encoding of full Orc into Join in which different evaluations of the same expression can be computed concurrently. This is achieved by taking advantage of the reflexive mechanism provided by Join and dynamic nets that allows for the dynamic creation of places and transitions. The main strategy of the encoding is to associate a fresh portion of a net to any evaluation of an Orc expression. That is, if the evaluation of an expression f can be represented by a net N_f, we assure that any evaluation of f is performed by a fresh copy of N_f. In this way confusions among concurrent evaluations of the same expression are avoided.

Definition 4.1. *Let* $\mathbb{O} = \langle \mathcal{D}, z :\in E(P) \rangle$ *be an* Orc *orchestrator. Then, the corresponding* Join *process is* $P_{\mathbb{O}} = \{\![\mathbb{O}]\!\}$, *where* $\{\![\_]\!\}$ *is inductively defined in Figure 5.*

We comment on the definitions in Figure 5. Any Orc definition $D \in \mathcal{D}$ becomes a local definition $\{\![D]\!\}$ of the corresponding Join process $P_{\mathbb{O}}$, while the initial expression $z :\in E(p_1, \ldots, p_n)$ becomes the active process $\{\![E(p_1, \ldots, p_n)]\!\}_z$. Note that the initial expression $E(p_1, \ldots, p_n)$ is encoded by considering a context z (i.e., the channel z encodes the homonymous variable). In this way, $P_{\mathbb{O}}$ will send a message $z\langle v \rangle$ for any value v obtained during the evaluation of $E(p_1, \ldots, p_n)$. Any Orc definition $E(x_1, \ldots, x_n) \triangleq f$ is translated as a basic rule $E(q_1, \ldots, q_n, z) \triangleright \{\![f]\!\}_z$, where z is a fresh name used for returning the values produced during the evaluation of f, i.e., z is used for implementing the usual continuation passing style of Join.

All remaining rules define the translation of expressions. In particular, the inert Orc expression 0 is translated as the inert Join process 0, while the constant expression c is encoded as $z\langle c \rangle$, i.e., as the assignment of the unique value c to z. Differently, the encoding of an expression consisting of a variable x is translated as a message $x\langle z \rangle$. In fact, as we will see later, we associate any Orc variable with a basic Join definition that answers any message $x\langle z \rangle$ with $z\langle v \rangle$ if x has been assigned a value v. Moreover, any request $x\langle z \rangle$ will be blocked until a value is assigned to x.

The invocation $M(p_1, \ldots, p_n)$ of a service M is translated as a process that starts by evaluating all actual parameters p_i. Since actual parameters can be only constants or variables, the evaluation of $\{\![p_i]\!\}_{y_i}$ will finish by producing messages $y_i\langle x_i \rangle$ on fresh names y_i. Hence, the unique local definition is enabled only when all actual parameters

$$\{[0 = \langle \mathcal{D}, z :\in E(P)\rangle]\} = \mathbf{def} \bigwedge_{D\in\mathcal{D}} \{[D]\} \mathbf{\ in\ } \{[E(P)]\}_z$$

$$\{[E(q_1,\ldots,q_n) \triangleq f]\} = E(q_1,\ldots,q_n,z) \triangleright \{[f]\}_z \quad \text{with } z \notin \{q_1,\ldots,q_n\}$$

$$\{[0]\}_z = 0$$

$$\{[c]\}_z = z\langle c\rangle$$

$$\{[x]\}_z = x\langle z\rangle$$

$$\{[M(p_1,\ldots,p_n)]\}_z = \mathbf{def\ } y_1\langle x_1\rangle | \ldots | y_n\langle x_n\rangle \triangleright \mathbf{def\ } k\langle v\rangle | tok\langle\rangle \triangleright z\langle v\rangle$$
$$\mathbf{in\ } M\langle x_1,\ldots,x_n,k\rangle \mid tok\langle\rangle$$
$$\mathbf{in\ } \{[p_1]\}_{y_1} | \ldots | \{[p_n]\}_{y_n}$$

$$\{[X(p_1,\ldots,p_n)]\}_z = \mathbf{def\ } y_1\langle x_1\rangle | \ldots | y_n\langle x_n\rangle | y\langle M\rangle \triangleright \mathbf{def\ } k\langle v\rangle | tok\langle\rangle \triangleright z\langle v\rangle$$
$$\mathbf{in\ } M\langle x_1,\ldots,x_n,k\rangle \mid tok\langle\rangle$$
$$\mathbf{in\ } \{[p_1]\}_{y_1} | \ldots | \{[p_n]\}_{y_n} | \{[X]\}_y$$

$$\{[E(p_1,\ldots,p_n)]\}_z = \mathbf{def\ } \bigwedge_{p\in\{p_1,\ldots,p_n\}\cap\mathcal{C}} fwd_p\langle k\rangle \triangleright k\langle p\rangle$$
$$\mathbf{in\ } E(\langle p_1\rangle,\ldots,\langle p_n\rangle,z)$$
$$\text{where } \langle p_i\rangle = p_i \text{ if } p_i \notin \mathcal{C} \text{ and } \langle p_i\rangle = fwd_{p_i} \text{ otherwise}$$

$$\{[f \mid g]\}_z = \{[f]\}_z \mid \{[g]\}_z$$

$$\{[f > x > g]\}_z = \mathbf{def\ } w\langle v\rangle \triangleright \mathbf{def\ } x\langle y\rangle \mid val_x\langle u\rangle \triangleright y\langle u\rangle \mid val_x\langle u\rangle$$
$$\mathbf{in\ } \{[g]\}_z \mid val_x\langle v\rangle$$
$$\mathbf{in\ } \{[f]\}_w$$

$$\{[g \text{ where } x :\in f]\}_z = \mathbf{def\ } x\langle y\rangle \mid val_x\langle u\rangle \triangleright y\langle u\rangle \mid val_x\langle u\rangle$$
$$\wedge\ w\langle v\rangle \mid tok\langle\rangle \triangleright val_x\langle v\rangle$$
$$\mathbf{in\ } \{[g]\}_z \mid \{[f]\}_w \mid tok\langle\rangle$$

Fig. 5. Encoding of an Orc Orchestrator in Join

have been completely evaluated. Moreover, the firing of the local rule creates two fresh ports: k and tok and a unique firing rule. Channel k indicates the port where the orchestrator awaits the answers of the invoked service (We assume the definition of any site to be extended in order to receive this extra parameter.) Channel tok assures that just one answer is considered for any invocation. In fact, there is only one message $tok\langle\rangle$, which is consumed (and it is not generated anymore) when the first message on k is received.

In case the name of the invoked service is the variable X, then X has to be evaluated before the invocation, just like any other actual parameter. The name of the site M will be returned as he value of X on port y.

The use of an Orc definition $E(p_1,\ldots,p_n)$ differs from the invocation of a service in the fact that definitions are called by following a lazy evaluation, i.e., parameters are not evaluated before the call. Hence, invocations of E can take place even though some of the formal parameters $p_1,\ldots,p_n$ have not been initialised. The local ports fwd_p introduced by the encoding if $p \in \mathcal{C}$ allow the constant parameters to be used as variables inside the expression defining E (see Example 4.1).

The encoding of a parallel composition $f|g$ corresponds to the parallel composition of the encodings of f and g. Note that both encoded expressions produce results on the same channel z. On the other hand, the sequential composition $f > x > g$ is translated as a process that starts by evaluating $\{[f]\}_w$ (i.e., the encoding of f) whose values will be sent as messages to the local port w. Hence, any message on w corresponds to the activation of a new evaluation of g. In fact, the local definition, which is enabled with a message $w\langle v\rangle$, will create a fresh copy of the encoding of g, which will evaluate g by considering the particular value v produced by f.

The last rule handles the translation of asymmetric parallel composition. Note that the encodings of f and g are activated concurrently. Unlike sequential composition, there is a unique copy of $\{[g]\}$ and a unique instance of the variable x. In fact, asymmetric composition requires to evaluate g just for one value of f. The unique message tok assures that only one value produced by $\{[f]\}$ will be set to the variable x.

Example 4.1. Let $\mathcal{O} = \langle\{d\}, z :\in Invoke(StockQuote, Sun)\rangle$,   with d : $Invoke(m, n)\underline{\Delta}\,m(n)$. The corresponding Join process is as follows.

$$\{[\mathcal{O}]\} = \mathbf{def}\ Invoke\langle m, n, z\rangle \rhd \mathbf{def}\ y_1\langle x_1\rangle|y\langle M\rangle \rhd \mathbf{def}\ k\langle v\rangle\mid tok\langle\rangle \rhd z\langle v\rangle$$
$$\mathbf{in}\ M\langle x_1, k\rangle\mid tok\langle\rangle$$
$$\mathbf{in}\ n\langle y_1\rangle\mid m\langle y\rangle$$
$$\mathbf{in}\ \mathbf{def}\ fwd_{StockQuote}\langle k\rangle \rhd k\langle StockQuote\rangle$$
$$\wedge\ fwd_{Sun}\langle k\rangle \rhd k\langle Sun\rangle$$
$$\mathbf{in}\ Invoke\langle fwd_{StockQuote}, fwd_{Sun}, z\rangle$$

Note the difference when calling a local definition (i.e., *Invoke*) and when invoking a service (i.e., *StockQuote*). In particular, actual parameters are not evaluated when calling a local definition. Moreover, a new forwarder is created for any constant parameter. In this case, the ports $fwd_{StockQuote}$ and fwd_{Sun} are introduced and are used as actual parameters. In this way the definition of *Invoke* may handle all its parameters as if they were variables. In fact, when rule $Invoke\langle m, n, z\rangle \rhd \ldots$ is fired by consuming the token $Invoke\langle fwd_{StockQuote}, fwd_{Sun}, z\rangle$, then the arguments m and n are evaluated by sending the messages $fwd_{Sun}\langle y_1\rangle$ and $fwd_{StockQuote}\langle y\rangle$, which will return the corresponding constants, i.e., the messages $y_1\langle Sun\rangle$ and $y\langle StockQuote\rangle$ will be produced.

The remaining part of this section is devoted to show the correspondence among Orc processes and their encoded form. The following definition introduces the equivalence notion we will use to compare Orc processes with their encoded form, which is a kind of weak bisimulation. In the following, given an Orc label α, the corresponding Join label is denoted with $\overline{\alpha}$ and it is defined as $\overline{M_k(v)} = \{k\}M\langle v, k\rangle$, $\overline{k?v} = k\langle v\rangle$, $\overline{!v} = \mathbb{0}z\langle v\rangle$.

Definition 4.2 (Weak Bisimulation). *Let* $\mathcal{O} = \langle\mathcal{D}, z :\in E(p_1, \ldots, p_n)\rangle$ *be an orchestrator, and P be a* Join *process. We call weak bisimulation any relation* $\mathcal{R}$ *satisfying the following condition:* $\mathcal{O}\,\mathcal{R}\,P$ *iff*

1. $\mathcal{O} \xrightarrow{\alpha} \mathcal{O}'$ *and* $\alpha \neq \tau$ *then* $P \to^* \xrightarrow{\overline{\alpha}} P'$ *and* $\mathcal{O}'\,\mathcal{R}\,P'$
2. $\mathcal{O} \xrightarrow{\tau} \mathcal{O}'$ *then* $P \xrightarrow{\tau}^* P'$ *and* $\mathcal{O}'\,\mathcal{R}\,P'$
3. $P \xrightarrow{\overline{\alpha}} P'$ *and* $\alpha \neq k\langle v\rangle$ *then* $\mathcal{O} \to^* \xrightarrow{\alpha} \mathcal{O}'$ *and* $\mathcal{O}'\,\mathcal{R}\,P'$
4. $P \xrightarrow{k\langle v\rangle} P'$ *then either (i)* $\mathcal{O} \xrightarrow{k?v} \mathcal{O}'$ *and* $\mathcal{O}'\,\mathcal{R}\,P'$, *or (ii)* $\mathcal{O}\xrightarrow{k?v}\!\!\!\!\!/$ *and* $\mathcal{O}\,\mathcal{R}\,P'$
5. $P \xrightarrow{\tau} P'$ *then* $\mathcal{O} \xrightarrow{\tau}^* \mathcal{O}$ *and* $\mathcal{O}\,\mathcal{R}\,P'$

The largest relation $\mathcal{R}$ *is said the weak bisimilarity and it is written* $\approx$.

All rules but the fourth one are quite standard. In fact, rule 4 handles the case in which a Join process performs an intrusion on an already extruded name. The only possibility is when the process receives an answer for a site call. Hence, such step should be mimicked by the orchestrator (i.e., the condition $\mathcal{O} \xrightarrow{k?v} \mathcal{O}'$). Nevertheless, this situation may take place only when the first answer is received. In fact, the Join encoding of an Orc site call ignores all the answers following the first one. On the other end, the open semantics of Join allows for the intrusion of those messages (even if they cannot be exploited). Hence, the weak bisimulation says that the intrusion of extra answers does not change the behaviour of the encoded form (i.e., $\mathcal{O} \xrightarrow{k?v}$ and $\mathcal{O} \, \mathcal{R} \, P'$).

In the following, we show that there exists a weak bisimulation among Orc orchestrators and their encoded form when considering a non-killing version of Orc, that is, a version in which asymmetric composition does not imply the killing of the residual of f. In fact we consider the following version of the rule (ASYMPRUNE).

$$\frac{f \xrightarrow{!c} f'}{g \text{ where } x :\in f \xrightarrow{\tau} g[c/x] \mid (0 \text{ where } z :\in f')} \text{ (NOTKILL-WHERE)}$$

Note that g is evaluated as in ordinary Orc just for one value produced by f. Nevertheless, the residual f' of f is allowed to continue its execution, but the obtained values are thrown away since 0 appears as the left-hand-side of the clause **where**. We remark that (NOTKILL-WHERE) does not significantly alters Orc's semantics and it can be envisaged as an implementation of the g **where** $x :\in f$ construct that simply ignores all values published by f but the first one.

Lemma 4.1 (Correspondence). *When considering rule* NOTKILL-WHERE, $\mathcal{O} \approx \{[\mathcal{O}]\}$.

Proof (Sketch). The proof follows by coinduction, showing that the following relation R is a weak bisimulation.

$$R = \{(\mathcal{O}, P) | \{[\mathcal{O}]\} \xrightarrow{\tau} {}^* P\} \cup \{(\mathcal{O}', P') | \mathcal{O} \xrightarrow{\alpha} \mathcal{O}' and \{[\mathcal{O}]\} \xrightarrow{\tau} {}^* \xrightarrow{\overline{\alpha}} \xrightarrow{\tau} {}^* P'\}$$

Actually the proof is up-to strong-bisimulation [15] on Join processes, since we consider terms up-to the relation $\equiv_e$ defined below

1. if $P \rightleftharpoons^* Q$ then $P \equiv_e Q$, i.e., P and Q are structural equivalent;
2. $P \equiv_e P | \text{def } D \text{ in } 0$, i.e., useless definitions are removed; and
3. if $Q \equiv \text{def}_S \, D \text{ in def}_{\{k\}} \, k\langle \vec{v} \rangle | tok\langle \rangle \triangleright z\langle v \rangle \text{ in } R \mid k\langle \vec{u} \rangle \rightarrow^* Q'$ implies $Q' \equiv \text{def}_S \, D' \text{ in}$ $\text{def}_{\{k\}} \, k\langle \vec{v} \rangle | tok\langle \rangle \triangleright z\langle \vec{v} \rangle \text{ in } R' \mid k\langle \vec{u} \rangle$ and $P \equiv \text{def}_S \, D \text{ in } R \rightarrow^* \text{def}_S \, D' \text{ in } R'$ and $tok \notin fn(R)$, then $P \equiv_e Q$, i.e., intruded messages that do not alter the behaviour of the process can be removed.

Note that $\equiv_e$ is a strong bisimulation (proved by standard coinduction).

Finally, we show that the computed values of ordinary Orc orchestrators corresponds with the computed values of their encoded form.

Theorem 4.1. $\mathcal{O} \rightarrow^* \xrightarrow{!v} \mathcal{O}'$ *iff* $\{[\mathcal{O}]\} \rightarrow^* \xrightarrow{z\langle v \rangle} P$

Proof (Sketch). The proof follows by (i) showing that the results computed by Orc and its not killing version are the same and (ii) by using Lemma 4.1.

5   Concluding Remarks

Orchestration paradigms can be roughly categorised into three key trends:

- technology-driven languages: all XML dialects and standardisation efforts (e.g., WS-BPEL [8], XLANG [27], WSFL [16]);
- model oriented: workflow aspects are prominent (e.g., Petri nets [24,3], YAWL [4]);
- process algebraic or messaging-based: the orchestration is ruled by communication primitives (e.g., CCS [17], pi-calculus [18], and Join calculus [14]).

A few years ago, when the series of WS-FM Workshop started, each trend contained several proposals substantially separated from the other two trends, with different background, scope and applications. For example, a still ongoing debate [25,1,2] adverses the use of workflow to that of pi-calculus and it has led to the establishment of an expert forum (the Process Modelling Group [22]) to investigate how the two different approaches can solve typical service composition challenges, like van der Aalst et al.'s *workflow patterns* [28,5], and compare the solutions. Workflow enthusiasts advocate that name mobility and message passing are not really necessary, while pi-calculus enthusiasts are confident that mobility aspects play a prominent role in dynamic assembling of services. The discussion has led also to the combined use of ideas from both world, like in the case of SMAWL [26], a CCS variant.

We have investigated the modelling of the orchestration language Orc in Petri nets and the Join calculus. Orc is an interesting proposal that can hardly fit in the orchestration categories discussed above. Our comparisons have allowed us to identify some key features of Orc, that are not so evident from its original definition. First, pipelining, site calls and asymmetric parallel composition involve dynamic creation of names and links, that cannot find a natural encoding in Petri nets with static topology, unless seriously restricting Orc. Second, the pruning associated with asymmetric conflict is a rather peculiar and powerful operation not common in process calculi. In fact, one can argue that it is also not very realistic to impose atomic cancelling of complex activities in a distributed setting (especially when side effects due to e.g. name passing and extrusion could have taken place). Nevertheless, from the point of view of process calculi, cancelling can be rendered as equivalent to the disabling of the input ports where the cancelled activities could send their data. In Petri nets and Join the disabling is modelled by void tokens that enable just one occurrence of certain events, but Join has the advantage of not introducing cleaning activities and serialisation of site calls, which are instead necessary for dealing with multiple invocations in the Petri net encodings of § 3.

Finally, we mention that Join appears to be adequate as coordination language since it can suitably encode Orc. Remarkably, Join, despite its thinness, also results a respectable language for choreography and computing. Finally, Join is perhaps also more suitable as coordination/orchestration language than e.g. pi-calculus because its join-pattern construct yields more flexible and convenient communication patterns.

Acknowledgement. The authors thank the anonymous reviewers for their valuable comments and suggestions that contributed to improve this work.

References

1. W.M.P. van der Aalst. Why workflow is NOT just a pi process. *BPTrends*, pages 1–2, 2004.
2. W.M.P. van der Aalst. Pi calculus versus Petri nets. *BPTrends*, pages 1–11, 2005.
3. W.M.P. van der Aalst and A.H.M. ter Hofstede. Workflow patterns: On the expressive power of (Petri-net-based) workflow languages. *Proc. of CPN'02*, volume 560 of *DAIMI*, pages 1–20. University of Aarhus, 2002.
4. W.M.P. van der Aalst and A.H.M. ter Hofstede. Yawl: yet another workflow language. *Inf. Syst.*, 30(4):245–275, 2005.
5. W.M.P. van der Aalst, A.H.M. ter Hofstede, B. Kiepuszewski, and A.P. Barros. Workflow patterns. *Distributed and Parallel Databases*, 14(1):5–51, 2003.
6. T. Araki and T. Kasami. Some decision problems related to the reachability problem for Petri nets. *TCS*, 3(1):85–104, 1976.
7. N. Benton, L. Cardelli, and C. Fournet. Modern concurrency abstractions for $C^{\sharp}$. *Proc. of ECOOP'02*, volume 2374 of *LNCS*, pages 415–440. Springer, 2002.
8. BPEL Specification (v. 1.1). http://www.ibm.com/developerworks/library/ws-bpel.
9. M. Buscemi and V. Sassone. High-level Petri nets as type theories in the join calculus. *Proc. of FoSSaCS'01*, volume 2030 of *LNCS*, pages 104–120. Springer, 2001.
10. S. Conchon and F. Le Fessant. Jocaml: Mobile agents for Objective-Caml. *Proc. of ASA/MA'99*, pages 22–29. IEEE Computer Society, 1999.
11. W.R. Cook, S. Patwardhan, and J. Misra. Workflow patterns in Orc, 2006. Submitted.
12. C. Dufourd, A. Finkel, and Ph. Schnoebelen. Reset nets between decidability and undecidability. *Proc. of ICALP'98*, volume 1443 of *LNCS*, pages 103–115. Springer, 1998.
13. M. J. Flynn and T. Agerwala. Comments on capabilities, limitations and correctness of Petri nets. *SIGARCH Computer Architecture News*, pages 81–86, 1973.
14. C. Fournet and G. Gonthier. The reflexive chemical abstract machine and the join calculus. *Proc. of POPL'96*, pages 372–385. ACM Press, 1996.
15. C. Fournet and C. Laneve. Bisimulations in the join calculus. *TCS*, 266:569–603, 2001.
16. F. Leymann. WSFL Specification (v. 1.0). http://www-306.ibm.com/software/solutions/webservices/pdf/WSFL.pdf.
17. R. Milner. *A Calculus of Communicating Systems*, volume 92 of *LNCS*. Springer, 1980.
18. R. Milner, J. Parrow, and J. Walker. A calculus of mobile processes, I and II. *Inform. and Comput.*, 100(1):1–40,41–77, 1992.
19. J. Misra and W. R. Cook. Orc - An orchestration language. http://www.cs.utexas.edu/~wcook/projects/orc/.
20. J. Misra and W. R. Cook. Computation orchestration: A basis for wide-area computing. *Journal of Software and Systems Modeling*, 2006. To appear.
21. C.A. Petri. *Kommunikation mit Automaten*. PhD thesis, Institut für Instrumentelle Mathematik, Bonn, 1962.
22. The Process Modelling Group web site. http://www.process-modelling-group.org/.
23. F. Puhlmann and M. Weske. Using the pi-calculus for formalising workflow patterns. *Proc. of BPM'05*, volume 3649 of *LNCS*, pages 153–168. Springer, 2005.
24. W. Reisig. *Petri Nets: An Introduction*. EATCS Monographs on Theoretical Computer Science. Springer Verlag, 1985.
25. H. Smith and P. Fingar. Workflow is just a pi process. *BPTrends*, pages 1–36, 2004.
26. C. Stefansen. SMAWL: A small workflow language based on CCS. *CAiSE'05 Short Paper Proceedings*, volume 161 of *CEUR Workshop Proceedings*. CEUR-WS.org, 2005.
27. S. Thatte. XLANG: Web Services for Business Process Design. http://www.gotdotnet.com/team/xml_wsspecs/xlang-c/default.htm, 2001.
28. Workflow Patterns web site. http://is.tm.tue.nl/research/patterns/.

Dynamic Constraint-Based Invocation of Web Services[*]

Diletta Cacciagrano, Flavio Corradini,
Rosario Culmone, and Leonardo Vito

University of Camerino, Polo Informatico, 62032, Camerino, Italy
`name.surname@unicam.it`

Abstract. For an automatic invocation of Web services, concrete platforms allow the client-side generation of stubs by means of suitable primitives of programming languages. In this setting, we propose a framework
that preserves static and dynamic integrity constraints of invocation parameters. The main ingredients of the framework are: (i) WSDL [16],
a Web services description language that describes the interface, the semantics and the protocol for invoking Web services, (ii) CLiX [10], a language for constraints specification in XML that allows the specification
of static and dynamic integrity constraints of Web service parameters by
means of logic formulas; (iii) reflection mechanisms for managing complex user-defined types. The proposed framework is entirely based on
XML-based technologies and allows only provably correct Web services
invocations be forwarded by client-side checking CLiX formulas.

1 A Fast Introduction of Web Services

It is often very hard to guarantee automatic interoperability among different
applications. A typical scenario is the Web, where clients applications may automatically invoke Web services. This is often very difficult to achieve for several
reasons (as, for instance, lack of semantic information exposed by interaction
interfaces or their heterogeneity). Object-oriented programming has suggested
a black-box approach, where the internal working of the system is hidden while
its functionalities are exposed to the environment via a suitable description of
the inputs and outputs. This way of doing has been indeed imported within the
Web Services technology. The functionality of a service over the Web is a special
signature that describes how it can be properly invoked. The Web Services Description Language (WSDL) [16] relies on this technique. It is an XML language
that contains information about the interfaces, the semantics and the protocol for invoking Web services. A WSDL document is analogous to a collection
of methods and their signatures, together with information about the syntax
of the inputs and the outputs. In particular, the parameters types are defined
by XML Schema [23]. Unfortunately, only simple static constraints can be expressed. Regarding communication protocols, one of the main WSDL proposal

---

[*] This work was supported by the Investment Funds for Basic Research (MIUR-FIRB)
project Laboratory of Interdisciplinary Technologies in Bioinformatics (LITBIO) and
by Halley Informatica.

M. Bravetti, M. Nuñes, and G. Zavattaro (Eds.): WS-FM 2006, LNCS 4184, pp. 138–147, 2006.
© Springer-Verlag Berlin Heidelberg 2006

is SOAP HTTP Binding. This allows services to be invoked by merely textual messages via HTTP protocol.

2   A Constraint-Based Interface

Concrete platforms provide the client-side generation of stubs from WSDL descriptions. Stubs allow Web services to be invoked by programming languages (e.g. Java). Their basic functionalities are marshalling and unmarshalling of service parameters. The former is used to serialize parameters to XML format while the latter acts as the vice versa; namely, it translates data from the serialized format (XML format) to the format suitable for the programming language.

However, a stub has also to allow a service to be properly invoked, e.g. it has to manage complex (user defined) types, and to respect static and dynamic integrity constraints of the invocation parameters. For instance, consider a Web service implementing banking functionalities. Suppose that

a. the input parameters represent a bank account: if the data on which the service is invoked do not represent a valid account number, then it is difficult to make proper use of it. This is an example of static constraint, since the validity of the data can be expressed by a static statement (e.g. *the account number must range over a given numeric set*).

b. the input parameters represent birth country and town of a customer: obviously, only some combinations of values are sound, since the hometown has to belong to the specified country. This is an example of inter-dependence constraint, since the parameters are related each other.

c. the input parameters represent an exempt from tax on profit investment, where the exemption holds only in the case the investment dates back more than a year ago: this is an example of dynamic constraint, since the soundness of the data depends on their values.

XML Schema does not allow complex constraints to be expressed: it is impossible to define inter-dependencies (example b) and dynamic constraints (example c). It follows that stubs, generated only from WSDL descriptions, do not allow Web services to be properly invoked.

To fill this gap, more expressive technologies have to support XML Schema.

A first approach is based on ontologies. XML metadata can be easily described as simplified ontologies, for instance in OWL-S language [19]. Numerous works (e.g. [3]) have shown that, when describing inputs and outputs using ontological concepts, the inferences supported by the underlying ontology language can be exploited in order to improve service discovery. However, this approach turns out to be expensive to express only integrity constraints, since client and service data structures have to be aligned (i.e. we need a mediator).

A second approach is based on logic languages. Describing parameters, types and constraints, not just by referencing a specific concept but via either a logic assertion model or some rule mechanism, is undoubtedly a more flexible technique, allowing an elaboration independent from the specific ontology. In a logic language, constraints can be expressed by logic sentences. RuleML [22], for instance, is an XML-based language that allows rules to be expressed as modular components in a declarative way. RuleML uses distinct, standard XML tags to define facts and rules; moreover, it can specify queries, inferences and mappings between Web ontologies. However, some inconvenient features have to be remarked:

- It handles mathematical operators like symbols, making mathematical operations difficult. We are unable to express rules using $>$ or $<$ operators that execute properly in the inference engines.
- Getting one RuleML file to execute in multiple languages is difficult, due to differences in fundamental processing between symbolic reasoning and Object-oriented programming. The use of variables and *individual* values in RuleML can set off a non-uniform execution of the rules.
- Building rules that fire properly is tricky in any inference engine: rules must be designed so that data can be captured as facts that trigger the firing of appropriate rules.

We believe that any approach considering XML metadata as simplified ontologies tries to merge two incomparable concepts. In fact:

- Ontologies are domain models and XML Schema defines document structures;
- Ontologies provide a structure and a vocabulary to describe the semantics contained in on-line information sources, while the purpose of XML Schema is prescribing the structure of documents and providing a shared vocabulary for the users of a specific XML application;
- In an ontological setting, the information is defined by means of semi-structured natural language, while XML Schema allows information to be expressed in a tabular style.

While a semantic-based approach - as ontologies and logic languages - is not agile and suitable to only express integrity constraints, a simple syntactic approach is powerful enough to this purpose.

The UML standard has been already equipped with an Object Constraint Language (OCL) [21], in order to allow modelers to express unambiguously nuances of meaning that the graphical elements (class diagrams) can not convey by themselves. It is a declarative language for the specification of functional behavior of single software system elements, as well as global constraints on valid system states. It supports as constraints mainly invariants on class diagrams, as well as functional specifications of methods by preconditions and postconditions. An OCL sentence can be written as follows:

```
context TypeName TypeRule: BooleanExpression
```

`BooleanExpression` is any boolean expression with operators, attributes and set of elements in the scope of `TypeName`: the result of any OCL sentence interpretation is a boolean value. `TypeName` denotes a set of either classes or operations subject to constraints, and `TypeRule` denotes the constraint type, namely invariant, precondition and postcondition, denoted by `inv`, `pre` and `post`, respectively. The keyword `context` introduces the expression context. Operators `forall` and `exists` can enrich boolean sentences: for this reason OCL can be considered a First-order logic language.

Unfortunately, OCL is not based on XML syntax: hence, it is not suitable to integrate WSDL descriptions and to share constraints within a limited scope of distributed networks.

Schematron [13] and CLiX [10] (Constraint Language in XML) are two of the most used XML-based constraint languages. However, CLiX turns out to be better to express constraints in XML, since it overcomes some drawbacks of the former language (missing hierarchical structure of tests, lacking recursive expressions, differing degree of expressiveness).

CLiX is a logic language, used both to constrain XML documents internally and to execute inter-document checks. It allows constraints to be described using a mixture of First-order logic and XPath expressions [15]. Existential and universal quantifiers are used to iterate over sets of nodes and boolean operators allow to build more complex formulas. Every construct in the language makes use of XPath to retrieve elements from documents for processing.

CLiX formulas can express referential integrity properties among complex data. For instance, suppose to define a graph in XML as follows:

```
<graph>
  <vertex id="0">
    <edge idref="5">
    <edge idref="6">
  </vertex>
<vertex id="5">
<vertex id="6">
</graph>
```

XML Schema is not powerful enough to define a semantic property like *the graph must be connex*. However, this property can be easily expressed by means of the following CLiX rule:

```
<rule id="valid edges">
  <forall var="eID" in="/vertex/edge/@to">
    <exists var="vID" in="/vertex/@id">
      <equal op1="$vID" op2="$eID" />
    </exists>
  </forall>
</rule>
```

3   A Constraint-Based XML Framework for Client-Side Stubs Automatic Generation

In this section, we show in detail an XML-based framework allowing the client-side automatic generation of stubs, for properly invoking Web services.

The service WSDL description is *enriched* with CLiX logic formulas, expressing static and dynamic integrity constraints of the invocation parameters. CLiX formulas are linked to the WSDL document by a namespace: it follows that CLiX is independent from the service description, i.e. every (XML) formalism can be freely chosen to describe the service.

The Web service makes available the WSDL description of its signature, the XML Schema modeling inputs and outputs and the set of its specific CLiX formulas. On the other side, the client activity consists on two steps:

1. producing a stub by means of a concrete platform, starting from the WSDL description and the XML Schema;
2. checking the (XML) serialized translation of the generated stub w.r.t. the set of CLiX formulas, before forwarding the service invocation.

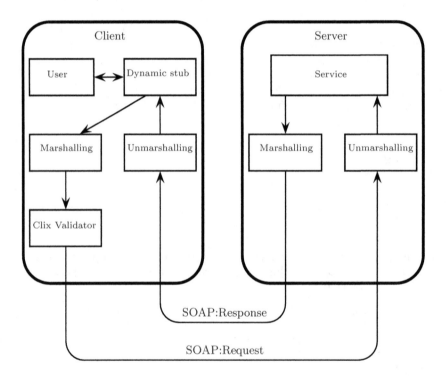

More in details, WSDL2Java [17] is the concrete platform used to translate any enriched WSDL file in a Java language stub. This phase consists of the standard XML Schema validation procedure and the management of complex (user defined) types by means of Java reflection mechanisms; CLiX constraints are ignored.

Then, the stub is serialized in XML format and checked w.r.t the associated CLiX formulas by OpenCLiXML [11], an open source CLiX validator.

Finally, the service invocation is forwarded by the client via SOAP only when checked correct: as a consequence, client and server need to exchange very few messages for successfully completing the invocation protocol.

Regarding performance aspects, on the one hand, CLiX constraints do not noticeably increase the SOAP messages size; on the other hand, the validation procedure weighs down the client elaboration. However, the considerable messages decrement over the network cancels out the overhead price.

Regarding semantic aspects, the meaning of parameters and service functionality is ignored: in fact, the framework enables a client to properly invoke a service, without knowing the semantics of its inputs and outputs. This is not a real shortcoming. Indeed, we can think of adding an ontological *mapping*, i.e. a semantic function which encodes identifiers into concepts, rather than a full ontological model, thanks to the fact that both inter-dependencies and dynamic constraints of the invocation parameters are expressed in XML syntax.

In the following, we give some more details about how to complex types and integrity constraints are handled.

3.1   Step 1: How to Handle Complex Types

WSDL2Java [17] is a concrete platform translating WSDL descriptions into stubs for invoking services by Java language.

A stub is a set of Java classes to set SOAP endpoints, as well as to handle complex types (input and output service parameters). For our purpose, WSDL2Java has been modified, in order to allow a complex types handling *on the fly*.

We show the main methods:

getAllOperation: The method returns the set of any available service operation.

getReturnType: The method takes an operation name and returns the output type name of the given operation.

getParametersType: The method takes an operation name and returns the set of its input parameters.

getClassParameter: The method takes a parameter name and returns the Class object of the specified parameter.

invokeMetod: The method takes an operation name (SOAP), a set of Object objects (the set of operation parameters) and returns the result of the Web service invocation in Object format.

3.2   Step 2: How to Handle Integrity Constraints

OpenCLiXML [11] is an open source Java implementation of the freely available CLiX specification from Systemwire [9]. The validator provides optimized rules processing against data represented in XML, including inter-document checks. For our purpose, the marshalling operation has been enriched with

OpenCLiXML, in order to support the validation of (XML) serialized stubs w.r.t. both XML Schema and CLiX formulas.

4 An Example: Electric Circuits and Kirchhoff's First Law

A lot of computational problems (flow control, GIS, optimization, etc.) make use of graphs; constraints can be very complex and can involve several parameters. Consider, for instance, a Web service able to elaborate descriptions of electric circuits verifying Kirchhoff's First law. The service models a circuit as an oriented and weighted graph. Vertexes and edges symbolize crossing points and conductors, respectively. The edges are oriented and weighted, since direction and intensity are parameters characterizing the electricity.

In this case, a circuit verifies Kirchhoff's First law if and only if

> At any point in it, where charge density is not changing in time, the sum of currents flowing towards that point is equal to the sum of currents flowing away from that point.

A *sound* electric circuit, i.e. an electric circuit verifying Kirchhoff's First law, can be modeled by a graph, equipped by the following constraints:

1. There is no loop;
2. There is no *source vertex*, i.e. vertex having no incoming edge;
3. There is no *shaft vertex*, i.e. vertex having no outgoing edge;
4. For every vertex, the sum of incoming edges values equals to the sum of outgoing edges values.

The following figure shows an instance of electric circuit, which verifies the above items.

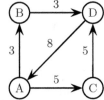

To obtain a sound electric circuit XML description, we proceed as follows. First, we model a graph in a UML Class diagram.

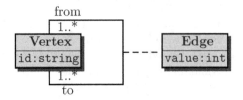

Then, we enrich it with OCL integrity constraints, expressing Kirchhoff's First
law.

```
context Vertex
inv:
    self.to->forall(n|n <> self) %----------------------------item 1
    self.edge[from]->size() > 0 %----------------------------item 2
    self.edge[to]->size() > 0 %----------------------------item 3
    self.edge[to].value.sum()=self.edge[from].value.sum() %--item 4
```

Notice that some integrity constraints can not be validated at run time, i.e. on
a partial graph, but only when the graph is completed. It suffices to consider item
4: whenever a vertex is created, the constraint expressed by item 4 does not hold
as long as appropriate edges are added. Even preconditions and postconditions
are not useful to validate this constraint before completing the graph. This fact
justifies the use of a validator *after* marshalling input and output parameters.

Figure 1 shows graphically the XML Schema, embedded in the service WSDL
document, modeling the input type (e.g. the graph).

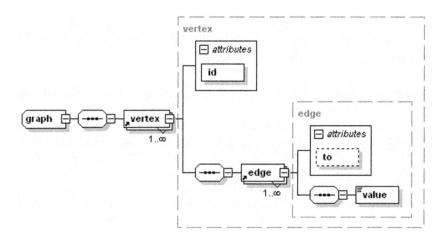

Fig. 1. XML Schema

The final step consists of translating each OCL assertion into an equivalent
CLiX rule. The following rules model the constraints expressed in items 1 and
2, respectively:

```
<clix:rule id="rule-item1">
    <clix:forall var="vertex" in="/graph/vertex">
        <clix:forall var="edge" in="$vertex/edge" >
            <clix:notEqual op1="$vertex/@id"  op2="$edge/@to" />
        </clix:forall>
    </clix:forall>
</clix:rule>
```

```
<clix:rule id="rule-item2">
    <clix:forall var="vertex" in="/graph/vertex">
      <clix:exists var="edge" in="/graph/vertex/edge" >
          <clix:equal op1="$vertex/@id"  op2="$edge/@to" />
      </clix:exists>
    </clix:forall>
</clix:rule>
```

Regarding item 3, both the constraint expressed by XML Schema (e.g. every vertex has at least one edge) and CLiX rule-item1 suffice to ensure that there is no shaft node in the input graph.

Finally, item 4 can be expressed in CLiX as follows:

```
<clix:rule id="rule-item4">
  <clix:forall var="vertex" in="/graph/vertex">
      <clix:forall var="edge" in="/graph/vertex/edge">
          <clix:equal op1="sum($edge/value)" op2="sum($edge/@to=$vertex@id)"/>
      </clix:forall>
  </clix:forall>
</clix:rule>
```

5   Conclusion and Future Work

Web Service Description Language (WSDL) is the most widely language used for Web service descriptions. In a model where application functionalities are exposed as a signature, a client can interact with a service only if it knows the content of the messages that need to be sent out to the service provider (automatic invocation). WSDL descriptions by themselves do not provide sufficient information to enable a client to properly perform the above activity.

In this scenario, we have proposed a framework for automatically and properly invoking Web services by means of client-side stubs. The key element is a service WSDL description, *enriched* with CLiX logic formulas: reflection mechanisms on the stubs manage complex (user defined) types, and CLiX logic formulas express static and dynamic integrity constraints of the invocation parameters. First, the WSDL description is elaborated to produce a stub; then, the XML translation of this stub is checked by a CLiX validator, according to CLiX logic formulas associated to the given description. In this way, a service invocation is forwarded only after the validator checking it correct w.r.t. service parameters integrity constraints, i.e. without waiting for either ack or error messages from the service provider.

As a future work, it is reasonable to think of enriching the model with an ontological description. This extension can be done in a quite natural way: we believe that an ontological *mapping*, i.e. a semantic function which encodes identifiers into concepts - like WSDL-S [24] and OWL-S [19] - can replace a full ontological model, thanks to the fact that both inter-dependencies and dynamic constraints of the invocation parameters are expressed in XML syntax.

References

1. Boley, H., Taber, S., Wagner, G.: Design Rationale of RuleML: A Markup Language for SemanticWeb Rules. Proc. of SWWS'01 (2001).
2. Wagner, G., Tabet, S. , Boley, H.: MOF-RuleML: The Abstract Syntax of RuleML as a MOF Model. OMG Meeting. Boston (2003).
3. Paolucci, M., Srinivasan, N., Sycara, K.: Adding OWL-S to UDDI, implementation and throughput. First International Workshop on Semantic Web Services and Web Process Composition (SWSWPC 2004).
4. Haase, P., Stojanovic, L.: Consistent Evolution of OWL Ontologies. Proc. of the Second European Semantic Web Conference (ESWC 2005). LNCS **3532** (2005) 182–197.
5. Richters, M., Gogolla, M.: On Formalizing the UML Constraint Language OCL. Proc. of 17th Int. Conf. Conceptual Modeling (ER'98). LNCS **1507** (1998) 449–464.
6. Horrocks, I., Patel-Schneider, P., Boley, H., Tabet, S., Grosof, B., Dean, M.: SWRL: A Semantic Web Rule Language: Combining OWL and RuleML. W3C Member Submission (2004). `http://www.w3. org/Submission/SWRL`.
7. Grosof, B., Volz, R., Decker, S.: Description logic programs: Combining logic programs with description logic. Proc. of the Twelfth International World Wide Web Conference (WWW 2003).
8. Warmer, J., Kleppe, A.: The Object Constraint Language: Precise Modeling with UML. Addison-Wesley (1998).
9. XlinkIt: A Consistency Checking and Smart Link Generation Service. ACM Transactions on Software Engineering and Methodology (2002) 155–185.
10. CLiX: Constraint Language in XML. `www.clixml.org/clix/1.0`.
11. Open CLiX: an open source CLiXML Schema Validator. `http://clixml. sourceforge.net`.
12. RuleML. The Rule Markup Initiative. Date 22nd October 2004. `www.ruleml.org`.
13. The Schematron Assertion Language. `http://www.ascc.net/xml/schematron`.
14. UML: Unified Model Language. `www.uml.org`.
15. XML Path Language (XPath) Version 2.0. W3C Recommendation. `http://www. w3.org/TR/xpath20`.
16. WSDL: Web Service Definition Language. `www.w3.org/TR/wsdl`.
17. WSDL2Java. `http://ws.apache.org/axis/java/user-guide.html`
18. W3C Web Services Activity. `www.w3.org/2002/ws`
19. OWL-S, DAML Web Service Ontology. `http://www.daml.org/services/owl-s`.
20. Klasse Objecten. OCL Center: OCL Tool. `http://www.klasse.nl/ocl/index.htm`.
21. Object Constraint Language Specification. version 2.0. `www.klasse.nl/ocl/ocl-subm.html`.
22. RuleML: the Rule Markup Initiative. `http://www.ruleml.org`.
23. W3C XML Schema. `www.w3.org/XML/Schema`.
24. Web Service Semantics: WSDL-S. `www.w3.org/Submission/WSDL-S`.

A Formal Account of Contracts for Web Services

S. Carpineti[1], G. Castagna[2], C. Laneve[1], and L. Padovani[3]

[1] Department of Computer Science, University of Bologna
[2] École Normale Supérieure de Paris
[3] Information Science and Technology Institute, University of Urbino

Abstract. We define a formal contract language along with subcontract and compliance relations. We then extrapolate contracts out of processes, that are a recursion-free fragment of CCS. We finally demonstrate that a client completes its interactions with a service provided the corresponding contracts comply. Our contract language may be used as a foundation of Web services technologies, such as WSDL and WSCL.

1 Introduction

The recent trend in Web services is fostering a computing scenario where loosely coupled parties interact in a distributed and dynamic environment. Such interactions are typically sequences of messages that are exchanged between the parties. The environment, being dynamic, makes it not feasible to define or assemble parties statically. In this context, it is fundamental for clients to be able to search at run-time services with the required capabilities, namely the format of the exchanged messages, and the protocol – or *contract* – required to interact successfully with the service. In turn, services are required to publish such capabilities in some known repository.

The Web Service Description Language (WSDL) [6,5,4] provides a standardized technology for describing the interface exposed by a service. Such description includes the service location, the format (or *schema*) of the exchanged messages, the transfer mechanism to be used (i.e. SOAP-RPC, or others), and the contract. In WSDL, contracts are basically limited to one-way (asynchronous) and request/response (synchronous) interactions. The Web Service Conversation Language (WSCL) [1] extends WSDL contracts by allowing the description of arbitrary, possibly cyclic sequences of exchanged messages between communicating parties.

Both WSDL and WSCL documents can be published in repositories [2,7] so that they can be searched and queried. However, this immediately poses an issue related to the *compatibility* between different published contracts. It is necessary to define precise notions of contract similarity and compatibility and use them to perform service discovery in the same way as, say, type isomorphisms are used to perform library searches [18,8]. Unfortunately, neither WSDL nor WSCL can effectively define these notions, for the very simple reason that they do not provide any formal characterization of their contract languages. This cries out

M. Bravetti, M. Nuñes, and G. Zavattaro (Eds.): WS-FM 2006, LNCS 4184, pp. 148–162, 2006.

for a mathematical foundation of contracts and the formal relationship between clients and contracts.

In this contribution we define a calculus for contracts along with a subcontract relation, and we formalize the relationship between contracts and processes (that is clients and services) exposing a given contract. Contracts are made of actions to be interpreted as either message types or communication ports. Actions may be combined by means of two choice operators: + represents the *external choice*, meaning that the interacting part decides which one of alternative conversations to carry on; $\oplus$ represents the *internal choice*, meaning that the choice is not left to the interacting part. As a matter of facts, contracts are behavioral types of processes that do not manifest internal moves and the parallel structure. They are *acceptance trees* in Hennessy's terminology [11,12].

Then we devise a *subcontract relation* $\preceq$ such that a contract σ is a subcontract of σ' if σ manifests less interacting capabilities than σ'. The subcontract relation can then be used for querying (Web services) repositories. A query for a service with contract σ may safely return services with contract σ' such that $\sigma \preceq \sigma'$. It is possible that interaction with a service that exposes a contract that is bigger than the client requires may result into unused capabilities on the server side. We argue that this is safe, because we are interested in the client's ability to complete the interaction. Such client completion property inspires a relationship between client contracts and service ones – the *contract completion* – that may be defined in terms of $\preceq$ and an appropriate complement operation over contracts.

To illustrate our contracts at work we consider a recursion-free fragment of the Calculus of Communicating Systems (CCS [13]). We define a *compliance* relation between processes such that a process – the client – interacting with another – the service – is guaranteed to *complete*. For instance the clients $(a.b \,|\, \overline{a}) \setminus a$ and $(a.b \,|\, a.c \,|\, \overline{a}) \setminus a$ respectively comply with the services $\overline{b}$ and $\overline{b} \,|\, \overline{c}$; the two clients do not comply with $\overline{c}$. We then extrapolate a contract out of a process by means of a type system defined using the expansion theorem in [15]. For instance, we are able to deduce $a.b \,|\, \overline{a} \vdash (a.(b.\overline{a} + \overline{a}.b) + \overline{a}.(a.b + b.a) + b) \oplus b$. Finally we prove our main result: *if the contract of a client complies with the contract of a service, then the client complies with the service.*

The expressiveness of our contract language is gauge by encoding WSDL message exchange patterns and some WSCL conversations into our contract language. Because of the $\preceq$ relation between contracts, we are able to draw some interesting considerations about similar exchange patterns, and order them according to the client's need. As we consider the recursion-free fragment of CCS, we are not able to deal with cyclic WSCL conversations, but we point out in the conclusions that their support requires well-known extensions to the contract language and to the subcontract relation.

Related Work. This research was inspired by "CCS without τ" [15] and by Hennessy's model of acceptance trees [11,12]. In facts, our contracts are an alternative representation of finite acceptance trees. While the use of formal models to describe communication protocols is not new (see for instance the exchange patterns in SSDL [19], which are based on CSP and the π-calculus), to the best of our knowledge the subcontract relation $\preceq$ is original. It is incomparable with may testing preorder and it is less discriminating than the must testing preorder [14]. The stuck free conformance relation in [10], which is inspired by the theory of refusal testing [16], is also more demanding than our subcontract relation. For instance $\mathbf{0}$ is not related with a in [10] whilst $\mathbf{0} \preceq a$.

It is worth noticing that both must testing and stuck free conformance are preserved by any CCS context without $+$ thus allowing modular refinement. This is not true for $\preceq$. For instance $a \preceq a + b$ so one might think that a service with contract a can be replaced by a service with contract $a + b$ in any context. However, the context $C = \bar{b} \,|\, b.\bar{a} \,|\, [\,]$ distinguishes the two services ($a + b$ can get stuck while a cannot). The point is that the context C, representing a client, does not comply with a, since it performs the actions b and $\bar{b}$ which are not allowed by the contract a.

Structure of the Paper. In Section 2 we formally define our language for contracts along with *subcontract* and *compliance* relations. In Section 3 we relate the language with existing technologies to specify service protocols. Our notion of compliance between contracts is lifted to a notion of *compliance* between processes in Section 4. Section 5 draws our conclusion and hints to future work.

2   The Contract Language

The syntax of contracts uses an infinite set of *names* $\mathcal{N}$ ranged over by a, b, c, ..., and a disjoint set of *co-names* $\overline{\mathcal{N}}$ ranged over by $\bar{a}$, $\bar{b}$, $\bar{c}$, ... We let $\bar{\bar{a}} = a$. Contracts σ are defined by the following grammar:

$\sigma ::=$		**contracts**
	$\mathbf{0}$	(*void*)
	$a.\sigma$	(*input prefix*)
	$\bar{a}.\sigma$	(*output prefix*)
	$\sigma + \sigma$	(*external choice*)
	$\sigma \oplus \sigma$	(*internal choice*)

Contracts are abstract definitions of conversation protocols between communicating parties. The contract $\mathbf{0}$ defines the empty conversation; the input prefix $a.\sigma$ defines a conversation protocol whose initial activity is to accept a message on the name a – representing URIs – and continuing as σ; the output prefix $\bar{a}.\sigma$ defines a conversation protocol whose initial activity is to send a message to the name a and continuing as σ. Contracts $\sigma + \sigma'$ and $\sigma \oplus \sigma'$ define conversation protocols that follow either the conversation σ or σ'; in the former ones the choice is left to the remote party, in the latter ones the choice being made locally. For example, $\mathtt{Login}.(\overline{\mathtt{Continue}} + \overline{\mathtt{End}})$ describes the conversation protocol of a service that is ready to accept $\mathtt{Logins}$ and will $\mathtt{Continue}$ or $\mathtt{End}$ the conversation according to client's request. This contract is different from $\mathtt{Login}.(\overline{\mathtt{Continue}} \oplus \overline{\mathtt{End}})$ where the decision whether to continue or to end is taken by the service.

In the rest of the paper, the trailing $\mathbf{0}$ is always omitted, α is used to range over names and co-names, and $\sum_{i \in 1..n} \sigma_i$ and $\bigoplus_{i \in 1..n} \sigma_i$ abbreviate $\sigma_1 + \cdots + \sigma_n$

and $\sigma_1 \oplus \cdots \oplus \sigma_n$, respectively. The *language* of σ, written $\mathcal{L}(\sigma)$, is the set of strings on names and co-names inductively defined as follows:

$$\mathcal{L}(\mathbf{0}) = \{\varepsilon\}$$
$$\mathcal{L}(\alpha.\sigma) = \{\alpha s \mid s \in \mathcal{L}(\sigma)\}$$
$$\mathcal{L}(\sigma_1 + \sigma_2) = \mathcal{L}(\sigma_1 \oplus \sigma_2) = \mathcal{L}(\sigma_1) \cup \mathcal{L}(\sigma_2)$$

2.1 Subcontract Relation and Dual Contracts

Contracts retain an obvious compatibility relation that relates the conversation protocols of two communicating parties: a contract σ of a party *complies with* σ' of another party if the corresponding protocols match when they interact. Such a definition of subcontract would require the notions of communicating party, which is a process, and of contract exposed by it. We partially explore this direction in Section 4; here we give a direct definition by sticking to a structured operational semantics style. We begin by defining two notions that are preliminary to compliance: *subcontract* and *dual contract*.

Definition 1 (Transition). *Let* $\sigma \overset{\alpha}{\not\longmapsto}$ *be the least relation such that*

$$\mathbf{0} \overset{\alpha}{\not\longmapsto}$$
$$\beta.\sigma \overset{\alpha}{\not\longmapsto} \quad \textit{if } \alpha \neq \beta$$
$$\sigma \oplus \sigma' \overset{\alpha}{\not\longmapsto} \quad \textit{if } \sigma \overset{\alpha}{\not\longmapsto} \textit{ and } \sigma' \overset{\alpha}{\not\longmapsto}$$
$$\sigma + \sigma' \overset{\alpha}{\not\longmapsto} \quad \textit{if } \sigma \overset{\alpha}{\not\longmapsto} \textit{ and } \sigma' \overset{\alpha}{\not\longmapsto}$$

The transition relation *of contracts, noted* $\overset{\alpha}{\longmapsto}$*, is the least relation satisfying the rules:*

$$\alpha.\sigma \overset{\alpha}{\longmapsto} \sigma$$

$$\frac{\sigma_1 \overset{\alpha}{\longmapsto} \sigma_1' \quad \sigma_2 \overset{\alpha}{\longmapsto} \sigma_2'}{\sigma_1 + \sigma_2 \overset{\alpha}{\longmapsto} \sigma_1' \oplus \sigma_2'} \qquad \frac{\sigma_1 \overset{\alpha}{\longmapsto} \sigma_1' \quad \sigma_2 \overset{\alpha}{\not\longmapsto}}{\sigma_1 + \sigma_2 \overset{\alpha}{\longmapsto} \sigma_1'}$$

$$\frac{\sigma_1 \overset{\alpha}{\longmapsto} \sigma_1' \quad \sigma_2 \overset{\alpha}{\longmapsto} \sigma_2'}{\sigma_1 \oplus \sigma_2 \overset{\alpha}{\longmapsto} \sigma_1' \oplus \sigma_2'} \qquad \frac{\sigma_1 \overset{\alpha}{\longmapsto} \sigma_1' \quad \sigma_2 \overset{\alpha}{\not\longmapsto}}{\sigma_1 \oplus \sigma_2 \overset{\alpha}{\longmapsto} \sigma_1'}$$

and closed under mirror cases for external and internal choices. We write $\sigma \overset{\alpha}{\longmapsto}$ *if there exists* σ' *such that* $\sigma \overset{\alpha}{\longmapsto} \sigma'$.

The relation $\overset{\alpha}{\longmapsto}$ is different from standard transition relations for CCS processes [13]. For example, there is always at most one contract σ' such that $\sigma \overset{\alpha}{\longmapsto} \sigma'$, while this is not the case in CCS (the process $a.b+a.c$ has two different a-successor states: b and c). This mismatch is due to the fact that contract transitions define the evolution of conversation protocols *from the perspective of the communicating parties*. Thus $a.b + a.c \overset{a}{\longmapsto} b \oplus c$ because, once the activity a has been done, the communicating party is not aware of which conversation path has been chosen. On the contrary, CCS transitions define the evolution of processes *from the perspective of the process itself*.

We write $\sigma(\alpha)$ for the unique continuation of σ after α, that is the contract σ' such that $\sigma \overset{\alpha}{\longmapsto} \sigma'$.

Definition 2 (Ready sets and subcontracts). *Let* R *range over finite sets of names and co-names, called* ready sets.

$\sigma \Downarrow$ R *is the least relation such that:*

$$\mathbf{0} \Downarrow \emptyset$$
$$\alpha.\sigma \Downarrow \{\alpha\}$$
$$(\sigma + \sigma') \Downarrow \mathrm{R} \cup \mathrm{R}' \qquad \textit{if } \sigma \Downarrow \mathrm{R} \textit{ and } \sigma' \Downarrow \mathrm{R}'$$
$$(\sigma \oplus \sigma') \Downarrow \mathrm{R} \qquad \textit{if either } \sigma \Downarrow \mathrm{R} \textit{ or } \sigma' \Downarrow \mathrm{R}$$

The subcontract relation $\preceq$ *is the largest relation such that* $\sigma_1 \preceq \sigma_2$ *implies:*
  1. *if* $\sigma_2 \Downarrow \mathrm{R}_2$ *then* $\sigma_1 \Downarrow \mathrm{R}_1$ *with* $\mathrm{R}_1 \subseteq \mathrm{R}_2$,
  2. *if* $\sigma_1 \overset{\alpha}{\longmapsto} \sigma_1'$ *and* $\sigma_2 \overset{\alpha}{\longmapsto} \sigma_2'$ *then* $\sigma_1' \preceq \sigma_2'$.
  Let $\sigma_1 \simeq \sigma_2$, *called* contract compatibility, *if both* $\sigma_1 \preceq \sigma_2$ *and* $\sigma_2 \preceq \sigma_1$.

The relation $\sigma \preceq \sigma'$ verifies whether the external non-determinism of σ' is greater than the external non-determinism of σ and that this holds for every α-successor of σ and σ', *provided both have such successors*. For example $a.(b \oplus c) \simeq a.b + a.c \simeq a.b \oplus a.c$ and $a.b \oplus b \preceq b$ and $b \preceq b + a.c$. It is worth to remark that $\preceq$ is not transitive: the last two relations *do not entail* $a.b \oplus b \preceq b + a.c$, which is false. This transitivity failure is not very problematic because σ and σ' are intended to play different roles in $\sigma \preceq \sigma'$, as detailed by the compliance relation. However, transitivity of $\preceq$ holds under lightweight conditions.

Proposition 1. *If* $\sigma_1 \preceq \sigma_2$ *and* $\sigma_2 \preceq \sigma_3$ *and either* $\mathcal{L}(\sigma_1) \subseteq \mathcal{L}(\sigma_2)$ *or* $\mathcal{L}(\sigma_3) \subseteq \mathcal{L}(\sigma_2)$, *then* $\sigma_1 \preceq \sigma_3$.

The relation $\preceq$ is incomparable with may testing semantics [12]: we have $a \oplus \mathbf{0} \preceq b$, while these two processes are unrelated by may testing; conversely, $a \oplus b$ and $a + b$ are may-testing equivalent, while $a + b \not\preceq a \oplus b$. The relation $\preceq$ is less discriminating than must testing semantics [12]: a and $a + b$ are unrelated in must testing while $a \preceq a + b$.

The notion of *dual contract* is used to revert the capabilities of conversation protocols. Informally, the dual contract is obtained by reverting actions with co-actions, $+$ with $\oplus$, and conversely. For example the dual contract of $a \oplus \bar{b}$ is $\bar{a} + b$. However, this naïve transformation is fallible because in the contract language some external choices are actually internal choices in disguise. For example, $a.b + a.c \simeq a.(b \oplus c)$ but their dual contracts are respectively $\bar{a}.\bar{b} \oplus \bar{a}.\bar{c}$ and $\bar{a}.(\bar{b} + \bar{c})$, and they tell very different things. In the first one, the communicating party cannot decide which action to perform after $\bar{a}$, whereas this possibility is granted in the second one. To avoid such misbehavior, we define dual contracts on contracts in normal form. We use the same forms introduced in [12]. Let the *normed contract* of σ, noted $\mathbf{nc}(\sigma)$, be

$$\mathbf{nc}(\sigma) \overset{\mathrm{def}}{=} \bigoplus\nolimits_{\sigma \Downarrow \mathrm{R}} \sum\nolimits_{\alpha \in \mathrm{R}} \alpha.\mathbf{nc}(\sigma(\alpha)) .$$

For example

$$\mathbf{nc}((a.b \oplus b.c) + (a.b.d \oplus c.b)) = \begin{aligned} & a.b.(\mathbf{0} \oplus d) \\ & \oplus (a.b.(\mathbf{0} \oplus d) + c.b) \\ & \oplus (a.b.(\mathbf{0} \oplus d) + b.c) \\ & \oplus (b.c + c.b) \end{aligned}$$

Lemma 1. $\sigma \simeq \mathbf{nc}(\sigma)$ *and* $\mathcal{L}(\sigma) = \mathcal{L}(\mathbf{nc}(\sigma))$.

Definition 3 (Dual contracts). *The* dual contract *of* σ, *noted* $\overline{\sigma}$, *is defined as*

$$\overline{\sigma} \stackrel{\text{def}}{=} \sum_{\sigma \Downarrow R} \bigoplus_{\alpha \in R} \overline{\alpha.\sigma(\alpha)}$$

where, by convention, we have $\bigoplus_{\sigma \in \emptyset} \sigma = \mathbf{0}$.

The dual operator is not contravariant with respect to $\preceq$. For example, $a \preceq a.b$, but $\overline{a.b} = \overline{a}.\overline{b} \not\preceq \overline{a}$. For similar reasons, contract compatibility is not preserved. For example, $\mathbf{0} \simeq \mathbf{0} \oplus a$ but $\overline{\mathbf{0}} = \mathbf{0} \not\simeq \mathbf{0} + \overline{a} = \overline{\mathbf{0} \oplus a}$. However a limited form of contravariance, which will result fundamental in the following, is satisfied by the dual operator.

Lemma 2. $\overline{\sigma} \preceq \overline{\sigma \oplus \sigma'}$.

2.2 Contract Compliance

Every preliminary notion has been set for the definition of contract compliance.

Definition 4 (Contract compliance). *A* contract σ complies with σ', *noted* $\sigma \ll \sigma'$, *if and only if* $\overline{\sigma} \preceq \sigma'$.

The notion of contract compliance is meant to be used for querying a Web service repository. A client with contract σ will interact successfully with every service with contract σ' provided $\sigma \ll \sigma'$. For example, consider a client whose conversation protocol states that it intends to choose whether to be notified either on a name a or on a name b. Its contract might be $a \oplus b$. Querying a repository for compliant services means returning every service whose conversation protocol is $\overline{a} + \overline{b}$, or $\overline{a} + \overline{b} + a$, or $\overline{a}.c + \overline{b}$, etc. The guarantee that we provide (see Section 4) is that, whatever service returned by the repository is chosen, the client will conclude his conversation. This asymmetry between the left hand side of $\preceq$ (and of $\ll$) and the right hand side is the reason of the failure of transitivity. More precisely, in $a.b \oplus b \preceq b$ and in $b \preceq a.c + b$, we are guaranteeing the termination of clients manifesting the two left hand sides contracts with respect to services manifesting the two right hand side contracts. This property is not transitive.

3 On the Expressive Power of the Contract Language

In this section we relate our contract language to existing technologies for specifying service protocols.

3.1   Message Exchange Patterns in WSDL

The Web Service Description Language (WSDL) Version 1.1 [6] permits to describe and publish abstract and concrete descriptions of Web services. Such descriptions include the schema [9] of messages exchanged between client and server, the name and type of *operations* that the service exposes, as well as the locations (URLs) where the service can be contacted. In addition, it defines four interaction patterns determining the order and direction of exchanged messages. For instance, the *request-response* pattern is used to describe a synchronous operation where the client issues a request and subsequently receives a response from the service.

The second version of WSDL [3,4,5] allows users to agree on message exchange patterns (MEP) by specifying in the required **pattern** attribute of operation elements an absolute URI that identifies the MEP. It is important to notice that these URIs act as global identifiers (their content is not important) for MEPs, whose semantics is usually given in plain English. In particular, WSDL 2.0 [4] predefines four message exchange patterns (each pattern being uniquely identified by a different URI) for describing services where the interaction is initiated by clients (four further MEPs are provided for interactions initiated by servers). Let us shortly discuss how the informal plain English semantics of these patterns can be formally defined in our contract language. Consider the WSDL 2.0 fragment

```
<operation name="A" pattern="http://www.w3.org/2006/01/wsdl/in-only">
  <input messageLabel="In"/>
</operation>
<operation name="B"
           pattern="http://www.w3.org/2006/01/wsdl/robust-in-only">
  <input messageLabel="In"/>
  <outfault messageLabel="Fault"/>
</operation>
<operation name="C" pattern="http://www.w3.org/2006/01/wsdl/in-out">
  <input messageLabel="In"/>
  <output messageLabel="Out"/>
  <outfault messageLabel="Fault"/>
</operation>
<operation name="D" pattern="http://www.w3.org/2006/01/wsdl/in-opt-out">
  <input messageLabel="In"/>
  <output messageLabel="Out"/>
  <outfault messageLabel="Fault"/>
</operation>
```

which defines four operations named A, B, C, and D. The first two operations are *asynchronous* by accepting only an incoming message labeled In. The last two operations are *synchronous* by accepting an incoming message labeled In and replying with a message labeled Out. In the B operation a fault message can occur after the input. The C operation always produces an output message (see **in-out** in its **pattern** attribute), unless a fault occurs. In the D operation the reply is optional, as stated by the `in-opt-out` exchange pattern attribute, and again it may fail with `Fault`.

We can encode the contract of the pattern of the A operation in our contract language as $\mathtt{inOnly} = \mathtt{In}.\overline{\mathtt{End}}$, that is an input action representing the client's request followed by a message $\overline{\mathtt{End}}$ that is sent from the service to notify the client that the interaction has completed.

The B operation can be encoded as

$$\mathtt{robustInOnly} = \mathtt{In}.(\overline{\mathtt{End}} \oplus \overline{\mathtt{Fault}.\mathtt{End}})$$

where after the client's request, the interaction may follow two paths, representing successful and faulty computations respectively. In the former case the end of the interaction is immediately signaled to the client. In the latter case a message `Fault` is sent to the client, followed by `End`. The use of the internal choice for combining the two paths states that it is the service that decides whether the interaction is successful or not. This means that a client compliant with this service can either stop after the request or it must be able to handle both the `End` and `Fault` messages: the omission of handling, say, `Fault` would result into an uncaught exception.

The need for an explicit `End` message to signal a terminated interaction is not immediately evident. In principle, the optional fault message could have been encoded as $\mathtt{In}.(\mathbf{0} \oplus \overline{\mathtt{Fault}})$. A client compliant with this service must be able to receive and handle the `Fault` message, but it must also be able to complete the interaction without further communication from the service. The point is that the client cannot distinguish a completed interaction where the service has internally decided to behave like $\mathbf{0}$ from an interaction where the service has internally decided to behave like `Fault`, but it is taking a long time to respond. By providing an explicit `End` message signaling a completed interaction, the service tells the client not to wait for further messages. By this reasoning, the `End` message after `Fault` is not strictly necessary, but we write it for uniformity.

By similar arguments the contract of the C operation can be encoded as

$$\mathtt{inOut} = \mathtt{In}.(\overline{\mathtt{Out}.\mathtt{End}} \oplus \overline{\mathtt{Fault}.\mathtt{End}})$$

and the contract of the D operation as

$$\mathtt{inOptOut} = \mathtt{In}.(\overline{\mathtt{End}} \oplus \overline{\mathtt{Out}.\mathtt{End}} \oplus \overline{\mathtt{Fault}.\mathtt{End}})$$

It is worth noticing how these contracts are ordered according to our definition of $\preceq$. We have $\mathtt{inOptOut} \preceq \mathtt{robustInOnly}$ and $\mathtt{robustInOnly} \preceq \mathtt{inOnly}$. Indeed, a client compliant with `inOptOut` must be able to complete immediately after the request, but it is also able to handle a `Out` message and a `Fault` message. The `robustInOnly` can only produce an `End` message or a `Fault` message, hence it is "more deterministic" than `inOptOut`. Similarly, `inOnly` is more deterministic than `robustInOnly` since it can only send an `End` message after the client's request. Finally, note that $\mathtt{inOptOut} \preceq \mathtt{inOut}$ also holds.

3.2   Conversations in WSCL

The WSDL message exchange patterns cover only the simplest forms of interaction between a client and a service. More involved forms of interactions, in
particular stateful interactions, cannot be captured if not as informal annotation within the WSDL interface. The Web service conversation language WSCL [1]
provides a more general specification language for describing complex *conversations* between two communicating parties, by means of an activity diagram. The
diagram is basically made of *interactions* which are connected with each other
by means of *transitions*. An interaction is a basic one-way or two-way communication between the client and the server. Two-way communications are just a
shorthand for two sequential one-way interactions. Each interaction has a *name*
and a list of *document types* that can be exchanged during its execution. A transition connects a *source* interaction with a *destination* interaction. A transition
may be *labeled* by a document type if it is active only when a message of that
specific document type was exchanged during the previous interaction.

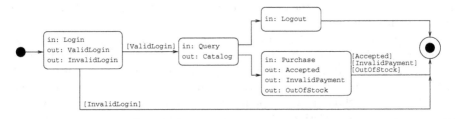

Fig. 1. Contract of a simple e-commerce service as a WSCL diagram

Below we encode the contract σ of a simplified e-commerce service (Figure 1)
where the client is required to login before it can issue a query and thus receive
a catalog. From this point on, the client can decide whether to purchase an item
from the catalog or to logout and leave. In case of purchase, the service may
either report that the purchase was successful, or that the item is out-of-stock,
or that the client's payment was refused:

$$\sigma \stackrel{\text{def}}{=} \text{Login}.(\overline{\text{InvalidLogin}.\text{End}} \oplus \overline{\text{ValidLogin}}.\text{Query}.\overline{\text{Catalog}}.(\\ \text{Logout}.\overline{\text{End}} + \text{Purchase}.(\\ \overline{\text{Accepted}.\text{End}} \oplus \overline{\text{InvalidPayment}.\text{End}} \oplus \overline{\text{OutOfStock}.\text{End}})))$$

Notice that unlabeled transitions in Figure 1 correspond to external choices
in σ, whereas labeled transitions correspond to internal choices. It is also interesting to notice that WSCL explicitly accounts for a termination message (called
"empty" in the WSCL specification, the final interaction on the right end in Figure 1) that is used for modeling the end of a conversation. The presence of this
termination message finds a natural justification in our formal contract language,
as explained above.

Now assume that the service is extended with a booking capability, so that after looking at the catalog the client may book an item to be bought at some later time. The contract of the service would change to σ' as follows:

$$\sigma' \stackrel{\text{def}}{=} \ldots \texttt{Logout.}\overline{\texttt{End}} + \texttt{Book.}\overline{\texttt{End}} + \texttt{Purchase.}(\ldots)$$

We notice that $\sigma \preceq \sigma'$ and $\mathcal{L}(\sigma) \subseteq \mathcal{L}(\sigma')$, that is σ' offers more capabilities than σ.

4   Compliance

Compliance relates a client process with a service process. A client is compliant with a service if the client terminates (i.e. it has no more interactions to perform) for every possible interaction with the service. That is, compliance induces a *completion property* for the client but not for the service. In order to formalize compliance we define processes and their dynamics. Then we demonstrate that it is possible to associate a contract to a process such that (process) compliance follows by the compliance of the corresponding contracts.

In this contribution, processes are finite CCS terms. The extension to CCS terms is not trivial and left for future work. For the sake of simplicity we do not include choice and relabeling operators. The transition relation is standard; therefore we omit comments.

Definition 5. *Processes P are defined by the following grammar:*

$$P ::= \quad \mathbf{0} \quad | \quad a.P \quad | \quad \overline{a}.P \quad | \quad P \setminus a \quad | \quad P \,|\, P$$

Let μ range over $\mathcal{N} \cup \overline{\mathcal{N}} \cup \{\tau\}$. The transition relation of processes, noted $\stackrel{\mu}{\longrightarrow}$, is the least relation satisfying the rules:

(IN)
$$a.P \stackrel{a}{\longrightarrow} P$$

(OUT)
$$\overline{a}.P \stackrel{\overline{a}}{\longrightarrow} P$$

(RES)
$$\frac{P \stackrel{\mu}{\longrightarrow} Q \quad \mu \notin \{a, \overline{a}\}}{P \setminus a \stackrel{\mu}{\longrightarrow} Q \setminus a}$$

(PAR)
$$\frac{P \stackrel{\mu}{\longrightarrow} Q}{P \,|\, R \stackrel{\mu}{\longrightarrow} Q \,|\, R}$$

(COM)
$$\frac{P \stackrel{\alpha}{\longrightarrow} P' \quad Q \stackrel{\overline{\alpha}}{\longrightarrow} Q'}{P \,|\, Q \stackrel{\tau}{\longrightarrow} P' \,|\, Q'}$$

The transitions of $P \,|\, Q$ have mirror cases that have been omitted.
We write $\Longrightarrow$ for $\stackrel{\tau}{\longrightarrow}{}^{*}$ and $\stackrel{\alpha}{\Longrightarrow}$ for $\stackrel{\tau}{\longrightarrow}{}^{*}\stackrel{\alpha}{\longrightarrow}\stackrel{\tau}{\longrightarrow}{}^{*}$.

The compliance of a client process with a service is defined as follows.

Definition 6 (Compliance). *Let $P \,\|\, Q \longrightarrow P' \,\|\, Q'$ be the least relation such that:*

- if $P \xrightarrow{\tau} P'$ then $P \parallel Q \longrightarrow P' \parallel Q$;
- if $Q \xrightarrow{\tau} Q'$ then $P \parallel Q \longrightarrow P \parallel Q'$;
- if $P \xrightarrow{\alpha} P'$ and $Q \xrightarrow{\bar{\alpha}} Q'$ then $P \parallel Q \longrightarrow P' \parallel Q'$.

Let $P \ll Q$, read P complies with Q, if one of the following holds:

1. $P \xrightarrow{\alpha}\!\!\!/\,$, or
2. $P \parallel Q \longrightarrow P' \parallel Q'$ and $P' \ll Q'$.

Process compliance has been noted in the same way as contract compliance in Section 2. This abuse is justified because the two notions are strongly related, as we will prove shortly.

Processes expose (principal) contracts. This is defined by an inference system that uses two auxiliary operators over contracts:

1. $\sigma \setminus a$ is defined by induction on the structure of σ:

$$
\begin{aligned}
\mathbf{0} \setminus a &= \mathbf{0} \\
(\alpha.\sigma) \setminus a &= \begin{cases} \mathbf{0} & \text{if } \alpha \in \{a, \bar{a}\} \\ \alpha.(\sigma \setminus a) & \text{otherwise} \end{cases} \\
(\sigma + \sigma') \setminus a &= \sigma \setminus a + \sigma' \setminus a \\
(\sigma \oplus \sigma') \setminus a &= \sigma \setminus a \oplus \sigma' \setminus a
\end{aligned}
$$

2. The operator "$|$" is commutative with $\mathbf{0}$ as identity, such that $\sigma \mid (\sigma' \oplus \sigma'') = (\sigma \mid \sigma') \oplus (\sigma \mid \sigma'')$, and $\sigma \mid (\sigma' + (\sigma'' \oplus \sigma''')) = \sigma \mid ((\sigma' + \sigma'') \oplus (\sigma' + \sigma'''))$. This allows us to define $\sigma \mid \sigma'$ when σ and σ' are external choices of prefixes. Our definition corresponds to the *expansion law* in [15]. Let $\sigma = \sum_{i \in I} \alpha_i.\sigma_i$ and $\sigma' = \sum_{j \in J} \alpha'_j.\sigma'_j$, then

$$
\sigma \mid \sigma' \overset{\text{def}}{=} \begin{cases} \sum_{i \in I} \alpha_i.(\sigma_i \mid \sigma') + \sum_{j \in J} \alpha'_j.(\sigma \mid \sigma'_j) \\ \qquad\qquad\qquad\qquad \text{if } \alpha_i \neq \overline{\alpha'_j} \text{ for every } i \in I,\ j \in J \\[2ex] \left(\sum_{i \in I} \alpha_i.(\sigma_i \mid \sigma') + \sum_{j \in J} \alpha'_j.(\sigma \mid \sigma'_j) + \bigoplus_{\alpha_i = \overline{\alpha'_j}}(\sigma_i \mid \sigma'_j) \right) \\ \oplus \bigoplus_{\alpha_i = \overline{\alpha'_j}}(\sigma_i \mid \sigma'_j) \qquad\qquad\qquad\qquad\qquad \text{otherwise} \end{cases}
$$

Definition 7. *Let $P \vdash \sigma$ be the least relation such that*

$$
\mathbf{0} \vdash \mathbf{0} \qquad \frac{P \vdash \sigma}{a.P \vdash a.\sigma} \qquad \frac{P \vdash \sigma}{\bar{a}.P \vdash \bar{a}.\sigma} \qquad \frac{P \vdash \sigma}{P \setminus a \vdash \sigma \setminus a} \qquad \frac{P \vdash \sigma \quad Q \vdash \sigma'}{P \mid Q \vdash \sigma \mid \sigma'}
$$

As anticipated, compliance of processes may be inferred from compliance of the corresponding contracts. This property, formalized in Theorem 1, requires few preliminary statements.

Lemma 3. *Let $P \vdash \sigma$, $P \xrightarrow{\mu} P'$, and $P' \vdash \sigma'$*

(a) *if $\mu = \tau$ then $\sigma \preceq \sigma'$, $\overline{\sigma'} \preceq \overline{\sigma}$, and $\mathcal{L}(\sigma') \subseteq \mathcal{L}(\sigma)$;*
(b) *if $\mu = \alpha$ then $\sigma(\alpha) \preceq \sigma'$, $\overline{\sigma'} \preceq \overline{\sigma(\alpha)}$, and $\mathcal{L}(\sigma') \subseteq \mathcal{L}(\sigma(\alpha))$.*

Proof. (Sketch) We proceed by induction on the derivation of $P \xrightarrow{\mu} P'$.

The base case corresponds to the application of either (IN) or (OUT). Since P has the form $\alpha.P'$ we have $\sigma(\alpha) = \sigma'$. Therefore we conclude $\sigma(\alpha) \preceq \sigma'$, $\overline{\sigma'} \preceq \overline{\sigma(\alpha)}$, and $\mathcal{L}(\sigma') = \mathcal{L}(\sigma(\alpha))$.

In the inductive case there are several sub-cases corresponding to the last rule that has been applied. We discuss (COM) and (PAR).

- (COM) implies $P = Q \,|\, R$ with $Q \xrightarrow{\alpha} Q'$ and $R \xrightarrow{\overline{\alpha}} R'$. Let $Q \vdash \sigma_1, Q' \vdash \sigma'_1$, $R \vdash \sigma_2$, and $R' \vdash \sigma'_2$. By definition of "$|$", we have $\sigma_1 \,|\, \sigma_2 = \bigoplus_{i \in I} \sigma''_i$ with $\sigma''_j = \sigma'_1 \,|\, \sigma'_2$ for some $j \in I$. Hence $\sigma_1 \,|\, \sigma_2 \preceq \sigma'_1 \,|\, \sigma'_2$ follows by definition of $\preceq$ and $\overline{\sigma'_1 \,|\, \sigma'_2} \preceq \overline{\sigma_1 \,|\, \sigma_2}$ follows by Lemma 2. It remains to show $\mathcal{L}(\sigma'_1 \,|\, \sigma'_2) \subseteq \mathcal{L}(\sigma_1 \,|\, \sigma_2)$. This is a straightforward consequence of the definition of "$|$" and $\mathcal{L}(\cdot)$.
- (PAR) implies $P = Q \,|\, R$ with $Q \xrightarrow{\mu} Q'$ and $Q \vdash \sigma_1, R \vdash \sigma_2$, and $Q' \vdash \sigma'_1$.
  - If $\mu = \tau$, by definition of "$|$", we have $\sigma_1 = \bigoplus_{i \in I} \sigma''_i$ with $\sigma''_j = \sigma'_1$ for some $j \in I$. Then $\sigma_1 \,|\, \sigma_2 = (\bigoplus_{i \in I} \sigma''_i) \,|\, \sigma_2 = \bigoplus_{i \in I} (\sigma''_i \,|\, \sigma_2)$ and $\sigma_1 \,|\, \sigma_2 \preceq \sigma'_1 \,|\, \sigma_2$ follows by definition of $\preceq$ while $\overline{\sigma'_1 \,|\, \sigma_2} \preceq \overline{\sigma_1 \,|\, \sigma_2}$ follows by Lemma 2. By definition of $\mathcal{L}(\cdot)$ we also conclude that $\mathcal{L}(\sigma'_1 \,|\, \sigma_2) \subseteq \mathcal{L}(\sigma_1 \,|\, \sigma_2)$.
  - If $\mu = \alpha$, by the inductive hypothesis we have $\sigma_1(\alpha) \preceq \sigma'_1$ and $\overline{\sigma'_1} \preceq \overline{\sigma(\alpha)}$. Since $Q \xrightarrow{\alpha} Q'$, by definition of "$|$" we have that $\sigma_1 \,|\, \sigma_2$ has the shape $\rho_1 \oplus (\rho_2 + \alpha.(\sigma'_1 \,|\, \sigma_2) + \rho_3) \oplus \rho_4$ where an arbitrary number of the ρ_i's may be missing. Hence $(\sigma_1 \,|\, \sigma_2)(\alpha) = \cdots \oplus (\sigma'_1 \,|\, \sigma_2) \oplus \cdots$. Then $(\sigma_1 \,|\, \sigma_2)(\alpha) \preceq \sigma'_1 \,|\, \sigma_2$ follows by definition of $\preceq$ and $\overline{\sigma'_1 \,|\, \sigma_2} \preceq \overline{(\sigma_1 \,|\, \sigma_2)(\alpha)}$ by Lemma 2. By definition of $\mathcal{L}(\cdot)$ we also conclude that $\mathcal{L}(\sigma'_1 \,|\, \sigma_2) \subseteq \mathcal{L}((\sigma_1 \,|\, \sigma_2)(\alpha))$. $\square$

Theorem 1. *If $P \vdash \sigma$, $Q \vdash \sigma'$, and $\sigma \ll \sigma'$ then $P \ll Q$.*

Proof. A maximal computation of the system $P \,\|\, Q$ is a sequence of systems $P_1 \,\|\, Q_1, \ldots, P_n \,\|\, Q_n$ such that $P_1 = P$, $Q_1 = Q$, for every $i = \{1, \ldots, n-1\}$ we have $P_i \,\|\, Q_i \longrightarrow P_{i+1} \,\|\, Q_{i+1}$, and $P_n \,\|\, Q_n \nrightarrow$. The proof is by induction on n.

If $n = 0$, then $P \,\|\, Q \nrightarrow$. We have two possibilities: if $P \xrightarrow{\alpha}$ then by definition $P \ll Q$. So let us suppose, by contradiction, that whenever $P \xrightarrow{\alpha}$ we have $Q \xrightarrow{\overline{\alpha}} \nrightarrow$. Since $P \vdash \sigma$ and $Q \vdash \sigma'$ this means that for any ready set R of σ there is no ready set S of σ' such that $\overline{\text{R}} \cap \text{S} \neq \emptyset$. From $P \xrightarrow{\alpha}$ and $P \vdash \sigma$ we know that $\sigma \Downarrow \text{R}$ and $\alpha \in \text{R}$ for some ready set R. That is, σ has at least one nonempty ready set. Thus, from the definition of $\overline{\sigma}$, we know that *every* ready set of $\overline{\sigma}$ is not empty. By definition of contract compliance we know that $\overline{\sigma} \preceq \sigma'$ and from the definition of $\preceq$ we have that any ready set S of σ' shares at least an action with $\overline{\text{R}}$ for some ready set R of σ, which is absurd.

If $n > 0$, assume that the theorem is true for any computation of length $n-1$. We have three cases:

$(P \longrightarrow P')$ Assume $P' \vdash \sigma''$, then from Lemma 3(a) we know that $\overline{\sigma''} \preceq \overline{\sigma}$ and $\mathcal{L}(\overline{\sigma''}) \subseteq \mathcal{L}(\overline{\sigma})$, hence by Proposition 1 we have $\overline{\sigma''} \preceq \sigma'$ that is $\sigma'' \ll \sigma'$. By the induction hypothesis we conclude that $P' \ll Q$ hence $P \ll Q$.

$(Q \longrightarrow Q')$ Assume $Q' \vdash \sigma''$, then from Lemma 3(a) we know that $\sigma' \preceq \sigma''$ and $\mathcal{L}(\sigma'') \subseteq \mathcal{L}(\sigma')$, hence by Proposition 1 we have $\overline{\sigma} \preceq \sigma''$ that is $\sigma \ll \sigma''$. By the induction hypothesis we conclude that $P \ll Q'$ hence $P \ll Q$.

$(P \xrightarrow{\alpha} P'$ **and** $Q \xrightarrow{\overline{\alpha}} Q')$ Assume that $P' \vdash \sigma''$ and $Q' \vdash \sigma'''$. From Lemma 3(b) know that $\overline{\sigma''} \preceq \overline{\sigma(\alpha)}$ and $\mathcal{L}(\overline{\sigma''}) \subseteq \mathcal{L}(\overline{\sigma(\alpha)})$, and by definition of dual contract we have $\overline{\sigma(\alpha)} = \overline{\sigma}(\overline{\alpha})$. Again from Lemma 3(b) we know that $\sigma'(\alpha) \preceq \sigma'''$ and $\mathcal{L}(\sigma''') \subseteq \mathcal{L}(\sigma'(\alpha))$. By Proposition 1 we have $\overline{\sigma''} \preceq \sigma'''$ that is $\sigma'' \ll \sigma'''$. The computation starting from $P' \parallel Q'$ has length $n - 1$, by the induction hypothesis we have $P' \ll Q'$ so we conclude $P \ll Q$.   □

5   Conclusion and Future Work

In this paper we have started an investigation aimed at the definition of a formal contract language suitable for describing interactions of clients with Web services. We have defined a precise notion of compatibility between services, called subcontract relation, so that equivalent services can be safely replaced with each other. This notion of compatibility is immediately applicable in any query-based system for service discovery, as well as for verifying that a service implementation respects its interface. To the best of our knowledge, this relation is original and it does not coincide with either must, or may, or testing preorders. Based on the subcontract relation, we have provided a formal notion of compliance, such that clients that are verified to be compliant with a contract are guaranteed to successfully complete the interaction with any service that exports that contract.

We have based our investigation on a very simple model of concurrency, the Calculus of Communicating Systems [13] without recursion, since this is but the first step of our investigation. Starting from this basis, we plan to pursue several lines of research. First and foremost we want to explore whether it is possible to modify our subcontract relation so that it is transitive, while preserving its main properties. The lack of transitivity has a non negligible impact on the use our relation. For instance, while it is possible to replace a given service with a new service whose subcontract is greater than the original service's contract, it is not possible to renew this operation without taking into account the original contract. After that we plan to study the addition of some form of recursion in order to model protocols whose length is not statically bound, as well as a better support of optional contracts. While these last points should not pose any particular problem, the passage from a CCS-like formalism to a π-calculus one will be much a more challenging task. Nevertheless this passage to a higher order formalism looks crucial for more than one reason. First it will allow us to take into account and generalize the forthcoming versions of WSDL. Also, it will more faithfully mimic WSCL protocols which discriminate on the content of messages. Besides, the type of these parameters could also be used to define contract isomorphisms to improve service discovery. In particular we will study *provable* isomorphisms, that is, isomorphisms for which it is possible to exhibit a process that "converts" the two contracts: for instance, imagine that we search for a service that implements the contract In(Int).In(Int), that is, a service that sequentially waits twice for an integer on the port In; the query may return a reference to a service with a contract isomorphic to it, say, In(Int×Int) together with a process that "proves" that these two contracts are isomorphic, that is, in the specific case, a process that buffers the two inputs and sends the pair of them on In: by composing this process with the original client (written for the first contract) one obtains a client complying with the discovered service.

On the linguistic side we would like to explore new process constructions that could take into account information available with contracts. For instance imagine a client that wants to use a service exporting the contract $(a + b) \oplus a$; in the simple language of Section 2 the client cannot specify that it wants to connect with b if available, and on a otherwise. We want also to devise query languages for service discovery, in particular we aim to devise a simple set-theoretic interpretation of contracts as sets of processes, use it to add union, intersection, and negation operators for contracts, and subsequently use these as query primitives.

A final issue brought by higher-order and whose exploration looks promising is that higher-order channels will allow us to use a continuation passing style (CPS) of programming. It is well-known that CPS can be used for stateless implementation of interactive web-sessions [17], thus we plan to transpose such a technique to contracts and resort to CPS to describe stateful interactions of services.

Acknowledgments. This work was partially funded by the ACI project "Transformation Languages for XML: Logics and Applications" (TraLaLA).

References

1. A. Banerji, C. Bartolini, D. Beringer, V. Chopella, et al. *Web Services Conversation Language (*WSCL*) 1.0*, Mar. 2002. http://www.w3.org/TR/2002/NOTE-wscl10-20020314.
2. D. Beringer, H. Kuno, and M. Lemon. *Using* WSCL *in a* UDDI *Registry 1.0*, 2001. UDDI Working Draft Best Practices Document, http://xml.coverpages.org/HP-UDDI-wscl-5-16-01.pdf.
3. D. Booth and C. K. Liu. *Web Services Description Language (*WSDL*) Version 2.0 Part 0: Primer*, Mar. 2006.
4. R. Chinnici, H. Haas, A. A. Lewis, J.-J. Moreau, et al. *Web Services Description Language (*WSDL*) Version 2.0 Part 2: Adjuncts*, Mar. 2006. http://www.w3.org/TR/2006/CR-wsdl20-adjuncts-20060327.
5. R. Chinnici, J.-J. Moreau, A. Ryman, and S. Weerawarana. *Web Services Description Language (*WSDL*) Version 2.0 Part 1: Core Language*, Mar. 2006. http://www.w3.org/TR/2006/CR-wsdl20-20060327.
6. E. Christensen, F. Curbera, G. Meredith, and S. Weerawarana. *Web Services Description Language (*WSDL*) 1.1*, 2001. http://www.w3.org/TR/2001/NOTE-wsdl-20010315.
7. J. Colgrave and K. Januszewski. Using WSDL in a UDDI registry, version 2.0.2. Technical note, OASIS, 2004. http://www.oasis-open.org/committees/uddi-spec/doc/tn/uddi-spec-tc-tn-wsdl-v2.htm.

8. R. D. Cosmo. *Isomorphisms of Types: from Lambda Calculus to Information Retrieval and Language Desig.* Birkhauser, 1995. ISBN-0-8176-3763-X.

9. D. C. Fallside and P. Walmsley. *XML Schema Part 0: Primer Second Edition*, Oct. 2004. http://www.w3.org/TR/xmlschema-0/.

10. C. Fournet, C. A. R. Hoare, S. K. Rajamani, and J. Rehof. Stuck-free conformance. Technical Report MSR-TR-2004-69, Microsoft Research, July 2004.

11. M. Hennessy. Acceptance trees. *JACM: Journal of the ACM*, 32(4):896–928, 1985.

12. M. C. B. Hennessy. *Algebraic Theory of Processes.* Foundation of Computing. MIT Press, 1988.

13. R. Milner. *A Calculus of Communicating Systems.* Springer-Verlag New York, Inc., Secaucus, NJ, USA, 1982.

14. R. D. Nicola and M. Hennessy. Testing equivalences for processes. *Theor. Comput. Sci*, 34:83–133, 1984.

15. R. D. Nicola and M. Hennessy. CCS without tau's. In *TAPSOFT '87/CAAP '87: Proceedings of the International Joint Conference on Theory and Practice of Software Development, Volume 1: Advanced Seminar on Foundations of Innovative Software Development I and Colloquium on Trees in Algebra and Programming*, pages 138–152, London, UK, 1987. Springer-Verlag.

16. I. Phillips. Refusal testing. *Theor. Comput. Sci.*, 50(3):241–284, 1987.

17. C. Queinnec. Inverting back the inversion of control or, continuations versus page-centric programming. *SIGPLAN Not.*, 38(2):57–64, 2003.

18. M. Rittri. Retrieving library functions by unifying types modulo linear isomorphism. *RAIRO Theoretical Informatics and Applications*, 27(6):523–540, 1993.

19. Savas Parastatidis and Jim Webber. *MEP SSDL Protocol Framework*, Apr. 2005. http://ssdl.org.

Execution Semantics for Service Choreographies

Gero Decker[1], Johannes Maria Zaha[2], and Marlon Dumas[2]

[1] SAP Research Centre, Brisbane, Australia
g.decker@sap.com
[2] Queensland University of Technology, Brisbane, Australia
{j.zaha, m.dumas}@qut.edu.au

Abstract. A service choreography is a model of interactions in which a set of services engage to achieve a goal, seen from the perspective of an ideal observer that records all messages exchanged between these services. Choreographies have been put forward as a starting point for building service-oriented systems since they provide a global picture of the system's behavior. In previous work we presented a language for service choreography modeling targeting the early phases of the development lifecycle. This paper provides an execution semantics for this language in terms of a mapping to π-calculus. This formal semantics provides a basis for analyzing choreographies. The paper reports on experiences using the semantics to detect unreachable interactions.

1 Introduction

A trend can be observed in the area of service-oriented architectures towards increased emphasis on capturing behavioral dependencies between service interactions. This trend is evidenced by the emergence of languages such as the Business Process Execution Language for Web Services (BPEL) [1] and the Web Service Choreography Description Language (WS-CDL) [7].

There are two complementary approaches to capture service interaction behavior: one where interactions are seen from the perspective of each participating service, and the other where they are seen from a global perspective. This leads to two types of models: In a *global model* (also called a *choreography*) interactions are described from the viewpoint of an ideal observer who oversees all interactions between a set of services. Meanwhile, a *local model* captures only those interactions that directly involve a given service. Local models are suitable for implementing individual services while choreographies are useful during the early phases of system analysis and design.

This paper reports on ongoing work aimed at bridging these two viewpoints by defining a service interaction modeling language (namely *Let's Dance*) as well as techniques for analyzing and relating global and local models of service interactions. In previous work [14], we defined this language informally. This paper introduces a formal execution semantics for the language using π-calculus and discusses the analysis of models using this semantics.

M. Bravetti, M. Nuñes, and G. Zavattaro (Eds.): WS-FM 2006, LNCS 4184, pp. 163–177, 2006.

The next section gives an overview of the Let's Dance language. The semantics and an example are given in Section 3 while Section 4 discusses the analysis of choreographies. In Section 5 related work is presented and section 6 concludes.

2   Language Overview

2.1   Language Constructs

A choreography is a set of interrelated service interactions corresponding to message exchanges. At the lowest level of abstraction, an interaction is composed of a message sending action and a message receipt action (referred to as communication actions). Communication actions are represented by non-regular pentagons (symbol $\triangleright$ for send and $\trianglerighteq$ for receive) that are juxtaposed to form a rectangle denoting an elementary interaction. A communication action is performed by an actor playing a role. The role is indicated in the top corner of a communication action. Role names are written in uppercase while the actor playing this role (or more specifically: the "actor reference") is written in lowercase between brackets.

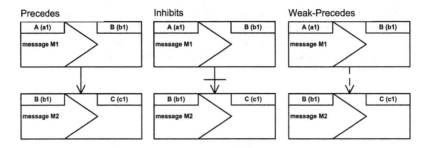

Fig. 1. Relationships in Let's Dance

Interactions can be inter-related using the constructs depicted in Figure 1. The relationship on the left-hand side is called "precedes" and is depicted by a directed edge: the source interaction can only occur after the target interaction has occurred. That is, after the receipt of a message "M1" by "B", "B" is able to send a message "M2" to "C". The middle relationship is called "inhibits", depicted by a crossed directed edge. It denotes that after the source interaction has taken place, the target interaction can no longer take place. That is, after "B" has received a message "M1" from "A", it may not send a message "M2" to "C". Finally, the relationship on the right-hand side, called "weak-precedes", denotes that "B" is not able to send a message "M2" until "A" has sent a message "M1" or until this interaction has been inhibited. That is, the target interaction can only occur after the source interaction has reached a final status, which may be "completed" or "skipped" (i.e. "inhibited").

Interactions can be grouped into composite interactions as shown on the left-hand side of Figure 2. Composite interactions can be related with other interactions through precedes, inhibits and weak-precedes relationships. A composite

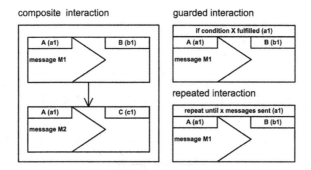

Fig. 2. Constructs of Let's Dance

interaction is completed if all sub-interactions have been executed or inhibited. The composite interaction in Figure 2 is completed if "A" has exchanged a message "M1" with "B" and a message "M2" with "C", since there is no way for the elementary interactions in question to be inhibited. The upper-right corner of Figure 2 shows a guard attached to an elementary interaction: The respective interaction is only executed if the guard evaluates to true. The actor evaluating the guard is named between brackets next to the guard. The last construct is depicted in the lower-right corner of Figure 2. It corresponds to the repetition of an interaction. Repetitions can be of type "while", "repeat until" or "for each" (the example shown in the figure is a "repeat until"). Repetitions of type "for each" have an associated "repetition expression" which determines the collection over which the repetition is performed. A repeated interaction (regardless of its type) has an associated stop condition. The actor responsible for evaluating the stop condition (and the repetition expression if applicable) is designated between brackets. Let's Dance does not impose a language for writing guards, stop conditions or repetition expressions. In this paper, we treat these as free-text.

2.2   Example

Figure 3 shows a simple order management choreography involving an actor "b1" playing the role "Buyer" and an actor "s1" playing the role "Supplier". Each interaction has a label assigned to it for identification purposes (e.g. "P" for exchanging message "PaymentNotice" in the example). The first interaction to be enabled is "O", whereby a supplier receives a message from a seller (and thus these actor references are bound to specific actors). Following this interaction, two elementary interactions ("OR" and "CO") are enabled: one where the buyer receives a number of "Order Responses" from the supplier, and another where the buyer receives a "Cancel Order" message from the supplier.

Interaction "OR" has an associated stop condition which is evaluated by actor "s1" (the supplier). This repeated interaction is of type "repeat ... until" and it completes once the supplier has no more "Order Response" messages to send (i.e. once all the line items in the purchase order have been processed). If all order responses are exchanged before a "Cancel Order" message materializes,

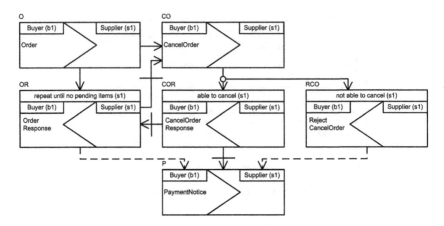

Fig. 3. Order Management Scenario

interaction "CO" is inhibited. This entails that any interaction that follows it in the "Precedes" graph can no longer be performed. If on the other hand the "Cancel Order" message materializes while "Order Response" messages are still being exchanged, the supplier may either reject or accept the cancellation request. In case of acceptance, a "Cancel Order Response" is exchanged and all other potentially active interactions are inhibited (namely "OR" and "P"). If the cancellation's is rejected, the supplier notifies it to the buyer (interaction "RCO") and all remaining interactions are allowed to complete. The choreography (instance) completes normally after the buyer and the supplier have exchanged a payment notice (interaction "P").

3 Formalization

3.1 Abstract Syntax

A *choreography* is a tuple $(I, RI, RT, GI, A, c_0, Precedes, WeakPrecedes,$ *Inhibits, Parent, Performs, Evaluates, Executes*) such that:

- I is a set of Interactions
- $RI \subseteq I$ is a set of Repeated Interactions
- A function RT: RI → {w, r, fs, fc} linking repeated interactions to a repetition type, which is either While, Repeat Until, For-each Sequential or For-each Concurrent
- $GI \subseteq I$ is a set of Guarded Interactions
- A is a set of Actors
- $c_0 \in I$ is the top-level interaction of the choreography
- *Precedes, WeakPrecedes, Inhibits* $\subseteq I \times I$ are three binary relations over the set of interactions I.
- *Parent* $\subseteq I \times I$ is the relation between interactions and their sub-interactions.
- A function *Performs*: I → $\wp(A)$ linking interactions to actors

- A function *Evaluates*: GI → ℘(A) linking guarded interactions to actors
- A function *Executes*: RI → ℘(A) linking repeated interactions to actors

Not captured in the above definition are the notions of "conditional" and "repetition" expressions since these can be abstracted away when formalizing the control-flow semantics of the language. However, it is useful to have these in mind to understand certain choices in the semantics. Each guarded interaction is associated to a conditional expression (i.e. a boolean function) that determines whether the interaction is performed or not. In the abstract syntax, we only capture the actor responsible for evaluating this conditional expression (function *Evaluates*) and not the expression itself. Likewise, every repeated interaction is associated with a conditional expression (called the "stop condition") that when evaluated to true implies that the iteration must stop (in the case of "repeat" and "for each") or must continue (in the case "while"). Again, the abstract syntax only captures the actor responsible for evaluating this expression (function *Executes*). Finally, "for each" repeated interactions have a "repetition expression" attached to it that, at runtime, is used to compute the ordered collection over which the iteration is performed. The actor responsible for evaluating the "repetition expression" is the same that evaluates the "stop condition".

The constraints below are assumed to be satisfied by any Let's Dance model.

- Each interaction has one and only one parent: $\forall i \in I \mid \exists! j \in I[j\ Parent\ i]$
- No relation crosses the boundary of a repeated (composite) interaction:
  $\forall i, j \in I\ \forall k \in RI[(k\ Ancestor\ i \wedge (i\ Precedes\ j \vee i\ WeakPrecedes\ j \vee i\ Inhibits\ j)) \rightarrow k\ Ancestor\ j \vee k = j]$ (where $Ancestor = Parent^+$).

3.2   Background on π-Calculus

The π-calculus is a process algebra for mobile systems [9]. In π-calculus, communication takes place between different π-processes. Names are a central concept in π-calculus. Links between processes as well as messages are names. This allows for link passing from one process to another. The scope of a name can be restricted to a set of processes but may be extruded as soon as the name is passed to other processes.

We will use the following syntax throughout the paper:

$$P ::= M \mid P|P' \mid (\nu\ z)P \mid\ !P$$
$$M ::= 0 \mid \pi.P \mid M + M'$$
$$\pi ::= \overline{x}\langle y\rangle \mid \overline{x} \mid x(y) \mid x \mid \tau$$

Concurrent execution is denoted as $P|P'$, the restriction of the scope of z to P as $(\nu\ z)P$ and an infinite number of concurrent copies of P as $!P$. Inaction of a process is denoted as 0. A non-deterministic choice between M and M' as $M + M'$, sending y over x as $\overline{x}\langle y\rangle$, sending an empty message over x as $\overline{x}$ and receiving an empty message over x as x. The prefix $x(y)$ receives a name over x and continues as P with y replaced by the received name. τ is the unobservable action. Communication between two processes can take place in the case of matching send- and receive-prefixes. Furthermore, we denote the parallel and sequential execution of the prefixes π_i, $i \in I$ as $\Pi_{i \in I}\, \pi_i$ and $\{\pi_i\}_{i \in I}$, respectively. To restrict the scope of the set of names z_i, $i \in I$ we use the abbreviation $[z_i]_{i \in I}$.

3.3 Formalization

We chose π-calculus for the formalization of Let's Dance since it has proved to be a suitable formalism for describing interactions in a service-oriented environment (cf. the formalization of the Service Interaction Patterns [8]). Although we do not exploit the full power of π-calculus in this paper, we are dependent on the concept of name passing as soon as correlation issues and actor reference passing find their way into the formalization. Also, conformance between global and local models – a central issue for choreographies in practice – calls for advanced reasoning techniques such as π-calculus' weak open bi-simulation.

To improve understandability, we decompose the formalization of an interaction into four levels covering different aspects as depicted in figure 4.

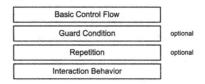

Fig. 4. Formalization levels for interactions

- *Basic Control Flow* covers the coordination between different interactions. The three different relationship types *Precedes*, *WeakPrecedes* and *Inhibits* and the notion of propagating skipping are formalized here.
- *Guard Condition* formalizes the possibility to skip an enabled interaction instance if a guard condition evaluates to false. Since evaluating the conditions themselves is not formalized, we introduced a non-deterministic choice. *Guard Condition* only applies to guarded interactions.
- *Repetition* covers the repetition types "while", "repeat", "for each (sequential)" and "for each (concurrent)". It only applies to repeated interactions.
- *Interaction Behavior* contains the formalization for elementary interactions and composite interactions. In the case of composite interactions enabling and skipping sub-interactions are formalized in this layer.

A π-process is introduced for each of these levels and for each interaction in a choreography. Communication between π-processes realizes the coordination between different interactions as well as between the different layers of each interaction. For inter-level-communication we introduce the private links *enable*, *complete* and *skip*. Figure 5 illustrates how these private links are used.

Sending a message over *enable* indicates that the interaction instance is enabled. Sending a message over *complete* back indicates that the interaction has executed successfully. *skip* is used to propagate skipping to sub-level-processes.

Case of executed interactions

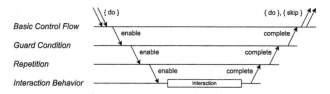

Case of skipped interactions

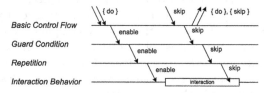

Fig. 5. Inter level communication

Formalization of Basic Control Flow. For every $A \in I$ the formalization of the corresponding interaction instances is:

$$A = (\nu\ perform, enable, complete, skip)(\{do_A\}_{i \in P}\ .\ \overline{perform} \tag{1}$$

$$|\ (perform\ .\ (\overline{enable}\ .\ (complete\ .\ A_{completed} \tag{2}$$

$$+ skip_A\ .\ (A_{skipped}\ |\ !skip_A))) \tag{3}$$

$$+ skip_A\ .\ (perform\ .\ A_{skipped}\ |\ !skip_A)) \tag{4}$$

$$|\ InnerProc(enable, complete, skip)) \tag{5}$$

$$A_{completed} = \{\overline{skip_i}\}_{i \in Q}\ .\ (\overline{done}_{Parent(A)}\ |\ \Pi_{i \in R}\ \overline{do_i})\ |\ !skip_A \tag{6}$$

$$A_{skipped} = \overline{skip}\ .\ \{\overline{skip_i}\}_{i \in S}\ .\ (\overline{done}_{Parent(A)}\ |\ \Pi_{i \in R}\ \overline{do_i}) \tag{7}$$

$$\textbf{where } P = \{x \in I \mid x\ Precedes\ A \vee x\ WeakPrecedes\ A \vee x = Parent(A)\}$$

$$Q = \{x \in I \mid A\ Inhibits\ x\}$$

$$R = \{x \in I \mid A\ Precedes\ x \vee A\ WeakPrecedes\ x\}$$

$$S = \{x \in I \mid A\ Precedes\ x\}$$

$$InnerProc = \begin{cases} Guard_A & \textbf{if } A \in GI \\ NoGuard_A & \textbf{if } A \notin GI \end{cases}$$

The names do_A and $skip_A$ are introduced for the coordination between A and all interactions that are the source of a relation where A is the target:

- *Precedes:* If the source interaction has completed an empty message is sent over do_A. If the source interaction was skipped then first a message is sent over $skip_A$ and then another message over do_A. This order is crucial for ensuring that first skipping is propagated before enabling takes place.
- *WeakPrecedes:* A message is sent over do_A if the source interaction has completed or was skipped.
- *Inhibits:* A message is sent over $skip_A$ if the source interaction has completed.

For every *Precedes* and *WeakPrecedes* relation a message over do_A has to arrive before anything else can happen inside the interaction instance. That is why the private name *perform* was introduced (lines 1, 2, 4). Even if a message over $skip_A$ arrives before all messages over do_A have arrived (line 4) the process has to wait for the remaining messages before sending a message over *perform*.

When all do_A-messages arrive before a $skip_A$-message, the interaction instance is enabled and an empty message is sent over *enable* to the process of the layer below (line 2). Once the interaction instance is enabled, the instance either completes (a *complete*-message is received) or a $skip_A$-message arrives. The latter causes the instance to be skipped immediately without waiting for the completion of the execution. In the first case, i.e. the instance completes, the follow-up actions in $A_{completed}$ apply which consist of first sending $skip_A$-messages to all target interactions of outgoing *Inhibits*-relations. Then *do*-messages are sent to all target interactions of outgoing *Precedes*- and *WeakPrecedes*-relations. *done*-messages will be explained in the section "Interaction behavior".

In the case where a $skip_A$-message arrives before all do_A-messages have arrived, the alternative in line 4 is chosen. After the *perform*-message has arrived (i.e. that all do_A-messages have arrived) the follow-up actions in $A_{skipped}$ apply. After skipping is propagated to the lower levels, *skip*-messages are sent to all target interactions of *Precedes*-relations. Finally, *do*- and *done*-messages are sent like it was already the case in $A_{skipped}$.

$!skip_A$ serves as a "garbage collector" for $skip_A$-messages that arrive without causing any effect: After the instance has already completed (line 6) or after a $skip_A$-message has already caused skipping the instance (lines 3, 4).

Example. Interaction OR from Figure 3 is not guarded and has one incoming *Precedes*-relation, one incoming *Inhibits*-relation, one outgoing *Inhibits*-relation and one outgoing *WeakPrecedes*-relation which leads to the following π-processes:

$$OR = !(\nu\ perform, enable, complete, skip)(do_{OR} \cdot \overline{perform}$$
$$|\ (perform \cdot (\overline{enable} \cdot (complete \cdot OR_{completed}$$
$$+skip_{OR} \cdot (OR_{skipped}\ |\ !skip_{OR})))$$
$$+skip_{OR} \cdot (perform \cdot OR_{skipped}\ |\ !skip_{OR}))$$
$$|\ NoGuard_{OR}(enable, complete, skip))$$
$$OR_{completed} = \overline{skip_{CO}} \cdot \overline{do_P}\ |\ !skip_{OR}$$
$$OR_{skipped} = \overline{skip} \cdot \overline{do_P}$$

Interaction Instance Lifecycle. When observing the communication between the *Basic-Control-Flow*-layer-process and the process of the level below we can easily identify the state an interaction instance is in. Figure 6 depicts the life cycle of an interaction instance.

Each interaction instance starts in the state *initialized*. Now a message over either *enable* or *skip* can be sent. In the case of *skip* the interaction instance is skipped and cannot execute any more. In the case of *enable* a message over

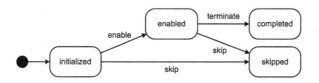

Fig. 6. Interaction instance life cycle

complete or *skip* can be sent. As already mentioned *complete* indicates that the interaction has executed successfully. Therefore, the instance changes to the state *completed*. A message over *skip* results in skipping the instance.

Formalization of Guard Conditions

$$Guard_A(e, c, s) = (\nu\ enable, complete, skip)(s\ .\ \overline{skip} \tag{1}$$
$$|\ (e\ .\ (\tau_0\ .\ \overline{skip_A} + \tau_0\ .(\overline{enable}\ .\ complete\ .\ \overline{c} \tag{2}$$
$$|\ InnerProc(enable, complete, skip))))) \tag{3}$$
$$NoGuard_A(e, c, s) = InnerProc(e, c, s) \tag{4}$$

$$\textbf{where} \quad InnerProc = \begin{cases} While_A & \textbf{if}\ A \in RI \wedge RT(A) = w \\ Repeat_A & \textbf{if}\ A \in RI \wedge RT(A) = r \\ ForEachSeq_A & \textbf{if}\ A \in RI \wedge RT(A) = fs \\ ForEachConc_A & \textbf{if}\ A \in RI \wedge RT(A) = fc \\ NoRepetition_A & \textbf{if}\ A \notin RI \end{cases}$$

The links e, c and s are used for the communication with the *Basic Control Flow* layer. The new names *enable*, *complete* and *skip* serve as communication links to the process of the layer below.

A guard will not be evaluated until the interaction instance is enabled. That is why a message has to be received over e before the non-deterministic choice can take place (line 2). If the first alternative is chosen a *skip*-message is sent back to the *Basic-Control-Flow*-layer-process which causes the interaction instance to be skipped. If the second alternative is chosen the layer below is enabled.

Example. Interaction COR from Figure 3 leads to the following π-process:

$$Guard_{COR}(e, c, s) = (\nu\ enable, complete, skip)(s\ .\ \overline{skip}$$
$$|\ (e\ .\ (\tau_0\ .\ \overline{skip_A} + \tau_0\ .(\overline{enable}\ .\ complete\ .\ \overline{c}$$
$$|\ NoRepetition_{COR}(enable, complete, skip)))))$$

Interaction OR from Figure 3 is translated as

$$NoGuard_{OR}(e, c, s) = Repeat_{OR}(e, c, s)$$

Formalization of Repetitions. "While" and "For each (sequential)" have identical semantics at the level of abstraction of control flow. In both cases the interaction instance is executed an arbitrary number of times. We assume that the repetition will terminate at some point in time. "Repeat until" repetitions have similar semantics as "While" except that in this case the interaction instance is executed at least once. The formalization below is based on recursion.

$$While_A(e, c, s) = ForEachSeq_A(e, c, s) = (\nu\ enable, complete, skip)$$
$$(s\ .\ \overline{skip}\ |\ e\ .\ R)$$
$$R = \tau_0\ .\ \overline{c} + \tau_0\ .\ (\overline{enable}\ .\ complete\ .\ R$$
$$|\ InnerProc(enable, complete, skip))$$
$$Repeat_A(e, c, s) = (\nu\ enable, complete, skip)(s\ .\ \overline{skip}\ |\ e\ .$$
$$(\overline{enable}\ .\ complete\ .\ R$$
$$|\ InnerProc(enable, complete, skip)))$$
$$R = \tau_0\ .\ \overline{c} + \tau_0\ .\ (\overline{enable}\ .\ complete\ .\ R$$
$$|\ InnerProc(enable, complete, skip))$$
$$\textbf{where}\quad InnerProc = \begin{cases} Elementary_A\ \textbf{if}\ A \notin CI \\ Composite_A\ \ \ \textbf{if}\ A \in CI \end{cases}$$

"For each (concurrent)" is the most complex type of repetitions. All interaction instances are executed concurrently. Informally, when a repeated interaction is performed, one instance of the contained interaction is started for each element in the collection obtained from the evaluation of the repetition expression. These instances execute concurrently. Each time that one of these instances completes, the stop condition is evaluated. If the stop condition evaluates to true, the execution of the remaining instances is stopped and the execution of the repeated interaction is considered to be completed.

The formalization of the "For each (concurrent)" construct below is inspired from the π-formalization for the workflow pattern "Multiple Instances with a-priori Runtime Knowledge" given in [10]. We introduce a linked list of processes that use links c for notifying the previous process in the list that the interaction instance has completed successfully and sk to notify the next process that the instance has been skipped. Figure 7 illustrates this. There can be cases where not all instances have to completed before the repetition is considered to be completed. Arbitrary stop conditions can be defined for a repetition and after a given instance completes a non-deterministic choice either leads to waiting for *complete* or sending a message over st right away. The latter results in propagating *stop*-messages that lead to the completion of the repeated interaction. The formalization of this construct is given below. The Symbol *InnerProc* is defined as for "While" repetitions (see above).

$$ForEachConc_A(e, c, s) = (\nu\ comp, sk)(e\ .R(comp, comp, sk)\ |\ comp\ .\ \overline{c}\ |\ s\ .\ \overline{sk})$$
$$R(c, st, s) = (\nu\ comp, stop, sk)(\tau_0\ .\ \overline{c} + \tau_0\ .\ (R(comp, stop, sk)$$
$$|\ (\nu\ enable, complete, skip)(s\ .\ (\overline{sk}\ |\ \overline{skip})$$
$$|\ \overline{enable}\ .\ (stop\ .\ (\overline{st}\ |\ \overline{skip}) + complete\ .$$
$$(\tau_0\ .\ (comp.\overline{c} + stop.\overline{st}) + \tau_0\ .\ (\overline{st}\ |\ \overline{sk})))$$
$$|\ InnerProc(enable, complete, skip))))$$

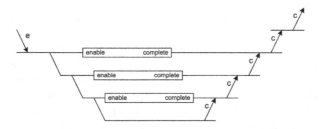

Fig. 7. Linked list of processes realizing three concurrent interaction instances

Example. π-processes for interaction OR from Figure 3:

$$Repeat_{OR}(e, c, s) = (\nu\; enable, complete, skip)(s.\overline{skip} \mid e.(\overline{enable}.complete.R$$
$$\mid Elementary_{OR}(enable, complete, skip)))$$
$$R = \tau_0 . \bar{c} + \tau_0 . (\overline{enable} . complete . R$$
$$\mid Elementary_{OR}(enable, complete, skip))$$

Formalization of Interaction Behavior. Elementary interactions are assumed to be atomic. Since we only focus on the control flow aspects of choreographies we do not incorporate an actual communication between two business partners in the π-formalization. We simply denote this interaction as $\tau_{interact}$.

$$Elementary_A(e, c, s) = e . \tau_{interact} . \bar{c} \mid s$$
$$Composite_A(e, c, s) = (\nu\; [do_i]_{i \in Q}, [done_i]_{i \in Q}, [skip_i]_{i \in Q})(\Pi_{B \in Q}\; B$$
$$\mid e .(\Pi_{i \in P} \overline{do_i} \mid \{done_A\}_{i \in P} . \bar{c})$$
$$\mid s . (\Pi_{i \in P} \overline{skip_i} . \overline{do_i}))$$

where $P = \{x \in I \mid A = Parent(x)\}$
$$Q = \{x \in I \mid A \in RI \wedge A\; Ancestor\; x$$
$$\wedge \neg \exists y \in RI(A\; Ancestor\; y \wedge y\; Ancestor\; x)\}$$

Sub interactions of composite interactions must not execute until the parent interaction has been enabled. In the formalization of *Basic Control Flow* we have seen that *do*-messages are expected from all source interactions of *Precedes*- and *WeakPrecedes*-relations as well as from all direct parent interactions.

As soon as an interaction instance has completed or is ready for propagating skipping a *done*-message is sent to the direct parent interaction. These *done*-messages are collected in the *Composite_A* process and as soon as all messages have arrived the *complete*-message is sent to the super-level-process. This behavior guarantees that all sub interaction instances are already in one of the states completed or skipped before further enabling and skipping takes place for outgoing relations from A.

In case of the receipt of a *skip*-message, *skip*-messages are sent to all sub interactions. If a sub interaction has already completed or has been skipped, this message does not have any effect.

If A is a repeated interaction we have to start executing the π-processes for all sub interactions at this point in time. That way we create multiple interaction instances for each sub interaction (one instance per repetition cycle). By creating new *do-* and *skip*-names we make sure that the inter-interaction-instance-coordination takes place within the same repetition cycle.

Creating new names only in the case of repeated interactions also implements the fact that *Precedes-*, *WeakPrecedes-* and *Inhibits*-relations can cross the boundaries of a composite interaction i if i is not repeated.

Example. Interaction OR from Figure 3 leads to the following formalization:

$$Elementary_{OR}(e, c, s) = e \cdot \tau_{interact} \cdot \bar{c} \mid s$$

Putting it All Together. We have shown how the behavior of individual interaction instances can be expressed using π-calculus. It now only takes a small step to come to a π-formalization of a whole choreography C:

$$C = (\nu \; [do_i]_{i \in P}, [done_i]_{i \in P}, [skip_i]_{i \in P}) \; \Pi_{A \in P} \; A$$
$$\textbf{where} \quad P = \{x \in I \mid \neg \exists y \in RI(y \; Ancestor \; x)\}$$

The π-processes for all interaction instances that are not sub interactions of repeated interactions are executed in parallel. Sub interactions of repeated interactions are executed in the $Composite_A$-process.

4   Reachability Analysis for Choreographies

The translation of Lets Dance choreographies into π-processes as it is shown in the previous section allows for reasoning on these choreographies. A typical means to examine π-processes is to use bi-simulation equivalence. The first definitions for bi-simulation, namely early and late bi-simulation, were introduced by Milner, Parrow and Walker ([9]). However, the most prominent definition for bi-simulation was introduced by Sangiorgi ([11]) and is called open bi-simulation. Using this bi-simulation equivalence relation $\sim_o$ we know whether two π-processes have the same transition behavior and thus simulate each other.

In the case of weak open bi-simulation the non-observable transitions are ignored. This bi-simulation definition is suitable for our purposes: We want to focus on certain interactions in our choreographies and consider everything else as non-observable to the bi-simulation analysis.

One interesting property of an interaction in a choreography is whether it is reachable (i.e. it may execute successfully) or if it is not-reachable (i.e. it never executes). If we examine an elementary interaction it is sufficient to check whether $\tau_{interact}$ may be executed. However, according to the definition given at the beginning of section 3 this action is unobservable. To change this we can replace the $\tau_{interact}$ of the interaction in question by the send-prefix $\overline{interact}$. The π-process would look like

$$Elementary_A(e, t, s) = e \cdot \overline{interact} \cdot \bar{t} \mid s$$

If we now define the link *interact* to be the only observable part in the choreography then we can compare it to other π-processes. E.g. a comparison to the π-process 0 tells us whether an interaction is reachable or not. If the choreography is weak open bi-simulation related to 0 the interaction in question is not-reachable otherwise the interaction must be reachable.

Doing bi-simulation analysis using tools such as the Mobility Workbench ([12]) is not possible if the choreography contains repeated interactions. The formalizations in the previous section introduce a non-deterministic choice for the stop condition of repetitions which causes the tool to run into an infinite loop. However, we can simply omit the *Repetition* layer for the reachability analysis while preserving correct results.

5   Related Work

Industry-driven initiatives have attempted to standardize notations for global description of service interactions. An early attempt was BPSS [5] where global models are captured as flows of interactions using flowchart-like constructs. WSCI [2] represents another approach wherein global service interaction models are defined as collections of inter-connected local models. Control dependencies are described within each individual local model. A formal semantics of a subset of WSCI is sketched in [3]. More recently, the WS-CDL initiative [7] led to a language that follows the line of BPSS insofar as global service behavior is described as flows of interactions. WS-CDL goes further than BPSS in the level of details at which interaction flows are described. In fact, WS-CDL can be seen as a programming-in-the-large language for Web services: it deals with global interactions as the basic primitive but relies on imperative programming constructs such as variable assignment, sequence and block-structured choice and parallel branching. Several formal semantics of WS-CDL or subsets thereof have been defined. Yang et al. [13] propose a small-step operational semantics of WS-CDL. It is not clear however that this semantics provides a suitable basis for reasoning about service choreographies, such as determining whether or not a local model complies to a choreography, or performing reachability analysis as discussed above. Other authors have defined subsets of WS-CDL and captured them in terms of process calculi. Busi et al. [4] define a formal language corresponding to a subset of WS-CDL and use it as a foundation to capture relationships between choreographies and local models. It is unclear though that this formalization provides a suitable basis for automated analysis of choreographies.

Unlike WS-CDL, Let's Dance does not target application developers, but rather analysts and designers. Accordingly, it avoids reliance on imperative programming constructs with which analysts are usually unfamiliar. Still, Let's Dance models can be used for simulation and verification as discussed above.

Several authors have considered the use of communicating state machines as a basis for modeling global models of service interactions [6]. While state machines lead to simple models for sequential scenarios, they usually lead to spaghetti-like models when used to capture scenarios with parallelism and cancellation. Thus, state machines may provide a suitable foundation for reasoning about service interactions, but their suitability for choreography modeling is questionable.

6 Conclusion and Outlook

This paper has introduced a formal semantics for a service interaction modeling language, namely Let's Dance, which supports the high-level capture of both global models (i.e. choreographies) and local models of service interactions. The semantics is defined by translation to π-calculus. At present, the semantics focuses on control-flow aspects. However, π-calculus is well-suited for capturing actor bindings and passing binding information across actors. Ongoing work aims at extending the current semantics along this direction.

The presented semantics has been used as a blueprint for the implementation of a simulation engine and as a basis for analyzing Let's Dance choreographies. We have shown in this paper how weak open bisimulation can be used to check reachability of interactions. Ongoing work aims at applying a similar technique to compliance checking, i.e. checking whether a local model complies to a choreography. However, when interactions in the choreography and those in the local models do not map one-to-one, or when a local model implements several choreographies, pure weak open bi-simulation approaches reach their limits.

Another problem that deserves further attention and can be addressed on the basis of the formalization is that of *local enforceability* of choreographies [15]. It turns out that not all choreographies defined as flows of interactions (the paradigm adopted in Let's Dance) can be mapped into local models that satisfy the following conditions: (i) the local models contain only interactions described in the choreography; and (ii) they collectively enforce all the constraints in the choreography. Proposals around WS-CDL skirt this issue. Instead, they assume the existence of a state (i.e. a set of variables) shared by all participants. Participants synchronize with one another to maintain the shared state up-to-date. Thus, certain interactions take place between services for the sole purpose of synchronizing their local view on the shared state and these interactions are not defined in the choreography. In the worst case, this leads to situations where a business analyst signs off on a choreography, and later it turns out that to execute this choreography a service provided by one organization must interact with a service provided by a competitor, unknowingly of the analyst. Thus, it is desirable to provide tool support to analyze choreographies to determine whether or not they are enforceable by some set of local models. In [15], we have defined an algorithm for determining local enforceability of Let's Dance choreographies. The formal semantics presented in this paper can provide a basis for validating the correctness of the transformation rules encoded in this algorithm.

Acknowledgments. The second author is funded by SAP. The third author is funded by a fellowship co-sponsored by Queensland Government and SAP.

References

1. T. Andrews, F. Curbera, H. Dholakia, Y. Goland, J. Klein, F. Leymann, K. Liu, D. Roller, D. Smith, S. Thatte, I. Trickovic, S. Weerawarana: *Business Process Execution Language for Web Services, version 1.1*, May 2003. http://www-106. ibm.com/developerworks/webservices/library/ws-bpel
2. A. Arkin et al.: *Web Service Choreography Interface (WSCI) 1.0*, 2002. www.w3. org/TR/wsci/
3. A. Brogi, C. Canal, E. Pimentel, A. Vallecillo: *Formalizing Web Service Choreographies*. In Proceedings of 1st International Workshop on Web Services and Formal Methods, Pisa, Italy, February 2004, Elsevier.
4. N. Busi, R. Gorrieri, C. Guidi, R. Lucchi, G. Zavattaro: *Choreography and Orchestration Conformance for System Design*. In Proceedings of 8th International Conference on Coordination Models and Languages (COORDINATION'06), Bologna, Italy, June 2006, Springer Verlag.
5. J. Clark, C. Casanave, K. Kanaskie, B. Harvey, N. Smith, J. Yunker, K. Riemer (Eds.): *ebXML Business Process Specification Schema Version 1.01*, UN/CEFACT and OASIS Specification, May 2001. http://www.ebxml.org/specs/ebBPSS.pdf
6. R. Hull, J. Su: *Tools for composite web services: a short overview*. SIGMOD Record 34(2): 86-95, 2005.
7. N. Kavantzas, D. Burdett, G. Ritzinger, Y. Lafon: *Web Services Choreography Description Language Version 1.0*, W3C Candidate Recommendation, November 2005. http://www.w3.org/TR/ws-cdl-10
8. G. Decker, F. Puhlmann, M. Weske: *Formalizing Service Interactions*. In Proceedings of BPM 2006, Vienna, Austria, 2006, Springer Verlag.
9. R. Milner, J. Parrow, D. Walker: *A calculus of mobile processes*, Information and Computation, 100:1–40, 1992.
10. F. Puhlmann, M. Weske: *Using the π-Calculus for Formalizing Workflow Patterns*. In Proceedings of BPM 2005, Nancy, France, September 2005, pp 153-168, Springer Verlag.
11. D. Sangiorgi: *A theory of bisimulation for the π-calculus*. In Acta Informatica 16(33): 69-97, 1996.
12. B. Victor, F. Moller, M. Dam, L.H. Eriksson: *The Mobility Workbench*. Uppsala University, 2006. http://www.it.uu.se/research/group/mobility/mwb
13. H. Yang, X. Zhao, Z. Qiu, G. Pu, S. Wang: *A Formal Model for Web Service Choreography Description Language (WS-CDL)*. Preprint, School of Mathematical Sciences, Peking University, January 2006. www.math.pku.edu.cn: 8000/var/preprint/7021.pdf
14. J. M. Zaha, A. Barros, M. Dumas, A. ter Hofstede: *Lets Dance: A Language for Service Behavior Modeling*. Preprint # 4468, Faculty of IT, Queensland University of Technology, February 2006. http://eprints.qut.edu.au/archive/00004468
15. J. M. Zaha, M. Dumas, A. ter Hofstede, A. Barros, G. Decker: *Service Interaction Modeling: Bridging Global and Local Views*. In Proceedings of the 10th International EDOC Conference, Hong Kong, 2006.

Analysis and Verification of Time Requirements Applied to the Web Services Composition

Gregorio Díaz, María-Emilia Cambronero, M. Llanos Tobarra,
Valentín Valero, and Fernando Cuartero

Department of Computer Science
University of Castilla-La Mancha
Escuela Politécnica Superior de Albacete. 02071 - Spain
{gregorio, emicp, llanos, valentin, fernando}@dsi.uclm.es

Abstract. This work presents a new approach to the analysis and verification of the time requirements of Web Services compositions via goal-driven models and model checking techniques. The goal-driven model used is an extension of the goal model KAOS and the model checker engine is the UPPAAL tool. The goal model specifies the properties that the system must satisfy and how they should be verified by using the model checker engine. In order to illustrate this approach, we apply these techniques to a basic Internet purchase process.

1 Introduction

A basic activity in the design of software system and by extension to Web Services is the analysis and verification of the requirements that the system must satisfy. However, before performing the analysis and verification, the software engineer must gather these requirements in an standardized specification.

In this work, we have focused our efforts on those systems where time plays an important role. Thus, in the literature we can find related works for the specification of software system requirements, as for instance [17]. However, we have based this work on the work of Lamsweerde et al [1,8,20]. Thus we have extended this work in order to describe more complex goal-driven requirement models. Once we have captured the system requirements and implemented the system by means of Web Services composition [5,4] (concretely by using the Web Service Choreography Description Language, WS-CDL [12]), these Web Services are translated into Timed Automata [2] by using the technique presented in [11]. After the translation, we can verify the time requirements by using the model checker, UPPAAL [9,10,15].

This work is structured in seven sections. In the first section we have already seen a brief introduction to the work. The second section presents the methodology approach. The third section specifies the study case that we follow in this work. The fourth section shows a goal-driven model for gathering time requirements. The fifth section performs a brief summary about WS-CDL, timed automata and the translation process between them. In the sixth section, we will see how to perform the verification process. Finally, the seventh section deals with the conclusions and future works.

M. Bravetti, M. Nuñes, and G. Zavattaro (Eds.): WS-FM 2006, LNCS 4184, pp. 178–192, 2006.

2   The Methodology Approach

The proposed methodology is divided into three phases (Fig. 1): Analysis, design and verification. The analysis is performed by using an extension of the goal model KAOS. This goal model allows analysts and specifiers to gather time requirements of software systems in a hierarchic order, i.e., from general and strategic goals to concrete requirements.

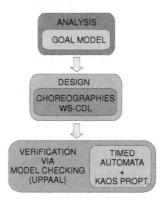

Fig. 1. The proposed Methodology for Web Services composition

The design is performed via composed specifications written in Web Services choreographies (WS-CDL), which are known as Web Services choreography specifications. These specifications appear as a necessary result of composing Web Services and implement mechanisms to deal with compositional problems, as for instance concurrency and time aspects.

The verification phase in the literature is useful taken together with the design phase. However, during the last few years, there has been a growing consensus that verification is a key instrument for developing software systems, in that sense Hoare [14], Clarke [7] together with a large number of authors have agreed in its importance [13]. Thus, we have considered that the verification is substantial enough to be taken apart from previous phases, although, we should not forget how close this phase is to the design. In this phase we have used a translation algorithm presented in [11] in order to translate the choreographies specified in the design into timed automata, which are the formalism used by the model checker UPPAAL. The timed automata captures in a proper manner the time behaviors of the different Web Services involved in a choreography. Once this translation is successfully finished, the verifiers can check whether the requirements, now transformed into properties, are fulfilled by the timed automata or not. If the verifiers find that the timed automata do not satisfy a property, then they can use the counterexample obtained from the verification to locate where exactly the error lies. This error can occur for several reasons, in which are included: Requirement specification errors, choreography specification errors and, the most desirable case, errors in the real system.

3   The Study Case: An Internet Purchase Process

This example is based upon a typical purchase process that uses Internet as a business context for a transaction. There are three actors in this example: a customer, a seller and a carrier. The Internet purchase works as follows: *"A customer wants to buy a product by using Internet. There are several sellers that offer different products in Internet Servers based on Web-pages. The customer contacts a seller in order to buy the desired product. The seller checks the stock and contacts with a carrier. Finally, the carrier delivers the product to the customer."*

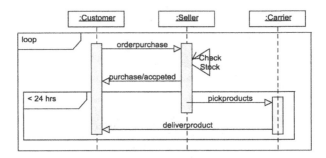

Fig. 2. The diagram for a purchase process by Internet

Figure 2 depicts the diagram that represents this purchase process. This process consists of three participants: the customer, the seller and the carrier. The behavior of each participant is defined as follows:

- Customer: He contacts the seller to buy a product. He must send the seller the information about the product and the payment method. After the payment, he waits to receive the product from a carrier within the agreed time, twenty four hours.
- Seller: He receives the customer order and the payment method. The seller checks if there is enough stock to deliver the order and sends an acceptance notification to the customer . If there is stock to deliver the order, then he contacts with a carrier to deliver the product.
- Carrier: He picks up the order and the customer information in order to deliver the product to the customer. The interval to deliver the product is the time that the seller has stipulated, one day, which is the main temporal constraint.

4   The Analysis Phase

The requirements, properties and characteristics of the system must be gathered in order to be checked. However, they must be expressed in a formalized manner. There are several languages, graphical diagrams, etc. to perform this, but we apply those in which time requirements are well captured. In this sense, goal-oriented requirements engineering emerges as a natural choice. The key activity in goal-oriented requirements engineering is the construction of the goal model.

Goals are objectives the system under construction must achieve. Goal formulations thus refer to intended properties to be ensured. They are formulated at different levels of abstraction from high-level, strategic concerns to low-level technical concerns. Goal models also allow analysts to capture and explore alternative refinements for a given goal. The resulting structure of the goal model is an AND-OR graph. The specific goal-oriented framework considered here is an extension of KAOS methodology [1,6,8,20] which has a two-level language: (1) an outer semi-formal layer for capturing, structuring and presenting requirements engineering concepts; (2) an inner formal assertion layer for their precise definition and for reasoning about them.

4.1   The Inner Formal Assertions Layer: TCTL Style Requirements

The formal assertions, in which the goals are written, use the UPPAAL language for specifying properties. This language is a subset of timed computation tree logic (TCTL) [19,18], where atomic expressions are location names, variables and clocks from the modeled system. The properties are defined using local properties that are either true or false depending on a specific configuration.

Definition 1. (Local Property) *Given an UPPAAL model* $\langle A, Vars, Clocks, Chan, Type \rangle$. *A formula* φ *is a local property iff it is formed according to the following syntactical rules:*

$$\varphi ::= deadlock$$

$$| \ A.l \qquad \qquad for \ A \in A \ and \ l \in L_A$$
$$| \ x \bowtie c \qquad \qquad for \ x \in Clocks, \bowtie \in \{<, <=, ==, >=>\}, c \in \mathbb{Z}$$
$$| \ x - y \bowtie c \qquad for \ x, y \in Clocks, \bowtie \in \{<, <=, ==, >=>\}, c \in \mathbb{Z}$$
$$| \ a \bowtie b \qquad \qquad for \ a, b \in Vars \bigcup \mathbb{Z}, \bowtie \in \{<, <=, ! =, ==, >=>\}$$
$$| \ (\varphi_1) \qquad \qquad for \ \varphi_1 \ a \ local \ property$$
$$| \ not \ \varphi_1 \qquad \quad for \ \varphi_1 \ a \ local \ property$$
$$| \ \varphi_1 \ or \ \varphi_2 \qquad for \ \varphi_1, \varphi_2 \ logical \ properties \ (logical \ OR)$$
$$| \ \varphi_1 \ and \ \varphi_2 \quad for \ \varphi_1, \varphi_2 \ logical \ properties \ (logical \ AND)$$
$$| \ \varphi_1 \ imply \ \varphi_2 \ for \ \varphi_1, \varphi_2 \ logical \ properties \ (logical \ implication)$$

In Definition 1 we have expressed the syntax of the temporal logic that UPPAAL uses. Now, let us see the definition of the five different property classes that UPPAAL may check.

Definition 2. (Temporal Properties) *let* $M = \langle A, Vars, Clocks, Chan, Type \rangle$ *be an UPPAAL model and let* φ *and* ψ *be local properties. The correctness of temporal properties is defined for the classes* $A[\ ]$, $A <>$ *and* $-->$ *as follows:*

$$M \vDash A[\ ] \ \varphi \qquad iff \ \forall \{(l, e, v)\}^K \in \tau(M). \ \forall k \le K. \ (l, e, v)^k \vDash_{loc} \varphi$$
$$M \vDash A <> \varphi \qquad iff \ \forall \{(l, e, v)\}^K \in \tau(M). \ \exists k \le K. \ (l, e, v)^k \vDash_{loc} \varphi$$
$$M \vDash \varphi --> \psi \ iff \ \forall \{(l, e, v)\}^K \in \tau(M). \ \forall k \le K$$
$$(l, e, v)^k \vDash_{loc} \varphi \Rightarrow \exists k' \ge k. \ (l, e, v)^{k'} \vDash_{loc} \psi$$

The two temporal property classes dual to $A[\ ]$ *and* $A <>$ *are defined as follows:*

$$M \vDash E <> \varphi \ iff \ \neg (M \vDash_{loc} A[\ ] \ not(\varphi))$$
$$M \vDash E[\ ] \ \varphi \quad iff \ \neg (M \vDash_{loc} A <> not(\varphi))$$

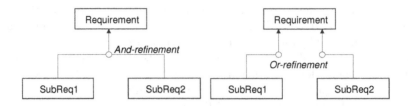

Fig. 3. And-refinement and Or-refinement goal models

4.2   The Outer Semi-formal Layer: The Goal-Driven Model

Two key elements are used as building elements for the definition of a goal model: *goals* and *requirements*. A goal prescribes intended behaviors of the system. It may refer to services to be provided (functional goals) or to the quality of service (non-functional goals). A requirement is a leaf goal that requires co-operation between different parties, which are called *agents*. Agents are active components that play a role in achieving goal satisfaction. To build Goal Models, goals are organized in an AND/OR refinement - abstraction hierarchy where higher-level goals are, in general, strategic, coarse-grained and involve multiple agents whereas lower-level goals are, in general, technical, fine-grained and involve fewer agents. In such structures, AND-refinement links relate a goal to a set of subgoals (called refinement) possibly conjoined with domain properties; this means that satisfying all subgoals in the refinement is a sufficient condition in the domain for satisfying the goal, as seen in the left-hand side of Figure 3. OR-refinement links may relate a goal to a set of alternative refinements, as seen in right-hand side of Figure 3.

Requirements must be checked by the model checker and are formalized in a real-time temporal logic that we have shown above. Keywords such as *Achieve* (reachability), *Avoid* (not safety), *Maintain* (safety), *possibly always*, *inevitably* and *unbounded response*, are used to name goals according to the temporal behavior pattern they prescribe. They are depicted in the goal model as follows:

Temporal Behavior	Goal Model Representation
Maintain (Safety) $A[\,]\,\varphi$	Requirement
Achieve (Reachability) $E <> \varphi$	Requirement
Possibly Always $E[\,]\,\varphi$	Requirement
Inevitably $A <> \varphi$	Requirement
Unbounded Response $\varphi -\!-> \psi$	Requirement

Once we have defined the goal model, we can apply this technique to our example. We must identify the crucial requirements for the Internet purchase process that we have described above. For this we have identified two different kinds of requirements. One kind refers to the obligation that both the seller and carrier have agreed to deliver the product on time, while the other refers to the quality of service. The time restriction establishes that the seller and carrier have twenty four hours to deliver the product. So, the seller must prepare the order for the carrier to send the product within the interval. The service quality is determined by two different requirements that are closely linked. The service must be rapid and also efficient. Due to this close relationship between these two requirements, if one of them is fulfilled then the other is fulfilled too.

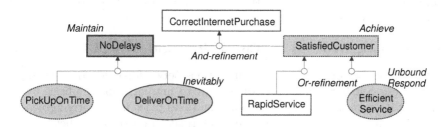

Fig. 4. The goal-model for the Internet Purchase Process

Figure 4 depicts the goal-model that we have developed for this example. The root goal *"CorrectInternetPurchase"* is decomposed into two subgoals by an And-refinement, which means that each one must be fulfilled in order to achieve the root goal. The first one, *"NoDelays"*, that is of type "maintain", is refined by another And-refinement with two leaf goals that inherit the maintain character. The first leaf goal *"PickupOnTime"* is of type "Unbound Respond". This goal represents the situation that the carrier must pick up the order on time and is formalized as follows:

$$Customer.WaitOrder \; - \; - >$$
$$(Carrier.PickUp \wedge Clock_{deliver} < 24hours) \tag{1}$$

The second leaf goal *"DeliverOnTime"* is of type "Inevitably" and specifies that the carrier must deliver the order on time. The goal is defined as follows:

$$A <> (Carrier.Deliver \wedge Clock_{deliver} < 24hours) \tag{2}$$

The second one, *"SatisfiedCustomer"*, of type "Achieve", is formed by two leaf goals. These leaf goals refine the parent goal by an Or-refinement, which means that if one of them is satisfied then the parent goal is satisfied too. The leaf goal *"RapidService"*, that determines that the customer will receive the order on time, is specified as follows:

$$E <> (Customer.ReceiveOrder \wedge Clock_{deliver} < 24hours) \tag{3}$$

The leaf goal *"EfficientService"* has the behavior of an "Unbounded Response" requirement. This goal indicates that when the seller accepts the order, then in the future, the customer will receive the order. This goal is formalized as follows:

$$Seller.AcceptOrder -- > Customer.ReceiveOrder \qquad (4)$$

5   The Design Phase

In the design phase, designers must specify the system by implementing it with the Web Service Choreography Description Language. Once we have this choreography specification, we can use the work presented in [11] in order to obtain the equivalent timed automata.

5.1   Designing Web Services Composition with WS-CDL

WS-CDL describes interoperable collaborations between parties. In order to facilitate these collaborations, services commit to mutual responsibilities by establishing Relationships. Their collaboration takes place in a jointly agreed set of ordering and constraint rules, whereby information is exchanged between the parties. The WS-CDL model consists of the following entities:

- **Participant Types, Role Types and Relationship Types** within a Choreography. Information is always exchanged between parties within or across trust boundaries. A Role Type enumerates the observable behavior a party exhibits in order to collaborate with other parties. A Relationship Type identifies the mutual commitments that must be made between two parties for them to collaborate successfully. A Participant Type groups together those parts of the observable behavior that must be implemented by the same logical entity or organization.
- **Information Types, Variables and Tokens.** Variables contain information about commonly observable objects in a collaboration, such as the information exchanged or the observable information of the Roles involved. Tokens are aliases that can be used to reference parts of a Variable. Both Variables and Tokens have Types that define the structure of what the Variable contains or the Token references.
- **Choreographies** define collaborations between interacting parties:
  - **Choreography Life-line:** This shows the progression of a collaboration. Initially, the collaboration is established between the parties; then, some work is performed within it, and finally it completes either normally or abnormally.
  - **Choreography Exception Block:** This specifies the additional interactions that should occur when a Choreography behaves in an abnormal way.
  - **Choreography Finalizer Block:** This describes how to specify additional interactions that should occur to modify the effect of an earlier successfully completed Choreography (for instance to confirm or undo the effect).

- **Channels** establish a point of collaboration between parties by specifying where and how information is exchanged.
- **Work Units** prescribe the constraints that must be fulfilled for making progress and thus performing actual work within a Choreography.
- **Activities and Ordering Structures.** Activities are the lowest level components of the Choreography that perform the actual work. Ordering Structures combine activities with other Ordering Structures in a nested structure to express the ordering conditions in which information within the Choreography is exchanged.
- **Interaction Activity** is the basic building block of a Choreography, which results in an exchange of information between parties and possible synchronizations of their observable information changes, and the actual values of the exchanged information.

Figure 5 shows a piece of the WS-CDL specification corresponding to this purchase process.

5.2   Timed Automata

By definition, a timed automaton is a standard finite-state automaton extended with a finite collection of real valued clocks. The clocks are assumed to proceed at the same rate and their values may be compared with natural numbers or reset to 0. UPPAAL extends the notion of timed automata to include integer variables, i.e. integer valued variables that may appear freely in general arithmetic expression used in guards as well as in assignments.

The model also allows clocks not only to be reset, but also to be set to any non-negative integer value.

Definition 3. (Atomic Constraints) *Let C be a set of real valued clocks and I a set of integer valued variables. An atomic clock constraint over C is a constraint of the form: $x \sim n$ or $x - y \sim n$, for $x, y \in C$, $\sim \in \{\leq, \geq, =\}$ and $n \in \mathbf{N}$. An atomic constraint over I is a constraint of the form: $i \sim n$, for $i \in I$, $\sim \in \{\leq, \geq, =\}$ and $n \in \mathbf{Z}$.*

By $C_c(C)$ we will denote the set of all clock constraints over C, and by $C_i(I)$ we will denote the set of all integer constraints over I.

Definition 4. (Guards) *Let C be a set of real valued clocks, and I a set of integer valued variables. A guard g over C and I is a formula generated by the following syntax: $g ::= c | g \wedge g$, where $c \in (C_c(C) \bigcup C_i(I))$.*

$\mathcal{B}(C, I)$ will stand for the set of all guards over C and I.

Definition 5. (Assignments) *Let C be a set of real valued clocks and I a set of integer valued variables. A clock assignment over C is a tuple $\langle v, c \rangle$, where $v \in C$ and $c \in \mathbf{N}$. An integer assignment over I is a tuple $\langle w, d \rangle$ representing the assignment $w = d$, where $w \in I$ and $d \in \mathbf{Z}$.*

We will use $\mathcal{A}(C, I)$ to denote the power-set of all assignments over I and C.

```
<interaction name="createPO" channelVariable="tns:seller-channel"
             operation="handlePurchaseOrder" align="true" initiate="true">
  <participate relationshipType="tns:CostIntSellCarrRS"
               fromRole="tns:Customer" toRole="tns:Seller"/>
  <exchange name="request" informationType="tns:purchaseOrderType"
            action="request">
    <send variable="cdl:getVariable("tns:purchaseOrder", "", "")" />
    <receive variable="cdl:getVariable("tns:purchaseOrder", "", "")"
             recordReference="record-the-channel-info" />
  </exchange>
  <exchange name="response" informationType="purchaseOrderAccepted"
            action="respond">
    <send variable="cdl:getVariable("tns:purchaseOrderAcceted","","")"/>
    <receive variable="cdl:getVariable("tns:purchaseOrderAccepted","","")"/>
  </exchange>
  <exchange name="NoStockAckException" informationType="NoStockAckType"
            action="respond">
    <send variable="cdl:getVariable('tns:NoStockAck', '', '')"
          causeException="true" />
    <receive variable="cdl:getVariable("tns:NoStockAck","","")"
             causeException="true"/>
  </exchange>
  <record name="record-the-channel-info" when="after">
    <source variable="cdl:
                 getVariable("tns:purchaseOrder,"","PO/CustomerRef")"/>
    <target variable="cdl:getVariable("tns:customer-channel", "", "")"/>
  </record>
  <record name="reset-clock" when="after">
    <source variable="00:00"/>
    <target variable="cdl:getVariable("tns:Clock1", "", "")"/>
  </record>
</interaction>
<interaction name="PickUpProductPO" channelVariable="tns:deliver-channel"
             operation="PickUpPurchaseOrder" align="true" initiate="true">
  <participate relationshipType="tns:CustIntSellCarrRS"
               fromRole="tns:Seller" toRole="tns:Carrier"/>
  <exchange name="request"
            informationType="tns:purchaseOrderType" action="request">
    <send variable="cdl:getVariable("tns:purchaseOrder", "", "")" />
    <receive variable="cdl:getVariable("tns:purchaseOrder", "", "")"
             recordReference="record-the-channel-info" />
  </exchange>
</interaction>
<interaction name="DeliverProductPO" channelVariable="tns:customer-channel"
             operation="DeliverProductOrder" align="true" initiate="true">
  <participate relationshipType="tns:CostIntSellCarrRS"
               fromRole="tns:Carrier" toRole="tns:Customer"/>
  <exchange name="request" informationType="tns:purchaseOrderType"
            action="request">
    <send variable="cdl:getVariable("tns:purchaseOrder", "", "")" />
    <receive variable="cdl:getVariable("tns:purchaseOrder", "", "")"
             recordReference="record-the-channel-info" />
  </exchange>
  <timeout  time-to-complete=
            "cdl:minor(cdl:getVariable("tns:Clock1","",""),"48:00")"/>?
</interaction>
```

Fig. 5. WS-CDL interaction specification of the Internet purchase process

Definition 6. (Timed automata) *A timed automaton A over a finite set of actions Act, clocks C and integer variables I is a tuple $\langle L, l_0, E, V \rangle$, where L is a finite set of nodes (control-nodes), l_0 is the initial node, $E \subseteq L \times \mathcal{B}(C, I) \times$*

$Act \times \mathcal{A}(C, I) \times L$ *corresponds to the set of edges, and* $V : L \rightarrow \mathcal{B}(C, I)$ *assigns invariants to locations. For a brief notation, we will denote* $l \xrightarrow{g,a,r} l'$ *by the edge* $\langle l, g, a, r, l' \rangle \in E.$

5.3   Translation Process: WS-CDL into Time Automata

For each component of a WS-CDL description we have the following correspondence in timed automata (see Fig. 6 for a schematic presentation of this correspondence):

Role: These are used to describe the behavior of each class of party that we are using in the choreography. Thus, this definition matches with the definition of a *template* in timed automata terminology.

Relation type: These are used to define the communications between two roles, and the needed channels for these communications. In timed automata we just need to assign a new channel for each one of these channels, which are the parameters of the templates that take part in the communication.

Participant type: These define the different parties that participate in the choreography. In timed automata they are processes participating in the system.

Channel types: A channel is a point of collaboration between parties, together with the specification of how the information is exchanged. As stated above, channels of WS-CDL correspond with channels of timed automata.

Variables: These are easily translated, as timed automata in UPPAAL support variables, which are used to represent some information.

Now the problem is to define the behavior of each template. This behavior is defined by using the information provided by the flow of choreographies. Choreographies are sets of workunits or sets of activities. Thus, activities and workunits are the basic components of the choreographies, and they capture the behavior of each component. Activities can be obtained as result of a composition of other activities, by using sequential composition, parallelism and choice. In terms of timed automata these operators can be easily translated:

- The sequential composition of activities is translated by concatenating the corresponding timed automata.
- Parallel activities are translated by the cartesian product of the corresponding timed automata.
- Choices are translated by adding a node into the automata which is connected with the initial nodes of the alternatives.

Finally, time restrictions are associated in WS-CDL with workunits and interaction activities. These time restrictions are introduced in timed automata by means of guards and invariants. Therefore, in the event of a workunit of an activity having a time restriction we associate a guard to the edge that corresponds to the initial point of this workunit in the corresponding timed automaton.

Thus, by applying these rules we obtain three timed automata: one corresponding to the **customer** (Fig. 7), another one to the **seller** (left-hand side of Fig. 8) and the last one to the **carrier** (right-hand side of Fig. 8).

Role = Template
Relation Type = Channel$^+$
Participant Type = Process$^+$
Channel Type = Channel
Variables = Variables
Choreography = Choreography$^+$ | Activity
Activity = Work Unit | Sequence | Paralelism | Choice
Sequence = Activity$^+$
Parallelism = Activity$^+$
Choice = Activity$^+$
Work Unit = State & Guard & Invariant

where the symbols +, | are BNF notation, and & is used to join information

Fig. 6. Schematic view of the translation

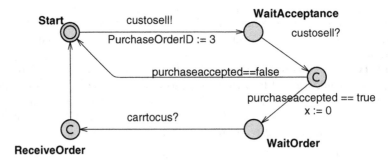

Fig. 7. The customer automaton

6   The Verification Phase: Via Model Checking

The model checking algorithm that UPPAAL uses is based on the symbolic model checking [3,16] that uses constraint solving. The algorithm checks if a state in a timed automata is reachable from the initial state or not. When searching the state space we need two buffers that we can call "wait" and "passed" respectively. The wait buffer holds the states not yet explored and the passed buffer holds the states explored so far.

Algorithm 1. *Forward Reachability Analysis*
   If we do forward reachability analysis we initially store $\langle l_0, U_0 \rangle$ in the wait buffer. We then repeat the following:

1. *Pick a state $\langle l_i, U_i \rangle$ from the wait buffer.*
2. *Check if $l_i = l_f \wedge U_i \subseteq U_f$. If that is the case, return the answer yes.*
3. *If $l_i = l_j \wedge U_i \subseteq U_j$, for some $\langle l_i, U_i \rangle$ in the passed buffer, drop $\langle l_i, U_i \rangle$ and go to step 1. Otherwise save $\langle l_i, U_i \rangle$ in the passed buffer. If $U_j \subset U_i$ we can replace the state $\langle l_j, U_j \rangle$ with $\langle l_i, U_i \rangle$. (To save space)*

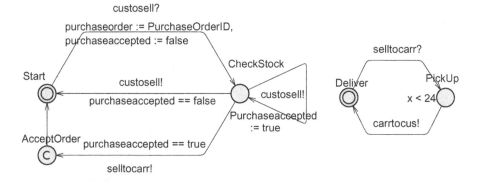

Fig. 8. Seller and carrier automata

4. *Find all l_k that are reachable from l_i in one step regardless of the assignments, taking only actions into account. Let g_k be the set of guards on the performed transition and a_k the set of resets*
5. *Now set $U_k = reset(sp(U_i) \cap g_k, a_k)$. If $U_k \neq \emptyset$, store $\langle l_k, U_k \rangle$ in the wait buffer.*
6. *If the wait buffer is not empty go to step 1, otherwise return the answer no.*

Thus, we can use the verifier of UPPAAL in order to check the properties that were identified. Notice that these properties must be adapted to consider the particular names of variables and clocks that are used in UPPAAL. For instance, the first property *"PickupOnTime"* (1) is rewritten as follows:

$$Customer.WaitOrder --> (Carrier.PickUp \wedge x < 24) \qquad (5)$$

The second property, *"DeliverOnTime"* (2) is rewritten as:

$$A <> (Carrier.Deliver and x < 24) \qquad (6)$$

The third property *"SatisfiedCustomer"* (3) is rewritten as follows:

$$E <> (Customer.ReceiveOrder and x < 24) \qquad (7)$$

The fourth property *"EfficientService"* (4) is rewritten as follows:

$$Seller.AcceptOrder --> Customer.ReceiveOrder \qquad (8)$$

Observe that the clocks $Clock_{deliver}$ is renamed to x.

We find an error in the verification of a property, concretely in Property 5 (Fig. 9). The problem appears when the seller sends the "acceptorder", but he does not send the "PickUp" message to the carrier within 24 hours. Then the carrier cannot deliver the product on time and the property is not fulfilled.

In order to correct this problem it is necessary to force the seller to send the "PickUp" message on time. For that purpose, we add an invariant to the

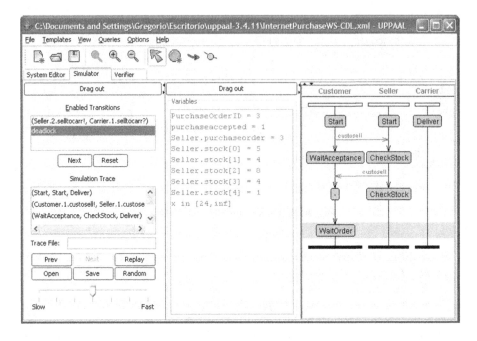

Fig. 9. The Uppaal trace for property 5

seller state "CheckStock" labeled x < 2. With this invariant the seller must send
the message within 2 hours since he has sent the message "PurchaseAccepted".
Thus, the seller automaton would be replaced with the automaton depicted in
Fig. 10 and the WS-CDL interaction that represents it would be rewritten as
shown in Fig. 11.

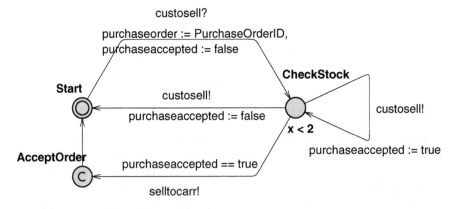

Fig. 10. Corrected Seller automaton

```
<interaction name="PickUpProductPO" channelVariable="tns:deliver-channel"
              operation="PickUpPurchaseOrder" align="true" initiate="true">
  <participate relationshipType="tns:CustIntSellCarrRS"
               fromRole="tns:Seller" toRole="tns:Carrier"/>
  <exchange name="request"
            informationType="tns:purchaseOrderType" action="request">
    <send variable="cdl:getVariable("tns:purchaseOrder", "", "")" />
    <receive variable="cdl:getVariable("tns:purchaseOrder", "", "")"
             recordReference="record-the-channel-info" />
  </exchange>
  <timeout  time-to-complete=
            "cdl:minor(cdl:getVariable("tns:Clock1","",""),"02:00")"/>?
</interaction>
```

Fig. 11. Corrected interaction

7   Conclusions and Future Work

In this work, we have presented a proposal for the analysis and verification of Web Services choreographies with time requirements. The gathering of time requirements via goal-driven diagrams, such as the KAOS extension presented in the fourth section, is a powerful tool for developing systems where time aspects determine whether the implementation presents the proper behaviors or not. However, in order to achieve this conclusion, this technique must be used together with formal specifications and formal techniques that can perform a verification process. For this purpose, the model checking technique has shown itself to be, in a wide range of systems, one of the most feasible formal method techniques.

As future work, we are working on the application of these techniques to other fields like Web Services orchestrations (WS-BPEL).

References

1. A. van Lamsweerde A. Dardenne and Stephen Fickas. Goal-directed requirements acquisition. page 350.
2. R. Alur and D. Dill. Automata for modeling real–time systems. In *In Proceedings of the 17th International Colloquium on Automata, Languages and Programming*, volume 443. Springer–Verlag, 1990.
3. Johan Bengtsson and Wang Yi. Timed automata: Semantics, algorithms and tools. In W. Reisig and G. Rozenberg, editors, *In Lecture Notes on Concurrency and Petri Nets*. Springer-Verlag, 2004.
4. Mario Bravetti, Claudio Guidi, Roberto Lucchi, and Gianluigi Zavattaro. Supporting e-commerce systems formalization with choreography languages. In *SAC '05: Proceedings of the 2005 ACM symposium on Applied computing*, pages 831–835, New York, NY, USA, 2005. ACM Press.
5. Mario Bravetti, Roberto Lucchi, Gianluigi Zavattaro, and Roberto Gorrieri. Web services for e-commerce: guaranteeing security access and quality of service. In *SAC '04: Proceedings of the 2004 ACM symposium on Applied computing*, pages 800–806, New York, NY, USA, 2004. ACM Press.

6. A. Rifaut J.F. Molderez A. van Lamsweerde C. Ponsard, P. Massonet and H. Tran Van. Early verification and validation of mission critical systems. In *Ninth International Workshop on Formal Methods for Industrial Critical Systems*, 2004.
7. Edmund M. Clarke, Jr., Orna Grumberg, and Doron A. Peled. *Model Checking*. MIT Press, 1999.
8. R. Darimont and A. van Lamsweerde. Formal refinement patterns for goaldriven requirements elaboration. In *Ninth International Workshop on Formal Methods for Industrial Critical Systemse, FSE-4 - 4th ACM Symp. on the Foundations of Software Engineering*, October 1996.
9. Gregorio Díaz, Fernando Cuartero, Valentín Valero Ruiz, and Fernando L. Pelayo. Automatic verification of the tls handshake protocol. In *SAC '04: Proceedings of the 2004 ACM symposium on Applied computing*, pages 789–794. ACM Press, 2004.
10. Gregorio Díaz, Kim Guldstrand Larsen, Juan José Pardo, Fernando Cuartero, and Valentin Valero. An approach to handle real time and probabilistic behaviors in e-commerce: validating the set protocol. In *SAC '05: Proceedings of the 2005 ACM symposium on Applied computing*, pages 815–820. ACM Press, 2005.
11. Gregorio Díaz, Juan José Pardo, María-Emilia Cambronero, Valentin Valero, and Fernando Cuartero. Automatic translation of ws-cdl choreographies to timed automata. In *EPEW/WS-FM*, volume 3670 of *Lecture Notes in Computer Science*, pages 230–242. Springer, 2005.
12. Nickolas Kavantzas et al. Web service choreography description language (wscdl) 1.0. http://www.w3.org/TR/ws-cdl-10/.
13. Constance Heitmeyer and Dino Mandrioli. *Formal Methods for Real-Time Computing*. John Wiley & Sons, 1996.
14. Tony Hoare. The verifying compiler: A grand challenge for computing research. *J. ACM*, 50(1):63–69, 2003.
15. K. Larsen, P. Pettersson, and Wang Yi. Uppaal in a nutshell. *Journal on Software Tools for Technology Transfer*, 1, 1997.
16. Kim G. Larsen, Paul Pettersson, and Wang Yi. Compositional and Symbolic Model-Checking of Real-Time Systems. In *Proc. of the 16th IEEE Real-Time Systems Symposium*, pages 76–87. IEEE Computer Society Press, Dec 1995.
17. Elena Navarro, Pedro Sanchez, Patricio Letelier, Juan A. Pastor, and Isidro Ramos. A goal-oriented approach for safety requirements specification. In *13th Annual IEEE International Conference and Workshop on the Engineering of Computer Based Systems (ECBS'06)*, pages 319–326. IEEE Computer Society, 2006.
18. Costas Courcoubetis Rajeev Alur and David L. Dill. Model-checking in dense real-time. In *Journal of Information and Computation*, 1993.
19. J. Sifakis T.A. Henzinger, X. Nicollin and S. Yovine. Symbolic model checking for real-time systems. In *In Proceedings of the IEEE Conference on Logics in Computer Science (LICS)*, 1992.
20. A. van Lamsweerde. Requirements engineering in the year 00: a research perspective. In *International Conference on Software Engineering*, page 519, 2000.

A Formal Approach to Service Component Architecture*

José Luiz Fiadeiro[1], Antónia Lopes[2], and Laura Bocchi[1]

[1] Department of Computer Science, University of Leicester
University Road, Leicester LE1 7RH, UK
{bocchi, jose}@mcs.le.ac.uk
[2] Department of Informatics, Faculty of Sciences, University of Lisbon
Campo Grande, 1749-016 Lisboa, Portugal
mal@di.fc.ul.pt

Abstract. We report on a formal framework being developed within the SEN-SORIA project for supporting service-oriented modelling at high levels of abstraction, i.e. independently of the hosting middleware and hardware platforms, and the languages in which services are programmed. More specifically, we give an account of the concepts and techniques that support the composition model of SENSORIA, i.e. the mechanisms through which complex applications can be put together from simpler components, including modelling primitives for the orchestration of components and the definition of external interfaces.

1 Introduction

One of the goals of SENSORIA – an IST-FET Integrated Project on *Software Engineering for Service-Oriented Overlay Computers* – is to define a formal framework that can support a Reference Modelling Language (SRML) that operates at the higher levels of abstraction of "business" or "domain" architectures. The term "service-oriented" is taken within SENSORIA in a broad sense that encompasses the general principles and techniques either available or envisioned for Web Services [1], as well as other manifestations such as Grid Computing [11]. The aim is to develop concepts and techniques that are independent of what are sometimes called "global computers", i.e. the technologies that provide the middleware infrastructure over which services can be deployed, published and discovered. In this sense, our aims are in tune with the goal of the industrial consortium that is developing the Service Component Architecture (SCA) [14]. Like in SCA, we are aiming to support ways through which

> *[...] relatively coarse-grained business components can be exposed as services, with well-defined interfaces and contracts, removing or abstracting middleware programming model dependencies from business logic.*

* This work was partially supported through the IST-2005-16004 Integrated Project *SENSORIA: Software Engineering for Service-Oriented Overlay Computers*, and the Marie-Curie TOK-IAP MTK1-CT-2004-003169 *Leg2Net: From Legacy Systems to Services in the Net.*

M. Bravetti, M. Nuñes, and G. Zavattaro (Eds.): WS-FM 2006, LNCS 4184, pp. 193–213, 2006.
© Springer-Verlag Berlin Heidelberg 2006

The main concern of SCA in developing this middleware-independent layer is to provide an open specification "allowing multiple vendors to implement support for SCA in their development tools and runtimes". This is why SCA offers specific support for a variety of component implementation and interface types such as BPEL processes with WSDL interfaces, and Java classes with corresponding interfaces. Our work explores a complementary direction: our research aims for a mathematical semantics of a Service Component Architecture that can provide a uniform model of service behaviour in a way that is independent of the languages and technologies used for programming and deploying services. Besides SCA, we also take into account recent advances on Web Services such as [1,6], and stay as close as possible to the terminology that is being adopted in the area.

More specifically, we develop a minimalist formal framework based on a core set of primitives and a language that is "small" enough to be formalised relatively easily and yet "powerful" enough to capture the essence of a new modelling paradigm centred on services. In this paper, we report on some of the efforts made so far in the development of this language by presenting fragments of its composition model, what we call SRML-P: the techniques through which one can model individual business components and interconnect them to build complex applications in a service-oriented way. A more detailed account of our approach is available in [9]. Issues related with dynamic configuration, such as service discovery and binding, are also being addressed over the model that we outline here.

In Section 2, we provide an overview of the composition model that we support in SRML-P. In Section 3, we present the primitives that we use for describing interactions. In Section 4, we discuss the modelling of components as orchestrations of interactions maintained with other parties. In Section 5, we show how external interfaces can be described in terms of sentences of a formal logic that model conversations. In Section 6, we discuss the way components can be wired to each other and to external interfaces in order to produce modules. In the concluding remarks, we point to other aspects that are being investigated and discuss the way we are taking this programme forwards. For illustration, we use a typical procurement business process involving a supplier, a warehouse and a local stock.

2   The Composition Model

SRML-P provides a language for modelling composite services, understood as services whose business logic involves a number of interactions among more elementary service components as well the invocation of services provided by other parties. As in SCA, interactions are supported on the basis of service interfaces defined in a way that is "independent of the hardware platform, the operating system, hosting middleware and the programming language used to implement the service" [14].

Central to the composition model is the notion of *service component*, or component for short. In SRML-P, a component is a computational unit that is modelled by means of an execution pattern involving a number of interactions that it can maintain with other parties. We refer to the execution pattern of a component as an *orchestration element*, or *orchestration* for short. The W3C Web Services Glossary[1] defines orchestration as

[...] the sequence and conditions in which one Web service invokes other Web services in order to realize some useful function.

In our context, the orchestration of the service provided by a module is the composition of the orchestrations defined within the components and the way they are wired together.

Each orchestration element is defined independently of the language in which the component is programmed and the platform in which it is deployed; it may be a BPEL process, a Java program, a wrapped-up legacy system, inter alia. In addition, the orchestration is independent of the specific parties that are actually interconnected with the component in any given run-time configuration; a component is totally independent in the sense that it does not invoke services of any specific co-party (i.e. an external service or another component) – it just offers an interface of two-way interactions in which it can participate.

As such, service components do not provide any business logic: the units of business logic are *modules* that use such components to provide services when they are interconnected with a number of other parties offering a number of required services. In a SRML-P module, both the provided services and those required from other parties are modelled as *external interfaces*, or interfaces for short. Each such interface specifies a stateful interaction between a service component and the corresponding party, i.e. SRML-P supports both "syntactic" and "behavioural" interfaces.

The external interface offered by a module to be used by clients, what in SCA corresponds to an "entry point", specifies constraints on the interactions that the module supports as a service provider such as the order in which it expects invocations or deadlines for the user to commit; it is the responsibility of the clients to adhere to these protocols, meaning that the provider may not be ready to engage in interactions that are not according to the specified constraints. Other properties are specified that any client may expect such as pledges on given parameters of the delivered services. The external interfaces to services required from other parties, what in SCA corresponds to "external services", specify the conversations that the module expects relative to each party.

Service components and external interfaces are connected to each other within modules through *internal wires* that bind the interactions that both parties declare to support. In SRML-P, all names are local, which implies that any interconnection needs to be made explicit through a wire that binds the names used locally in each party. The idea is to support reuse of both service components and external interfaces, thus facilitating the process of designing business applications. The coupling of service components within modules can be seen to be tight and performed at design time, reflecting the fact that they offer an (atomic) unit of business logic.

The table below establishes a relationship between the terminology that we use in SRML-P and the W3C Web Services Glossary. However, as already mentioned, in

---

[1] http://www.w3.org/TR/ws-gloss/

SRML-P we are aiming for higher-levels of abstraction in service-oriented modelling, which explains why this relationship is not a one-to-one mapping.

W3C	SRML-P	Relationship
Service	Module	A **module** defines how a certain **service** is provided through the coordination of a set of internal components and external services.
Service Description	External Interface (Provides/Requires)	**External Interfaces** correspond to **service descriptions** that include the interface and the interactive behaviour of the services provided/required by a module.
Orchestration	Orchestration	In SRML-P, **orchestration** is spread among all the components within a module.

In order to illustrate how applications are modelled in SRML-P, we use a typical procurement business process involving a supplier, a warehouse, a local stock, and a price look-up facility. The decision to make the local stock a component of the module reflects the tight coupling that exists with the supplier in business terms. The choice of warehouse should probably be made at run-time, for instance taking into account properties of the customer like its location, which justifies that it is represented in the module as an external interface. The price look-up facility is also a good example of an external service that may be shared among several suppliers.

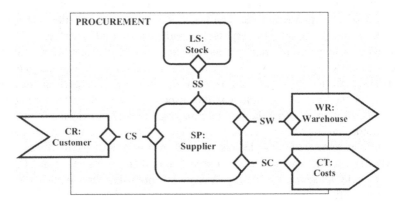

This module declares two components: *SP* and *LS*. Components are typed by what we call *business roles*, which are discussed in Section 4; in this case, *SP* plays the business role of *Supplier* and *LS* of *Stock*. Three external interfaces are declared: one provides-interface – *CR* – and two requires-interfaces – *WR* and *CT*. Each such interface is typed by what we call a *business protocol* as discussed in Section 5; in the example, the business protocols are *Customer, Warehouse* and *Costs*, respectively. Finally, four wires connect components and interfaces: *CS, SS, SW* and *SC*. Each wire is labelled by an *interaction protocol* as discussed in Section 6; the labelling of wires is not easily depicted in figures such as above and is normally given in the textual definition of the module only. More details on the notion of module, including an algebraic semantics, can be found in [9].

3 The Language of Interactions

In this section, we provide a short account of the primitives that are being defined for describing interactions, taking into account proposals that have been made for Web-Services [4], in orchestration languages such as ORC [13], and in calculi such as Sagas [5]. However, because our aim is to support an abstract and declarative style of specification, our language will use some of these concepts (e.g. compensations, pledges, locking-properties, deadlines and timeouts) in a somewhat different way.

In SRML, we distinguish several types of interactions as shown in the table below. Interactions involve two parties and can be in both directions, i.e. they can be conversational. Interactions are described from the point of view of the party in which they are declared, i.e. "receive" means invocations received by the party and sent by the co-party, and "send" means invocations made by the party. Interactions can be synchronous, implying that the party waits for the co-party to reply or complete, or asynchronous, in which case the party does not block. The reason for choosing to have non-blocking asynchronous interactions is that we can leave it to the orchestration of the components to engage or not in other interactions while waiting for a reply.

r&s	The interaction is initiated by the co-party, which expects a reply. The co-party does not block while waiting for the reply.
s&r	The interaction is initiated by the party and expects a reply from its co-party. While waiting for the reply, the party does not block.
rcv	The co-party initiates the interaction and does not expect a reply.
snd	The party initiates the interaction and does not expect a reply.
ask	The party synchronises with the co-party to obtain data.
rpl	The party synchronises with the co-party to transmit data.
tll	The party requests the co-party to perform an operation and blocks.
prf	The party performs an operation and frees the co-party that requested it.

Notice that r&s and s&r interactions are durative/conversational. We distinguish several events that can occur during such interactions:

interaction⊴	The event of initiating *interaction*.
interaction⊠	The reply-event of *interaction*.
interaction✓	The commit-event of *interaction*.
interaction✗	The cancel-event of *interaction*.
interaction☀	The deadline-event of *interaction*.
interaction⚰	The revoke-event of *interaction*.

Further to these events, each such interaction may have an associated *pledge* – a condition that is guaranteed to hold from the moment a positive reply-event occurs until either the commit, the cancel or the deadline-event happens, whichever comes first. We denote this condition by *interaction*$\mathcal{S}$. A reply-event *interaction*⊠ is positive iff the distinguished Boolean parameter *Reply* is true.

The sequence diagrams below illustrate the intuitive semantics of these primitives when a pledge is offered. In the case on the left, the initiator commits to the pledge; a revoke may occur later on compensating the effects of *interaction*. In the case in the middle, there is a cancellation; in this situation, a revoke is not available. In the case on the right, the deadline-event occurs without a commit or cancel having occurred; this implies that no further events for that interaction will occur. In Section 4, we give examples of the usage of these primitives.

Events can be referred to from the point of view of the party that initiate them, in which case we use the notation *event!*, or the party that receives them, in which case we use *event?*. Events occur during state transitions in both parties involved in the interaction and require that the parties are available to perform the event; in other words, events are blocking in the sense that a party wishing to issue *event!* needs to wait for its co-party to be able to perform *event?*.

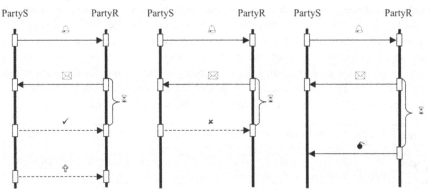

Interactions can have parameters for transmitting data when they are initiated, declared as ⌂, and for carrying a reply, declared as ⊠. Notice that the boolean ⊠-parameter *Reply* is always available, indicating if the reply is positive Only the additional parameters required for carrying data associated with the reply need to be declared. Key parameters, marked as ↦, can also be declared which are used for generating different instances of a given class of events.

We assume that there are a number of "global" interactions provided by "the environment" such as time-related activities. This is necessary for parties to have some common understanding of issues like deadlines. In this paper, we will make use of the interaction *alertDate*, which is initiated by a party with a ↦-parameter – *Ref* of type *string*, and a ⌂-parameter – *Interval* of type *date*. The agreed meaning is that the environment publishes *alertDate*⊠ when *Interval* units of time have elapsed. Any party can subscribe to that event.

We make use of a number of connectives to formulate behavioural properties, examples of which are given throughout the paper. The following table summarises the intuitive meaning and the way some of them can be formulated in a branching time logic with linear past (see [12]).

a **before** b	If b holds then a must have been true.	$\mathbf{AG(b \supset Pa)}$
b **exceptif** a	b can occur iff b and a have never occurred.	$\mathbf{AG(\neg Pa \wedge H(\neg b) \equiv Eb)}$
a **enables** b	b can occur iff a has already occurred but not b.	$\mathbf{AG(Pa \wedge H(\neg b) \equiv Eb)}$
a **ensures** b	b will occur after a occurs, but b cannot occur without a having occurred.	$\mathbf{AG(b \supset Pa \wedge a \supset Fb)}$

The syntax and semantics of the logic supporting the specification of behavioural properties are currently being developed. In this logic, some properties of the underlying computational and interaction model will be fixed, such as:

- The initiation of an r&s interaction enables and ensures that a reply will be issued; we are working on an extension of the language that will provide primitives for assigning quality-of-service attributes such as the delay in which the reply is sent.
- A positive reply sets the pledge, which holds until the deadline, the commit or the deadline event occurs; the commit and the deadline events are enabled until either of them or the deadline occurs.
- Events occur only once during each "session", i.e. during each lifetime of an instance of a party.

We should point out that the style of specification that we adopt is quite different from recent proposals in the area of Semantic Web-Services (METEOR-S, OWL-S, SWSL, WSMF), which go little beyond a black-box, transformational approach based on concepts like pre- and post-conditions. These contribute to some extent towards a behavioural description of services but are confined to static/transformational aspects of black-box behaviour that only takes into account initial and final states of service execution. Therefore, they are not suitable for reasoning about conversational and stateful interactions as modelled in SRML-P. An exception is [15], which adopts an assumption/commitment style of specification as used for concurrent processes.

4   Components and Business Roles

In SRML-P, components instantiate *business roles*, which are specified by declaring a set of interactions and the way they are orchestrated. As an example, consider the business role of a supplier. A supplier can be involved in the following interactions:

```
INTERACTIONS
    r&s requestQuote
        ⏃ which:product
        ⊠ cost:money
    r&s orderGoods
        ⏃ many:nat
        ⊠ much:money
    s&r checkShipAvail
        ⏃ which:product, many:nat
    rcv confirmShip
    rcv makePayment
    snd shipOrder
    ask how(product):money
    ask checkStock(product,nat):bool
    tll incStock(product,nat)
    tll decStock(product,nat)
```

Notice that the co-parties of the supplier in these interactions are not named; the specification models the business role played by the component independently of the way it is instantiated within any given system. Components are linked to their co-parties within modules through explicit wires as described in Section 6.

The way the declared interactions are orchestrated is specified through a set of variables that provide an abstract view of the state of the component, and a set of transitions that model the activities performed by the component, including the way it interacts with its co-parties.

A transition has an optional name and a number of possible features. For instance:

```
transition TQuote
    triggeredBy requestQuote⌂?
    guardedBy s=0
    effects which'=requestQuote.which
        ∧ much'=how(requestQuote.which)*1.2
        ∧ inStock'=false
        ∧ timeoutQuote'=false
        ∧ s'=1
    sends requestQuote⌧!
        ∧ requestQuote.cost=much'
        ∧ requestQuote.Reply=true
        ∧ alertDate⌂!
        ∧ alertDate.Ref="quote"
        ∧ alertDate.Interval=7
```

- A trigger is a condition: typically, the occurrence of a receive-event.
- A guard is a condition that identifies the states in which the transition can take place – in *TQuote*, the state in which *s=0*. If the guard is false, a component that plays the specified role will not engage in the interaction.
- A sentence specifies the effects of the transition in the local state. We use *var'* to denote the value that a state variable *var* has after the transition. In the case above, we store business data and initialise the state variables *much*, *inStock* and *timeoutQuote*. Notice that, in the example, we use the synchronous interaction *how* to compute the cost that is going to be quoted. We will see that the co-party in this interaction is an external service that lists the current prices of goods.
- Another sentence specifies the events that are sent, including the values taken by their parameters. In this sentence, we use variables and primed variables as in the "effects"-section; the separation between the two sections is just logical and there are no dependencies between them. In the example, this consists in issuing the reply quoting the costs computed as mentioned and setting an *alertDate* with a 7-day interval – the period during which the quoted price is guaranteed.

Notice that, even if it is relatively easy to model a state machine in SRML-P, the way we model control flow is much more flexible because transitions are decoupled from interactions and changes to state variables. For instance, the transition *TAlert* can occur in any state after the request was issued:

```
transition TAlert
    triggeredBy alertDate⌧?
    guardedBy
    effects alertDate.Ref="quote" ⊃ timeoutQuote'=true
        ∧ alert.Ref="goods" ∧ s=2 ⊃ s'=8
```

```
sends alertDate.Ref="quote" ∧ s=1 ⊃ requestQuote◆*!
    ∧ alert.Ref="goods" ∧ s=2 ⊃ orderGoods◆*!
        ∧ incStock(which,many)
```

This transition is triggered when the supplier receives a notification from an *alert-Date*; if the alert is concerned with the quote, it simply sets an internal timeout state variable so that the supplier knows how to calculate the costs of a subsequent order and it alerts its co-party that the timeout has occurred; if the alert is concerned with the goods and no commitment has been received, the supplier notifies its co-party and replenishes the local stock – *incStock(which,many)*. Notice that the latter is a synchronous interaction.

5   External Interfaces and Business Protocols

Besides components, a module in SRML-P may declare a number of (external) interfaces. These provide abstractions (types) of parties that can be interconnected with the components declared in the module either to provide or request services; this is what, in SCA, corresponds to "Entry Points" and "External Services".

External interfaces are specified through *business protocols*. Like orchestrations, protocols declare the interactions in which the external entities can be involved as parties. The difference is that, instead of an orchestration, we provide a set of properties that model the protocol that the co-party is expected to adhere to. For instance, the behaviour that a supplier expects from a warehouse is as follows:

```
BUSINESS PROTOCOL Warehouse is

    INTERACTIONS
        r&s check&lock
            ⌂ which:product, many:nat
        snd confirm
    BEHAVIOUR
        check&lock⌂? exceptif true
        check&lock⊠! ∧ check&lock.Reply ⊃
            alertDate⌂! ∧ alertDate.Interval=3 ∧
                    alertDate.Ref="goods"
        check&lock◆*! ⊃ alertDate⊠? ∧ alertDate.Ref="goods"
        check&lock⚡ ⊃ (check&lock✓? ensures confirm⌂!)
        check&lock✓? ⊃ (check&lock⚐? exceptif confirm⌂!)
```

Notice that the interactions are again named from the point of view of the party concerned – the warehouse in the case at hand. The properties require the following:

- In the initial state the warehouse is ready to engage in *check&lock*.
- The deadline associated with *check&lock* is a timeout of 3 days with reference "goods" set when the reply is issued.
- A positive reply sets the pledge associated with *check&lock*, which ensures that *confirm* will be issued upon but not before receiving the commit.
- After the commit, *check&lock* can be revoked until *confirm* has been issued.

Protocols are also used for modelling the behaviour that users can expect from a service. This subsumes what, in [2], are called *external specifications*:

In particular, a trend that is gathering momentum is that of including, as part of the service description, not only the service interface, but also the business protocol supported by the service, i.e., the specification of which message exchange sequences are supported by the service, for example expressed in terms of constraints on the order in which service operations should be invoked.

This is the case of customers:

BUSINESS PROTOCOL Customer **is**

   INTERACTIONS
      s&r howMuch
         ⌂ which:product
         ⊠ cost:money
      s&r buy
         ⌂ many:nat
         ⊠ much:money
      snd pay
      rcv ackShip

   BEHAVIOUR
      howMuch⌂? **exceptif** true
      howMuch⊠? **enables** buy⌂!
      howMuch⊠? ⊃ alertDate⌂! ∧ alertDate.Interval=7
        ∧ alertDate.Ref="quote"
      howMuch●*? ⊃ alertDate⊠? ∧ alertDate.Ref="quote"
      howMuch⊠? ⊃ howMuch.Reply
      howMuch⊠ ⊃ (buy⌂! **ensures**
        (buy⊠? ∧ buy.Reply ⊃ buy.much=buy.many*howMuch.much))
      buy⊠? ∧ buy.Reply ⊃ alertDate⌂! ∧ alertDate.Interval=3
        ∧ alertDate.Ref="goods"
      buy●*? ⊃ alertDate⊠? ∧ alertDate.Ref="goods"
      buy⊠ ⊃ (pay⌂! **ensures** ackShip⌂?)
      pay⌂! ≡ buy✓!
      buy✓! ⊃ buy⚕! **exceptif** ackShip⌂?

The properties offer the following behaviour:

- A request for *howMuch* is enabled at the start.
- A request for *buy* will be accepted after and only after a reply to *howMuch*.
- The deadline associated with *howMuch* is a timeout of 7 days set when the reply is received.
- A reply to *howMuch* is always positive; the corresponding pledge ensures that the cost associated with a subsequent order placed before the deadline will be the quoted one.
- The deadline associated with *buy* is a timeout of 3 days. This is why the warehouse is being requested to provide the same timeout.
- The pledge associated with *buy* ensures that *ackShip* will be issued upon and never before payment is issued.
- Payment is a commit to *buy*.
- *buy* can be revoked until *ackShip* has been issued.

Notice again that components and external interfaces are independent entities in the sense that they do not name the co-parties involved in the interactions that they support. These entities become connected in modules through internal wires.

6   Wires and Interaction Protocols

A module consists of a number of components and external interfaces (provides/requires) wired to one another. Wires are labelled by connectors that coordinate the interactions in which the parties are jointly involved. In SRML-P, we model the interaction protocols involved in these connectors as separate, reusable entities.

Just like business roles and protocols, an interaction protocol is specified in terms of a number of interactions. The "semantics" of the protocol is provided through a collection of sentences that establish how the interactions are coordinated, which may include routing events and transforming sent data to the format expected by the receiver. As an example, consider the following protocol:

```
INTERACTION PROTOCOL Custom1 is

    INTERACTIONS
        ask  S₁(product,nat):bool
        tll  S₂(product,nat)
        tll  S₃(product,nat)
        rpl  R₁(product):nat
        prf  R₂(product,nat)

    COORDINATION
        S₁(p,n) = R₁(p)≥n
        S₂(p,n) ⊃ R₂(p,R₁(p)+n)
        R₁(p)≥n ∧ S₃(p,n) ⊃ R₂(p,R₁(p)−n)
        R₁(p)<n ⊃ ¬S₃(p,n)
```

This protocol is used by the wire *SS* that connects *Supplier* and *Stock* as follows:

SP Supplier				LS Stock
ask checkStock	S₁		R₁	rpl get
tll incStock	S₂	Custom1	R₂	prf set
tll decStock	S₃			

The name bindings thus declared establish the following protocol:

```
checkStock(p,n)=(get(p)≥n)
incStock(p,n) ⊃ set(p,get(p)+n)
get(p)≥n ∧ decStock(p,n) ⊃ set(p,get(p)−n)
get(p)<n ⊃ ¬decStock(p,n)
```

That is, the boolean value returned by *checkStock(p,n)* as invoked by the supplier is computed by the local stock by checking if the value returned by *get(p)* is greater or equal to *n*. Notice that these are synchronous interactions. The protocol also stipulates that to a request from the supplier for *incStock(p,n)* the local stock executes *set(p,get(p)+n)*. Likewise, to a request from the supplier for *decStock(p,n)* the local stock executes *set(p,get(p)−n)* only if *get(p)* returns a value greater than or equal to *n*; otherwise, the request is not accepted.

The names used in interaction protocols are generic to facilitate reuse. In fact, families of protocols may be defined by parameterising the specification with the data sorts involved in the interactions. For instance, the following protocol is used between *Supplier* and *Customer*:

INTERACTION PROTOCOL Straight.I(d_1)O(d_2) **is**

    INTERACTIONS
        s&r S_1
             ⌂ i_1:d_1
             ⊠ o_1:d_2
        r&s R_1
             ⌂ i_1:d_1
             ⊠ o_1:d_2
    COORDINATION
         S_1 ≡ R_1
         $S_1.i_1 = R_1.i_1$
         $S_1.o_1 = R_1.o_1$

This is a "standard" protocol that connects directly two entities over two interactions with one ⌂– and one ⊠-parameter. This protocol is used twice in the following wire to connect different interactions between *Supplier* and *Customer:*

SP Supplier ◇		CS		◇	CR Customer
r&s requestQuote	R_1		S_1		**s&r** howMuch
⌂ which	i_1	Straight	i_1		⌂ which
⊠ cost	o_1		o_1		⊠ cost
r&s orderGoods	R_1		S_1		**s&r** buy
⌂ which	i_1	Straight	i_1		⌂ which
⊠ cost	o_1		o_1		⊠ cost
rcv makePayment	R_1	Straight	S_1		**snd** pay
snd shipOrder	S_1	Straight	R_1		**rcv** ackShip

The other protocol used in this wire is an even simpler version involves no parameters:

INTERACTION PROTOCOL Straight **is**

    INTERACTIONS
        snd S_1
        rcv R_1
    COORDINATION
         S_1 ≡ R_1

The name bindings establish straightforward connections such as:

```
howMuch ≡ requestQuote
howMuch.which = requestQuote.which
howMuch.cost = requestQuote.cost
buy ≡ orderGoods
buy.which = orderGoods.which
buy.much = orderGoods.much
pay ≡ makePayment
ackShip ≡ shipOrder
```

Interaction protocols are considered as first-class objects because we want to use them to assign properties to wires that reflect constraints on the underlying run-time environment. These may concern data transmission, synchronous/asynchronous connectivity, distribution, and other non-functional properties such as security.

7   Concluding Remarks and Further Work

In this paper, we have described some of the primitives that are being proposed for the SENSORIA Reference Modelling Language in order to support building systems in service-oriented architectures using "technology agnostic" terms. More specifically, we have focused on the language that supports the underlying composition model. This is a minimalist language that follows a recent proposal for a Service Component Architecture [14] that "builds on emerging best practices of removing or abstracting middleware programming model dependencies from business logic". However, whereas the SCA-consortium concentrates on the definition of an open specification that supports a variety of component implementation and interface types, and on the deployment, administration and configuration of SCA-based applications, our goal is to development a mathematical framework in which service-modelling primitives can be formally defined and application models can be reasoned about.

This is why we are developing a logic for specifying and reasoning about interactions in the conversational mode that characterises services. The primitives that we are proposing take into account proposals that have been made for Web-Service Conversation [4], in other modelling languages such as ORC [13], and in calculi such as Sagas [5]; they take into account that interactions are stateful and provide first-class notions such as reply, commit, compensation and pledge.

The core of our paper focused on the notion of module, which we adapted from SCA. Modules in SRML-P are the basic units of composition. They include external interfaces for required and provided services, and a number of components whose orchestrations ensure that the properties offered on the provides-external interfaces are guaranteed by the connections established by the wires assuming that the services requested satisfy the properties declared on the requires-external interfaces. An algebraic formalisation of this notion of module can be found in [9], which includes the correctness condition. We have also added a notion of parameter through which we can configure chosen aspects of a module such as timeouts; such parameters can be instantiated at run-time as part of a negotiation process.

Modules can be assembled together to make complex systems in a way that is similar to SCA, i.e. by linking requires-external interfaces of a module with provides-external interfaces of other modules via external wires. External wires carry a proof-obligation to ensure that the properties offered by the provides-interface imply those declared by the requires-interface.

SRML-P also supports a way of offering a system as a module, i.e. of turning an assembly of services into a composite service that can be published and discovered on its own. This can be useful, for instance, when one wants to put together a number of services that, individually, offer only partial matches for a given required external interface but, in a suitable configuration, can provide a suitable match. The operation

An assembly of modules defining a SRML-P system; EW–external wire

that collapses a system into a module internalises the external wires and forgets the external specifications. An algebraic semantics of module interconnection and composition can be found in [9] based on categorical constructions similar to those used in algebraic specification [7] and software architecture [10].

Finally, we are also developing a notion of configuration for SRML-P. A configuration is a collection of components wired together that models a run-time composition of service components. A configuration results from having one or more clients using the services provided by a given module, possibly resulting from a complex system, with no external interfaces, i.e. with all required external interfaces wired-in. It is at the level of configurations that we address run-time aspects of service composition such as sessions, as well as notions of persistence. Research is under way to provide primitives for managing configurations with a semantics based on graph-transformations [7], as used, for instance, in [3,16].

Acknowledgments

J. Fiadeiro was partially supported by a grant from the Royal Society (UK) and A. Lopes by the Foundation for Science and Technology (Portugal) during an extended stay at the University of Pisa during April and May 2006. We wish to thank our hosts for the facilities and opportunities for discussion. We would like to thank Luís Andrade, Roberto Bruni, Rocco de Nicola, Giorgios Koutsoukos, Ugo Montanari and Martin Wirsing for their comments on previous versions of this paper.

References

1. G. Alonso, F. Casati, H. Kuno, V. Machiraju (2004) *Web Services*. Springer, Berlin Heidelberg New York
2. K. Baïna, B. Benatallah, F. Casati, F. Toumani (2004) Model-driven web service development. In A. Persson, J. Stirna (eds): *CAiSE'05. LNCS, vol 3084*. Springer, Berlin Heidelberg New York, pp 290–306
3. L. Baresi, R. Heckel, S, Thöne, D. Varró (2003) Modeling and validation of service-oriented architectures: Application vs style. In A. Persson, J. Stirna (eds): *ESEC'03. LNCS, vol 3084*. Springer, Berlin Heidelberg New York, pp 290–306

4. B. Benatallah, F. Casati, F. Toumani (2004) Web service conversation modelling. *IEEE Internet Computing* 8(1):46–54

5. R. Bruni, H. Melgratti, U. Montanari (2005) Theoretical foundations for compensations in flow composition languages. In *POPL'05*. ACM Press, New York, pp 209-220

6. F. Curbera, R. Khalaf, N. Mukhi, S. Tai, S. Weerawarana (2003) The next step in web services. *CACM* 46(10):29–34

7. H. Ehrig, K. Ehrig, U. Prange, G. Taentzer (2006) *Fundamentals of Algebraic Graph Transformation*. EATCS Monographs on Theoretical Computer Science. Springer, Berlin Heidelberg New York

8. H. Ehrig, B. Mahr (2005) *Fundamentals of Algebraic Specification 2: Module Specifications and Constraints*. EATCS Monographs on Theoretical Computer Science, vol 21. Springer, Berlin Heidelberg New York

9. J. L. Fiadeiro, A. Lopes, L. Bocchi (2006) *The SENSORIA Reference Modelling Language: Primitives for Service Description*. Available from www.sensoria-ist.eu

10. J. L. Fiadeiro, A. Lopes, M. Wermelinger (2003) A mathematical semantics for architectural connectors. In: R. Backhouse, J. Gibbons (eds) *Generic Programming. LNCS, vol 2793*. Springer, Berlin Heidelberg New York, pp 190–234

11. I. Foster, C. Kesselman (eds) (2004) *The Grid 2: Blueprint for a New Computing Infrastructure*. Morgan Kaufmann, San Francisco, CA

12. R. Goldblatt (1987) *Logics of Time and Computation*. CSLI, Stanford

13. J. Misra, W. Cook (2006) Computation orchestration: A basis for wide-area computing. *Journal of Software and Systems Modelling*. To appear

14. SCA Consortium (2005) *Building Systems using a Service Oriented Architecture*. Whitepaper available from www-128.ibm.com/developerworks/library/specification/ws-sca/

15. M. Solanki, A. Cau and H. Zedan (2004) Augmenting semantic web service description with compositional specification. In *WWW'04*. ACM Press, New York, pp 544–552

16. M. Wermelinger, A. Lopes, J. L. Fiadeiro (2001) A graph-based architectural (re)-configuration language. In V.Gruhn (ed): *ESEC/FSE'01*. ACM Press, New York, pp 21–32

Appendix – The Procurement Service

In this appendix, we model the procurement business process used in the paper, involving a supplier, a warehouse, a local stock, and a price look-up facility.

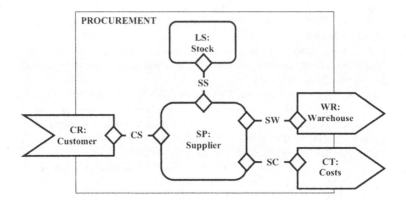

PROCUREMENT consists of:

- CR – the external interface of the service provided by the module, of type *Customer*;
- WR – the external interface of a service required for shipping the product if it is not available locally, of type *Warehouse*;
- CT – the external interface of a service required for quoting the current market costs of products, of type *Costs*;
- SP – a component that coordinates the business process, of type *Supplier*;
- LS – a component that provides local storage of products, of type *Stock*
- CS, SS, SW, SC – four internal wires that make explicit the partner relationship between *CR* and *SP*, *SP* and *LS*, *SP* and *WR*, and *SP* and *CT*, respectively.

The components, external interfaces and protocols required for the definition of PRO-CUREMENT are collected at the end of the appendix.

MODULE Procurement **is**

COMPONENTS

    SP: Supplier
    LS: Stock

PROVIDES

    CR: Customer

REQUIRES

    WR: Warehouse
    CT: Costs

WIRES

SP Supplier		SS		LS Stock	
ask checkStock	S_1		R_1	**rpl** get	
tll incStock	S_2	Custom1	R_2	**prf** set	
tll decStock	S_3				

SP Supplier		SC		CT Costs	
ask how	S_1	AskTll	R_1	**tll** much	

SP Supplier		SW		WH Warehouse	
s&r checkShipAvail	S_1		R_1	**r&s** check&lock	
⌂ which	i_1	Straight	i_1	⌂ which	
many	i_2		i_2	many	
rcv confirmShip	R_1	Straight	S_1	**snd** confirm	

SP Supplier		CS		CR Customer	
r&s requestQuote	R_1		S_1	**s&r** howMuch	
⌂ which	i_1	Straight	i_1	⌂ which	
⊠ cost	o_1		o_1	⊠ cost	
r&s orderGoods	R_1		S_1	**s&r** buy	
⌂ which	i_1	Straight	i_1	⌂ which	
⊠ cost	o_1		o_1	⊠ cost	
rcv makePayment	R_1	Straight	S_1	**snd** pay	
snd shipOrder	S_1	Straight	R_1	**rcv** ackShip	

END MODULE

SPECIFICATIONS

BUSINESS ROLE Stock **is**

> **INTERACTIONS**
> > **rpl** get(product):nat
> > **prf** set(product,nat)
>
> **ORCHESTRATION**
> > **local** qoh:product→nat
> > **transition**
> > > **triggeredBy** get(p)
> > > **sends** qoh(p)
> > **transition**
> > > **triggeredBy** set(p,n)
> > > **effects** qoh(p)'=n

BUSINESS ROLE Supplier **is**

> **INTERACTIONS**
>> **r&s** requestQuote
>>> 🔔 which:product
>>> ✉ cost:money
>>
>> **r&s** orderGoods
>>> 🔔 many:nat
>>> ✉ much:money
>>
>> **rcv** makePayment
>> **snd** shipOrder
>> **s&r** checkShipAvail
>>> 🔔 which:product, many:nat
>>
>> **rcv** confirmShip
>> **ask** how(product):money
>> **ask** checkStock(product,nat):bool
>> **tll** incStock(product,nat)
>> **tll** decStock(product,nat)
>
> **ORCHESTRATION**
>> **local** s:[0..8], inStock:bool, which:product, many:nat,
>>   much:money, timeoutQuote:bool   .
>>
>> **initialisation**
>>> s=0
>>
>> **termination**
>>> s=8
>>
>> **transition** TQuote
>>> | **triggeredBy** requestQuote🔔?
>>> | **guardedBy** s=0
>>> | **effects** which'=requestQuote.which
>>> | ∧ much'=how(requestQuote.which)*1.2
>>> | ∧ inStock'=false
>>> | ∧ timeoutQuote'=false
>>> | ∧ s'=1
>>> | **sends** requestQuote✉!
>>> | ∧ requestQuote.cost=much'
>>> | ∧ requestQuote.Reply=true
>>> | ∧ alertDate🔔!
>>> | ∧ alertDate.Ref="quote"
>>> | ∧ alertDate.Interval=7
>>
>> **transition** TAlert
>>> | **triggeredBy** alertDate✉?
>>> | **guardedBy**
>>> | **effects** alert.Ref="quote" ∧ s=1 ⊃ timeoutQuote'=true
>>> | ∧ alert.Ref="goods" ∧ s=2 ⊃ s'=8
>>> | **sends** alert.Ref="quote" ∧ s=1 ⊃ requestQuote💣*!
>>> | ∧ alert.Ref="goods" ∧ s=2 ⊃ orderGoods💣*!
>>> | ∧ incStock(which,many)
>>
>> **transition** TimeoutOrder
>>> | **triggeredBy** checkShipAvail💣*?
>>> | **guardedBy**
>>> | **effects** s=4 ⊃ s'=8
>>> | **sends** s=4 ⊃ orderGoods💣*!

```
transition TOrder
  triggeredBy orderGoods⌂?
  guardedBy s=1
  effects many'=orderGoods⌂.many
      ∧ timeoutQuote ⊃
          much'=orderGoods.many*how(requestQuote.which)*1.2
      ∧ ¬timeoutQuote ⊃ much'=orderGoods.many*much
      ∧ checkStock(which,orderGoods.many) ⊃ s'=2
                    ∧ inStock'=true
      ∧ ¬checkStock(which,orderGoods.many) ⊃ s'=3
                    ∧ inStock'=false
  sends inStock' ⊃ decStock(which,many)
                    ∧ orderGoods⊠!
                    ∧ orderGoods.much=much'
                    ∧ orderGoods.Reply=true
                    ∧ alertDate⌂!
                    ∧ alertDate.Ref="goods"
                    ∧ alertDate.Interval=3
      ∧ ¬inStock' ⊃ checkShipAvail⌂!
                    ∧ checkShipAvail.which=which
                    ∧ checkShipAvail.many=many'

transition TWare
  triggeredBy checkShipAvail⊠?
  guardedBy s=3
  effects checkShipAvail.Reply ⊃ s'=4
      ∧ ¬checkShipAvail.Reply ⊃ s'=8
  sends checkShipAvail.Reply ⊃ orderGoods⊠!
                    ∧ orderGoods.Reply=true
                    ∧ orderGoods.much=much
      ∧ ¬checkShipAvail.Reply ⊃ orderGoods⊠!
                    ∧ orderGoods.Reply=false

transition TPay
  triggeredBy makePayment⌂?
  guardedBy (s=2 ∨ s=4)
  effects s=2 ⊃ s'=5
      ∧ s=4 ⊃ s'=6
  sends s=4 ⊃ checkShipAvail✓!

transition TConfirm
  triggeredBy confirmShip⌂?
  guardedBy s=6
  effects s'=7

transition TShip
  triggeredBy
  guardedBy s=5 ∨ s=7
  effects s'=8
  sends shipOrder⌂!

transition TAbort
  triggeredBy orderGoods♱?
  guardedBy (s=5 ∨ s=6)
  effects s'=8
  sends s=5 ⊃ incStock(which,many)
      ∧ s=6 ⊃ checkShipAvail♱!
```

BUSINESS PROTOCOL Warehouse **is**

   INTERACTIONS

      r&s check&lock
         ⌂ which:product, many:nat
      snd confirm

   BEHAVIOUR

      check&lock⌂? **exceptif** true
      check&lock⊠! ∧ check&lock.Reply ⊃
        alertDate⌂! ∧ alertDate.Interval=3 ∧
            alertDate.Ref="goods"
      check&lock☀! ⊃ alertDate⊠? ∧ alertDate.Ref="goods"
      check&lock⧖ ⊃ (check&lock✓? **ensures** confirm⌂!)
      check&lock✓? ⊃ (check&lock✝? **exceptif** confirm⌂!)

BUSINESS PROTOCOL Costs **is**

   INTERACTIONS

      rpl much(product):money

BUSINESS PROTOCOL Customer **is**

   INTERACTIONS

      s&r howMuch
         ⌂ which:product
         ⊠ cost:money
      s&r buy
         ⌂ many:nat
         ⊠ much:money
      snd pay
      rcv ackShip

   BEHAVIOUR

      howMuch⌂? **exceptif** true
      howMuch⊠? **enables** buy⌂!
      howMuch⊠? ⊃ alertDate⌂! ∧ alertDate.Interval=7
        ∧ alertDate.Ref="quote"
      howMuch☀? ⊃ alertDate⊠? ∧ alertDate.Ref="quote"
      howMuch⊠? ⊃ howMuch.Reply
      howMuch⧖ ⊃ (buy⌂! **ensures**
        (buy⊠? ∧ buy.Reply ⊃ buy.much=buy.many*howMuch.much))
      buy⊠? ∧ buy.Reply ⊃ alertDate⌂! ∧ alertDate.Interval=3
        ∧ alertDate.Ref="goods"
      buy☀? ⊃ alertDate⊠? ∧ alertDate.Ref="goods"
      buy⧖ ⊃ (pay⌂! **ensures** ackShip⌂?)
      pay⌂! ≡ buy✓!
      buy✓! ⊃ buy✝! **exceptif** ackShip⌂?

INTERACTION PROTOCOL Straight **is**

   INTERACTIONS
      snd S_1
      rcv R_1
   COORDINATION
      $S_1 \equiv R_1$

INTERACTION PROTOCOL Straight.I(d_1)O(d_2) **is**

    INTERACTIONS

      s&r S_1

          ✉ $i_1:d_1$

          ✉ $o_1:d_2$

      r&s R_1

          ✉ $i_1:d_1$

          ✉ $o_1:d_2$

    COORDINATION

      $S_1 = R_1$

      $S_1.i_1 = R_1.i_1$

      $S_1.o_1 = R_1.o_1$

INTERACTION PROTOCOL Straight.I(d_1,d_2) **is**

    INTERACTIONS

      s&r S_1

          ✉ $i_1:d_1$, $i_2:d_2$

      r&s R_1

          ✉ $i_1:d_1$, $i_2:d_2$

    COORDINATION

      $S_1 = R_1$

      $S_1.i_1 = R_1.i_1$

      $S_1.i_2 = R_1.i_2$

INTERACTION PROTOCOL Custom1 **is**

    INTERACTIONS

      ask S_1(product,nat):bool

      tll S_2(product,nat)

      tll S_3(product,nat)

      rpl R_1(product):nat

      prf R_2(product,nat)

    COORDINATION

      $S_1(p,n) = R_1(p) \geq n$

      $S_2(p,n) \supset R_2(p,R_1(p)+n)$

      $R_1(p) \geq n \wedge S_3(p,n) \supset R_2(p,R_1(p)-n)$

      $R_1(p) < n \supset \neg S_3(p,n)$

INTERACTION PROTOCOL AskTll(d_1,d_2) **is**

    INTERACTIONS

      ask $S_1(d_1):d_2$

      tll $R_1(d_1):d_2$

    COORDINATION

      $S_1(x) = R_1(x)$

Evaluating the Scalability of a Web Service-Based Distributed e-Learning and Course Management System

Stephen Gilmore and Mirco Tribastone

LFCS, University of Edinburgh
{stg, mtribast}@inf.ed.ac.uk

Abstract. A growing concern of Web service providers is *scalability*. An implementation of a Web service may be able at present to support its user base, but how can a provider judge what will happen if that user base grows? We present a modelling approach based on process algebra which allows service providers to investigate how models of Web service execution scale with increasing client population sizes. The method has the benefit of allowing a simple model of the service to be scaled to realistic population sizes without the modeller needing to aggregate or re-model the system.

1   Introduction

Web Services are gaining more and more popularity as an approach to distributed computing. This flourishing is in part due to the use of well-known standard protocols for message exchange such as HTTP [1], XML [2], SOAP [3], and WSDL (Web Service Description Language) [4], as well as a large number of frameworks to improve developer's productivity (e.g. Apache AXIS [5], and Java WSDP [6]). Web Services are also being supported by businesses (e.g., [7]) to provide programmer-friendly interfaces for their services.

This paper addresses scalability performance aspects of e-Learning oriented Web Services. We present a scenario in which Web Service technology is used to implement a Distributed Course Management System (DCMS). One of the most severe problems a DCMS has to deal with is the performance degradation occurring when many users are requesting the service simultaneously. Let us imagine a DCMS is available for collecting final course projects of a class. Teaching staff usually put a deadline on those activities, and students are likely to get their projects ready very close to the due date. The DCMS has to cope with a flash crowd-like effect, as server resources (i.e. memory, CPU and bandwidth) have to be shared among a large number of users, thus paving the way for performance penalties experienced by users. In order to assess scalability properties of the system, we first develop a simple analytical model of the request/response message exchange pattern in SOAP, the Web Service communication protocol. This model constitutes the basis for the DCMS model where concurrent clients performing SOAP requests are taken into account.

M. Bravetti, M. Nuñes, and G. Zavattaro (Eds.): WS-FM 2006, LNCS 4184, pp. 214–226, 2006.

2   Related Work

Performance issues of traditional Web servers have been extensively investigated (for example, [8,9]). Research on performance evaluation of Web Services has been primarily focused on comparing SOAP implementations [10,11] or investigating performance of SOAP approaches to scientific computing [12,13].

In comparison to this, less effort has been invested in modelling the newer technology of Web Services. In [14] a profile-driver model for cluster-based web services is presented. Application profiles are obtained by mapping workload characteristics to resource (i.e. CPU, disk, memory) utilisation using linear fitting. Results shows that remote invocation overhead is important for the accuracy of the model; however, in our work we disregard method call overhead as in our scenario we focus on the most constrained system activity occurring at rate which turns out to be several order of magnitudes slower than SOAP processing. [15] propose an analytical model for a multi-tier web service based on a network of queues, where each queue represents an application tier. Although this work shares some common ideas (chain multi-tier approach), we propose a much simpler model where server overload, tier replication and multiple session classes are not taken into account. A general account of Web Service scalability is found in [16].

Structure of This Paper: The remainder of this paper is structured as follows. In Section 3 we briefly introduce PEPA, the stochastic process algebra employed for our modelling. In Section 4 we develop the model of request/response message exchange for Web Services. In Section 5 we discuss methodology and numerical results of parameter estimation. In Section 6 the DCMS case study is shown and a preliminary model is given. Stiffness problems in model evaluation are solved by means of the simplified model which is presented in Section 7. Numerical results are presented in Section 8. Section 9 concludes the paper.

3   Overview of Performance Evaluation Process Algebra

In Performance Evaluation Process Algebra (PEPA) [17], a system is viewed as a set of *components* which carry out *activities* either individually or in cooperation with other components. Activities which are private to the component in which they occur are represented by the distinguished action type, τ. Each activity is characterized by an *action type* and a duration which is exponentially distributed. This is written as a pair such as (α, r) where α is the action type and r is the *activity rate*. This parameter may be any positive real number, or may be unspecified. We use the distinguished symbol $\top$ to indicate that the rate is not specified by this component. This component is said to be *passive* with respect to this action type and the rate of the shared activity is defined by another component.

3.1 Combinators of the Language

PEPA provides a set of combinators which allow expressions to be built which define the behaviour of components via the activities that they engage in. These combinators are presented below.

Prefix: $(\alpha, r).P$: Prefix is the basic mechanism by which the behaviours of components are constructed. This combinator implies that after the component has carried out activity (α, r), it behaves as component P.

In this paper we will make use of *functional rates* [18] which allow the rate at which an activity is performed to depend on the current state of the model. (In Petri nets terms, a "marking-dependent" rate.)

Choice: $P_1 + P_2$: This combinator represents a competition between components. The system may behave either as component P_1 or as P_2. All current activities of the two components are enabled. The first activity to complete distinguishes one of these components and the other is then discarded.

Cooperation: $P_1 \bowtie_L P_2$: This describes the synchronization of components P_1 and P_2 over the activities in the cooperation set L. The components may proceed independently with activities whose types do not belong to this set. A particular case of the cooperation is when $L = \emptyset$. In this case, components proceed with all activities independently. The notation $P_1 \parallel P_2$ is used as a shorthand for $P_1 \bowtie_\emptyset P_2$. In a cooperation, the rate of a shared activity is defined as the rate of the slowest component.

Hiding: P/L This component behaves like P except that any activities of types within the set L are *hidden*, i.e. such an activity exhibits the unknown type τ and the activity can be regarded as an internal delay by the component. Such an activity cannot be carried out in cooperation with any other component: the original action type of a hidden activity is no longer externally accessible, to an observer or to another component; the duration is unaffected.

Constant: $A \stackrel{def}{=} P$ Constants are components whose meaning is given by a defining equation: $A \stackrel{def}{=} P$ gives the constant A the behaviour of the component P. This is how we assign names to components (behaviours). An explicit recursion operator is not provided but components of infinite behaviour may be readily described using sets of mutually recursive defining equations.

One process constant is pre-defined. The deadlocked process named *Stop* enables no activities [19].

3.2 Formal Semantics of the Language

Process algebras are concise formally-defined modelling languages for the precise description of concurrent, communicating systems. The PEPA process algebra benefits from formal semantic descriptions of different characters which are appropriate for different uses. The structured operational semantics presented in [17] maps the PEPA language to a Continuous-Time Markov Chain (CTMC) representation. A denotational semantics for the language maps PEPA models to elements of metric spaces [20]. A continuous-space semantics maps PEPA models to a system of ordinary differential equations (ODEs) [21], admitting different solution procedures. We use both the CTMC and ODE semantics in the present paper.

3.3 Analysis Tools for PEPA

The reason to have a formally-defined high-level language for performance modelling is that it is possible to implement software tools which evaluate models according to the formal semantics of the language. In the present study we used the PRISM probabilistic model-checker [22], which accepts PEPA as one of its input languages, to perform transient analysis of the CTMC. We used the PEPA Workbench [23] to compile the PEPA model to a differential equation form which we could solve using a fifth-order Runge Kutta numerical integrator.

Because we are modelling in a high-level language it is possible to apply these very different numerical evaluation procedures to compute performance results from the same model. This is a freedom which we would not have if we had coded a Markov chain or differential equation-based representation of the model directly in a numerical computing platform such as Matlab.

4 Model of a Request/Response SOAP Exchange

Web Services use SOAP as the underlying protocol for inter-process communication. Being based on XML, it requires more resources than traditional binary-based RPC protocols such as, e.g. CORBA or RMI. Moreover, sending binary data over XML-based protocol is a critical performance issue.

Several approaches have been presented so far to allow efficient transmission of binary data over SOAP. SOAP with Attachments (SwA) [24] uses the MIME mechanism [25] to send MultiPart/Related messages. DIME [26] is a specification from Microsoft which encapsulates SOAP messages and attachments into binary records. DIME is no longer supported and has been replaced by MTOM [27], a WC3 Recommendation which enables optimised MIME serialisation of SOAP messages.

4.1 Message Life Cycle

We describe a fair approximation of a SOAP message life cycle, as we used to model the system. Although SOAP also supports asynchronous (one-way) messages, we focus on the Request/Response exchange pattern. Moreover, let us suppose that the client may transmit a binary file with the request. We assume the attachment is being sent according to the SwA specification, though our model is consistent with other mechanisms as well.

The client is the originator of the request. We may describe it as a process which evolves through the following series of activities:

1. *Message creation.* This involves XML formatting activities.
2. *File attachment.* This phase depends on the mechanism employed (e.g. SwA, DIME, MTOM, Base64 Encoding) and the file size.

3. *Message sending.* Key factors are message size and network bandwidth.
4. *Response awaiting.* Performance issues are related to the server throughput and network available bandwidth.
5. *Response processing.* HTTP and XML parsing are taken into account.

The server performs the following activities:

1. *Request processing.* This involves both HTTP and XML parsing.
2. *Attachment processing.* This depends on how many processing resources are needed by the server in order to deal with the attachment.
3. *Response creation.* This phase includes server's method invocation and XML response message formatting.
4. *Response sending.* This is dependent on the available network bandwidth.

Setup of the Model. We consider the model in the optimistic scenario where hardware and software failures are assumed to occur sufficiently infrequently that we will not represent them. Further, the server is sufficiently well-provisioned that we may also neglect the possibility failures caused by out-of-memory errors or overrunning the thread limit on the JVM hosting the Web container. We will return to review these optimistic assumptions after we compute performance results from our model.

4.2   PEPA Model of the System

It is straightforward to obtain a PEPA representation from the system description presented in Section 4.1. Figure 1 shows the model of a request/response message exchange. The system here is made up of only two components that perform a single exchange by synchronising on all of their common activities.

$$ClientA \stackrel{def}{=} (create, \alpha).ClientB$$
$$ClientB \stackrel{def}{=} (attach, \beta).ClientC$$
$$ClientC \stackrel{def}{=} (queue, \lambda).ClientD$$
$$ClientD \stackrel{def}{=} (request, \top).ClientE$$
$$ClientE \stackrel{def}{=} (response, \top).ClientF$$
$$ClientF \stackrel{def}{=} (processResponse, \gamma).Stop$$

$$ServerA \stackrel{def}{=} (queue, \top).ServerB$$
$$ServerB \stackrel{def}{=} (request, \mu).ServerC$$
$$ServerC \stackrel{def}{=} (save, \theta).ServerD$$
$$ServerD \stackrel{def}{=} (processRequest, \eta).ServerE$$
$$ServerE \stackrel{def}{=} (response, \phi).Stop$$

$$ClientA \underset{\{queue, request, response\}}{\bowtie} ServerA$$

Fig. 1. PEPA model of request/response message exchange

5   Parameter Estimation

5.1   Experimental Design

We conducted experiments to estimate the appropriate numerical values for the parameters used in our model. We implemented a simple Web Service in which SwA was enabled to allow it to save a binary file attached by the client. The implementation of the server interface as well as the method for processing attachments are timed methods, in order to let us gather measurement data on their invocation.

The client makes a designer-tunable number of service calls, the attachment file size being passed as application argument. The designer may also set an inter-message idle period; however, our results were not affected by changes in this parameter.

5.2   Test Environment

We performed our tests with both client and server running on the same host, although our Web Services was implemented to be remotely accessible. We used a desktop with the following configuration: Intel Dual Xeon 3.2 GHz processor and 2 GB RAM running Microsoft Windows XP 64bit Edition. Our Web Service framework uses Sun Java Application Server Platform Edition 8.2, Java 2 Platform Standard Edition 5.0, Java WSDP 1.6 and JavaBeans Application Framework 1.0.2. Class binding, automatic WSDL file generation and application deployment were supported by NetBeans IDE 5.0.

We used 200 ms inter-message idle period and 1000 service invocations for each experiment; file size was 20 MB. Table 1 shows experimental results we obtained in our tests.

Table 1. Experimental results

Activity Name	Mean (ms)
create	0.592
attach	0.040
processResponse	0.154
save	81.100
processRequest	0.775

6   Distributed Course Management System Model

In order to assess the scalability issues of a Web Service-based distributed application we consider the following scenario. A Web Service is implemented for distributed e-Learning and Course Management System. We restrict our analysis to a case where one single course is being managed. We assume that no other services simultaneously run on the server; thus, the server download capacity c_s as well as server upload capacity μ_s are fully available for the Web Service.

The clients' (i.e. students) arrival process is assumed to be well-described by a Poisson distribution with rate λ. The system allows a maximum number of students (course size) N. We assume that all students have the same values for download capacity c_c and upload capacity μ_c. Like the server, we also suppose that no other process but the Web Service client-side application consumes network resources.

When multiple clients are involved, the server has to share its bandwidth among them. A model of the behaviour of the network is therefore necessary. We address this issue by developing a simple model for characterising service performance of the system. In this model we assume an ideal network in which no loss occurs and network nominal *capacity* means *available bandwidth*. We also suppose that transmissions are established on top of TCP connections where fairness against concurrent requests is perfect.

Given the above assumptions, if we denote i ($i > 0$) as the number of uploading clients at any point in time, the uploading rate of each connection *request* is:

$$request = \min \left\{ \frac{c_s}{i}, \mu_c \right\} \tag{1}$$

Similarly, if j is the number of downloading clients (i.e., clients who are receiving the response message), the downloading rate of each connection *response* is:

$$response = \min \left\{ \frac{\mu_s}{j}, c_c \right\} \tag{2}$$

6.1   PEPA Model of the System

We present the model of the DCMS by taking into account the behaviour of server bandwidth when multiple connections are allowed. Local activities are unaffected by concurrent requests. Thus, the model of the client is the same as in Fig. 1. As for the server, we need to distinguish each of the possible number of clients which upload to him simultaneously. Let $Server_i$ be the process description of the server downloading from i concurrent clients. The model of the server as well as the description of the system are described in Fig. 2.

Model analysis has been carried out by setting local activity rates as they were obtained in our experimental tests (cfr. Tab. 1). Table 2 shows the complete parameter set. It is worthwhile to observe that network parameters represent bandwidths normalised by the message size being sent. For instance, $c_s = 0.001$ means that the server is able to get the entire message completed in 1000 s; this value resembles a realistic situation where a server equipped with a 10 Mbps connection has to download a file about 1 GB long. We also would like to point out that server upload capacity is much faster than its download capacity because of the size of the message being transmitted: here we have assumed 1 KB long SOAP response messages in our parameter set. The value of λ is to consider flash crowd-like effect, such that triggered for instance by simultaneous service requests when a deadline is due.

As our model considers client components which perform only one request, transient analysis has to be carried out for evaluating the performance of the

$$Server_0 \stackrel{def}{=} (queue, \top).Server_1$$

$$Server_i \stackrel{def}{=} (queue, \top).Server_{i+1} + (request, \min\{\tfrac{c_s}{i}, \mu_c\}).(save, \theta).$$
$$(processRequest, \eta).(response, \min\{\tfrac{\mu_s}{i}, c_c\}).Server_{i-1}$$
$$(0 < i < N)$$

$$Server_N \stackrel{def}{=} (request, \min\{\tfrac{c_s}{N}, \mu_c\}).(save, \theta).(processRequest, \eta).$$
$$(response, \min\{\tfrac{\mu_s}{N}, c_c\}).Server_{N-1}$$

$$\left(\underbrace{ClientA \parallel ClientA \parallel \ldots \parallel ClientA}_{N} \right) \underset{queue, request, response}{\bowtie} Server_0$$

Fig. 2. Model of the server in DCMS

system. In the following we describe some preliminary studies which have been conducted in order to assess scalability issues of the model.

Table 2. Parameter set for model analysis

Parameter	Meaning	Rate (s^{-1})
α	create	1689.20
β	attach	25000.00
γ	processResponse	6493.50
θ	save	12.33
η	processRequest	1290.32
λ	queue	20.00
N	Population size	100
c_s	Server download bandwidth	0.001
μ_s	Server upload bandwidth	$c_s/3$
c_c	Client download bandwidth	$(c_s/10) \cdot 10^6$
μ_c	Client upload bandwidth	$c_c/30$

We mapped the PEPA model to CTMC representation. We found the underlying Markov chain does not scale with the number of model components. We calculated different state space sizes by varying N, as shown in Tab.3. We argue that the CTMC representation highlights lack of scalability which makes performance analysis intractable even for unrealistic values of N.

It is well known that the ODE-based representation of the model offers better scalability, as the size of the space vector does not change for N varying. However, we encountered stiffness problems when running time-series analysis, as the expected time to obtain model results was high (i.e., 10^8 s) even if the state vector size would suggest easy computability. We conjecture these problems are due to the differences of several order of magnitude between some activity rates (e.g., μ_c against β). We actually modified the parameter set by imposing unreal-

Table 3. CTMC State space sizes for N varying

N	State space size
1	9
2	72
3	540
4	3888
5	27216
6	186624

istic values (all close to 1) which made the running much faster, as we obtained results in 10^{-2} s.

7   A Simplified Model

The scalability problems discussed above lead us to a simplified model where all activities which occur at fast rate have been disregarded. The model is shown in Fig. 3.

$$ClientIdle \stackrel{def}{=} (queue, \lambda).ClientUploading$$
$$ClientUploading \stackrel{def}{=} (request, \top).Stop$$
$$Server_0 \stackrel{def}{=} (queue, \top).Server_1$$
$$Server_i \stackrel{def}{=} (queue, \top).Server_{i+1} + (request, \min\{\tfrac{c_s}{i}, \mu_c\}).Server_{i-1}$$
$$(0 < i < N)$$
$$Server_N \stackrel{def}{=} (request, \min\{\tfrac{c_s}{N}, \mu_c\}).Server_{N-1}$$

$$\left(\underbrace{ClientIdle \parallel ClientIdle \parallel \ldots \parallel ClientIdle}_{N} \right) \underset{\{queue, request, response\}}{\bowtie} Server_0$$

Fig. 3. Simplified PEPA model of the DCMS

When mapping the PEPA model to CTMC representation, we found that the model is still not scalable as the space state size is 3^N. In the continuous-space representation the rates are separated by fewer orders of magnitude and performance results could be evaluated at low computational cost. In particular, we required only 0.03 seconds of compute time to obtain a 10^6 seconds time series analysis.

8   Numerical Results

We obtained numerical results using the parameter set as follows. We considered a maximum number of users $N = 100$, requesting service according to a flash

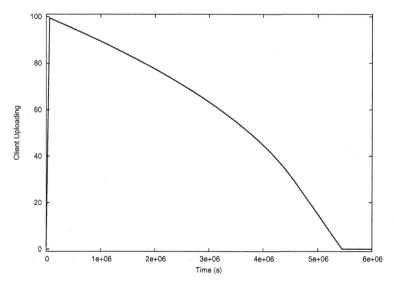

Fig. 4. Evolution of the number of clients uploading

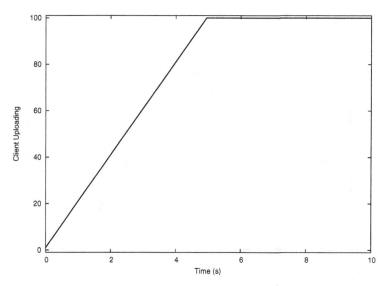

Fig. 5. Flash crowd effect in DCMS

crowd-like effect at rate $\lambda = 20$. Server download capacity c_s was set to 0.001, and client upload capacity $\mu_c = c_s/30$.

Figure 4 shows a time series plot of the number of client uploading to the server. The initial burstiness of requests is shown in Figure 5.

Figure 6 plots service durations for different server bandwidths (i.e., $c_s = 0.01, 0.02$, and 0.1). Finally, Figure 7 shows service durations for different values of N, when $c_s = 0.1$ and $\mu_c = c_s/30$.

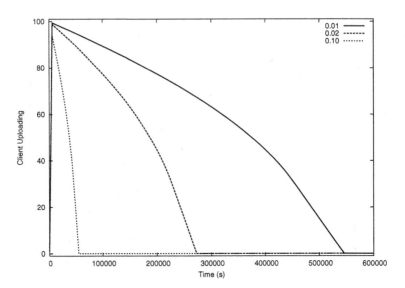

Fig. 6. Time series for different server bandwidths

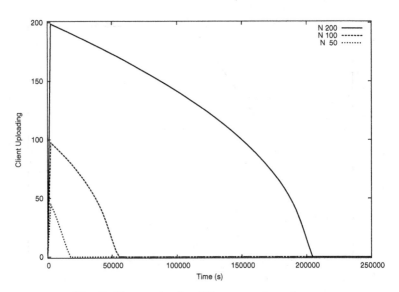

Fig. 7. Time series for different number of users

Commentary on the Results: We note that the system requires a significant amount of time to get every client request completed. Earlier we outlined a series of assumptions about the model setup which included the optimistic assumptions of absence of failure of various kinds, and did not include the possibility of users aborting long-running file uploads only to restart them again later. Since unsuccessful file transfers (of whatever kind) will only tend to delay things more we can safely interpret the results presented above as saying that even in this very optimistic setting the system is impractical for use.

9 Conclusions

This paper has assessed the scalability of a Web service which supports secure distributed file upload using the Web service attachments API. The issue of scalability extends basic evaluation of performance: a service may have acceptable performance at present, but the question is how this performance will be likely to change as greater numbers of service subscribers are added.

Models of distributed systems which are based on a discrete-state interleaving semantics are limited by the well-known state-space explosion problem: the size of the system as a whole is bounded by the product of the state space size of the individual components which it contains. Markovian models (whether obtained from process algebras, Petri nets or another modelling formalism) are victims of this problem. By mapping to a continuous-state differential equation representation the PEPA language allows modellers to assess scalability. The state-space is never constructed, making it possible to have a scalable analysis process. We move directly from the model with parameters fitted from measurement data to time series plots showing the changes in the number of each kind of component over time. The solution to a system of differential equations is definitive, as the solution of a Markov chain is, thus there is no repetition cost as found in other modelling approaches used to assess scalability (such as simulation). The numerical procedures used have low computational cost.

Acknowledgements. This work was supported by the EU IST-3-016004-IP-09 project SENSORIA.

References

1. W3C. HTTP protocol specification. http://www.w3.org/Protocols/rfc2616/rfc2616.html.
2. W3C. XML protocol specification. http://www.w3.org/TR/2004/REC-xml-20040204/.
3. W3C. SOAP protocol specification. http://www.w3.org/TR/soap/.
4. W3C. WSDL protocol specification. http://www.w3.org/TR/wsdl.
5. Apache AXIS. http://ws.apache.org/axis/.
6. Java Web Services Development Pack. http://java.sun.com/webservices/jwsdp/index.jsp.
7. Google web APIs. http://www.google.com/apis/.
8. M. Arlitt and L. Williamson C. Internet web servers: Workload characterization and performance implications. In *IEEE/ACM Transaction on Networking*, October 1997.
9. L. Slothouber. A model of web server performance. In *Proceedings 5th International World Wide Web Conference*, 1996.

10. D. Davis and M. Parashar. Latency performance of SOAP implementations. In *Proceedings 2nd IEEE International Symposium on Cluster Computing and the Grid*, 2002.
11. M. Govindaraju, A. Slominski, K. Chiu, P. Liu, R. van Engelen, and M. Lewis. Toward characterizing the performance of SOAP toolkits. In *Proceedings 5th IEEE/ACM International Workshop on Grid Computing*, pages 365–372, November 2004.
12. R. van Engelen. Pushing the SOAP envelope with web services for scientific computing. In *Proceedings International Conference on Web Services (ICWS'03)*, pages 346–354, 2003.
13. K. Chiu and M. Govindaraju. Investigating the limits of SOAP performance for scientific computing. In *Proceedings 11th IEEE International Symposium on High-Performance Distributed Computing*, 2002.
14. C. Stewart and K. Shen. Performance modeling and system management for multi-component online services.
15. B. Urgaonkar, G. Pacifici, P. Shenoy, M. Spreitzer, and A. Tantawi. An analytical model for multi-tier internet services and its application. In *Proceedings of the ACM SIGMETRICS*, June 2005.
16. Robert van Engelen. Are web services scale free? `http://www.cs.fsu.edu/~engelen/powerlaw.html`, June 2005.
17. J. Hillston. *A Compositional Approach to Performance Modelling*. Cambridge University Press, 1996.
18. J. Hillston and L. Kloul. An efficient Kronecker representation for PEPA models. In L. de Alfaro and S. Gilmore, editors, *Proceedings of the first joint PAPM-PROBMIV Workshop*, volume 2165 of *Lecture Notes in Computer Science*, pages 120–135, Aachen, Germany, September 2001. Springer-Verlag.
19. N. Thomas and J. Bradley. Terminating processes in PEPA. In K. Djemame and M. Kara, editors, *Proceedings of the Seventeenth UK Performance Engineering Workshop*, pages 143–154, University of Leeds, July 2001.
20. M. Kwiatkowska and G. Norman. Metric denotational semantics for PEPA. In M. Ribaudo, editor, *Proceedings of the Fourth Annual Workshop on Process Algebra and Performance Modelling*, pages 120–138. Dipartimento di Informatica, Università di Torino, CLUT, July 1996.
21. J. Hillston. Fluid flow approximation of PEPA models. In *Proceedings of the Second International Conference on the Quantitative Evaluation of Systems*, pages 33–43, Torino, Italy, September 2005. IEEE Computer Society Press.
22. A. Hinton, M. Kwiatkowska, G. Norman, and D. Parker. PRISM: A tool for automatic verification of probabilistic systems. In *Proceedings 12th International Conference on Tools and Algorithms for the Construction and Analysis of Systems (TACAS'06)*, 2006. To appear.
23. S. Gilmore and J. Hillston. The PEPA Workbench: A Tool to Support a Process Algebra-based Approach to Performance Modelling. In *Proceedings of the Seventh International Conference on Modelling Techniques and Tools for Computer Performance Evaluation*, number 794 in Lecture Notes in Computer Science, pages 353–368, Vienna, May 1994. Springer-Verlag.
24. W3C. SOAP with Attachments. `http://www.w3.org/TR/SOAP-attachments`.
25. MIME Multipart/Related Content-type RFC. `http://www.ietf.org/rfc/rfc2387.txt`.
26. DIME protocol specification. `msdn.microsoft.com/library/en-us/dnglobspec/html/draft-nielsen-dime-02.txt`.
27. W3C. MTOM. `http://www.w3.org/TR/2005/REC-soap12-mtom-20050125/`.

Choreography Conformance Analysis: Asynchronous Communications and Information Alignment*

Raman Kazhamiakin and Marco Pistore

DIT, University of Trento
via Sommarive 14, 38050, Trento, Italy
{raman, pistore}@dit.unitn.it

Abstract. Web service choreography languages provide a way to describe the collaboration protocol of multiple services that exchange information in order to achieve a common goal. This description may be seen as a specification that should be respected by the joint behavior of the set of services implementing the choreography. Such a conformance requires that (i) the observable behavior of the implementation corresponds to the behavior described by the protocol specification, and (ii) the business information is properly managed, guaranteeing that the participants have a shared knowledge about it, according to what is specified in the choreography. In this paper we present a choreography conformance analysis approach that addresses both the behavioral correspondence and the business information management. The key features of the approach are the capability to deal with asynchronous interactions and the ability to model and analyse the data managed and exchanged in the protocol, thus providing more accurate verification results. We also present symbolic techniques based on these formalizations that can be used for model checking of the choreography conformance.

1 Introduction

Web service technology enables the development of complex heterogeneous, distributed applications, facilitating the specification, deployment, and enactment of remote software components accessible on the web via standardized protocols. The ability to integrate the existing services owned and managed by distinct stakeholders, obtaining new composite business applications, is one of the fundamental ideas underlying the Web service technology paradigm. Among the various aspects that need to be specified to fully describe a Web service composition, the representation of a stateful and coordinated behavior of the composition plays a prominent role. A wide range of Web service standards and languages has been proposed for these purposes [1,2,3]. The Web Services Choreography Description Language (WS-CDL, [3]) is particularly relevant for the specification

---

* This work is partially funded by the MIUR-FIRB project RBNE0195K5, "KLASE", by the MIUR-PRIN 2004 project "STRAP", and by the EU-IST project FP6-016004 "SENSORIA".

M. Bravetti, M. Nuñes, and G. Zavattaro (Eds.): WS-FM 2006, LNCS 4184, pp. 227–241, 2006.

of the compositions, as it provides a way to describe the observable behavior of the collaboration from the global point of view. One of the main goals of the choreography description is to define a reference model of the composition that the real service implementations should conform to. *Conformance testing* refers to the verification that the joint behavior of the composition of the service implementations corresponds to that described in the choreography.

The conformance analysis, however, does not amount only to check the correspondence between the sequences of externally observable message exchanges generated by the composition of service implementations and the collaboration protocol specification. It is also necessary to verify that the information of the protocol is being managed and distributed accordingly, and that the participants have a common view of the business data described in the choreography. The management of business information in conformance testing is complicated by the fact that WS-CDL allows for specifying in a declarative way that certain pieces of information should be synchronized either as a result of a certain data exchange (interaction alignment) or of the protocol execution as a whole (choreography coordination), without explicitly describing and constraining the mechanisms that should implement them.

In this paper we present a formal analysis framework that allows for the verification of the conformance between the collaboration specification and the composition of service implementations. The presented framework is based on our previous work [4] that provides a formal model for the compositions of *local* participants implementations. The key feature of this framework is the ability to model and analyse compositions, where the interactions are asynchronous, and the messages may be reordered and stored in unbounded queues.

In this work, we extend the approach of [4] in two ways. First, we enrich the model with the capability to represent and manage data-related constructs (e.g., variables, conditions, assignments), thus providing a way to model the data-flow of the compositions. Second, we introduce a formalism for the *global* model that allows for the choreographic description of the compositions. Based on these formalisations, we define the choreography conformance as a kind of bisimulation relation, emphasizing the asynchrony of the message communications. We also present formal definitions for the most common information alignment requirements, such as the interaction coordination alignment rules presented by WS-CDL. Furthermore, we define a symbolic representation of the underlying models, and propose finite-state model checking techniques for verifying the conformance between the implementing composition and the choreography specifications.

The paper is structured as follows. Section 2 introduces the conformance problem using variants of a simple example. Section 3 defines the formal models for the data- and control-flow of the underlying systems from the global perspective and as a composition of interacting local services. In Sect. 4 we present the notions of the asynchronous conformance relation and the information alignment rules, and discuss the symbolic analysis techniques suitable for the conformance verification. Concluding remarks and related works are discussed in Sect. 5.

2   Modelling Web Services Compositions

In order to illustrate the problems related to the conformance between the specification of a Web service composition and its implementation, we consider several variants of the Request For Quotation (RFQ) case study. The goal of the composition is to combine purchasing and delivery functionalities in a single business process, involving several participants. Thus, the composition describes the interactions of three independent services, namely a *buyer*, a *seller*, and a *shipper*.

We model the scenario using a WS-CDL [3] specification that describes the collaborations between the participants from the global perspective. WS-CDL specifications identify the participants of the composition, their variables, the interactions between the partners, and the dependencies between these interactions, such as control-flow and data-flow dependencies, transactional requirements etc. An example of the choreography specification is represented as a UML activity diagram in Fig. 1(a). The elementary actions in the diagram represent message exchanges, like `request` or `offer`; the decisions points, like the choice to accept or reject the offer; the silent internal activities, like the `verify` activity used to check the presence of the product.

The composition implementation is represented as a set of local specifications, one for each participant of the collaboration, defined in an appropriate language, e.g. BPEL [1]. These local models may represent either the real services, or rather the behavioral interfaces of the participants, to which the real implementations should conform [5]. Each local specification describes the (stateful) behavior of a particular service. It defines the operations that are triggered upon the invocation of the service. These operations include variables assignments, invoking other services and receiving responses, and structured activities like sequences, loops, conditional choices, etc. Examples of the local protocols, as those of the buyer and the seller, are represented as UML diagrams in Fig. 1(b).

It is important to note that the implementation description may include significantly more activities and even participants than is specified in the choreography description. These auxiliary elements are used to ensure the protocol, coordinating and aligning the main parts of the system.

2.1   Behavioral Correctness

The choreography model represented in Fig. 1(a) describes the following business scenario. First, the buyer asks the seller for a particular good, sending a request for quote. The offer is prepared and sent back to the buyer. In this moment two situations are possible: either the buyer accepts the message and the process continues with the confirmation and a shipment engagement; or the acceptance does not happen within a certain time limit, the offer is considered invalid, and the whole procedure terminates.

This choreography specification defines the requirements to the implementing compositions. That is, an implementation should satisfy all the control-flow and data-flow requirements of the model. Consider the BPEL processes that are supposed to implement the participants of the above scenario (Fig. 1(b)). It is easy

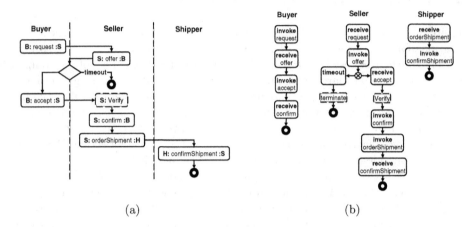

(a)   (b)

Fig. 1. RFQ case study

to see that these processes, when composed together, satisfy the specified choreography only under the assumption that the interactions are *synchronous*, i.e.,
a message emission is possible only if it is immediately followed by a reception.
This assumption, often used in modelling of Web service compositions, may be
violated in real settings due to the *asynchronous* nature of Web service interactions. Indeed, since the buyer and the seller are independent, it is possible that
the former emits the acceptance message simultaneously with the timeout of the
seller. This leads to a state, where the seller has terminated the execution, while
the buyer waits for the offer confirmation. This scenario may not be detected if
the assumption on synchronous interactions is applied.

In order to satisfy the choreography specification, some auxiliary activities
should be performed. In particular, the `accept` message should follow some availability checking interaction, where the the buyer asks for the possibility to accept
the order. In case of positive response, the acceptance is invoked, otherwise the
buyer terminates. On the other side, the seller waits for this availability checking
message, and responds negatively only if the timeout has expired.

2.2   Information Alignment

Figure 2(a) represents a modified choreography specification of the RFQ case
study. Here, instead of termination on timeout, the seller iteratively provides the
buyer with the updated information about the requested product (interaction
`refresh`), until the latter does not accept the offer.

The process implementations of the participants are presented in Fig. 2(b). In
the buyer process the decision to accept the offer is performed in parallel with
the loop, where the offer information is continuously updated on the reception
of `refresh` message. Analogously, the seller repeatedly waits for either an acceptance message or for a timeout expiration. The boolean variables (`done` and
`accepted`) are used to control termination of the loops.

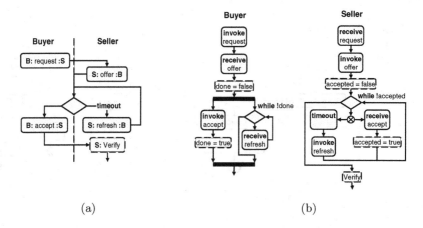

Fig. 2. RFQ case study: iterative quoting

The most relevant property that this choreography should satisfy is the *information alignment* between the participants. In particular, when the offer is accepted after several updates, both the buyer and the seller should have a common knowledge on the current offer instance. Such a requirement is modelled in a declarative way in WS-CDL, by marking certain interactions (e.g. `refresh` and `accept`), as *aligned* interactions.

It is easy to see that the given implementation may violate this requirement. Since the partners are independent, the timeout and acceptance invocations may happen simultaneously. As a result, the local values of the accepted offer may be different. Another negative scenario happens when the acceptance is performed after several updates. If the message queue of the buyer service is not ordered, there is no guarantee that the accepted offer is the last emitted by the seller. The necessity to guarantee the correctness on the information alignment requires the analysis techniques that go beyond the verification of the behavioral correctness.

2.3   Composition Coordination

Apart from the alignment of a particular interaction, it is often required that the participants of the choreography agree on the final state of the collaboration activity. This requirement, referred in WS-CDL as choreography coordination, states that either all the participants suffered an exception, or all of them completed successfully (and, consequently, their finalization is also agreed). In WS-CDL notation it is allowed to declare a coordination requirement without explicitly modelling the corresponding coordination interactions. A choreography implementation, however, should satisfy this requirement by providing special coordination message exchanges.

Consider the choreography model represented in Fig. 3(a). After the confirmation of the availability of the product, the seller interacts with a new actor, namely Credit Card Agency (CCA), in order to verify the payment information

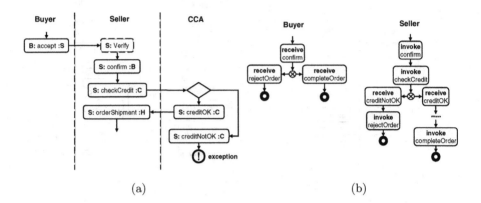

(a)   (b)

Fig. 3. RFQ case study: coordination management

of the buyer. This verification may result in a fault message, and the seller enters its exception state. In order to guarantee that the exception is propagated to the buyer, an auxiliary communication should be instantiated between these actors. The corresponding implementation is presented in Fig. 3(b). After the reception of the order confirmation the buyer waits for the additional messages that allow to distinguish the resulting state of the protocol. If the credit check failed, the seller sends the `rejectOrder` message to the buyer, and the latter knows that the exception occurred and the composition terminated abnormally.

These examples illustrate two important problems that should be addressed by a formal framework for validation of choreography specifications against compositions of service implementations. First, it is necessary to check the conformance of the behavior of the composition of services to the behavior, described in the choreography model. Doing this, it is important to take into account the asynchronous nature of the Web service communications, i.e., the possibility of message intersections and reorderings, variety of the implementations of the queueing mechanisms. Second, it is necessary to validate that the implementation satisfies the alignment requirements, declared in the choreography model, as those reflecting the interaction alignment and the choreography coordination.

3   Formalization

The formal model we use as a basis for the required analysis techniques consists of three parts, namely the *data model*, the *choreography model*, and the *implementation model*. The data model provides a formalisation of the data manipulated by the services and is used to reason on the data flow of the compositions. The control flow on the other hand, is defined by the choreography model, used to represent a behavior of the WS-CDL specification, and by the implementation model, used to represent a behavior of the composition of several existing services, specified, e.g., in BPEL [1].

3.1   Data Model

We model the data manipulation in Web service compositions using the following notations. Given a set of typed variables $\mathcal{V}$ and a set of typed functions $\mathcal{F}$, the expressions and terms over the variables and functions are defined as follows:

- $E \equiv (t_1 = t_2) \mid \neg e \mid (e_1 \wedge e_2)$ that is equality between terms, negation or disjunction of expressions;
- $T \equiv v \mid f(t_1, \ldots, t_n)$, with $v \in \mathcal{V}$ and $f \in \mathcal{F}$, that is a variable or function call on terms.

We assume a fixed interpretation of typed functions. For the interpretation of variables, instead, we use *valuation* functions g that map variables $v \in \mathcal{V}$ to their values. We write $g \models e$ to denote that the expression e evaluates to true under the valuation g. A *condition* $\phi \in \Phi$ is an expression of the form presented above. An *assignment* $\omega \in \Omega$ has the form $(v := t)$. We denote an *update* of the valuation g with the assignment ω as $upd(g, \omega)$.

3.2   Choreography Model

The formal model of choreography is based on the notion of *roles* and *actions*. A role represents the behavior of a particular participant of the composed system. During the protocol execution, the role can be in one of its possible *states* and can evolve to new states as a result of performing some actions. Moreover, each role is possibly equipped with a set of typed variables.

We model message communications actions as *interactions* defined on a set of service operations (or message types) M. The signature of the interaction has the form $(r_s, r_d, \mu, \bar{v}_s, \bar{v}_d)$, where r_s and r_d are the roles of the sender and receiver respectively, μ is the service operation, and variables $\bar{v}_d$ of the receiver are populated with the values of the corresponding variables $\bar{v}_s$ of the sender. Set of interactions is denoted as $\mathcal{A}_O$.

We also define *internal actions* $\mathcal{A}_\tau$, which are used to represent evolutions of the system that do note involve interactions between services. An internal action a_τ has the form $(\mathcal{R}_\tau, \tau)$, where $\mathcal{R}_\tau \subseteq \mathcal{R}$ denotes a subset of roles that perform an action, and τ is used to denote the internal action itself[1]. The set of all actions is denoted as $\mathcal{A}$.

We model a choreography behavior as a *Global Transition System* (GTS). Informally, we represent a *global state* of the choreography as a vector $\bar{s} = \langle s_1, \ldots, s_n \rangle$, where s_i is a local state of the role r_i. We denote a vector with component s_i updated to s_i' as $\bar{s}[s_i'/s_i]$. The behavior of the choreography is defined by the *global transition relation* $\mathcal{T}$. The relation defines *conditions*, under which the action can be performed, and *effects* of these executions, which specify the modification of the states and variables of the participants.

---

[1] The possibility of a group of participants to participate to an internal action is used in WS-CDL to model that the branching condition may be evaluated simultaneously by a group of roles.

Definition 1 (GTS). *A global transition system representing the choreography of n roles is a tuple* $\Sigma_p = \langle \mathcal{V}, \mathcal{S}, \mathcal{S}_0, \mathcal{A}, \mathcal{T} \rangle$, *where*

- $\mathcal{V} = \bigcup_i \mathcal{V}_i$ *is a set of all the role variables;*
- $\mathcal{S} \subseteq \mathcal{S}_i \times \cdots \times \mathcal{S}_n$ *is a finite set of global states and* $\mathcal{S}_0 \subseteq \mathcal{S}$ *is a set of initial states;*
- $\mathcal{A} = \mathcal{A}_\tau \cup \mathcal{A}_O$ *is a set of actions;*
- $\mathcal{T} \subseteq \mathcal{S} \times \Phi \times \mathcal{A} \times \Omega^* \times \mathcal{S}$ *is a global transition relation. A transition* $(\bar{s}, \phi, a, \Omega, \bar{s}') \in \mathcal{T}$ *if*
    - $a = (r_a, r_b, \mu, \bar{v}_s, \bar{v}_d)$ *and* $\bar{s}' = \bar{s}[s'_a/s_a, s'_b/s_b]$, *or*
    - $a = (\mathcal{R}_\tau, \tau)$ *and* $\bar{s}' = \bar{s}[s'_i/s_i]$ *for each* $r_i \in \mathcal{R}_\tau$.

Let $\gamma = \langle \bar{s}, g \rangle$ be a *configuration* of the choreography. The transition of GTS $(\bar{s}, \phi, a, \Omega, \bar{s}')$ is fireable in γ only if $g \models \phi$. The resulting configuration is defined as $\langle \bar{s}', upd(g, \Omega) \rangle$. We write $\gamma \xrightarrow{\mu} \gamma'$, if the action a has the form $(r_s, r_d, \mu, \bar{v}_s, \bar{v}_d)$, and $\gamma \xrightarrow{\tau} \gamma'$ otherwise. We denote a set of transitions, fireable in γ, as $out(\gamma)$.

3.3 Implementation Model

We model a system that implements a given choreography specification as a composition of *local transition systems* (LTSs). Each LTS represents the behavior of one of the participants. The implementation model may include more participants, interactions and operations than those declared in the choreography specification. In particular, these participants and/or operations may describe the low-level mechanisms that are used to implement the coordination requirements, declared in the choreography specification.

The behavior of the participant is defined using set of local variables and local actions. The local actions of the ith participant are divided into *input actions* $\mathcal{I}^i$, representing the reception of message α, denoted as $\overleftarrow{\alpha}$; *output actions* $\mathcal{O}^i$, representing the emission of message α, denoted as $\overrightarrow{\alpha}$; and *internal actions* $\mathcal{A}^i_\tau$. A message $\alpha \in M_\alpha$ has the form $\mu(\bar{x})$, where μ is the service operation, and $\bar{x}$ denotes a message content.

Definition 2 (LTS). *A local transition system representing the* i^{th} *participant of the implementation model is a tuple* $\langle \mathcal{V}^i, \mathcal{S}^i, \mathcal{S}^i_0, \mathcal{A}^i, \mathcal{T}^i \rangle$, *where*

- $\mathcal{V}^i$ *is a set of local variables;*
- $\mathcal{S}^i$ *and* $\mathcal{S}^i_0$ *are the finite sets of local states and initial local states respectively;*
- $\mathcal{A}^i = \mathcal{I}^i \cup \mathcal{O}^i \cup \mathcal{A}^i_\tau$ *is a set of local actions;*
- $\mathcal{T}^i \subseteq \mathcal{S}^i \times \Phi \times \mathcal{A}^i \times \Omega^* \times \mathcal{S}^i$ *is a local transition relation.*

We define a composition of local participants as follows. During the execution, the composition participants evolve independently, exchanging messages with other participants through a certain communication medium, represented as a set of queues. We refer to this medium as *communication model*. The behavior of the composition strongly depends on the structure of the communication model: the number of queues, queue ordering, queue bounds etc. An example of this dependency is illustrated in Sect. 2.1, where the composition of service implementations conforms to the specification behavior under the synchronous communication model, but violates it under a more realistic asynchronous model. Therefore, the implementation model should be correct with respect to the choreography specification regardless to the communication model applied for the composition representation.

In our previous work [4], we present a hierarchy of communication models and introduce the notion of the *most general communication model* (MG-model). We show that under this model any composition of LTSs exhibits more behaviors than the composition under any other communication model. The MG-model is defined as a structure with one unbounded and unordered queue. That is, all the exchanged messages are stored in and consumed from this queue regardless their ordering[2]. We will use this model to represent and analyse the composition of the local transition systems.

Let $\mathbb{N}^{M_\alpha}$ be a set of multisets of M_α, i.e. set of mappings from M_α to natural number $\mathbb{N}$. Given two elements w and w', we write $w.w'$ to denote the multiset union, if $w, w' \in \mathbb{N}^{M_\alpha}$. Thus, the queue content is defined as a multiset w.

Definition 3 (CTS). *A composition transition system representing the composition of n participants is a tuple $\Sigma_c = \langle \mathcal{V}^c, \mathcal{S}^c, \mathcal{S}^c_0, \mathcal{A}^c, \mathcal{T}^c \rangle$, where*

- $\mathcal{V}^c = \bigcup_i \mathcal{V}_i$ *is a set of all local variables;*
- $\mathcal{S}^c$ *is a set of composition states of the form $\langle \bar{s}, w \rangle$;*
- $\mathcal{S}^c_0 \subseteq \mathcal{S}^c$ *is a set of initial composition states with empty queue $w = \epsilon$;*
- $\mathcal{A}^c = \bigcup_i \mathcal{A}^i$ *is a set of actions;*
- $\mathcal{T}^c \subseteq \mathcal{S}^c \times \Phi \times \mathcal{A}^c \times \Omega^* \times \mathcal{S}^c$ *is a composition transition relation. The transition $(\langle \bar{s}, w \rangle, \phi, a, \Omega, \langle \bar{s}', w' \rangle) \in \mathcal{T}^c$ if for some i there exists a transition $(s_i, \phi, a, \Omega, s'_i) \in \mathcal{T}^i$ such that $\bar{s}' = \bar{s}[s'_i/s_i]$ and*
  - *if $a = \overrightarrow{\alpha}$, then $w' = w.\alpha$;*
  - *if $a = \overleftarrow{\alpha}$, then $w = \alpha.w'$;*
  - *if $a = \tau$, then $w' = w$.*

The behavior of the composition is defined analogously. Let us denote the configuration of the composition as a triple $\gamma = \langle \bar{s}, g, w \rangle$. The transition of CTS $(\langle \bar{s}, w \rangle, \phi, a, \Omega, \langle \bar{s}', w' \rangle)$ is fireable in γ only if $g \models \phi$. The resulting configuration is defined as $\langle \bar{s}', upd(g, \Omega), w' \rangle$. We write $\gamma \xrightarrow{\overrightarrow{\mu}} \gamma'$, if the action a has the form $\overrightarrow{\mu}(\bar{x})$, $\gamma \xrightarrow{\overleftarrow{\mu}} \gamma'$, if the action a has the form $\overleftarrow{\mu}(\bar{x})$, and $\gamma \xrightarrow{\tau} \gamma'$ otherwise.

A (possibly infinite) sequence $\pi = \gamma_0, a_0, \gamma_1, a_1, \ldots$ is a *run* of the CTS, if $\gamma_0 \in \mathcal{S}^c_0$, and for any $i \geq 0$ $\gamma_i \xrightarrow{a_i} \gamma_{i+1}$.

4   Choreography Validation

An important issue in the analysis of Web service specification is verifying that the given composition of existing services satisfies the requirements of the spec-

---

[2] If certain interaction constraints (e.g., synchronizability, message ordering) should be satisfied by the composition, a corresponding communication model may be used instead of MG-model. See [4] for the details on the analysis and implementation.

ified global choreography protocol. This analysis has to address the following problems. First, it has to check that the behavior exhibited by the composition corresponds to those described in the choreography document. This problem is referred to as *conformance checking* [6]. Second, it is often needed that the participants agree on the state of the protocol as a result of its execution. In other words, they expect to have a common knowledge on certain variables that describe the state of the protocol. This problem is referred to as *information alignment*.

4.1 Choreography Conformance

In [7] the notion of conformance between choreography and orchestration (i.e. implementation specification) was introduced as a bisimulation-like relation. However, some crucial aspects are ignored in that framework. The model of the composition, adopted in this framework, relies on the assumption that the message exchanges are synchronous, which is often not realistic in the Web service environments. As a consequence, it is not always possible to reveal the implementation problems like, e.g., the message losses, queue unboundedness, message intersections and disorder.

We extend the presented approach in the following way. Given an implementation specification, we model the composition of participants in the most "liberal" (i.e., with respect to the possible behaviors) settings, that is, under the most general communication model. We require that the following properties hold on the resulting composition:

- the composition specification is *complete*, i.e. all the messages send by any participant should be eventually consumed by the recipient;
- the composition is *bounded*, that is there exists such a constant K that in every reachable configuration of the composition the number of messages in the queue is less than this constant: $|w| \leq K$;
- the (relevant part of) observable behavior of the implementation is *similar* to the behavior of the choreography specification.

More formally, we define the notion of conformance as follows. Let M^p be a set of service operations of the choreography specification. In order to hide irrelevant operations of the implementation, we use the operator $[\cdot]$. That is, given an action $a \in \mathcal{A}^c$, we write $[a] = \mu$, if $a = \overrightarrow{\mu}(\bar{x})$ and $\mu \in M^p$, and $[a] = \tau$ otherwise. We write $\gamma^c \xrightarrow{\tau}{}^* \gamma_1^c$ to denote that γ_1^c is reachable from γ^c through (zero or more) irrelevant operations. Analogously, $\gamma^p \xrightarrow{\tau}{}^* \gamma_1^p$ means that γ_1^p is reachable from γ^p through (zero or more) internal actions.

The conformance relation requires that conversations of the implementing composition reflects all and only the conversations of the choreography.

Definition 4 (Conformance Relation). *Let γ^p and γ^c be configurations of Σ_p and Σ_c respectively. We say that the relation $R(\gamma^p, \gamma^c)$ is a conformance relation if for any transition label a*

- *if $\gamma^p \xrightarrow{a} \gamma_1^p \wedge a = \mu$, then $\gamma^c \xrightarrow{\tau}{}^* \gamma_2^c \wedge \gamma_2^c \xrightarrow{\overrightarrow{\mu}} \gamma_1^c \wedge R(\gamma_1^p, \gamma_1^c)$;*

- if $\gamma^c \xrightarrow{a} \gamma_1^c \wedge [a] = \mu$, then $\gamma^p \xrightarrow{\tau}^* \gamma_2^p \wedge \gamma_2^p \xrightarrow{\mu} \gamma_1^p \wedge R(\gamma_1^c, \gamma_1^p)$;
- if $\gamma^p \xrightarrow{a} \gamma_1^p \wedge a = \tau$, then $\gamma^c \xrightarrow{\tau}^* \gamma_1^c \wedge R(\gamma_1^p, \gamma_1^c)$;
- if $\gamma^c \xrightarrow{a} \gamma_1^c \wedge [a] = \tau$, then $\gamma^p \xrightarrow{\tau}^* \gamma_1^p \wedge R(\gamma_1^c, \gamma_1^p)$.

We write $\Sigma_p \approx \Sigma_c$ if there exists a conformance relation R, such that any initial configuration of Σ_p conforms to some initial configuration of Σ_c, and vice versa.

Definition 5 (Asynchronous Choreography Conformance). *An implementing composition Σ_c is asynchronously conformant to the choreography Σ_p, if Σ_c is complete, bounded, and $\Sigma_c \approx \Sigma_p$.*

4.2   Information Alignment

An interesting property being modelled in the choreography specifications is the information alignment, i.e. the ability to control that the participating roles agree on the outcome of the interactions or even of the execution of the whole protocol [3]. In particular, in the scenario in Fig. 2(a) it is required that both the buyer and the seller have a have a common view on the offer value. That is, the partners may need to have a common knowledge on the information they exchange (interaction based alignment). As a result of such an alignment the participants act on the basis of their shared knowledge. In other cases, like those illustrated in Fig. 3(a), this property expresses a requirement that the participant will agree on the way the choreography ended, regardless the alignment of intermediate interactions (choreography coordination). In either case, the implementing system should ensure that the specified requirements are satisfied (i.e., the interaction complete and the partner have the same information understanding, or choreography termination state is agreed).

Following the above patterns, we distinguish two kinds of properties to be modelled and validated on the implementing composition. The properties of the first group are used to check the proper interaction completion and the corresponding data alignment. The property of the second group are used to verify that the participants have a common view on the termination state.

More formally, let $a = (r_s, r_r, \mu, \bar{v}_s, \bar{v}_r) \in \mathcal{A}_O$ be an interaction action whose alignment has to be ensured. Let also ϕ be an expression over the variables of the partners that is expected to evaluate to true on the completion of the interaction. The interaction alignment rule requires that any emitted message should be eventually consumed, a new message can not be emitted until the previous is consumed, and the values of the variables should satisfy the expression on the interaction.

Definition 6 (Interaction Alignment Rule). *An interaction alignment rule $\langle (r_s, r_r, \mu, \bar{v}_s, \bar{v}_r), \phi \rangle$ requires that for any run $\pi = \gamma_0, a_0, \gamma_1, a_1, \ldots$ of Σ_c, if $\gamma_i \xrightarrow{\overrightarrow{\mu}} \gamma_{i+1}$ for some $i \geq 0$, then*

- *there exists $j > i$, such that $\gamma_j \xrightarrow{\overleftarrow{\mu}} \gamma_{j+1}$, and*
- *for any $i < k < j$ $a_k \neq \overrightarrow{\mu}$, and*
- *$\gamma_{j+1} \models \phi$.*

Consider an example choreography and implementation in Fig. 2(a) and 2(b) respectively. The interaction alignment rule for the `refresh` interaction has the form $\langle (s, b, refresh, sOffer, bOffer), (sOffer = bOffer) \rangle$. It is easy to see that the rule is violated by the implementation.

The coordination alignment rule requires that the participants agree on the information in a termination state of the choreography. Given some termination state $\bar{s}$, let $\phi_{\bar{s}} = \phi_{\bar{s}}^1 \wedge \cdots \wedge \phi_{\bar{s}}^n$ be an expression over the implementation that evaluates to true if and only if the participants are in the required state. Let E be a set of the all the expressions of the terminating states: $E = \{\phi_{\bar{s}}\}$.

Definition 7 (Coordination Alignment Rule). *A coordination alignment rule $E = \{\phi_{\bar{s}}\}$ requires that*

- *for each γ^c of Σ_c, with $out(\gamma^c) = \emptyset$, there exists $\phi_{\bar{s}} \in E$, such that $\gamma^c \models \phi_{\bar{s}}$;*
- *for each $\phi_{\bar{s}} \in E$, there exists γ^c of Σ_c, such that $out(\gamma^c) = \emptyset$ and $\gamma^c \models \phi_{\bar{s}}$.*

The coordination requires that each termination state of the implementation should correspond to some termination state of the choreography, and every termination state of the choreography is also a termination state of the implementation.

For the protocol represented in Fig. 3(a) the coordination alignment rule is formulated as follows:

$$E = \left\{ \begin{array}{l} (b.state = done \wedge s.state = done \wedge c.state = ok \wedge h.state = done), \\ (b.state = fail \wedge s.state = fail \wedge c.state = fail \wedge h.state = init) \end{array} \right\}$$

That is, either all the partners are in their successful states, or the buyer the seller and the CCA services fail, and the shipper is not initiated.

4.3   Choreography Analysis

The formal model represented above allows for the definition of systems with potentially infinite number of reachable configurations. This makes the application of formal analysis techniques very complex, if at all possible. In order to be able to perform the choreography conformance validation, the model should be made finite. For these purposes, we recall the approach of [8,9], and for the lack of space we only sketch the formalization here.

Symbolic Representation. We represent the composition models using an abstraction-based approach [8,9]. In this model the variables and their valuations are given in terms of valuations of the set of propositions. These propositions may express certain facts about the composition states, variables, relations between them, function values, etc. More formally, we allow the proposition to have a form of expression: $p \equiv (t_1 = t_2) \mid \neg p \mid p_1 \wedge p_2$. We will refer to the set of propositions as $\mathcal{P}^A$.

We define an abstract model corresponding to the concrete one, based on the set $\mathcal{P}^A$. An abstract valuation g^A is simply a mapping from $\mathcal{P}^A$ to $\{true, false\}$.

Since the set $\mathcal{P}^A$ is finite, a set of concrete valuations corresponds to an abstract valuation g^A: $\{g \mid$ for each $p \in \mathcal{P}^A$, $g \models p$ iff $g^A(p) = true\}$. We denote such set as a *interpretation* of the abstract valuation, written as $\mathcal{I}(g^A)$.

According to the definition[3], the transition $(\bar{s}, \phi, a, \Omega, \bar{s}')$ of Σ_p is fireable in a (concrete) configuration $\gamma = \langle \bar{s}, g \rangle$, if the valuation satisfies the transition guard. The resulting valuation is defined as $upd(g, \Omega)$. Given an *abstract configuration* $\gamma^A = \langle \bar{s}, g^A \rangle$, the transition is fireable in γ^A, if $g^A \models \phi$. Analogously, the result of the transition is some valuation $upd^A(g^A, \Omega)$, such that there exists $g \in \mathcal{I}(g^A)$, for which $upd(\gamma, \Omega) \in \mathcal{I}(upd^A(\gamma^A, \Omega))$. The run of the abstract model as defined in the same way. It is easy to see that the abstract model is finite.

Symbolic Analysis Techniques. As we discussed above, the analysis of the correspondence between the choreography and the implementation requires that the following three properties are satisfied: the implementation is complete (i.e., all the messages are received), bounded, and the asynchronous conformance relation is satisfied. The algorithm that allows for the boundedness and completeness analysis of the above implementation model is presented in [4]. The verification of the asynchronous conformance relation between Σ_p and Σ_c models may be done symbolically, based on the abstractions for these models. The symbolic algorithm, adopted for the conformance checking analysis is presented in [10]. In particular, it is shown how the equivalence relation may be represented symbolically, and verified using BDD-based model checking algorithm.

Symbolic model checking algorithms may be used also for the verification of the alignment rules. We exploit the Computational Tree Logic (CTL, [11]) for this purposes. Given an alignment rule, a corresponding CTL formula ϕ_R is constructed, which holds when the implementation satisfies the rule.

More formally, let $IR = \langle (r_s, r_r, \mu, \bar{v}_s, \bar{v}_r), e_{IR} \rangle$ be an interaction alignment rule. Let $\phi_{\overrightarrow{\mu}}$ (respectively, $\phi_{\overleftarrow{\mu}}$) be an expression, which is true if and only if the message μ is emitted (resp. received). A CTL formula ϕ_{IR} is defined as follows:

$$\phi_{IR} = \text{AG}(\phi_{\overrightarrow{\mu}} \Rightarrow ((\text{AF}(\phi_{\overleftarrow{\mu}} \wedge \phi_{IR})) \wedge \text{A}(\neg\phi_{\overrightarrow{\mu}}\text{U}\phi_{\overleftarrow{\mu}}))) .$$

In other words, from each state, where the aligned interaction is started, (*i*) the state, where the interaction is complete, should be always reachable, (*ii*) the information alignment condition should be satisfied, and (*iii*) there should not be any intermediate emissions.

Analogously, let $CR = \{\phi_{\bar{s}}\}$ be a coordination alignment rule. The corresponding CTL formula is defined as follows:

$$\phi_{CR} = (\text{AF} \bigvee_{\bar{s}} \text{AG}\phi_{\bar{s}}) \wedge (\bigwedge_{\bar{s}} \text{EF AG}\phi_{\bar{s}}) .$$

The formula states that some of the allowed termination states is always reachable, and each of them may be reached by some execution of the composition.

---

[3] The abstraction of CTS may be defined analogously.

5   Conclusions and Related Work

In this paper we presented a formal framework for the verification of the conformance between the choreography specification and the composition of service implementations. The formalism allows for modelling the data- and control-flow of the Web service compositions, defined as a global protocol and as a set of interacting local services. The key feature of the framework is the asynchronous message exchange, where the messages may be reordered and stored in unbounded queues. We exploit this feature for the definition of asynchronous choreography conformance, thus allowing for more accurate analysis of a wider class of compositions. We also formalize advanced declarative synchronization requirements exploited by WS-CDL, such as the interaction alignment and the coordination alignment rules. Finally, we presented symbolic reasoning techniques for model checking choreography specifications against the implementing compositions.

The work close to ours is presented in [7]. The choreography and the orchestration languages are formalized, and the notion of conformance between the specifications is presented. Here we extends the model of [7] in several directions. First, our approach allows for representation and management of data. Second, we adopt asynchronous communication model, while the interactions are defined in [7] as synchronous. Third, we also aim at addressing the information alignment problem, thus covering more essential choreography properties.

The problem of verification of the global protocol specification against the implementing composition is also discussed in [12,13,14]. In [12] the notion of conformance is defined by means of automata and is restricted only to compositions of two services. In [13] the choreography specifications are used to represent the service obligations rules, and then are verified against the implementations defined as compositions of interacting BPEL processes. Again, the analysis does not consider the data-flow of the composition, and relies on the synchronous communication model, which is not realistic for a wide class of composition scenarios. The work of [14] concentrates on checking that the choreography specification is respected by the implementing services at run time. The formalisation is given in terms of Petri Nets.

The formalization of the Web service choreography models are also presented in [15,16,17]. In particular, in [17] the global and the local (end-point) calculi are introduces to describe the choreography and the behavior of compositions of local implementations. The work discusses the relation between the two paradigms, and presents the potential problems related to the asynchronous exchanges and message reorderings. The problem of synchronous versus asynchronous interactions in global models is also discussed in [18], where the notion of the protocol synchronizability is presented together with the sufficient conditions. The results of [4] extend this approach and provide a way to determine an appropriate level of asynchronism and a suitable communication model for the given composition.

References

1. Andrews, T., Curbera, F., Dolakia, H., Goland, J., Klein, J., Leymann, F., Liu, K., Roller, D., Smith, D., Thatte, S., Trickovic, I., Weeravarana, S.: Business Process Execution Language for Web Services (version 1.1) (2003)

2. OMG: Business Process Modeling Language (BPML). (2005) [http://www.bpmi.org].

3. W3C: (Web Services Choreography Description Language Version 1.0. W3C Candidate Recommendation 9 November 2005) [http://www.w3.org/TR/ws-cdl-10/].

4. Kazhamiakin, R., Pistore, M., Santuari, L.: Analysis of Communication Models in Web Service Compositions. In: Proc. WWW'06. (2006)

5. Dijkman, R.M., Dumas, M.: Service-Oriented Design: A Multi-Viewpoint Approach. Int. J. Cooperative Inf. Syst. **13**(4) (2004) 337–368

6. Guerin, F., Pitt, J.: Verification and compliance testing. In: Communication in Multiagent Systems. (2003) 98–112

7. Busi, N., Gorrieri, R., Guidi, C., Lucchi, R., Zavattaro, G.: Choreography and Orchestration: A Synergic Approach for System Design. In: Proc. ICSOC'05. (2005)

8. Graf, S., Saidi, H.: Construction of abstract state graph with PVS. In: Proc. CAV'97. (1997)

9. Chaki, S., Clarke, E., Groce, A., Ouaknine, J., Strichman, O., Yorav, K.: Efficient verification of sequential and concurrent C programs. In: Proc. FMSD'04. (2004)

10. Burch, J., Clarke, E., McMillan, K., Dill, D., Hwang, L.: Symbolic Model Checking: 10^{20} States and Beyond. In: Proceedings of the Fifth Annual IEEE Symposium on Logic in Computer Science, IEEE Computer Society Press (1990)

11. Clarke, E., Emerson, E., Sistla, A.: Automatic Verification of Finite-state Concurrent Systems Using Temporal Logic Specifications. ACM Transactions on Programming Languages and Systems **8**(2) (1986)

12. Baldoni, M., Baroglio, C., Martelli, A., Patti, V., Schifanella, C.: Verifying the Conformance of Web Services to Global Interaction Protocols: a First Step. In: Proc. EPEW/WS-FM. (2005)

13. Foster, H., Uchitel, S., Magee, J., Kramer, J.: Model-Based Analysis of Obligations in Web Service Choreography. In: Proc. AICT-ICIW'06. (2006)

14. van der Aalst, W.M., Dumas, M., Ouyang, C., Rozinat, A., Verbeek, H.: Choreography Conformance Checking: An Approach based on BPEL and Petri Nets. Technical report, BPM Center Report BPM-05-25 (2005)

15. Brogi, A., Canal, C., Pimentel, E., Vallecillo, A.: Formalizing Web Services Choreographies. In: Proc. WS-FM'04. (2004) ENTCS.

16. Bravetti, M., Guidi, C., Lucchi, R., Zavattaro, G.: Supporting e-commerce systems formalization with choreography languages. In: Proc. SAC '05. (2005)

17. Carbone, M., Honda, K., Yoshida, N.: A theoretical basis of communication-centred concurrent programming (2005) [http://lists.w3.org/Archives/Public/public-ws-chor/2005Nov/att-0015/part1_Nov25.pdf].

18. Fu, X., Bultan, T., Su, J.: Synchronizability of Conversations among Web Services. IEEE Transactions on Software Engineering **31**(12) (2005) 1042–1055

Application of Model Checking to AXML System's Security: A Case Study*

Il-Gon Kim and Debmalya Biswas

IRISA/INRIA, Campus de Beaulieu, 35042 Rennes cedex, France
{ikim, dbiswas}@irisa.fr

Abstract. An Active XML (AXML in short) has been developed to provide efficient data management and integration by allowing Web services calls to be embedded in XML document. AXML documents have new security issues due to the possibility of malicious documents and attackers. To solve this security problem, document-level security with embedded service calls has been proposed to overcome the limitation of traditional security protocols.

The aim of this paper is to show how existing model checking technique, with CSP and FDR, used for traditional message-based security protocols, can be adapted to specify and verify AXML document-based security. To illustrate our approach, we present the framework for modelling and analyzing AXML document's security. Then, we demonstrate how this technique can be applied to analyze electronic patient record taken from [13]. Finally, we show the possible vulnerabilities due to delegated query and malicious service call.

1 Introduction

In the context of Web services and XML, data integration and management have been an important issue, due to the heterogeneity and autonomy of data sources. Active XML (AXML in short) has been developed to provide efficient data management and integration by allowing Web services calls to be embedded in XML document[1][3]. For example, the possibility of *intensional* data(embedded service calls) in AXML document leads to powerful data management by allowing dynamic collaboration with distributed systems and discovering new relevant data sources at run-time.

However, AXML has also brought the following security issues: 1) it is necessary to protect peers from malicious AXML documents, and 2) it is required to protect AXML documents from malicious peers. To solve the above security problems, document-level security with embedded service calls as well as XML Encryption and XML Signature has been studied[6][13].

Over the last decade, great attention has been paid to the question of developing formal methods for analyzing security protocols over the last decade. While some methods have been successfully applied to verify security properties

---

* This work is supported by the INRIA projects ARC-ASAX and RNRT-SWAN.

M. Bravetti, M. Nuñes, and G. Zavattaro (Eds.): WS-FM 2006, LNCS 4184, pp. 242–256, 2006.

of traditional message-based security protocols, they have not yet been applied to analyze security problems specific to AXML document-based systems. For example, AXML documents support query delegation by invoking embedded service calls, which are not considered in SOAP message security. In addition, it is worth noting that the formal specification and verification issues related with AXML documents include new types of security aspects not considered in traditional message-based protocols. For example, an AXML document is basically an XML document and service calls. As such, it is necessary to develop an abstract model by analyzing XML tagging and embedded service calls. AXML document invokes embedded security-related service calls in order to obtain a key and generate encrypted or signed document. This means that an abstract model could be extracted from two viewpoints: 1) before invoking a security service call, and 2) after invoking a security service call. Besides, it also needs to reflect the fact that there would be more security threats in addition to traditional one such as overhearing and modifying transmitted messages. For example, an intruder could embed enormous amount of false data or additional service calls in the returned AXML document to the intended recipient after intercepting the original document.

In this paper, we show how existing model checking technique, generally used for analyzing message-based protocols, can be adapted to verify new vulnerabilities of AXML systems. To do this, we have chosen formal analysis techniques based on Casper/CSP and FDR because it has already been proven to be very successful for verifying traditional protocols[20] as well as SOAP message-based protocols[14][16].

The remainder of this paper is organized as follows. Section 2 gives a brief overview of AXML and its security services. In Section 3, we show how to specify and analyze AXML documents by invoking security service calls. In Section 4, we describe how AXML documents encrypted or signed with XML Encryption and XML Signature could be translated systematically to an abstract security notation. In Section 5, we demonstrate the case study of analyzing electronic patient record. Section 6 describes some related works. Finally, we conclude in Section 7.

2   Overview of AXML Document and Security Service Calls

AXML documents are basically XML documents where some parts of data are explicitly denoted and other parts are given intensionally, by embedded service calls within the documents. The <sc></sc> tags in an AXML document represents a service call and its children subtrees denote the parameters of the Web service calls. After invoking an embedded service call on the document, a corresponding Web service is executed. Then the results of invoking the embedded service calls are appended at the location of the service call in the document. We use the terminology *materialization*, which means that the associated Web service is invoked, and its result is returned to the location of the service call.

Thus, an AXML system consists of a set of AXML documents plus the services in those documents.

The corresponding security services consist of a tuple *(p, s)*, where $p \in P$ is the identity of a peer providing the service, and $s \in S$ is the name for a security service such as encryption. The algebraic expressions for an AXML document(in short, a document), tree, function node, Web service, and service evaluation on peers are simply expressed as below[2] :

- *d@p* : a document *d* at peer *p*
- *q@p* : a query *q* at peer *p*
- *s@p* : a service *s* provided by peer *p*
- $f(para_1,...,para_n)@p$: a function node *f* to invoke a corresponding security service *s* defined on peer *p*, with parameters, $para_1,...,para_n$
- *Result(Z)* : evaluation result *Z* of service *s* (defined on *p*) on peer *p*

In the rest of this paper, the above algebraic expressions will be used to describe the document exchange between peers and the document *d* represents all or some forest of AXML documents. For more details about AXML syntax and semantics, see [3].

3   Modelling and Analyzing AXML Document Embedded with Security Service Call

3.1   Framework for Modelling and Analysis

In Fig. 1(a), the framework for modelling and analyzing security services in AXML system is illustrated. In this framework, Casper[18] (Compiler for the Analysis of Security Protocols) is a compiler that converts a high level description of a protocol into CSP (Communicating Sequential Processes) code that can be run in a model checker FDR (Failure-Divergence Refinement). CSP[9] is a process algebra language to describe systems as a number of processes which operate independently and communicate with each other over well-defined channels. FDR[11] is a model checking tool for state machines, with foundations in the theory of concurrency based on CSP.

Given an AXML system, its model can be considered from two viewpoints: 1) *an AXML document before invoking a service call*, and 2) *an AXML document after invoking a service call*. We denote the former as 'd_1' and the latter as 'd_2'. These two models('d_1' and 'd_2') are transformed into a high-level security notation according to derivation rules of the δ mapping function.

First, the common security notation of Casper input is created($\delta(d_1) = \delta(d_2)$), after applying the δ functions to d_1 and d_2. Next, CSP code is generated automatically using Casper's compilation function. Then, the FDR model checker shows the possible attacker scenarios if the CSP code doesn't hold any given security property. Thus, the verification results will be helpful for a designer to modify an AXML system to be robust against security vulnerabilities.

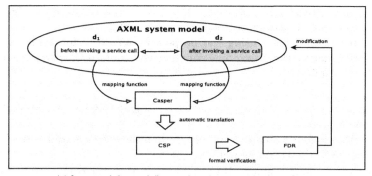

(a) framework for modelling and analyzing security services

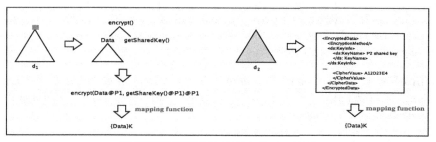

(b) service call processes of encryption and decryption

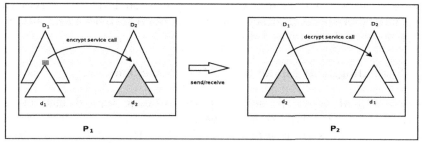

(c) mapping function to generate Casper input

Fig. 1. Model-based verification of security services in an AXML system

Fig. 1(b) shows the process of encryption and decryption in AXML documents. P_1 is an AXML peer and it invokes a local service call, *encrypt*(denoted by a square), and d_1 refers to a subtree including a service call node and data to be encrypted. d_2 is the materialized result after evaluating the *encrypt* service call and it is encoded based on XML Signature and XML Encryption standards. For example, P_1 could obtain the shared key by using the function node *getSharedKey*, then it could invoke the *encrypt* service call, *encrypt(Data, EncryptedData)*, to encrypt the data with the shared key. Then encrypted AXML document is encoded according to the standard format defined in XML Encryption(see Fig. 1(c)). Similarly, if the function node related with signature(e.g., *sign(Data, getPrivateKey()))* is called, the AXML document would be signed according to the standard format defined in XML Signature.

The main advantages of using the proposed framework for analyzing security and constructing the δ mapping function to generate Casper input can be summarized as follows:

- Using the δ mapping functions enables us to generate Casper input systematically.
- If an attack is found on $\delta(d_1)$ and $\delta(d_2)$, then the corresponding attack exists on a real AXML system as well.
- If an attack is found on a real AXML system, then the corresponding attack exists on $\delta(d_1)$ and $\delta(d_2)$ as well.
- If an attack is found on an AXML document before invoking a service call, then the corresponding attack still exists in the AXML document after materialization of the service call.

3.2   Extending CSP Model for AXML Documents

***Document* Datatype.** Analogous to the *Message* type defined in [17], AXML *document* datatype could be based on the *Atom* set where security function nodes are such as *getSharedKey()@p* $\subseteq$ *Atom*, *getPublicKey()@p* $\subseteq$ *Atom*, *getPrivateKey()@p* $\subseteq$ *Atom*, *Hash(data)@d* $\subseteq$ *Atom*, *encrypt(data, getSharedKey()@p)@p* $\subseteq$ *Atom*, *encrypt(data, getPublicKey()@p)@p* $\subseteq$ *Atom*, and *sign(data, getPrivateKey()@p)@p* $\subseteq$ *Atom*. Simple definition of the *Document* datatype by the BNF(Backus-Naur Form) expression could be similar to the *Message* type as shown below:

Definition 1. *A document d or data value $v \in$ Document might be an atom (Atom), concatenated data(v.v), data encrypted with a key($\{v\}_K$), or a digested message with hash function h.*

$a \in Atom ::= P \mid N \mid K$

$f(para_1,...,para_n)@p ::= a$

$d \in Document ::= v \mid d.d \mid \{d\}_K \mid h(d)$

$v \in Data ::= a \mid v.v \mid \{v\}_K \mid h(v)$

where P ranges over the set Agent of agent names, K over the set Key of keys(e.g., PK(p) : public key of agent p, SK(p) : private key of agent p), and N over the nonce(random number) set. The concatenation notation '.' is associative.

AXML document security allows *selective encryption* which means that it is possible to encrypt all or a specific part of an AXML document(denoted by $\{d\}_K$ and $\{v\}_K$, respectively). Here, the expression $f(para_1,...,para_n)@p$ could be considered as all or some parts of an AXML document before or after invoking a service call(see d_1 or d_2 in Fig. 1).

Intruder Model. In the classical CSP model for an attacker, it is generally assumed that an intruder has the following abilities to attack honest agents:

- overhear or intercept all messages flowing through the network
- construct and deliver spurious messages disguised as a trusted peer
- forward intercepted messages to another peer
- decrypt messages that are encrypted with his own public key

In addition to the above attack abilities, we assume that an intruder p_I could have the following new abilities : 1) manipulate the XML-based elements and 2) return falsified document d' containing other malicious service calls and fabricated data.

Because of the addition of two attack abilities in the CSP model, we also need to modify the traditional CSP model, based on the five basic deduction rules[17], that allow an intruder to construct new data or document. In the classical inference model, $B \vdash m$ represents that the intruder may derive message m from the set of messages B. For example, if the intruder can produce an encrypted message and the corresponding decrypting key, then he could decrypt the message. This sample decryption rule instance for an intruder can be adapted as follows:

decryption rule : $B \vdash \{d\}_k \wedge B \vdash k \Longrightarrow B \vdash d$
AXML system's decryption :
$B \vdash$ <EncryptedData>
    <EncryptionMethod.../ >
    <KeyInfo><KeyName> shared key k < /KeyName>< /KeyInfo>
    <CipherData><CipherValue>A12D23E< /CipherValue>< /CipherData>
   < /EncryptedData>
$\wedge B \vdash$ <KeyInfo><KeyName> shared key k < /KeyName>< /KeyInfo>
$\Longrightarrow B \vdash$ <document>...< /document>

The intruder CSP process in an AXML system consists of three main channels: 1)*send* to intercept every document or data sent by the honest peers, 2) *receive* to forward intercepted document or data disguised as an honest peer, and 3) *leak* to decrypt secret information and create falsified document d'.

$$Intruder(B) \mathrel{\widehat{=}} \mathop{\square}_{d \in Document} \quad send?P_1 ?P_2!d \; \rightarrow \; Intruder(close(B \cup \{d\}))$$

$$\mathop{\square}_{d \in Document, B \vdash d} \quad receive?P_1 ?P_2!d \; \rightarrow \; Intruder(B)$$

$$\mathop{\square}_{d \in Document, B \vdash d} \quad leak.d \; \rightarrow \; Intruder(B)$$

The initial state of the intruder is *Intruder(IK)* containing initial knowledge *IK* which is a member of *facts*(such as all peer's identity, all kinds of keys that peers' possess). The function close(B) calculates all *facts*(simply B) that are deducible or buildable from B under the deduction rules.

The complete AXML system is constructed similarly with a classical CSP model. For more detail information about CSP model for a traditional security protocol, see [20].

$$\text{SYSTEM}_{AXML} \mathrel{\widehat{=}} (P_1 \;|||\; P_2 \;|||\; \ldots \;|||\; P_n) \;||\; \text{INTRUDER}_{PI}$$

Fault-Preserving Simplifying Transformation. Hui et al.[10] have proved that if one can verify the transformed protocol, then it will have the same effect as the verification of the original protocol. Based on this fault-preserving technique, E. Kleiner et al. have [15] proved that even if automatic translation function is used to generate Casper input from WS-Security SOAP messages, it preserves the same inference process of intruder and the corresponding attacks in the real WS-Security application. We can apply this proof to the AXML system model. Thus, the abstract CSP model($SYSTEM_{AXML}$) for AXML systems satisfies the following two conditions for fault-preserving as shown in [10],[15]:

1. $\forall B \in \mathbb{P}(Document); d \in Document \bullet B \cup IK \vdash d \Rightarrow \delta(B) \cup IK_{AXML} \vdash \delta(d)$
2. $\delta(IK) \subseteq IK_{AXML}$

The first condition means that if an intruder can deduce the document or data in the original *SYSTEM*, he would be able to deduce the equivalent one d in the transformed $SYSTEM_{AXML}$. The second condition represents that all the corresponding *facts* of an intruder's initial knowledge *IK* in the original *SYSTEM* is a subset of the transformed $SYSTEM_{AXML}$.

Therefore, we can say that if an attack is found on the abstract $SYSTEM_{AXML}$, then the corresponding attack can also be found on the original *SYSTEM* and vice versa.

4   Case Study: Electronic Patient Record

Step 1: Dr. Kim(p_1) sends query q_1 to Paris hospital(p_2) by invoking the service call *"diagnosis@p_2"* in order to look into the patient record of the patient *Suzzanne* before diagnosing her.

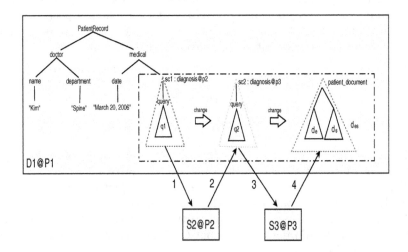

Fig. 2. Service call steps of AXML document in peer p_1

Step 2: Paris hospital(p_2) performs access control by enforcing the relevant access control rules(denoted "AC") and the query "q_1" gets rewritten into "q_2" . In this example, we assume that a corresponding access control rule for Dr. Kim is defined in the access control systems of Paris hospital :

AC: Dr. Kim, /PatientRecord/(name ∪ ssn ∪ visit/(medical_doctor ∪ diagnosis ∪ xray))

Now, suppose the query q_1 and the filtered query q_2 are :

$\mathbf{q_1}$: /PatientRecord[name="Suzzanne", ssn="123-45-6789"]
$\mathbf{q_2}$: /PatientRecord[name="Suzzanne", ssn="123-45-6789"]/(name ∪ ssn ∪ visit/(medical_doctor ∪ diagnosis ∪ xray))

For details of the access control mechanism proposed for AXML systems, the reader is referred to [5].

Paris hospital filters the query q_1 as q_2 and it finds that there is no patient related after evaluating the query q_2. Given this, let us assume that the Paris hospital(p_2) finds out that Rennes hospital(p_3) has related a patient record. Paris hospital also subscribes to regular patient record updates from other hospitals such as Rennes hospital. Then, it returns a query signed by itself for delegating Dr. Kim to invoke a service provided by Rennes hospital(*query delegation*).

Step 3: Dr. Kim invokes the service call "*diagnosis@p_3*" with the parameter of "q_2" signed by Paris hospital so that the query will be evaluated by Rennes hospital.

Step 4: Rennes hospital verifies the query q_2 using its own public key and assures itself that Dr. Kim has been delegated to invoke the service call "*diagnosis@p_3*" and use q_2. After evaluating the service call, Rennes hospital returns the diagnosis record for *Suzzanne*, encrypted with a shared key k and signed by Rennes hospital (the shared key k itself is encrypted by the public key of *Dr. Kim*). It is extremely important that a patient record should be protected from any unauthorized modification, whether accidental or not.

4.1 Model Construction from d_1

As mentioned in Section 4, we show how to construct an AXML system model from d_1 which is the document before invoking a security service call. First, we describe a model in AXML algebraic expression(see Section 2), then we write it in Casper notation(see Section 4.3).

AXML Expression

1. $p_1 \rightarrow p_2$: *q1@p_1* [p_2 computes : q_2]
2. $p_2 \rightarrow p_1$: *encrypt(q_2@p_2, getPrivateKey()@p_2)@p_2*
3. $p_1 \rightarrow p_3$: *Result(Z)*
4a. $p_3 \rightarrow p_1$: *encrypt(d@p_3, getSharedKey(random()@p_3)@p_3)@p_3,*
     encrypt(getSharedKey()@p_3, getPublicKey()@p_1)@p_3
4b. $p_3 \rightarrow p_1$: *encrypt(digest(d@p_3)@p_3, getPrivateKey()@p_3)@p_3*

The message sequences listed above represent exchanges of queries, data, or documents. p_1, p_2, and p_3 are *Dr. Kim, Paris hospital,* and *Rennes hospital* peers, respectively. In step 3, *Result(Z)* represents the result document of evaluating the service call in step 2. The messages 4a and 4b show the nested service calls to generate encrypted and signed patient records, where $d@p_3$ is the document of patient diagnosis d on peer p_3. The first *encrypt* call and the second one are used to transform the d encrypted with a random shared key and generate the shared key encrypted with the public key of p_1, respectively. The two materialized results are combined into the XML Encryption encoded document, d_e. Similarly, the *encrypt* service in message 4b is used to generate the XML Signature encoded document, d_s. After finishing all the data exchanges, p_1 invokes the *decrypt* local service calls related to d_e and d_s.

4.2   Model Construction from d_2

We demonstrate how to construct an AXML system model from d_2 (see Section 3) by showing the translation process from the materialization results of the patient document $\delta(d_{es})$ to Casper input. The d_e and the d_s in d_{es} are encoded in XML based on the XML Encryption and XML Signature standards.

```
<EncryptedData xmlns="http://www.w3.org/2001/04/xmlenc#">
    <EncryptionMethod
        Algorithm="http://www.w3.org/2000/09/xmlenc#3des-cbc"/>
    <ds:KeyInfo xmlns:ds="http://www.w3.org/2000/09/xmldsig#">
        <EncryptedKey xmlns="http://www.w3.org/2001/04/xmlenc#">
            <EncryptedMethod
                Algorithm="http://www.w3.org/2001/04/xmlenc#rsa-1_5"/>
            <ds:KeyInfo xmlns:ds="http://www.w3.org/2000/09/xmldsig#">
                <ds:KeyName>
                    Dr. Kim's Public Key
                </ds:KeyName>
            </ds:KeyInfo>
            <CipherData>
                <CipherValue>A23B45C56 ... </CipherValue>
            </CipherData>
            <CarriedKeyName>
                Symmetric Key with Dr. Kim
            </CarriedKeyName>
        </EncryptedKey>
        <ds:KeyName> Symmetric Key with Dr. Kim </ds:KeyName>
    </ds:KeyInfo>
    <CipherData>
        <CipherValue>ErBGCQHKJOOaqbmiibhGk ... </CipherValue>
    </CipherData>
</EncryptedData>

<Signature xmlns="http://www.w3.org/2000/09/xmldsig#">
    <SignedInfo>
        <SignatureMethod
            Algorithm="http://www.w3.org/2000/07/xmldsig#rsa-sha1"/>
        <Reference URI="">
            <DigestMethod
                Algorithm="http://www.w3.org/2000/07/xmldsig#sha1"/>
            <DigestValue>j6lwx3rvEPOOvKtMup4NbeVu8nk=</DigestValue>
        </Reference>
    <SignedInfo>
    <SignatureValue>MCOCFFrVLtRlk=...</SignatureValue>
    <KeyInfo>
        <KeyName>Rennes Hospital's Integrity Key</KeyName>
    </KeyInfo>
</Signature>
```

We use '$\Rightarrow$' to represent the message derivation process from $\delta(d_e)$ and $\delta(d_s)$ to Casper input. The derivation rule for generating a Casper input is similar to [14], but our approach is different from it because the former is focused towards SOAP messages based on WS-Security.

$\delta(d_{es}) = \delta(d_e),\ \delta(d_s)$

$\delta(d_e)$
$\Rightarrow \delta(<\text{EncryptedData}>...</\text{EncryptedData}>)$
$\Rightarrow \delta(<\text{CipherData}>...</\text{CipherData}>)$
$\Rightarrow \delta(<\text{KeyInfo}>...</\text{KeyInfo}>),\ \delta(<\text{EncryptedMethod}.../>)$
$\Rightarrow \delta(<\text{KeyName}>...</\text{KeyName}>,\ R),\ \delta(<\text{EncryptedKey}>...</\text{EncryptedKey}>),$
  $\delta(<\text{EncryptedMethod Algorithm}="\text{http://www.w3.org.2001/04/xmlenc\#3des-cbc}"/>)$
$\Rightarrow \{d\}_k,\ \delta(<\text{CipherData}>...</\text{CipherData}>)$
$\Rightarrow \{d\}_k,\ \delta(<\text{KeyInfo}>...</\text{KeyInfo}>),\ \delta(<\text{EncryptedMethod}.../>)$
$\Rightarrow \{d\}_k,\ \delta(<\text{KeyName}>...</\text{KeyName}>,\ R),$
  $\delta(<\text{EncryptedMethod Algorithm}="\text{http://www.w3.org.2001/04/xmlenc\#rsa-1\_5}"/>)$
$\Rightarrow \{d\}_k,\ \{k\}_{PK(p3)}$

$\delta(d_s)$
$\Rightarrow \delta(<\text{Signature}>...</\text{Signature}>)$
$\Rightarrow \delta(<\text{SignatureValue}>...</\text{SignatureValue}>)$
$\Rightarrow \{\delta(<\text{SignedInfo}>...</\text{SignedInfo}>)\}\delta(<\text{KeyInfo}>...</\text{KeyInfo}>)$
$\Rightarrow \{\delta(<\text{SignatureMethod}...>...</\text{SignatureMethod}...>),\delta(<\text{Reference}...>...</\text{Reference}...>)\}$
$\delta(<\text{KeyInfo}>...</\text{KeyInfo}>)$
$\Rightarrow \{\delta(<\text{SignatureMethod Algorithm} = "\text{http://www.w3.org/2000/07/xmldsig\#rsa-sha1}"/>),$
$\delta(<\text{Reference URI}="">)\}\ \delta(<\text{KeyInfo}>...</\text{KeyInfo}>)$
$\Rightarrow \{\delta(<\text{DigestMethod}>...<\text{DigestMethod}>)\}\ \delta(<\text{KeyName}>...</\text{KeyName}>,\ Sig)$
$\Rightarrow \{\delta(<\text{DigestValue}>...<\text{DigestValue}>))\}\ SK(p3)$
$\Rightarrow \{sha(d)\}SK(p3)$

$\therefore\ d_{es} = \delta(d_e),\ \delta(d_s) = \{d\}_k,\ \{k\}_{PK(p1)},\ \{sha(d)\}_{SK(p3)}$

4.3   Analysis of Security Services

The design of security protocol using document-level security would be error-prone when considering security requirements in new emerging applications, complex communication steps with many peers, and a powerful attacker. In this subsection, we use Casper notation to model sequences of exchanging queries or documents depicted in Fig. 2. Then we analyze some security requirements (confidentiality and authentication) using FDR model checker:

security requirements:
  – authentication
    • *Dr. Kim(p_1)* must be sure that it received a patient record document from *Rennes hospital(p_3)*.
  – confidentiality
    • A confidential document of patient record d must not be leaked by an unauthorized peer.

For a security analysis, we assume that all encryption algorithms are secure and an intruder cannot perform any cryptanalysis. We also assume that an intruder p_I has the following initial knowledge set:

intruder knowledge:
  $\{p_1,\ p_2,\ p_3,\ PK(P),\ SK(p_I),\ K_I\} \in Intruder(IK)$ where K_I is an intruder's share key, and $\{p_1,\ p_2,\ p_3,\ p_I\} \in P$.

Here, we translate a protocol description into Casper syntax based on sequences for exchanging documents in Fig. 2. In addition, we generate Casper input systematically from AXML documents denoted in XML Encryption and XML Signature in a similar way to [14].

Sequences for exchanging queries or documents:

1. $p_1 \longrightarrow p_2 : q_1$
2. $p_2 \longrightarrow p_1 : \{q_2\}_{SK(p_2)}$
3. $p_1 \longrightarrow p_3 : \{q_2\}_{SK(p_2)}$
4. $p_3 \longrightarrow p_1 : \{d\}_k, \{k\}_{PK(p_1)}, \{\text{sha}(d)\}_{SK(p_3)}$

In casper notation, we use the expression $\{d\}_k$ to represent the data or document d encrypted with key k. The public key function is represented as PK and the private key function is expressed as SK. For example, a pair of public key and private key of peer 'p_1' is written in $PK(p_1)$ and $SK(p_1)$, respectively. The hash function $SHA\text{-}1$ in XML Signature is denoted as sha in protocol description. For example, the message 4 means that p_3 sends the messages of the patient record d encrypted with shared key k, encrypted shared key with the public key of p_1, and signed message digest with a hash function.

```
Secret(p3, d, [p1])
Secret(p1, d, [p3])
Secret(p3, k, [p1])
Secret(p1, k, [p3])
Agreement(p3, p1, [d, k])
```

We verified the confidentiality and authentication properties, which are defined in the above. The lines beginning with *Secret* represent the *confidentiality property*. For example, the statement '*Secret(p₃, d, [p₁])*' is interpreted as "p_3 believes that the confidential information d is a secret that should be known only to p_1".

The line starting with *Agreement* defines the *authentication property*. The *authentication property* represents the establishment guarantees when it has completed, concerning the party it has apparently been running with. For example, the fourth one means that "p_3 is authenticated to p_1 with d and k".

In particular, we assume that the intruder could generate the falsified document d' containing other embedded service calls in the materialization result. Then, this may lead to DoS(Denial-of-Service) attack in a peer if the following two properties of secrecy and authentication are not satisfied in CSP trace event sets tr of $SYSTEM_{AXML}$.

1. *signal.Claim_Secret.p_a.p_b.d* **in** $tr \wedge$ $p_a \in$ Honest $\wedge$ $p_b \in$ Honest $\Rightarrow \neg(leak.d$ **in** $tr)$
2. $p_b \in Honest \Rightarrow signal.Running.RESPONDER.p_b.p_a$
   precedes *signal.Commit.INITIATOR.p_a.p_b*

where:

- *signal. Claim_Secret.p_a.p_b.d* means that p_a thinks that the patient document d is a secret which should be known only to p_b.
- *signal. Running.RESPONDER.p_b.p_a* represents that the responder p_b thinks he started a protocol run apparently with the initiator p_a.
- *signal. Commit.INITIATOR.p_a.p_b* represents that the initiator p_a thinks that he has completed a protocol run apparently with the responder p_b.

After analyzing the property statements of '*Secret(p_3, d, [p_1])*' and '*Secret(p_3, k, [p_1])*', the FDR tool shows no counterexample about them. However, when the FDR is applied to other property statements, we found that the following attack scenario could be derived from its counterexample:

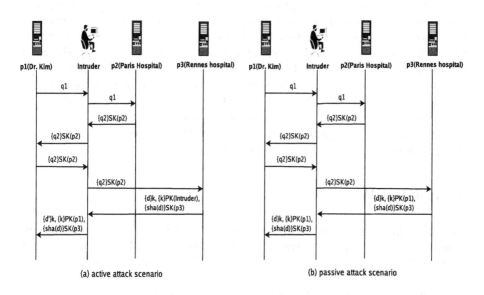

Fig. 3. Attack scenarios on the electronic patient record

Security Vulnerabilities. In Fig. 3, an intruder could monitor query q_1 and intercept the filtered query q_2 delegated by p_2. Then, the intruder could send the intercepted delegation query to p_3 disguised as an honest peer p_1. Here we can consider two different kinds of attack scenarios:

In the first case, p_3 might regard an attacker p_I as an honest peer because it has already been authorized and possesses q_2 delegated by p_2. This disguise is possible in a real Web service world because p_3 may not know who the original initiator of the service transaction is. Then, the intruder can successfully decrypt the encrypted patient record d and create the falsified patient record d'. A more intelligent intruder may return an original patient document without modification and instead he can embed other recursive service calls inside the document itself. Although p_1 uses *lazy query evaluation*[1] to filter irrelevant service calls, it must spend important resources wastefully such as CPU processor and memory space. Even in the worst case, this result might be linked to denial-of-service attack.

In the second case, (assumption) p_3 exactly knows p_1 as the initiator of Web Service transaction . Through the man-in-the middle attack, the intruder can intercept the encrypted signed documents($\{d\}_k$, $\{k\}_{PK(p_1)}$, $\{sha(d)\}_{SK(p_3)}$) from p_3. Even if the intruder can not decrypt the patient's record due to non possession of the private key of p_1, there might be potential attack that the received documents could be reused for a different patient next time. Eventually, mismatched patient records may has a dangerous effect on the patient's health.

The main vulnerability in this example is based on the insecure usage of *query delegation*, not the vulnerability of the document-level security itself. As such, the intruder could intercept the delegation query '$\{q_2\}_{SK(p_2)}$' that bypasses access control in p$_2$ and disguises as an honest p_1, even if the intruder has no proper right to request a patient record document of p_2. A simple solution to this attack scenario is to add the identity p_1 and the filtered query q_2 signed by itself in message 3, as p$_1$, $\{\{q_2\}_{SK(p_2)}\}_{SK(p_1)}$. This countermeasure prevents the intruder from generating a modified message and sending it to p_3, because p_3 checks who would be the intended responder for d through p_1's identity in the signed message. Another solution is to use a time-stamp with a short validity period against replay attack. More detailed information related to using a time-stamp against replay attack can be found in [20].

5   Related Works

Model checking with FDR has proved to be very successful for modelling and analyzing security aspects in traditional protocols[17],[18]. Relatively, few studies have been devoted to analyze Web services security with model checking technology.

Eldar Kleiner et al.[14] showed how the WS-Security specification[12] could be mapped to Casper and analyzed with FDR. Llanos Tobarra et al.[16] also used Casper/FDR tools and illustrated how to analyze some security properties of a Web service application as a licence server, developed by Microsoft Web Services Enhancement (WSE)[19]. Karthikeyan Bhargavan et al.[4] developed a tool called *TulaFale* to specify SOAP-based security protocols in pi-calculus and analyze its vulnerabilities.

The above approaches analyzed some vulnerabilities in existing XML-based Web service messages focusing only on the SOAP communication channel constructed by WS-Security. They do consider document-level security. To the best of our knowledge, there is no research to describe how to model AXML documents combined with embedded security service calls and analyze the vulnera-

---

[1] *Lazy query evaluation* was proposed to detect which calls may bring relevant data for query execution and to avoid the materialization of irrelevant information[1].

bilities due to delegated query and malicious service calls in the document. In this regard, we believe our approach to be different from the above related works.

6 Conclusion

Active XML (AXML) has been evolving as one of the new challenging researches in distributed, autonomous Web Services paradigm, by combining XML data and embedded Web services calls to allow simple and dynamic data management. Furthermore, security is one of the most vital topics in Web services development today and will in the foreseeable future.

In this paper, we have shown how existing model checking techniques with Casper/CSP and FDR, used for the verification of classical security protocols, could be applied to analyze vulnerabilities of AXML documents as well. To the best of our knowledge, this is the first approach to analyze the security of AXML documents using model checking.

We have explained the framework for adapting a classical CSP model to AXML systems and have shown how to build a Casper input from two models: 1) the document before invoking a service call, and 2) the document after invoking a service call.

Finally, we have demonstrated the usefulness of our approach by modelling and analyzing an electronic patient record. We found that a careless usage of delegated query could lead to security weakness and this vulnerability may induce falsification of data or DoS attacks by malicious document from an untrusted peer.

The analysis results also provide a hint that security services based on XML Encryption and XML Signature between AXML peers do not provide a complete security solution by themselves. The combination of other complementary security standards such as SAML and XACML would make an AXML system more robust against powerful, intellectual attacks in distributed networks.

Acknowledgements. We would like to thank Stefan Haar, Loic Helouet, Serge Abiteboul, Bogdan Cautis, and anonymous referees for their valuable feedback which helped to improve the work in the previous draft considerably.

References

1. S. Abiteboul, O. Benjelloun, B. Cautis, I. Manolescu, T. Milo, and N. Preda. *"Lazy Query Evaluation for Active XML"*, *Proceedings of ACM SIGMOD Conference*, pp.227-238, 2004.
2. S. Abiteboul, I. Manolescu, and F. Taropa, *"A Framework for Distributed XML Data Management"*, *Proceedings of EDBT 2006*, pp.1049-1058, 2006.
3. Active XML Home Page (AXML), *http://activexml.net*, 2004.
4. K. Bhargavan, C. Fournet, A. Gordon, and R. Pucellla. *"TulaFale: A security tool for web services"*, In *Formal Methods for Components and Objects: International Symposium, FMCO 2003*, volume 3188 of *Lecture Notes in Computer Science*, pp.197-22. 2003.

5. S. Abiteboul, B. Alexe, O. Benjelloun, B. Cautis, I. Fundulaki, T. Milo, and A. Sahuguet. *"An Electronic Patient Record on Steroids : Distributed, Peer-to-Peer, Secure and Privacy-conscious"*, *Proceedings of the 30th VLDB Conference*, pp.1273-1276, 2004.

6. S. Abiteboul, O. Benjelloun, B. Cautis, and T. Milo. *"Active XML, Security and Access Control"*, *Proceedings of the SBBD Workshop*, pp.13-22, 2004.

7. D. Eastlake, J. Reagle, T. Imamura, B. Dillaway, and E. Simon. *"XML-Encryption synatx and Proceeding"*, W3C Recommendation, 2001.

8. D. Eastlake, J. Reagle, D. Solo, M. Bartel, J. Boyer, B. Fox, B. LaMacchia, and E. Simon. *"XML-Signature Syntax and Processing"*, W3C Recommendation, 2002.

9. C.A.R. Hoare, *Communicating Sequential Processes*, 1985.

10. M.L. Hui and G. Lowe. Fault-preserving Simplifying Transformations for Security Protocols. *Journal of Computer Security*, 9(1/2):3-46, 2001.

11. Formal Systems(Europe) Ltd. FDR2 User Manual, Aug. 1999.

12. IBM, Microsoft, and VeriSign, Web Services Security(WS-Security), Version 1.0, April 2002.

13. I.G. Kim and D. Biswa. Secure Data Management based on AXML Document : Electronic Patient Record, 2006(submitted).

14. E. Kleiner and A.W. Roscoe. *"Web Services Security: a preliminary study using Casper and FDR"*, *Proceedings of Automated Reasoning for Security Protocol Analysis (ARSPA 04)*, 2004.

15. E. Kleiner and A.W. Roscoe. *"On the Relationship between Web Services Security and Traditional Protocols"*, DIMACS Workshop on Security of Web Services and E-Commerce, 2005.

16. L. Tobarra, D. Cazorla, F. Cuartero, and Gregorio Diaz. "Applicatoin of Formal Methods to the Analysis of Web Services Security", *2nd International Workshop on Web Services and Formal Methods*, pp.215-229, 2005.

17. G. Lowe. *"Breaking and fixing the Needham-Schroeder public-key protocol using FDR"*, *Proceedings of TACAS, number 1055 in LNCS. Springer*, pp.147-166, 1996.

18. G. Lowe, "A Compiler for the Analysis of Security Protocols", *Proceedings of the 10th Computer Security Foundations Workshop*, 1997.

19. Microsoft, Microsoft Web Services Enhancements (WSE) 2.0, *http://msdn. microsoft.com/webservices/building/wse. Proceedings of ACM SIGMOD*, pp.289-300, 2003.

20. P.Y.A. Ryan and S. A, Schneider. *Modelling and Analysis of Security Protocols: the CSP Approach*, Addison-Wesley, 2001.

Towards a Unifying Theory for Web Services Composition*

Manuel Mazzara[1] and Ivan Lanese[2]

[1] Faculty of Computer Science
Free University of Bozen-Bolzano, Italy
manuel.mazzara@unibz.it
[2] Computer Science Department
University of Bologna, Italy
lanese@cs.unibo.it

Abstract. Recently the term *orchestration* has been introduced to address composition and coordination of *web services*. Several languages used to describe business processes using this approach have been presented, and most of them use the concepts of *long-running transactions* and *compensations* to cope with error handling. WS-BPEL, which is currently the most used orchestration language, also provides a Recovery Framework. However its complexity hinders rigorous treatment. In this paper, we address the notion of orchestration from a formal point of view with particular attention to transactions and compensations. In particular, we introduce $web\pi_\infty$, an untimed version of $web\pi$, and the related theory, as a foundational unifying framework for orchestration able to meet composition requirements and to encode the whole BPEL itself.

1 Web Services

Service Oriented Computing (SOC) [7] is an emerging paradigm for distributed computing and e-business processing that finds its origin in object-oriented and component computing [17]. One of the main goals of SOC is enabling developers to build networks of integrated and collaborative applications, regardless of both the platform where the applications or services run (e.g., the operating system) and the programming language used to develop them.

Web services are a set of technologies supporting SOC. They provide a platform on which applications can be developed by taking advantage of the Internet infrastructure. A web service makes its functionalities available over the network through specific access points, in such a way that they can be exploited, in turn, by other services. Web services are an evolutionary technology, they did not just exist suddenly. There is no revolution about them, this technology has to be seen as an evolution based on the already existing Internet protocols.

1.1 Web Services Composition

The interesting thing in the web services programming model is that a service can itself use several other services and all of them are based on the same model.

---

* Research partially supported by the Project FET-GC II IST-2005-16004 Sensoria.

M. Bravetti, M. Nuñes, and G. Zavattaro (Eds.): WS-FM 2006, LNCS 4184, pp. 257–272, 2006.

This means that a composite business process can itself be exposed as a web service, enabling business processes to be aggregated to form higher-level processes. There is, indeed, a recursive use of the model where, notably, the overall scenario will be transparent to the final consumer. In this way, web services technologies provide a mechanism to build complex services out of simpler ones: this practice is called *web services composition*. A composition consists in the aggregation of services by programming the relative interactions and has the ability to make the created aggregations reusable [5]. To program a complex cross-enterprise task or a business transaction, for example, it is possible to logically chain discrete web service activities into inter-enterprise business processes.

Different organizations are presently working on additional layers which have to deal with the new approach of composing web services on a workflow base for business automation purposes. Two examples of past proposals for describing service compositions are IBM's WSFL (Web Services Flow Language) [9] and Microsoft's XLANG [18]. XLANG is a block-structured language with basic control flow structures such as `sequence`, `switch` (conditional), `while` (looping), `all` (parallel) and `pick` (choice based on timing or external events). Unlike XLANG, WSFL is not limited to block structures and it allows for arbitrary directed acyclic graphs. Iteration is only supported through exit conditions - that is, an activity iterates until its exit condition is met.

A more recent proposal (presently a working draft by OASIS), which aims at integrating WSFL and XLANG, is the Web Services Business Process Execution Language [2] (WS-BPEL or BPEL for short). It combines WSFL's graph-oriented process representation and XLANG's structural construct-based processes into a unified language for composition. However, while the graph based model used in WSFL has largely not evolved, block-structured programming, similar to the method of describing workflow in XLANG, has evolved incredibly in the last decades to encapsulate complexity and allow for greater manageability and maintainability. Some of the lessons learned from programming could improve business modeling using workflow. The use of block-structured programming can be cited as one of the main points in favor of the approach taken by XLANG and the BizTalk Orchestration framework [12], and in this paper we will focus on it.

Business process orchestration has to meet several requirements, including a way to address concurrency and asynchronous message passing, which form the basic paradigm of the distributed computation on the Internet. Another relevant aspect is the management of exceptions and transactional integrity [15]. BPEL covers all these aspects, but its current specification is rather involved. As far as error handling is concerned, for instance, it provides three different mechanisms for coping with abnormal situations: *fault handling, compensation handling* and *event handling*[1]. Documentation is informal and in many points it is not very clear, in particular when interactions among the different mechanisms are required. Therefore the language is difficult to use, and it is relevant to

---

[1] The BPEL event handling mechanism was not designed for error handling only. However, it can be used for this purpose and we concentrate here on this aspect.

address the issue of error recovering in a formal way to clarify all the controversial aspects.

In order to formally deal with the requirements, we start from the π-calculus [14,16] because the definition of XLANG (and then BPEL) has been strongly influenced by it. Unfortunately, the original π-calculus does not provide any transactional mechanism. For this reason, we consider an extension of the calculus called webπ [8], which extends the basic calculus with transactional facilities. In particular, we will present an untimed variant (while one of the main concerns of webπ is time) of it, that we call $\text{web}\pi_\infty$, and we analyze its semantic properties. We concentrate, in particular, on the weak behavioral equivalence, which abstracts from internal steps, and which is not meaningful in the webπ scenario, since time allows to find out internal steps anyway. In fact, internal steps make time to progress, and timeouts to trigger. The most common formalization of behavioral equivalence is through *barbed congruence*, which guarantees that equated processes are indistinguishable by external observers, even when put in arbitrary contexts. For instance equivalent web services remain indistinguishable also when composed to form complex business transactions. As main contributions we show that barbed congruence can be characterized via a labeled semantics that is easier to compute, and we show some examples on how this framework can be used to prove interesting properties about compensations and web services composition. The first author exploited $\text{web}\pi_\infty$ to formalize a simplification of the BPEL Recovery Framework unifying all the mechanisms (fault, compensation and event handling), as can be found in [10]. Thus the results therein can be used to derive also properties of BPEL. Further results in this sense and all the complete proofs just sketched in the paper can be found in the Ph.D. thesis of the first author [11].

2   The Orchestration Calculus $\text{web}\pi_\infty$

In this section we present $\text{web}\pi_\infty$, introducing its syntax and both a reduction semantics and a weak barbed congruence. Notably, $\text{web}\pi_\infty$ semantics is not just a simplification of webπ semantics, since, in the last one, time is used also for transaction commit, while here we have to deal with it differently. Also, we add input-guarded choice to the calculus, which was not present in [8].

The syntax of $\text{web}\pi_\infty$ *processes* relies on a countable set of channel *names*, ranged over by $x, y, z, u, \ldots$. Tuples of names (possibly empty) are written $\widetilde{u}$, and $|\widetilde{u}|$ is the length of tuple $\widetilde{u}$. When we write $i \in I$ we intend, if nothing is said, that I is a finite non-empty set of indexes.

$$
\begin{array}{lll}
P ::= \mathbf{0} & \textbf{(nil)} \\
\quad | \ \overline{x}\,\widetilde{u} & \textbf{(output)} \\
\quad | \ \sum_{i\in I} x_i(\widetilde{u_i}).P_i & \textbf{(guarded choice)} \\
\quad | \ (x)P & \textbf{(restriction)} \\
\quad | \ P \,|\, P & \textbf{(parallel composition)} \\
\quad | \ !x(\widetilde{u}).P & \textbf{(guarded replication)} \\
\quad | \ \langle\!| P \ ; \ P |\!\rangle_x & \textbf{(workunit)}
\end{array}
$$

A process can be the inert process $\mathbf{0}$, an output $\overline{x}\,\widetilde{u}$ sent on a name x that carries a tuple of names $\widetilde{u}$ (if $\widetilde{u}$ is empty we may write simply $\overline{x}$), a choice among input-guarded processes that consumes a message $\overline{x_i}\,\widetilde{w_i}$ and then behaves like $P_i\{\widetilde{w_i}/\widetilde{u_i}\}$, a restriction $(x)P$ that behaves as P except that inputs and messages on x are prohibited, a parallel composition of processes, a replicated input $!x(\widetilde{u}).P$ that consumes a message $\overline{x}\,\widetilde{w}$ and then behaves like $P\{\widetilde{w}/\widetilde{u}\}\,|\,!x(\widetilde{u}).P$, or a workunit (or simply a unit) $\langle\!\langle P \,;\, Q\rangle\!\rangle_x$ that behaves as the *body* P until an abort $\overline{x}$ is signaled (either by P or from the outside) and then behaves as the *event handler* Q.

We avoid to mix replication and choice since this simplifies the presentation and since this is not necessary for our aims (and notably to model BPEL semantics). The extension is however easy.

We use $+$ to denote binary choice. We use $\prod_{i \in I} P_i$ to denote the parallel composition of processes P_i for each $i \in I$. Names x in outputs, inputs, and replicated inputs are called *subjects*. It is worth to notice that the syntax of $\text{web}\pi_\infty$ processes essentially adds the workunit construct to the asynchronous π-calculus.

The input $x(\widetilde{u}).P$, restriction $(x)P$ and replicated input $!x(\widetilde{u}).P$ are binders of names $\widetilde{u}$, x and $\widetilde{u}$ respectively. The scope of these binders is the process P. We use the standard notions of *free* and *bound names* of processes, denoted as $\text{fn}(P)$ and $\text{bn}(P)$ respectively, and of α-equivalence.

2.1   The Reduction Semantics

We present here the reduction semantics for our calculus. We give it in two steps, following the approach of Milner [13], separating the structural congruence that governs the static relations among processes from the reductions that rule their interactions. A structural congruence relation equates all the processes we do not want to distinguish. It is introduced as a small collection of axioms that allow to manipulate the structure of processes. This relation is intended to express some basic facts about the operators, such as commutativity of parallel composition. The second step is defining the way in which processes evolve dynamically by means of an operational semantics. We simplify the second step by closing the allowed transitions w.r.t. the structural congruence.

Definition 1 (Structural congruence). *The* structural congruence $\equiv$ *is the least congruence satisfying the abelian monoid laws for parallel composition (associativity, commutativity and $\mathbf{0}$ as identity) and commutativity of choice, and which is closed under α-renaming and under the following axioms:*

1. *Scope laws:*
$$(u)\mathbf{0} \equiv \mathbf{0}, \qquad (u)(v)P \equiv (v)(u)P,$$
$$P\,|\,(u)Q \equiv (u)(P\,|\,Q), \quad \text{if } u \notin \text{fn}(P)$$
$$\langle\!\langle (z)P \,;\, Q\rangle\!\rangle_x \equiv (z)\langle\!\langle P \,;\, Q\rangle\!\rangle_x, \quad \text{if } z \notin \{x\} \cup \text{fn}(Q)$$

2. *Workunit laws:*
$$\langle\!\langle \mathbf{0} \,;\, Q\rangle\!\rangle_x \equiv \mathbf{0}$$
$$\langle\!\langle \langle\!\langle P \,;\, Q\rangle\!\rangle_y \,|\, R \,;\, S\rangle\!\rangle_x \equiv \langle\!\langle P \,;\, Q\rangle\!\rangle_y \,|\, \langle\!\langle R \,;\, S\rangle\!\rangle_x$$

3. *Floating law:*

$$\langle\!\langle \bar{z}\,\widetilde{u}\,|\,P \,;\, Q\rangle\!\rangle_x \equiv \bar{z}\,\widetilde{u}\,|\,\langle\!\langle P \,;\, Q\rangle\!\rangle_x$$

The scope laws are standard while novelties regard workunit and floating laws. The law $\langle\!\langle \mathbf{0} \,;\, Q\rangle\!\rangle_x \equiv \mathbf{0}$ defines a committed workunit, namely a workunit with $\mathbf{0}$ as body. Such a workunit cannot fail anymore and thus it is equivalent to $\mathbf{0}$. The law $\langle\!\langle \langle\!\langle P \,;\, Q\rangle\!\rangle_y \,|\, R \,;\, S\rangle\!\rangle_x \equiv \langle\!\langle P \,;\, Q\rangle\!\rangle_y \,|\, \langle\!\langle R \,;\, S\rangle\!\rangle_x$ moves workunits outside parents, thus flattening the nesting. Notwithstanding this flattening, parent workunits may still affect children, but this has to be programmed explicitly, exploiting the available communication primitives. The law $\langle\!\langle \bar{z}\,\widetilde{u}\,|\,P \,;\, Q\rangle\!\rangle_x \equiv \bar{z}\,\widetilde{u}\,|\,\langle\!\langle P \,;\, Q\rangle\!\rangle_x$ floats messages outside workunit boundaries. By this law, messages are particles that independently move towards their inputs. The intended semantics is the following: if a process emits a message, this message traverses the surrounding workunit boundaries until it reaches the corresponding input. In case an outer workunit fails, recovery for this message may be detailed inside the handler process. When a workunit fails we will take care of messages and other workunits inside it (which may also have been included by applying the structural axioms above in the opposite direction), and preserve them.

The dynamic behavior of processes is defined by the reduction relation below, where we use the shortcut:

$$\langle\!\langle P \,;\, Q\rangle\!\rangle \overset{\text{def}}{=} (z)\langle\!\langle P \,;\, Q\rangle\!\rangle_z \text{ where } z \notin \text{fn}(P) \,\cup\, \text{fn}(Q)$$

Definition 2 (Reduction semantics). *The reduction relation $\rightarrow$ is the least relation satisfying the axioms below, and closed under $\equiv$ and under the contexts $(x)_-\,,\,\_\,|\,R, \text{ and } \langle\!\langle \_ \,;\, R\rangle\!\rangle_z$:*

(R-COM)
$$\overline{x_i}\,\widetilde{v}\,|\,\textstyle\sum_{i\in I}\,x_i(\widetilde{u}_i).P_i \;\;\rightarrow\;\; P_i\{\widetilde{v}/\widetilde{u}_i\}$$

(R-REP)
$$\overline{x}\,\widetilde{v}\,|\,!x(\widetilde{u}).P \;\;\rightarrow\;\; P\{\widetilde{v}/\widetilde{u}\}\,|\,!x(\widetilde{u}).P$$

(R-FAIL)
$$\overline{x}\,|\,\langle\!\langle \textstyle\prod_{i\in I}\sum_{s\in S_i}\,x_{i,s}(\widetilde{u_{i,s}}).P_{i,s}\,|\,\prod_{j\in J}\,!x_j(\widetilde{u}_j).P_j \,;\, Q\rangle\!\rangle_x \;\;\rightarrow\;\; \langle\!\langle Q \,;\, \mathbf{0}\rangle\!\rangle$$
$$\text{where } J \neq \emptyset \vee I \neq \emptyset, S_i \neq \emptyset$$

Rules (R-COM) and (R-REP) are standard in process calculi and they model input-output interaction and lazy replication. Rule (R-FAIL) models workunit failures: when a unit aborts (receiving an empty message on its abort port), the corresponding body is terminated and the handler activated. On the contrary, aborts are not possible if the transaction is already terminated (namely every thread in the body has completed its own work). For this reason, when the handler is activated, we close the workunit by restricting its name. The reason to maintain the structure will be clear in the section relative to the labeled semantics (Section 3).

2.2   The Extensional Semantics

The extensional semantics of $web\pi_\infty$ relies on the notions of barb and context. We say that P has a *barb* at x, and write $P \downarrow x$, if P manifests an output on the free name x.

Definition 3. *We define $P \downarrow x$ as the least relation satisfying the rules:*

$$\overline{x}\,\widetilde{u} \downarrow x$$
$$(z)P \downarrow x \qquad \text{if } P \downarrow x \text{ and } x \neq z$$
$$P \mid Q \downarrow x \qquad \text{if } P \downarrow x \text{ or } Q \downarrow x$$
$$\langle P \,;\, Q \rangle_z \downarrow x \qquad \text{if } P \downarrow x$$

It is worth to notice that inputs (both simple and replicated) have no barb. This is standard in asynchronous calculi and represents the fact that an observer has no direct way of knowing whether the message (s)he has sent has been received.

Definition 4. Process contexts, *noted* $C_\pi[\cdot]$, *are defined by the following grammar:*

$$C_\pi[\cdot] ::= [\cdot] \mid (x)C_\pi[\cdot] \mid C_\pi[\cdot] \mid P \mid \textstyle\sum_{i \in I} x_i(\widetilde{u}_i).P_i + x(\widetilde{u}).C_\pi[\cdot] \mid !x(\widetilde{u}).C_\pi[\cdot] \mid$$
$$\langle C_\pi[\cdot] \,;\, P \rangle_x \mid \langle P \,;\, C_\pi[\cdot] \rangle_x$$

Barbed bisimilarity is usually defined as the largest bisimulation on the reduction relation such that the equated terms have the same barbs. Usually, such a relation is not a congruence and the barbed congruence is defined as the maximal barbed bisimulation that is also a congruence. In the following $\rightarrow_n$ stands for $\overbrace{\rightarrow \cdots \rightarrow}^{n}$. We write $\Rightarrow$ to denote $\rightarrow_n$ for some $n \geq 0$. We also write $P \Downarrow x$ for $\exists P'.P \Rightarrow P' \wedge P' \downarrow x$.

Definition 5 (Barbed congruence). *A* barbed bisimulation *is a symmetric binary relation S between processes such that $P \, S \, Q$ implies*

1. *if $P \downarrow x$ then $Q \Downarrow x$;*
2. *if $P \rightarrow P'$ then $Q \Rightarrow Q'$ and $P' \, S \, Q'$.*

Barbed congruence, *denoted as* $\approx$, *is the largest barbed bisimulation that is also a congruence.*

3   The Labeled Semantics

Barbed congruence requires quantification over all contexts, thus making direct proofs particularly difficult. A standard device to avoid such a quantification consists in introducing a labeled operational model and equipping it with a weak (asynchronous) bisimulation. If one can prove that bisimulation implies barbed congruence, then it can be used as a useful proof technique for behavioral equivalence.

We use some auxiliary machineries: the *extraction function* $\mathsf{xtr}(P)$, that extracts messages and units out of the process P, and is needed to define the abort of a unit:

$$
\begin{aligned}
\mathsf{xtr}(\mathbf{0}) &= \mathbf{0} \\
\mathsf{xtr}(\overline{x}\,\widetilde{v}) &= \overline{x}\,\widetilde{v} \\
\mathsf{xtr}(\textstyle\sum_{i\in I} x_i(\widetilde{u}_i).P_i) &= \mathbf{0} \\
\mathsf{xtr}((x)P) &= (x)\mathsf{xtr}(P) \\
\mathsf{xtr}(P\,|\,Q) &= \mathsf{xtr}(P)\,|\,\mathsf{xtr}(Q) \\
\mathsf{xtr}(!x(\widetilde{u}).P) &= \mathbf{0} \\
\mathsf{xtr}(\langle P \,;\, Q\rangle_x) &= \langle P \,;\, Q\rangle_x
\end{aligned}
$$

and the input predicate $\mathsf{inp}(P)$, which verifies whether a process contains an input that is not inside a workunit, which is used to find out whether a unit is still active. It is the least relation such that:

$$
\begin{aligned}
&\mathsf{inp}(\textstyle\sum_{i\in I} x_i(\widetilde{u}_i).P_i) \\
&\mathsf{inp}((x)P) && \text{if } \mathsf{inp}(P) \\
&\mathsf{inp}(P\,|\,Q) && \text{if } \mathsf{inp}(P) \text{ or } \mathsf{inp}(Q) \\
&\mathsf{inp}(!x(\widetilde{u}).P)
\end{aligned}
$$

In this section it will be useful to have clear the following property:

Proposition 1. *The extraction function is idempotent, i.e., if P is a $\mathtt{web}\pi_\infty$ process then $\mathsf{xtr}(P) = \mathsf{xtr}(\mathsf{xtr}(P))$.*

Proof. The proof is by structural induction on P. All the cases are straightforward. □

We can now define the labeled semantics. Let μ range over input labels $x(\widetilde{u})$, bound output labels $(\widetilde{z})\overline{x}\,\widetilde{u}$ where $\widetilde{z} \subseteq \widetilde{u}$, and the label τ. Let also $\mathrm{fn}(\tau) = \emptyset$, $\mathrm{fn}(x(\widetilde{u})) = \{x\}$, $\mathrm{fn}(\overline{x}\,\widetilde{u}) = \{x\}\cup\widetilde{u}$, and $\mathrm{fn}((\widetilde{z})\overline{x}\,\widetilde{u}) = \{x\}\cup\widetilde{u}\setminus\widetilde{z}$. Finally, let $\mathrm{bn}(\mu)$ be $\widetilde{z}$ if $\mu = (\widetilde{z})\overline{x}\,\widetilde{u}$, $\widetilde{u}$ if $\mu = x(\widetilde{u})$, and $\emptyset$ otherwise. We implicitly identify terms up to α-renaming $\equiv_\alpha$, that is, if $P \equiv_\alpha Q$, $P' \equiv_\alpha Q'$ and $P \overset{\mu}{\to} P'$ then $Q \overset{\mu}{\to} Q'$. In the following we will use again the shortcut:

$$
\langle P \,;\, Q\rangle \overset{\mathrm{def}}{=} (z)\langle P \,;\, Q\rangle_z \text{ where } z \notin \mathrm{fn}(P) \cup \mathrm{fn}(Q)
$$

Definition 6 (Labeled semantics). *The transition relation of* $\mathtt{web}\pi_\infty$ *processes, noted* $\overset{\mu}{\to}$, *is the least relation satisfying the rules:*

(IN)
$$
\sum_{i\in I} x_i(\widetilde{u}_i).P_i \xrightarrow{\;x_i(\widetilde{u}_i)\;} P_i
$$

(OUT)
$$
\overline{x}\,\widetilde{u} \xrightarrow{\;\overline{x}\,\widetilde{u}\;} \mathbf{0}
$$

(REPIN)
$$
!x(\widetilde{u}).P \xrightarrow{\;x(\widetilde{u})\;} P\,|\,!x(\widetilde{u}).P
$$

(RES)
$$
\frac{P \overset{\mu}{\to} P' \quad x \notin \mathrm{fn}(\mu)\cup\mathrm{bn}(\mu)}{(x)P \overset{\mu}{\to} (x)P'}
$$

(OPEN)
$$
\frac{P \xrightarrow{\;(\widetilde{v})\overline{x}\,\widetilde{u}\;} P' \quad w \neq x \quad w \in \widetilde{u}\setminus\widetilde{v}}{(w)P \xrightarrow{\;(w\widetilde{v})\overline{x}\,\widetilde{u}\;} P'}
$$

(PAR)
$$
\frac{P \overset{\mu}{\to} P' \quad \mathrm{bn}(\mu)\cap\mathrm{fn}(Q) = \emptyset}{P\,|\,Q \overset{\mu}{\to} P'\,|\,Q}
$$

(COM)
$$\frac{P \xrightarrow{(\widetilde{w})\overline{x}\,\widetilde{v}} P' \quad Q \xrightarrow{x(\widetilde{u})} Q' \quad \widetilde{w} \cap \mathrm{fn}(Q) = \emptyset \quad |\widetilde{v}| = |\widetilde{u}|}{P\,|\,Q \xrightarrow{\tau} (\widetilde{w})(P'\,|\,Q'\{\widetilde{v}/\widetilde{u}\})}$$

(ABORT)
$$\frac{\mathrm{inp}(P)}{\langle\!\langle P\,;\,Q\rangle\!\rangle_x \xrightarrow{x()} \langle\!\langle \mathrm{xtr}(P)\,|\,Q\,;\,\mathbf{0}\rangle\!\rangle}$$

(SELF)
$$\frac{P \xrightarrow{\overline{x}} P' \quad \mathrm{inp}(P)}{\langle\!\langle P\,;\,Q\rangle\!\rangle_x \xrightarrow{\tau} \langle\!\langle \mathrm{xtr}(P')\,|\,Q\,;\,\mathbf{0}\rangle\!\rangle}$$

(WUNIT)
$$\frac{P \xrightarrow{\mu} P' \quad \mathrm{bn}(\mu) \cap (\mathrm{fn}(Q) \cup \{x\}) = \emptyset}{\langle\!\langle P\,;\,Q\rangle\!\rangle_x \xrightarrow{\mu} \langle\!\langle P'\,;\,Q\rangle\!\rangle_x}$$

Rules involving parallel composition have mirror cases that we have omitted.

The first seven rules are standard in π-calculus. We just remind the role of the bound output $(u)\overline{x}\,u$ in $P \xrightarrow{(u)\overline{x}\,u} Q$. This kind of action means that P emits a private name u (a name bound in P) on the port x. Bound output actions arise from free output actions which carry names out of their scope as in the process $(u)\overline{x}\,u$. Let us discuss the rules related to workunits. Rule (WUNIT) is the simplest one: it lifts transitions to workunit contexts modeling the evolution of the body. In this sense it is very similar, for instance, to rules (PAR) and (RES). Rule (ABORT) models transaction termination due to an abort message. The premise checks that the unit body is still alive – it contains an active input – and, in this case, the compensation Q is triggered. We carefully do not erase the messages and the units in the body, which are extracted using the function $\mathrm{xtr}(\cdot)$. We remark that abort is not possible if the unit body P has completed, namely $\mathrm{inp}(P)$ is false. Rule (SELF) is similar to (ABORT), taking into account the case when the abort message is raised by the body of the unit. In this case, the handler Q can be spawned only if the body P cannot commit, i.e. if some input-guarded process is still waiting inside the process after the signaling of x.

Finally, two remarks deserve to be made: the first one concerns the shortcut $\langle\!\langle P\,;\,Q\rangle\!\rangle$. This shortcut is used in rules (ABORT) and (SELF) to preserve the workunit structure after its abort. This could appear to be a strange design choice because this structure could be considered a redundant information once the workunit has aborted. Instead, it is important to retain it to have the input predicate falsity stable w.r.t. the transition relation. Indeed, it is not reasonable that if $\neg\mathrm{inp}(P)$ and $P \xrightarrow{\mu} P'$ then $\mathrm{inp}(P')$, since this corresponds to undo a commit. Note that the opposite instead makes sense, i.e., if $\mathrm{inp}(P)$ and $P \xrightarrow{\mu} P'$ then $\neg\mathrm{inp}(P')$ (for example in $\overline{x}\,|\,x().\mathbf{0}$), since this models a commit. However, the proposition below shows that the input predicate is stable under output transitions, i.e., a process can never commit via an output.

The second remark regards the side condition $\mathrm{inp}(P)$ in the rule (SELF). It should be written $\mathrm{inp}(P')$, referring to the pending state of some input in the process P' *after* the x signal. Usually, it is not very elegant and it is not a common practice in transition systems to write down a side condition related to the right side of a premise. Anyway, it is safe to write $\mathrm{inp}(P)$ instead of $\mathrm{inp}(P')$. We will prove this fact with the following:

Proposition 2. *Let P be a* $\mathrm{web}\pi_\infty$ *process:*

1. *if* $P \xrightarrow{\overline{x}\,\widetilde{u}} Q$ *and* $\mathrm{inp}(P)$ *then* $\mathrm{inp}(Q)$
2. *if* $\neg\mathrm{inp}(P)$ *and* $P \xrightarrow{\mu} Q$ *then* $\neg\mathrm{inp}(Q)$.

Proof. We give just a brief sketch of the proof because of space constraints. Both the parts of the proof are by structural induction on P. In the first case one just has to consider the cases where $\mathrm{inp}(P)$, while in the second one the other cases have to be considered.   □

3.1 Weak Asynchronous Bisimilarity

Recalling the weak asynchronous bisimilarity presented in [1] we define a weak asynchronous bisimilarity for $\mathrm{web}\pi_\infty$. We then find a suitable variant, that we call *closed bisimilarity*, which can be used as a tool to prove weak barbed congruence.

Definition 7 (Weak asynchronous bisimilarity). *We define* $\overset{\tau}{\Rightarrow}$ *as the reflexive and transitive closure of* $\xrightarrow{\tau}$ *and* $\overset{\mu}{\Rightarrow}$ *as* $\overset{\tau}{\Rightarrow}\xrightarrow{\mu}\overset{\tau}{\Rightarrow}$.

A weak asynchronous bisimulation *is a symmetric binary relation* $\mathcal{R}$ *such that* $P\,\mathcal{R}\,Q$ *implies:*

1. *if* $P \xrightarrow{\tau} P'$, *then* $Q \overset{\tau}{\Rightarrow} Q'$ *and* $P'\,\mathcal{R}\,Q'$;
2. *if* $P \xrightarrow{(\widetilde{z})\overline{x}\,\widetilde{u}} P'$ *and* $\widetilde{z} \cap \mathrm{fn}(Q) = \emptyset$, *then* $Q \overset{(\widetilde{z})\overline{x}\,\widetilde{u}}{\Longrightarrow} Q'$ *and* $P'\,\mathcal{R}\,Q'$;
3. *if* $P \xrightarrow{x(\widetilde{u})} P'$ *then*
   (a) *either* $Q \overset{x(\widetilde{u})}{\Longrightarrow} Q'$, *and* $P'\,\mathcal{R}\,Q'$;
   (b) *or* $Q \overset{\tau}{\Rightarrow} Q'$, *and* $P'\,\mathcal{R}\,(Q'\,|\,\overline{x}\,\widetilde{u})$.

Weak asynchronous bisimilarity $\approx_a$ *is the largest weak asynchronous bisimulation.*

Unfortunately $\approx_a$ is not a congruence as it is instead in asynchronous π-calculus [16]. To show this fact consider the following counterexample. Let

$$P \overset{\mathrm{def}}{=} \mathbf{0}$$
$$Q \overset{\mathrm{def}}{=} (z)z()$$

then $P \overset{\cdot}{\approx}_a Q$ because they both cannot move. As you can easily see $\mathrm{inp}(Q)$ holds but $\mathrm{inp}(P)$ does not, so if you consider the context $\langle\!\langle \mathsf{C}_\pi[\cdot]\ ;\ \overline{y}\,\rangle\!\rangle_x$ and the rule (ABORT) you can see that the processes

$$\langle\!\langle \mathbf{0}\ ;\ \overline{y}\,\rangle\!\rangle_x$$
$$\langle\!\langle (z)z(\,)\text{;}\ \overline{y}\,\rangle\!\rangle_x$$

behave differently with respect to the asynchronous bisimilarity definition given above. To solve this problem and have an equivalence which is also a congruence it is necessary to close it under the input predicate according to the following definition:

Definition 8. *A binary relation* $\mathcal{R}$ *over processes is input predicate-closed if* $P\,\mathcal{R}\,Q$ *implies* $\mathsf{inp}(P) = \mathsf{inp}(Q)$.

Unfortunately this is not enough to get a congruence. Consider now the counterexample:

$$P \stackrel{\text{def}}{=} !x().y() \mid \langle\!\!| z().u() \; ; \; \mathbf{0} \rangle\!\!|$$
$$Q \stackrel{\text{def}}{=} z().u() \mid \langle\!\!| !x().y() \; ; \; \mathbf{0} \rangle\!\!|$$

P and Q behave in the same way in the sense that $P \stackrel{.}{\approx}_a Q$. Also it is easy to see that $\mathsf{inp}(P) = \mathsf{inp}(Q)$ but, unfortunately, $\mathsf{xtr}(P)$ and $\mathsf{xtr}(Q)$ are not bisimilar, since $\mathsf{xtr}(P) = \langle\!\!| z().u() \; ; \; \mathbf{0} \rangle\!\!|$ and $\mathsf{xtr}(Q) = \langle\!\!| x().y() \; ; \; \mathbf{0} \rangle\!\!|$, thus the two processes behave differently when inserted, e.g., in the context $\langle\!\!| \cdot \; ; \; \mathbf{0} \rangle\!\!|_x$. To solve this problem we also need an additional definition:

Definition 9. *A binary relation* $\mathcal{R}$ *over processes is extract-closed if* $P\,\mathcal{R}\,Q$ *implies* $\mathsf{xtr}(P)\,\mathcal{R}\,\mathsf{xtr}(Q)$.

Now, we can define a labeled bisimilarity, that we call *closed bisimilarity*, and prove that it is a congruence.

Definition 10 (Closed bisimilarity). *Closed bisimilarity* $\approx_a$ *is the largest weak asynchronous bisimulation that is input predicate-closed and extract-closed.*

We study now some properties of closed bisimilarity.

Theorem 1. *Closed bisimilarity* $\approx_a$ *is a congruence, i.e. given two processes* P *and* Q *such that* $P \approx_a Q$ *then* $\mathsf{C}_\pi[P] \approx_a \mathsf{C}_\pi[Q]$ *for each context* $\mathsf{C}_\pi[\cdot]$.

Proof. The proof is by structural induction over contexts, and each case requires a coinduction. Because of space constraints we give only the proof for workunit body and handler, the other cases being anyway similar to the corresponding cases of the analogous theorem for the asynchronous π-calculus (see [16]).

For the body we have to prove that $P \approx_a Q$ implies $\langle\!\!| P \; ; \; R \rangle\!\!|_x \approx_a \langle\!\!| Q \; ; \; R \rangle\!\!|_x$. Let us consider the three relevant cases of the definition. In the first case (rule (ABORT)), if $\langle\!\!| P \; ; \; R \rangle\!\!|_x \xrightarrow{x()} \langle\!\!| \mathsf{xtr}(P) \mid R \; ; \; \mathbf{0} \rangle\!\!|$ we must have $\mathsf{inp}(P)$ and, for the input closure, also $\mathsf{inp}(Q)$. Thus $\langle\!\!| Q \; ; \; R \rangle\!\!|_x \xrightarrow{x()} \langle\!\!| \mathsf{xtr}(Q) \mid R \; ; \; \mathbf{0} \rangle\!\!|$ and the statement follows from the coinductive hypothesis and the extract closure. The second case (rule (SELF)) is $\langle\!\!| P \; ; \; R \rangle\!\!|_x \xrightarrow{\tau} \langle\!\!| \mathsf{xtr}(P') \mid R \; ; \; \mathbf{0} \rangle\!\!|$ if $P \xrightarrow{\overline{x}} P'$. This also requires $\mathsf{inp}(P)$. This implies $\mathsf{inp}(Q)$ because of the input closure. Thus, since $P \approx_a Q$ we have $Q \stackrel{\overline{x}}{\Rightarrow} Q'$ and $P' \approx_a Q'$. Using rule (WUNIT) to lift the τ steps and rule (SELF) for the $\overline{x}$ step we get $\langle\!\!| Q \; ; \; R \rangle\!\!|_x \stackrel{\tau}{\Rightarrow} \langle\!\!| \mathsf{xtr}(Q') \mid R \; ; \; \mathbf{0} \rangle\!\!|$. Note, in fact, that, since outputs are asynchronous, we can always suppose that all the τ actions are performed before the output, that is when the workunit is still able to participate to the interaction. The statement follows from the coinductive hypothesis and the extract closure. For the last case (rule (WUNIT)) the proof is trivial because we simply lift the behavior of the body to the workunit context.

For the handler we have to prove that $P \approx_a Q$ implies $\langle R ; P \rangle_x \approx_a \langle R ; Q \rangle_x$. In this case P and Q can move only when shifted to the body part, as it happens in rule (ABORT) and rule (SELF). Since they are moved without being changed, then the thesis follows by coinduction. □

We prove now some auxiliary lemmas that will bring us nearer to our main goal.

Lemma 1. *Let P be a $\mathtt{web}\pi_\infty$ process. Then the following holds:*

1. *P can always be written in the form:*

$$P \equiv (\widetilde{z})(\prod_{i \in I} \sum_{s \in S_i} x_{i,s}(\widetilde{u_{i,s}}).P_{i,s} \mid \prod_{l \in L} !x_l(\widetilde{u}_l).P_l \mid \prod_{j \in J} \langle P_j ; Q_j \rangle_{x_j} \mid \prod_{k \in K} \overline{x_k}\,\widetilde{u_k})$$

2. *$\mathsf{xtr}(P)$ can always be written in the form:*

$$\mathsf{xtr}(P) \equiv (\widetilde{z})(\prod_{j \in J} \langle P_j ; Q_j \rangle_{x_j} \mid \prod_{k \in K} \overline{x_k}\,\widetilde{u_k})$$

Proof. For the first part it is necessary to apply structural congruence rules: in particular workunit laws to flatten the workunit structure, floating laws to extract output particles outside of workunits, parallel and summation laws to rearrange the order of processes and scope laws to factorize names in $\widetilde{z}$. For the second part, notice that all the structural axioms commute with function $\mathsf{xtr}(\cdot)$, thus it is enough to put P in the normal form above and then apply the extract function. □

Lemma 2. *Let P be a $\mathtt{web}\pi_\infty$ process. Then the following holds:*

1. *$P \xrightarrow{\overline{x}\,\widetilde{u}} P'$ only if $\mathsf{xtr}(P) \neq \mathbf{0}$*
2. *$P \xrightarrow{\overline{x}\,\widetilde{u}} P'$ if and only if $\mathsf{xtr}(P) \xrightarrow{\overline{x}\,\widetilde{u}} \mathsf{xtr}(P')$*

Proof. Both the parts are by induction on the structure of P. The first part is trivial, let us consider the second one. Thanks to Lemma 1, we can always divide a process in two parallel components P_1 and P_2, such that P_1 can not perform outputs and $\mathsf{xtr}(P_1) = \mathbf{0}$, and P_2 can perform outputs (unless it is $\mathbf{0}$) and $\mathsf{xtr}(P_2) = P_2$. The thesis follows trivially. □

Now we need to define a new concept of *input context* which is auxiliary to the next lemma.

Definition 11. Input contexts, *noted $\mathsf{N}[\cdot]$, are defined by the following grammar:*

$$\mathsf{N}[\cdot] ::= \sum_{i \in I} x_i(\widetilde{u}_i).P_i + [\cdot](\widetilde{v}).P$$
$$.P$$
$$\mathsf{N}[\cdot] \mid P$$
$$(z)\mathsf{N}[\cdot]$$
$$\langle \mathsf{N}[\cdot] ; P \rangle_z$$
$$\langle P ; Q \rangle_{[\cdot]}$$

Lemma 3. *Let P be a* webπ_∞ *process. Then*

1. $P \xrightarrow{(\widetilde{z})\overline{x}\,\widetilde{u}} P'$ *implies* $P \equiv (\widetilde{z})(P' \,|\, \overline{x}\,\widetilde{u})$
2. $P \xrightarrow{x(\widetilde{u})} P'$ *implies* $P \equiv \mathsf{N}[x]$

Proof. For the first part the proof is by induction on the proof tree of $P \xrightarrow{(\widetilde{z})\overline{x}\,\widetilde{u}}$ P'. The base case is when $\overline{x}\,\widetilde{u} \xrightarrow{\overline{x}\,\widetilde{u}} \mathbf{0}$ by the (OUT) rule and is trivial. The inductive cases are related to the rules (WUNIT), (PAR), (RES) and (OPEN). The proof is similar in all the cases. We just show the case of rule (WUNIT). By inductive hypothesis we know that $P \equiv (\widetilde{z})(P' \,|\, \overline{x}\,\widetilde{u})$. Then $\langle\!\langle P \;;\; Q \rangle\!\rangle_y \equiv (\widetilde{z})(\langle\!\langle P' \;;\; Q \rangle\!\rangle_y \,|\, \overline{x}\,\widetilde{u})$ using the floating law, as required.

For the second part the proof is by induction on the proof tree of $P \xrightarrow{x(\widetilde{u})} P'$. We have three base cases related to the rules (IN), (REPIN) and (ABORT). The cases follows directly by definition. The inductive cases are related to rules (RES), (PAR) and (WUNIT) and are trivial too.   □

The next lemma analyzes the relations between reduction semantics and barbs on one side, and labeled transitions on the other side.

Lemma 4. *Let P be a* webπ_∞ *process. Then*

1. $P \downarrow x$ *if and only if* $P \xrightarrow{(\widetilde{z})\overline{x}\,\widetilde{u}} Q$ *for some Q, $\widetilde{z}$ and $\widetilde{u}$*
2. $P \xrightarrow{\tau} Q$ *implies* $P \to Q$
3. $P \to Q$ *implies that there is R such that $R \equiv Q$ and* $P \xrightarrow{\tau} R$

Proof. We prove the three statements in the lemma separately.

1. Since barbs are preserved by structural congruence, the first part follows from Lemma 3.
2. We have to prove that $P \xrightarrow{\tau} Q$ implies $P \to Q$. The proof is by induction on the proof tree of $P \xrightarrow{\tau} Q$. The base cases are two and they are related to rules (SELF) and (COM), i.e., the rules that introduce the label τ in the tree. The inductive cases are instead related to all those rules that move the τ label from the premise to the conclusion of the inference, i.e. (WUNIT), (PAR) and (RES). For space reasons we describe only the workunit part. The base case follows from the first part of Lemma 3. For the inductive case we have to prove that $\langle\!\langle P \;;\; Q \rangle\!\rangle_z \xrightarrow{\tau} R$ implies $\langle\!\langle P \;;\; Q \rangle\!\rangle_z \to R$. The inductive case is when $P \xrightarrow{\tau} P'$ and $\langle\!\langle P \;;\; Q \rangle\!\rangle_z \xrightarrow{\tau} \langle\!\langle P' \;;\; Q \rangle\!\rangle_z$ for the (WUNIT) rule. In this case we can apply the inductive hypothesis obtaining $P \to P'$ and, since the reduction relation is closed under the workunit context, $\langle\!\langle P \;;\; Q \rangle\!\rangle_z \to \langle\!\langle P' \;;\; Q \rangle\!\rangle_z$.
3. We have to prove that $P \to Q$ implies that there is R such that $R \equiv Q$ and $P \xrightarrow{\tau} R$. The proof is by induction on the proof tree of $P \to Q$. The base cases are three and they are related to rules (R-COM), (R-REP) and (R-FAIL). The inductive cases are instead related to the closures under contexts and

structural congruence. We show only the workunit case: if $P \to P'$ we have $\langle P \; ; \; Q \rangle_z \to \langle P' \; ; \; Q \rangle_z$ for the the context closure of the reduction relation. By inductive hypothesis we also have $P \xrightarrow{\tau} R$ with $R \equiv P'$. From this fact, using rule (WUNIT) of the labeled semantics, we get $\langle P \; ; \; Q \rangle_z \xrightarrow{\tau} \langle R \; ; \; Q \rangle_z$ where $\langle R \; ; \; Q \rangle_z \equiv \langle P' \; ; \; Q \rangle_z$. □

Now we are ready to prove our main result, which shows that closed bisimilarity can be used as a tool to prove weak barbed congruence.

Theorem 2. *For each pair of* webπ_∞ *processes P and Q, $P \approx_a Q$ implies $P \approx Q$.*

Proof. Lemma 4 proved that $\approx_a$ is a weak barbed bisimulation. We have also proved (Theorem 1) that $\approx_a$ is a congruence. Since $\approx$ is the largest barbed bisimulation that is a congruence then the thesis follows. □

4 Relevant Examples

The theory developed so far allows us to prove interesting properties about webπ_∞ processes. In this section we show some examples of pattern reducibility proving them correct as far as weak barbed congruence is concerned, and using closed bisimilarity as technical tool. This also shows that closed bisimilarity, whose completeness has not been proved yet, can be applied in many interesting cases.

Handlers Reducibility. Let us consider the following processes where $x' \notin \mathrm{fn}(P) \cup \mathrm{fn}(Q), x' \neq x$.

$$\langle P \; ; \; Q \rangle_x$$
$$(x')(\langle P \; ; \; \overline{x'} \rangle_x \mid \langle x'().Q \; ; \; \mathbf{0} \rangle)$$

The following theorem states that any workunit can be rewritten in another unit where the handler consists of a single asynchronous output and all the remaining parts of the process are moved in a separate unit and activated when necessary.

Theorem 3. $\langle P \; ; \; Q \rangle_x \approx (x')(\langle P \; ; \; \overline{x'} \rangle_x \mid \langle x'().Q \; ; \; \mathbf{0} \rangle)$

Proof. The relation ϕ on webπ_∞ processes defined as follows is a closed bisimulation. Below we intend P and Q to range over all processes, and x, x' range over all the names such that $x' \notin \mathrm{fn}(P) \cup \mathrm{fn}(Q), x' \neq x$.

$$\phi = \{(P,P)\} \cup \{(\langle P \; ; \; Q \rangle_x, (x')(\langle P \; ; \; \overline{x'} \rangle_x \mid \langle x'().Q \; ; \; \mathbf{0} \rangle))\}$$
$$\cup \{(\langle \mathrm{xtr}(P) \mid Q \; ; \; \mathbf{0} \rangle, (x')(\langle \mathrm{xtr}(P) \; ; \; \mathbf{0} \rangle \mid \langle Q \; ; \; \mathbf{0} \rangle))\}$$

The full proof requires to show that the three conditions for closed bisimilarity are satisfied. This is quite easy, and the interested reader can refer to [11]. The thesis then follows thanks to Theorem 2. □

Decoupling of Service and Recovery Logics. Let us consider another couple of processes where $y \notin \mathrm{fn}(!z(u).P \,|\, Q) \cup \{v\}$:

$$\langle\!\!\!\mid !z(u).P \,|\, Q \,;\, \overline{v} \,\rangle\!\!\!\mid_x$$
$$(y)(\langle\!\!\!\mid !z(u).P \,;\, \overline{y} \,\rangle\!\!\!\mid_x \,|\, \langle\!\!\!\mid Q \,|\, (w)w(u) \,;\, \overline{v} \,\rangle\!\!\!\mid_y)$$

The following theorem shows the way in which a pattern expressing the service logic $!z(u).P \,|\, Q$ and the recovery logic for that service (intended as a single asynchronous output because of the previous theorem) can be decoupled and written separately by means of two different workunits. The property can be read also in the opposite sense, showing how two different workunits can be coupled in a single one.

Theorem 4. $\langle\!\!\!\mid !z(u).P \,|\, Q \,;\, \overline{v} \,\rangle\!\!\!\mid_x \approx (y)(\langle\!\!\!\mid !z(u).P \,;\, \overline{y} \,\rangle\!\!\!\mid_x \,|\, \langle\!\!\!\mid Q \,|\, (w)w(u) \,;\, \overline{v} \,\rangle\!\!\!\mid_y)$

Proof. The proof is similar to the one above, considering now as ϕ:

$$\phi = \{(P, P)\} \cup \{\langle\!\!\!\mid !z(u).P \,|\, Q \,;\, \overline{v} \,\rangle\!\!\!\mid_x, (y)(\langle\!\!\!\mid !z(u).P \,;\, \overline{y} \,\rangle\!\!\!\mid_x \,|\, \langle\!\!\!\mid Q \,|\, (w)w(u) \,;\, \overline{v} \,\rangle\!\!\!\mid_y)\}$$

where we intend P and Q to range over all processes, and z, u, v, x and y range over all the names such that $y \notin \mathrm{fn}(!z(u).P \,|\, Q) \cup \{v\}$. The only trick is that the addition of the deadlocked component $(w)w(u)$ is needed to ensure that the input predicate is true on the right hand side, as necessary to simulate the left hand side.   □

The applications above show that in some cases of interest closed bisimilarity allows to use quite easily writable relations, while using weak barbed congruence directly is far more complex.

5   Conclusion

In this paper we analyzed some semantic issues in the framework of $\mathrm{web}\pi_\infty$, a simple extension of the π-calculus with untimed long running transactions. A timed extension of $\mathrm{web}\pi_\infty$, called $\mathrm{web}\pi$, has been presented in [8] to meet the challenge of time in composition. There $\mathrm{web}\pi$ has been equipped with an explicit mechanism for time elapsing and timeout handling. Adding time allows to express another interesting aspect of systems. Remember however that if one is not interested in the timing details, timeouts can be simply expressed as choices between the normal behavior and the timeout behavior. Discussing the notion of orchestration without considering time constraints makes it possible to focus on information flow, message passing, concurrency and resource mobility. Also, it allows to have a more abstract view using the weak semantics, which does not make sense in the timed framework, and which is the desired level of abstraction in many cases. Notice for instance that processes in our sample applications are not equivalent according to a strong equivalence.

Another related calculus is c-join [3], which extends join calculus [6] with long running transactions and compensations. The main difference between $\mathrm{web}\pi_\infty$

and c-join is that in the latter the nesting of transactions matters, since when the external transaction is aborted all the internal transactions are aborted too. This forces a particular way to deal with related transactions, while in our case this decision can be taken in a case by case way, by explicit sending abort signals to the other transactions. Note that in c-join instead a process can only abort the innermost transaction containing it (but the compensation can be programmed to propagate the abort to the upper level). Finally, in c-join, communication between processes in different transactions causes the transactions to be merged.

Long running transactions have been analyzed also using Compensating CSP [4], but this approach is more focused on the definition of compensations for large processes starting from definitions of compensations for their components, and it provides neither synchronization (apart from sequential composition) nor mobility.

This work contributes with a powerful and expressive language, with a solid semantics, that allows formal reasoning. The language shows a clear relation with the π-calculus and the actual encoding is a feasible task, while it would be quite harder to get such an encoding for XLANG and other web services composition languages. Future developments building on the results achieved in this paper include software tools for static analysis of programs based on composition of services. A useful result we achieved in [11] that stem from this work is a streamlined definitions of syntax and semantics of BPEL, to get a simpler way to model involved transaction behaviors. The overall goal of these works is to allow for improvement of quality and applicability of real composition languages.

Acknowledgments. The authors would like to strongly acknowledge Cosimo Laneve for his huge support and contribution and Luiz Olavo Bonino Da Silva Santos, Roberto Bruni and Hernán Melgratti for theirs comments.

References

1. R. M. Amadio, I. Castellani, and D. Sangiorgi. On bisimulations for the asynchronous pi-calculus. *Theoret. Comput. Sci.*, 195(2):291–324, 1998.
2. A. Arkin, S. Askary, B. Bloch, F. Curbera, Y. Goland, N. Kartha, C. K. Liu, V. Mehta, S. Thatte, P. Yendluri, A. Yiu, and A Alves. Web services business process execution language version 2.0. Technical report, Oasis, December 2005. Working draft.
3. R. Bruni, H. C. Melgratti, and U. Montanari. Nested commits for mobile calculi: Extending join. In *Proc. of IFIP TCS'04*, pages 563–576. Kluwer Academics, 2004.
4. M. J. Butler, C. A. R. Hoare, and C. Ferreira. A trace semantics for long-running transactions. In *25 Years Communicating Sequential Processes*, volume 3525 of *Lect. Notes in Comput. Sci.*, pages 133–150. Springer, 2004.
5. F. Curbera, R. Khalaf, N. Mukhi, S. Tai, and S. Weerawarana. The next step in web services. *Commun. ACM*, 46(10):29–34, 2003.
6. C. Fournet and G. Gonthier. The reflexive CHAM and the join-calculus. In *Proc. of POPL'96*, pages 372–385. ACM Press, 1996.

7. M. N. Huhns and M. P. Singh. Service-oriented computing: Key concepts and principles. *IEEE Internet Computing*, 9(1):75–81, 2005.

8. C. Laneve and G. Zavattaro. Foundations of web transactions. In *Proc. of FoSSaCS'05*, volume 3441 of *Lect. Notes in Comput. Sci.*, pages 282–298. Springer, 2005.

9. F. Leymann. Web services flow language (WSFL 1.0). Technical report, IBM, May 2001.

10. R. Lucchi and M. Mazzara. A π-calculus based semantics for WS-BPEL. *J. Log. Algebr. Program.*, 2006. To appear.

11. M. Mazzara. *Towards Abstractions for Web Services Composition*. PhD thesis, Department of Computer Science, University of Bologna, 2006. Also available as Technical Report UBLCS-2006-08.

12. Microsoft BizTalk. `http://www.microsoft.com/biztalk/default.mspx`.

13. R. Milner. Functions as processes. *Math. Struct. in Comput. Sci.*, 2(2):119–141, 1992.

14. R. Milner, J. Parrow, and J. Walker. A calculus of mobile processes, I and II. *Inform. and Comput.*, 100(1):1–40,41–77, 1992.

15. C. Peltz. Web services orchestration and choreography. *IEEE Computer*, 36(10):46–52, 2003.

16. D. Sangiorgi and D. Walker. *The π-calculus: A theory of Mobile Processes*. Cambridge University Press, 2001.

17. C. Szyperski. *Component Software: Beyond Object-Oriented Programming, 2nd Ed.* Addison-Wesley/ACM Press, 2002.

18. S. Thatte. XLANG: Web services for businnes process design. Technical report, Microsoft Corporation, 2001. Downloadable from `www.gotdotnet.com/team/xml/wsspecs/xlang-c`.

Towards the Formal Model and Verification of Web Service Choreography Description Language*

Zhao Xiangpeng, Yang Hongli, and Qiu Zongyan

LMAM and Department of Informatics, School of Math.,
Peking University, Beijing 100871, China
{zxp, yhl, qzy}@math.pku.edu.cn

Abstract. The Web Services Choreography Description Language (WS-CDL) is a W3C specification for the description of peer-to-peer collaborations of participants from a global viewpoint. For the rigorous development and tools support for the language, the formal semantics of WS-CDL is worth investigating. This paper proposes a small language CDL as a formal model of the simplified WS-CDL, which includes important concepts related to participant roles and collaborations among them in a choreography. The formal operational semantics of CDL is given. Based on the formal model, we discuss further: 1) project a given choreography to orchestration views, which provides a basis for the implementation of the choreography by code generation; 2) translate WS-CDL to the input language of the model-checker SPIN, which allows us to automatically verify the correctness of a given choreography. An automatic translator has been implemented.

1 Introduction

Web services promise the interoperability of various applications running on heterogeneous platforms. Web service composition refers to the process of combining several web services to provide a value-added service, which has received much interest to support enterprise application integration. Two levels of view to the composition of web services exist, namely orchestration and choreography. The choreography view focuses on the composition of Web services from a global perspective, and it differs from the orchestration view which focuses on the interactions among one party and others.

The recently released web service choreography description language (WS-CDL) is a W3C [2] candidate recommendation for web service composition. WS-CDL is an XML-based language for the describing peer-to-peer collaborations of participants by defining, based on a global viewpoint, from their common and complementary observable behavior [15]. WS-CDL is neither an "executable business process description language" nor an implementation language. The execution logic of the application is covered by languages at another level, such as XLANG [19], BPEL [3], BPML [5], etc. WS-CDL focuses on describing the business protocol among different participant roles. All the behaviors are performed by the participants, and WS-CDL gives a global observation.

As discussed in [6], WS-CDL lacks the separation between its meta-model and its syntax, and lacks of a formal grounding. Due to the message-passing nature of web

---

* Supported by National Natural Science Foundation of China (No. 60573081).

M. Bravetti, M. Nuñes, and G. Zavattaro (Eds.): WS-FM 2006, LNCS 4184, pp. 273–287, 2006.

services interaction, many subtle errors can occur (e.g., message not received, dead-locks, incompatible behaviour, etc.) when a number of parties are collaborated with each other. To guarantee the correct interaction of independent, communicating web services becomes even more critical in the open-end world of web services [18]. As a language aimed to become a standard for the web service choreography, formal studies may clear the opaque points or inconsistencies in the language definition, and provide a grounding for tools development.

In this paper, we propose a small language called CDL as a formal model of the simplified WS-CDL. CDL includes many important concepts related to the participant roles and the collaborations among them in a choreography. The aim of this model is to focus on the core features of WS-CDL. Based on the formal model, it is possible 1) to generate orchestration views from a given choreography; 2) to reason about the proper-ties that should be satisfied by the specified system. We propose a projection function for orchestration generation and discussed the correctness issue of the projection. We also provide an automatic translation tool which can convert a choreography into the input language of the model checker SPIN [11]. Afterwards, we can either simulate or verify the choreography automatically. Besides, manual reasoning based on our model is also possible, as discussed in our previous report [12].

This paper is organized as follows: Section 2 is an informal overview of WS-CDL. We present the formal model of CDL in Section 3, including its syntax and operational semantics. In Section 4 we discuss the projection from choreography to orchestration, while in Section 5 we discuss how to model-check WS-CDL specification using our automatic translator. Some related work is discussed in Section 6, and section 7 con-cludes.

2   Overview of WS-CDL

This section provides an overview of WS-CDL, as defined in WS-CDL specification [15] released on 9th November 2005. A choreography defines collaborations among interacting participants. It can be recognized as a container for a collection of activities that may be performed by the participants. There are two types of activities in WS-CDL: basic activities and control-flow activities.

Basic activities include a *noAction* action, which does not do anything; an *assign* ac-tivity, which assigns, within one role, the value of one variable or an expression to an-other variable; and an *interaction* activity, which results in an exchange of information between participant roles and possible synchronization of their observable information changes and the actual values of the exchanged information.

An interaction activity is composed of: 1) the participant roles involved; 2) the ex-changed information and the corresponding direction(s); 3) the observable information changes; 4) the operation performed by the recipient. The information exchange type of interactions is described by the possible actions on the WS-CDL channel, which falls into three types: request, respond, or request-respond. According to the exchange type, there are three kinds of interactions. The operation in an interaction activity is performed after the request (if there is one) and before the response (if there is one).

The example below shows an interaction between two roles *Consumer* and *Retailer* as a request/response exchange on the channel *retailer-channel*. The message *po* is sent from *Consumer* to *Retailer* as a request; and the message *poAck* is sent back from *Retailer* to *Consumer* as a response. After the message exchange, the variable *Consumer-poState* is assigned by the value *sent* at *Consumer*, and *Retailer-poState* by *received* at *Retailer*, as specified in the *record* elements.

```
<interaction name="createPO" channelVariable="retailer-channel"
             operation="handlePurchaseOrder">
 <participate relationshipType="tn:ConsumerRetailer
              fromRoleTypeRef="tn:Consumer" toRoleTypeRef="tn:Retailer"/>
 <exchange name="request" informationType="tn:POType" action="request">
  <send variable="cdl:getVariable('tn:po','','')" recordReference="Consumer-poState" />
  <receive variable="cdl:getVariable('tn:po','','')" recordReference="Retailer-poState" />
 </exchange>
 <exchange name="response" informationType="POAckType" action="respond">
  <send variable="cdl:getVariable('tn:poAck','','')"/>
  <receive variable="cdl:getVariable('tn:poAck','','')"/>
 </exchange>
 <record name="Consumer-poState" when="after">
  <source expression="sent"/>
  <target variable="cdl:getVariable('tn:poState','','')"/>
 </record>
 <record name="Retailer-poState" when="after">
  <source expression="received"/>
  <target variable="cdl:getVariable('tn:poState','','')"/>
 </record>
</interaction>
```

The control-flow activities include sequence, parallel, choice and workunit. The *sequence*, *parallel* and *choice* activities have similar meanings as in the other programming languages. A *workunit* describes the conditional and repeated execution of an activity [6].

A role type enumerates the potential observable behaviors that a participant can exhibit in order to interact. Variables in WS-CDL are used to represent different types of information such as the exchanged information or the observable state information of the role involved. Unlike most programming languages, there are no independent variables in WS-CDL, i.e. each variable must belong to some role.

3   CDL: A Formal Model for WS-CDL

In this section we define a small language CDL, which can be viewed as a subset of WS-CDL. It models choreography with a set of participant roles and the collaboration among them. We give the syntax and an operational semantics here.

3.1   Syntax

In the definitions below, the meta-variable R ranges over role declarations; A and B range over activity declarations; r, f and t range over role names; x, y, u and v range over variable names; e, e_1 and e_2 ranges over XPath expressions; g, g_1, g_2 and p range over XPath boolean expressions; op ranges over the operations offered by the roles. We will use $\overline{R}$ as a shorthand for $R_1, \cdots, R_n$, for some n. (Similarly, for $\overline{x}, \overline{op}, \overline{e}$, etc.) We use $r.x$ to refer to the variable x in role r, and $r.\overline{x} := \overline{e}$ for $r.x_1 := e_1, \cdots, r.x_n := e_n$.

A choreography declaration includes a name C, some participant roles $\overline{R}$, and an activity A, with the form:

$$C[\overline{R}, A]$$

Each participant role R has some local variables $\overline{x}$ and observable behaviors represented as a set of operations $\overline{op}$. The signature and function of the operations are defined elsewhere and omitted here. A role with name r is defined as:

$$R ::= r[\overline{x}, \overline{op}]$$

The basic activities in CDL are the follows:

$$
\begin{array}{lll}
BA ::= & \text{skip} & \text{(skip)} \\
& |\, r.\overline{x} := \overline{e} & \text{(assign)} \\
& |\, \text{comm}\,(f.x \xrightarrow{c} t.y, rec, op) & \text{(request)} \\
& |\, \text{comm}\,(f.x \xleftarrow{c} t.y, rec, op) & \text{(response)} \\
& |\, \text{comm}\,(f.x \xrightarrow{c_t} t.y, f.u \xleftarrow{c_f} t.v, rec, op) & \text{(req-resp)}
\end{array}
$$

The skip activity does nothing. The assignment activity $r.\overline{x} := \overline{e}$ assigns, within the role r, the values of expressions $\overline{e}$ to the variables $\overline{x}$. Note that e must only contain variables that belong to the same role r. For remote assignments (i.e. assign some variable of one role to some variable of another role), we must use the interaction activity, which is either:

- a request interaction with the form comm $(f.x \rightarrow t.y, rec, op)$ in which the message is sent from $f.x$ to $t.y$;
- a response interaction with the form comm $(f.x \leftarrow t.y, rec, op)$ in which the response message is sent from $t.y$ to $f.x$;
- a request-response interaction comm $(f.x \rightarrow t.y, f.u \leftarrow t.v, rec, op)$ with a request message from $f.x$ to $t.y$ and a response message from $t.v$ to $f.u$.

In an interaction, the operation op specifies what the recipient should do when it receives the message. After the operation, some state change will be performed by rec, which is the shorthand for the assignments $f.\overline{x} := \overline{e_1}, t.\overline{y} := \overline{e_2}$. Here $\overline{x}$ and $\overline{y}$ are two lists of state variables on the roles f and t respectively.

The syntax of the control-flow activities is listed here:

$$
\begin{array}{lll}
A, B ::= & BA & \text{(basic)} \\
& |\, p?A & \text{(condition)} \\
& |\, p * A & \text{(repeat)} \\
& |\, g : A : p & \text{(workunit)} \\
& |\, A; B & \text{(sequence)} \\
& |\, A \sqcap B & \text{(non-deterministic)} \\
& |\, g_1 \Rightarrow A \,[\!]\, g_2 \Rightarrow B & \text{(general-choice)} \\
& |\, A \parallel B & \text{(parallel)}
\end{array}
$$

An activity is either a basic activity BA, a workunit, or a control-flow activity. The workunit introduced in WS-CDL is separately defined as three constructs here. Two of them are the condition construct $p?A$ and the repeat construct $p * A$, that work normally. The other is the workunit $(g : A : p)$, which will blocked until the guard g evaluates to "true". When the guard is trigged, the activity A is performed. If A terminates successfully, and if the repetition condition p evaluates to "true", the workunit will be considered again; otherwise, the workunit finishes. A control-flow activity is either a sequence activity $A; B$, a non-deterministic activity $A \sqcap B$, a general choice $g_1 \Rightarrow A \,[\!]\, g_2 \Rightarrow B$, or a parallel activity $A \parallel B$.

The WS-CDL specification includes many well-formedness and typing rules, such as "In an interaction, each information exchange variable has the same type on the sender and the receiver". We are developing a type system for CDL to statically verify the validity of all these rules. In this paper we do not consider well-formnedness problems, and assume that the CDL program under consideration is always well-formed.

3.2 Operational Semantics of CDL

In this section, a small-step operational semantics for CDL is presented. We define the configuration as a tuple $\langle A, \sigma \rangle$, where A is an activity, and σ is the state of the choreography which is a composition of each participant role's state. A role state, σ_{r_i}, $i = 1, \cdots, n$, is a function from the variable names of the role r_i to their values. We suppose that each variable name is decorated with the role name on which it resides, the values of variables are unknown initially. The state of the choreography

$$\sigma \stackrel{\text{def}}{=} \sigma_{r_1} \cup \sigma_{r_2} \cup \cdots \cup \sigma_{r_n}$$

is the composition of all the role states in the choreography.

For convenience, we use the form $\sigma \oplus \{r.x \mapsto e\}$ to denote the global state σ with some variable assignments on given role r. Moreover, we use $\langle \epsilon, \sigma \rangle$ to denote the terminal configuration.

Basic Activity. The semantics of the basic activities are defined as follows:

The execution of skip activity always terminates successfully, leaving everything unchanged.

$$\langle \text{skip}, \sigma \rangle \longrightarrow \langle \epsilon, \sigma \rangle \tag{SKIP}$$

The *assign* activity is a multiple assignment. The values of the variables $r.\overline{x}$ do not change until all the evaluations $\overline{e}$ are completed. Note that every variable appearing in $\overline{e}$ should belong to r, i.e. remote value fetch is not allowed.

$$\langle r.\overline{x} := \overline{e}, \ \sigma \rangle \longrightarrow \langle \epsilon, \sigma \oplus \{r.\overline{x} \mapsto \overline{e}\} \rangle \tag{ASS}$$

In an interaction activity, some information may exchange between two participant roles, namely a "from" role f and a "to" role t. After the operation op is accomplished, there may be some variable updates on both roles according to the assignments in rec. The semantics for op is not defined here; we can view op as an external atomic activity. As a result, we can define the trace of a choreography as the sequence of operations it performs.

$$\langle \text{comm} (f.x \xrightarrow{c} t.y, rec, op), \ \sigma \rangle \longrightarrow \langle rec, \sigma \oplus \{t.y \mapsto f.x\} \rangle \tag{REQ}$$

$$\langle \text{comm} (f.x \xleftarrow{c} t.y, rec, op), \ \sigma \rangle \longrightarrow \langle rec, \sigma \oplus \{f.x \mapsto t.y\} \rangle \tag{RESP}$$

$$\langle \text{comm} (f.x \xrightarrow{c_t} t.y, f.u \xleftarrow{c_f} t.v, rec, op), \ \sigma \rangle \longrightarrow \langle rec, \sigma \oplus \{t.y \mapsto f.x, f.u \mapsto t.v\} \rangle$$
$$\tag{REQ-RESP}$$

Control-Flow Activity. The behavior of the condition activity $(p?A)$ is the same as A when the boolean expression p evaluates to true. Otherwise, it does nothing and terminates successfully.

$$\frac{\sigma(p) = \textbf{false}}{\langle p?A, \sigma \rangle \longrightarrow \langle \epsilon, \sigma \rangle} \qquad \text{(IF-FALSE)}$$

$$\frac{\sigma(p) = \textbf{true}}{\langle p?A, \sigma \rangle \longrightarrow \langle A, \sigma \rangle} \qquad \text{(IF-TRUE)}$$

The repeat activity $(p * A)$ is executed by first evaluating p. When p is false, the activity terminates and nothing is changed. When p is true, the sequential composition $(A; (p * A))$ will be executed.

$$\frac{\sigma(p) = \textbf{false}}{\langle p * A, \sigma \rangle \longrightarrow \langle \epsilon, \sigma \rangle} \qquad \text{(REP-FALSE)}$$

$$\frac{\sigma(p) = \textbf{true}}{\langle p * A, \sigma \rangle \longrightarrow \langle A; p * A, \sigma \rangle} \qquad \text{(REP-TRUE)}$$

The workunit activity $(g : A : p)$ is blocked when the guard condition g evaluates to false. When g evaluates to true, A is executed. After the execution, repetition condition p is tested. If p evaluates to false, then the activity terminates; if true, then the workunit restarts. In the WS-CDL syntax, g and p can be omitted. An omitted condition means that it is always true.

$$\frac{\sigma(g) = \textbf{true}}{\langle g:A:p, \sigma \rangle \longrightarrow \langle A; p?(g:A:p), \sigma \rangle} \qquad \text{(BLOCK)}$$

The sequential composition $(A; B)$ first behaves like A; when A terminates successfully, $(A; B)$ continues by behaving like B. If A never terminates successfully, neither does $A; B$.

$$\frac{\langle A, \sigma \rangle \longrightarrow \langle A', \sigma' \rangle}{\langle A; B, \sigma \rangle \longrightarrow \langle A'; B, \sigma' \rangle} \qquad \text{(SEQ)}$$

$$\langle \epsilon; B, \sigma \rangle \longrightarrow \langle B, \sigma \rangle \qquad \text{(SEQ-ELIM)}$$

The non-deterministic choice $A \sqcap B$ behaves like either A or B, where the selection between them is non-deterministic, without referring the knowledge or control of the external environment.

$$\frac{\langle A, \sigma \rangle \longrightarrow \langle A', \sigma' \rangle}{\langle A \sqcap B, \sigma \rangle \longrightarrow \langle A', \sigma' \rangle} \qquad \text{(NON-DET)}$$

$$\frac{\langle B, \sigma \rangle \longrightarrow \langle B', \sigma' \rangle}{\langle A \sqcap B, \sigma \rangle \longrightarrow \langle B', \sigma' \rangle} \qquad \text{(NON-DET)}$$

The general choice $(g_1 \Rightarrow A \,[\!]\, g_2 \Rightarrow B)$ behaves like A if the guard g_1 is matched, otherwise behaves like B if g_2 is matched, where each guard is a boolean expression. If both g_1 and g_2 are matched, then the first is selected.

$$\frac{\sigma(g_1) = \textbf{true}, \ \sigma(g_2) = \textbf{false}}{\langle g_1 \Rightarrow A \,[\!]\, g_2 \Rightarrow B, \sigma \rangle \longrightarrow \langle A, \sigma \rangle} \qquad \text{(CHOICE)}$$

$$\frac{\sigma(g_1) = \textbf{false}, \ \sigma(g_2) = \textbf{true}}{\langle g_1 \Rightarrow A \,[\!]\, g_2 \Rightarrow B, \sigma \rangle \longrightarrow \langle B, \sigma \rangle} \qquad \text{(CHOICE)}$$

$$\frac{\sigma(g_1) = \textbf{true}, \ \sigma(g_2) = \textbf{true}}{\langle g_1 \Rightarrow A \,[\!]\, g_2 \Rightarrow B, \sigma \rangle \longrightarrow \langle A, \sigma \rangle} \qquad \text{(CHOICE)}$$

We use interleaving semantics for the parallel composition:

$$\frac{\langle A, \sigma \rangle \longrightarrow \langle A', \sigma' \rangle}{\langle A \parallel B, \sigma \rangle \longrightarrow \langle A' \parallel B, \sigma' \rangle} \qquad \text{(PARA)}$$

$$\frac{\langle B, \sigma \rangle \longrightarrow \langle B', \sigma' \rangle}{\langle A \parallel B, \sigma \rangle \longrightarrow \langle A \parallel B', \sigma' \rangle} \qquad \text{(PARA)}$$

$$\langle \epsilon \parallel B, \sigma \rangle \longrightarrow \langle B, \sigma \rangle \qquad \text{(PARA-ELIM)}$$

$$\langle A \parallel \epsilon, \sigma \rangle \longrightarrow \langle A, \sigma \rangle \qquad \text{(PARA-ELIM)}$$

Based on the formal semantics, we can do manual reasoning about the properties that should be satisfied by a given choreography. A purchase order choreography example is given in our previous work [12]. In this paper, we focus on automatic verification using model-checking, as described in Section 5.

4   Projection from CDL to Orchestration Views

As we have described, CDL provides a choreographical view of the interacting web services, which involves the interaction of many parties. For code generation, simulation and verification purposes, it is meaningful to generate orchestration views from a given choreography view, while each of them describes only the interaction behavior of one party with its related partners. In our example, the credit checker only deals with the seller, not the buyer nor the inventory. An orchestration view for the credit checker is a projection from the choreography that hides the behavior of all the unrelated parties.

In choreography, as at a higher level of view, we can always let the two-party interaction start without waiting, as explained informally by the following:

$$\mathsf{comm}\,(f.x \xrightarrow{ch} t.y, rec, op) \approx (ch!f.x \parallel ch?t.y) \approx t.y := f.x$$

In other words, the data transportation through channels is implicit under a choreography view. This explains the reason that we use variable assignment for the semantics of interaction. At the local view level, we remove the interaction activities from our syntax, while adding the channel communication activities:

$$BA_{orc} ::= \mathsf{skip} \mid f.\overline{x} := t.\overline{y} \mid ch!f.x \mid ch?t.y$$

The semantics of an orchestration is similar to a process in an ordinary process algebra, and we do not want to discuss the details here. Note that according to WS-CDL specification, we can only send some variable through a channel, rather than an arbitrary expression. Also, we suppose that the channel communications are all synchronous, since asynchronous channels may bring some difficulty in both modelling and verification [8].

We define a set of projection rules from a given choreography to a process of a given target role r_t as a function Pr, which maps an activity in choreography to an activity in the local view. For a choreography $C[\overline{r}\,,\, A]$ that has a root activity A and n roles $r_1, \cdots, r_n$, we define the projection from C to role r_i as $Pr(A, r_i)$.

$$Pr(\mathsf{skip}, r_t) \stackrel{def}{=} \mathsf{skip}$$

$$Pr(r.\overline{x} := \overline{e}, r_t) \overset{def}{=} \begin{cases} r.\overline{x} := \overline{e} \text{ if } r_t = r \\ \text{skip} \qquad \text{otherwise} \end{cases}$$

$$Pr(\text{comm } (f.x \overset{c}{\rightarrow} t.y, rec, op), r_t) \overset{def}{=} \begin{cases} c!f.x; Pr(rec, r_t) \quad \text{if } r_t = f \\ c?t.y; op; Pr(rec, r_t) \text{ if } r_t = t \\ \text{skip} \qquad\qquad\qquad \text{otherwise} \end{cases}$$

$$Pr(\text{comm } (f.x \overset{c}{\leftarrow} t.y, rec, op), r_t) \overset{def}{=} \begin{cases} c?t.y; op; Pr(rec, r_t) \text{ if } r_t = f \\ c!f.x; Pr(rec, r_t) \quad \text{if } r_t = t \\ \text{skip} \qquad\qquad\qquad \text{otherwise} \end{cases}$$

$$Pr(\text{comm } (f.x \overset{c_t}{\rightarrow} t.y, f.u \overset{c_f}{\leftarrow} t.v, rec, op), r_t)$$
$$\overset{def}{=} \begin{cases} c_t!f.x; c_f?t.y; Pr(rec, r_t) \quad \text{if } r_t = f \\ c_t?f.x; op; c_f!t.y; Pr(rec, r_t) \text{ if } r_t = t \\ \text{skip} \qquad\qquad\qquad\qquad\qquad \text{otherwise} \end{cases}$$

$$Pr(A; B, r_t) \overset{def}{=} Pr(A, r_t); Pr(B, r_t)$$

$$Pr(p?A, r_t) \overset{def}{=} p_{r_t}?Pr(A, r_t)$$

$$Pr(p * A, r_t) \overset{def}{=} p_{r_t} * Pr(A, r_t)$$

$$Pr(g : A : p, r_t) \overset{def}{=} g_{r_t} : Pr(A, r_t) : p_{r_t}$$

$$Pr(A \sqcap B, r_t) \overset{def}{=} Pr(A, r_t) \sqcap Pr(B, r_t)$$

$$Pr(g_1 \Rightarrow A [\!] g_2 \Rightarrow B, r_t) \overset{def}{=} g_{1_{r_t}} \Rightarrow Pr(A, r_t) [\!] g_{2_{r_t}} \Rightarrow Pr(B, r_t)$$

$$Pr(A \parallel B, r_t) \overset{def}{=} Pr(A, r_t) \parallel Pr(B, r_t)$$

Intuitively, if some activity is not related to the given role and should be hidden, we simply replace it with skip. For interaction activities, we will replace them with channel communications according to the direction of the interaction. The control-flow activities that do not have guards are not modified.

For those those activities that involve guards, there could be a problem of unconnectedness. For example, in $(A.x > 0)?(B.y := 1)$, we say the guard's role is *unconnected* with the assignment activity's role; while $(A.x > 0)?(A.z := 1)$ is *connected*. Although this is allowed by the WS-CDL specification, it is not possible to directly implement an unconnected specification, because B cannot remotely access the variable x on role A. We do not intend to address the unconnectedness problem in this paper. To simplify the definition, we add a requirement that every guard must have the form of $e_1 \wedge \cdots \wedge e_n$, where e_i is a term which only involves role r_i. In the projection of the guards, the projected guard g_{r_t} on role r_t has only a part of the original guard g that is related to the role, i.e. $g_{r_t} = e_t$. For example, a guard $A.x > 0 \wedge B.y > 0$ will be projected to $A.x > 0$ in the projected orchestration for role A, and $B.x > 0$ for B. This is rooted from the function globalizedTrigger $(e_1, r_1, \cdots, e_n, r_n)$ defined in WS-CDL specification.

Given a choreography, we can project it to each involved role $r \in \overline{R}$ with the rules above. After that, we can consider implementation, simulation or verification. Note that the generated orchestration may contain a lot of redundant skip, and some redundant structured activities. We have removed most of the redundancy in our automatic translator which is described in the next section.

5   Model-Checking CDL Specification

In this section we discuss how to verify a given WS-CDL specification using the SPIN model checker. The input language of SPIN is called Promela [11], which is a language for modeling finite-state concurrent processes. SPIN can verify or falsify (by generating counterexamples) LTL (Linear Temporal Logic) properties of Promela specifications using an exhaustive state space search. Given the XML specification of a CDL choreography, we generate a Promela specification, which consists of some communicating concurrent processes denoting different parties. We implement the translation in two steps: (1) from WS-CDL specification to projected orchestration specifications; (2) from the orchestration specifications to Promela processes with communication channels. The first phase has been discussed in the previous section, and we will focus on the second phase in this section.

5.1   Translation to Promela

We discuss our translation procedure using the annual tax statement example taken from [13]. In the choreography, the client asks an advisor to help him pay tax to the municipality according to the annual statement he provides. The client's request may be rejected directly by the advisor, or forwarded to the municipality, which will return a notification that either accepts the statement or rejects it. The WS-CDL source code is 300-lines-long and is difficult to read. An abridged version of the source code is shown in Figure 1.

We give the translated Promela code of this example in Figure 2. The first part of the code consists of some type declarations and variable declarations. We introduce a variable named r_x for each variable x under role r. Each information type variable is converted into a mtype variable; while each channel variable is converted into a channel chan. Although model-checkers have proved to be powerful in verifying the control flow of a system, it performance is quite poor when we allow the variables to have a wide range of possible values. As a prototype system, we only consider two states nil and something of each information variable, which denotes whether the variable has been assigned by some value or not. We also introduce some auxiliary boolean variables to implement parallelism, which are discussed later.

The second part of the code consists of several processes that denotes roles in the choreography. The init process instantiates three processes corresponding to each role. Based on the projection technique introduced in Section 4 we can give the execution logic of each process. Assuming the projection has been done, in Table 1 we give a mapping from orchestration specification of role r to Promela code. Since Promela supports most of the activities defined in our CDL semantics, most translation is quite straightforward.

In Promela, if statement is a blocking guarded choice. The system can proceed only if at least one guard is satisfied. If more than one guards are satisfied, then the system

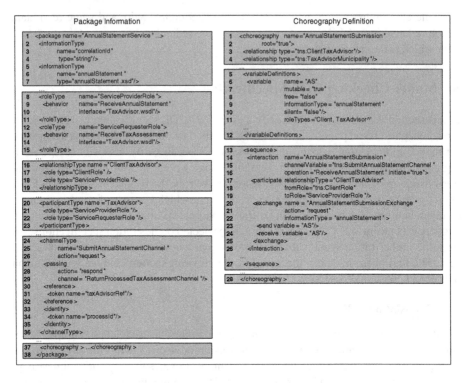

Fig. 1. WS-CDL Specification Example

will make a non-deterministic choice. The do statement is used for repeating, and is similar with if. For parallel activities, we first introduce some auxiliary processes with the prefix "para" for each block in the parallel activity, and then call the processes to start by a run statement. Since run is an asynchronous call in Promela, we need some extra mechanism to make the calling process wait until all the called processes have finished running. The auxiliary variables with prefix r_para_aux are introduced for this purpose. We use conditional expressions such as r_para_aux_A == true to block the execution of the calling process. The auxiliary variables such as r_para_aux_A are assigned by true only at the end of each called process, thus achieving the synchronous calling mechanism.

Finally, we add a label such as TaxAdvisor_end: at the end of each process, which is useful for expressing properties during verification.

5.2 Simulation and Verification

We have implemented an automatic translator[1] according to the translation rules using the XSLT (eXtensible Stylesheet Language Transformation) language. In the implementation, we reuse some source codes provided in [13]. We have also implemented a

---

[1] The tool can be downloaded at http://www.is.pku.edu.cn/~fmows/

```
/* Choreography: AnnualStatementSubmission */
mtype = {nil, something, };
chan SubmitAnnualStatementChannel = [0] of { mtype };
chan ReturnNotificationChannel ...
mtype ServiceProviderRole_AS = nil;
mtype ClientRole_AS = nil; ...
mtype ServiceProviderRole_RN = nil; ...
bool Client_para_aux_1 = false;
...
proctype TaxAdvisor() {
  SubmitAnnualStatementChannel ? ServiceProviderRole_AS;
  if
  :: ReturnNotificationChannel ! ServiceProviderRole_RN;
  :: {run TaxAdvisor_para_1();        /* parallel begin */
     run TaxAdvisor_para_2();
     TaxAdvisor_para_aux_1 == true;
     TaxAdvisor_para_aux_2 == true; /* parallel end */
     ReturnTaxAssessmentChannel ? ServiceRequesterRole_TA;
     ReturnProcessedTaxAssessmentChannel ! ServiceProviderRole_PTA; }
  fi;
  ServiceProviderRole_AS = something;
  TaxAdvisor_end: skip; /* ending label */
}
proctype Client() {...}
proctype Municipality() {...}
/* parallel auxiliary proctypes*/
proctype TaxAdvisor_para_1() {
  ReturnNotificationChannel ! ServiceProviderRole_AC;
  TaxAdvisor_para_aux_1 = true;
}
proctype Client_para_1() ...
init { atomic {
    run Client();
    run TaxAdvisor();
    run Municipality();
}}
```

Fig. 2. Promela Code Snippet

Java based user interface as the front-end of the translator. The user can easily translate a WS-CDL specification into a Promela file, and then simulate or verify the Promela processes with SPIN.

With our translator, the user can view the choreography in a graphical and interactive way in the simulator provided in SPIN. A simple simulation scenario of the buyer-seller example given in the WS-CDL specification [15] is shown in Figure 3.

Using LTL (Linear Temporal Logic), we can automatically verify or falsify useful properties of the choreography, such as:

- Every role will always reach the ending state eventually.

```
<> (Client@Client_End && TaxAdvisor@TaxAdvisor_End &&
   Municipality@Municipality_End)
```

- The client can always finish running while receiving the processed tax assessment (PTA) from the municipality. This property is not satisfied by the choreography, since the advisor may refuse the request. SPIN can detect the false property, and generate a counter example to illustrate the reason for the failure in a graphical way.

```
<> (Client@Client_End && ClientRole_PTA != nil)
```

Table 1. Translation to Promela for Role r

skip	skip
$r.x := e$	r_x = e
$ch!e$	ch ! e
$ch?r.x$	ch ? r_x
$p?A$	if :: p -> A :: !p-> skip fi
$p * A$	do :: p -> A :: !p-> break od
$g:A:p$	do :: g -> A; if :: p->skip :: !p->break fi :: !g-> break od
$A; B$	A; B
$g_1 \Rightarrow A \llbracket g_2 \Rightarrow B$	if :: g1 -> A :: g2 -> B fi
$A \sqcap B$	if :: A :: B fi

$A \parallel B$	atomic {
	run r_paraA();
	run r_paraB();
	};
	r_para_aux_A == true;
	r_para_aux_B == true;

- If the processed annual statement (PAS) is forwarded to the municipality, then the client will always receive the processed tax assessment eventually. Such acknowledgement is very useful in designing protocols.

```
[] (ServiceRequesterRole_PAS != nil -> (<> ClientRole_PTA != nil)
```

We have translated and verified several examples, including the buyer-seller example given in the WS-CDL specification [15], the purchase order process given in [12], and the annual tax statement process proposed in [13]. The verification procedure is speedy; for each example, it only costs several seconds on a Pentium 4 machine with 512MB memory.

6   Related Work and Discussion

Formal approaches are useful in analyzing and verifying properties of web services. There are some existing work on specifying and verifying web service compositions. Foster *et al.* [10] discussed a model-based approach to verify web service compositions and developed the tool LTSA that translates BPEL or WS-CDL specification to the FSP process algebra model. Salaun *et al.* developed a process algebra to derive the interactive behavior of a business process out from a BPEL specification [18]. Brogi *et al.* presented the formalization of Web Service Choreography Interface (WSCI) using a process algebra approach(CCS), and discussed the benefits of such formalization [4].

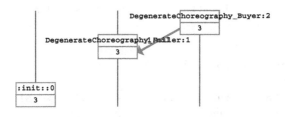

Fig. 3. A Simple Simulation Scenario

Fu *et al.* gave a translation from BPEL to Promela [8]. Aalst *et al.* discussed the different approaches of formalizing BPEL, and listed some challenges including defining a "real" choreography language [20]. Pi4SOA [1] is a tool for designing WS-CDL choreography with a nice graphical user interface, and supports projection from WS-CDL to BPEL or Java. It has a text-based simulator which is relatively difficult to use, and does not provide verification mechanism. There are also works on the formal semantics of web services languages. In our previous work, we presented an operational semantics to a simplified version of BPEL with some important concepts related to fault and compensation handling [9,16].

N.Busi *et al.* [7] proposed a simple choreography language and a simple orchestration language, and defined the concept conformance as a bi-simulation. It is a theoretical work and does not consider tool-based verification. Misra [14] proposed a new programming model for the orchestration of web services. It is relatively far from practice and needs further investigation. Mendling and Hafner [13] proposed a translation algorithm from BPEL to WS-CDL. Since they did not provide a formal model, the correctness of the translation remained to be proved.

The choreography working group of W3C has also recognized the importance of providing a formal grounding for WS-CDL language. Although WS-CDL appears to borrow terminologies from Pi-Calculus, the link to this or any other formalism is not clearly established [17].

We have noticed some debatable issues about the guard expressions during our investigation of WS-CDL. As discussed in Section 4, the semantics for the guards can bring the problem of unconnectedness. A workunit with the form of $r_1.x = 1 : \text{comm} (r_1.x \xrightarrow{c} r_2.y, rec, op) : true$ may be troublesome, since r_1 may send a few messages and then terminate according to the guard $r_1.x = 1$, while r_2 will wait for infinite number of messages because it does not have a guard. Therefore, a deadlock is inevitable. Moreover, even if we define the guard as $r_1.x = 1 \wedge r_2.y = 2$, we are still not sure whether the choreography is deadlock-free, because $r_1.x = 1$ and $r_2.y = 2$ may not become true (or false) simultaneously. Similarly, although the conditional activity $(r_1.x = 1)?(r_2.y := 1)$ is permitted by the specification, it is usually not a desirable choreography. In [1,13], after automatic projection to BPEL, blank guards for those unmentioned roles are generated for the user to fill in, which is obviously not a simple task.

In this paper, we have simplified the problem by adding a requirement that each variable appearing in the guard must be accessible by each role. Some clearer and more understandable structures should be investigated and designed in the future, which is a very interesting future work.

7   Conclusion and Future Work

The goal of the WS-CDL language is to propose a declarative, XML-based language that concerns about global, multi-party, peer-to-peer collaborations in the web services area. One of the important problems related to WS-CDL is the lack of separation between its meta-model and its syntax. A formal semantics can provide validation capabilities for WS-CDL.

In this paper, we define a simple language CDL which covers the features of WS-CDL related to the participant roles and the collaborations among roles. A formal operational semantics for the language is presented. Based on the semantics, we discussed how to 1) project a given choreography to orchestration views, which provides a basis for the implementation of the choreography by code generation; 2) apply model-checking technique to automatically verify the correctness of a given choreography. Given a system, we might check its consistency, and various properties (e.g. no deadlock), and the satisfaction with business constraints. We have developed an automatic translation tool from WS-CDL to the input language of the model checker SPIN. The user only needs to provide a WS-CDL specification, and then do simulation or verification automatically. We have tried several cases using our translation tool, and managed to verify some useful properties.

Towards the semantics and verification of full WS-CDL, CDL focuses on just a few key issues related to web service choreography. The goal in the designing of CDL is to make the proof of its properties as concise as possible, while still capturing the core features of WS-CDL. The features of WS-CDL that CDL does model include roles, variables, activities (control-flow, workunit, skip, assignment, interaction) and choreography. CDL omits some advanced features such as some details of the channel, exception and finalize blocks. Other features missing from CDL include base types (relationship type, participant type, information type), token, token locator, expressions and some basic activities such as silent and perform. Extending CDL to include more features of WS-CDL will be one direction of our further work.

For future work, we want to integrate the exception handling and finalize block mechanisms into our model, which are important facilities to support long-running interaction in WS-CDL. The conformance problem between orchestration and choreography, i.e. whether some given BPEL orchestration processes are consistent with the given WS-CDL choreography model, also needs further investigation.

Acknowledgements. We would like to thank Cai Chao, Dai Xiwu and Pu Geguang for many helpful comments.

References

1. Pi4soa. http://www.pi4soa.org/.
2. World wide web consortium. http://www.w3.org/.

3. Business process execution language for web services, version 1.1. May 2003. http://www-106.ibm.com/developerworks/webservices/library/ws-bpel.
4. A.Brogi, C.Canal, E.Pimentel, and A.Vallecillo. Formalizing web service choreographies. In *Proc. of WS-FM 2004, ENTCS Vol. 105*. Elsevier, 2004.
5. A. Arkin. Business process modeling language. November 2002. http://www.bpmi.org/.
6. A. Barros, M. Dumas, and P. Oaks. A Critical Overview of the Web Services Choreography Description Language. 2005. http://www.bptrends.com.
7. N. Busi, R. Gorrieri, C. Guidi, R. Lucchi, and G. Zavattaro. Choreography and orchestration: a synergic approach for system design. In *Proc. of ICSOC 2005, LNCS 3826*. Springer, 2005.
8. X. Fu, T. Bultan, and J. Su. Analysis of interacting BPEL web services. In *Proc. of WWW'04, pp. 621-630*. ACM Press, 2004.
9. G.Pu, X.Zhao, S.Wang, and Z.Qiu. Towards the semantics and verification of BPEL4WS. In *Proc. of WLFM 2005, ENTCS Vol. 151*. Elsevier, 2006.
10. H.Foster, S.Uchitel, J.Magee, and J.Kramer. Model-based analysis of obligations in web service choreography. In *Proc. of International Conference on Internet and Web Applications and Services 2006*. IEEE Computer Society, 2006.
11. G. J. Holzmann. *The SPIN Model Checker: Primer and Reference Manual*. Addison-Wesley, 2003.
12. H.Yang, X.Zhao, and Z.Qiu. A formal model of web service choreography description language(WS-CDL). Technical report, Preprint of the Institute of Mathematics, March 2006, Peking University, 2006. available at: http://www.is.pku.edu.cn/~fmows/.
13. J. Mendling and M. Hafner. From inter-organizational workflows to process execution: Generating BPEL from WS-CDL. In *Proc. of OTM 2005, LNCS 3762, Springer*, 2005.
14. J. Misra. A programming model for the orchestration of web services. In *Proc. of SEFM'04*. IEEE Computer Society, 2004.
15. N.Kavantzas, D.Burdett, G.Ritzinger, T.Fletcher, Y.Lafon, and C.Barreto. Web Services Choreography Description Language Version 1.0. November 9,2005. http://www.w3.org/TR/2005/CR-ws-cdl-10-20051109/.
16. Z. Qiu, S. Wang, G. Pu, and X. Zhao. Semantics of BPEL4WS-like fault and compensation handling. In *Proc. of FM 2005, LNCS 3582*. Springer, 2005.
17. S. Ross-Talbot. Web services choreography and process algebra. 29th April 2004.
18. G. Salaun, L. Bordeaux, and M. Schaerf. Describing and reasoning on web services using process algebra. In *Proc. of ICWS'04*. IEEE, 2004.
19. S.Thatte. XLANG: Web services for business process design. Technical report, Microsoft, 2001.
20. W.M.P. van der Aalst, M. Dumas, A. H. M. ter Hofstede, N. Russell, H. M. W. Verbeek, and P. Wohed. Life after BPEL? In *Proc. of WS-FM 2005, LNCS 3670*. Springer, 2005.

Author Index

Aiello, Marco   24
Alberti, Marco   58

Baraka, Rebhi   73
Bhargavan, Karthikeyan   88
Biswas, Debmalya   242
Bocchi, Laura   193
Boreale, M.   38
Brogi, Antonio   107
Bruni, Roberto   38, 123

Cacciagrano, Diletta   138
Caires, L.   38
Cambronero, María-Emilia   178
Carpineti, S.   148
Castagna, G.   148
Chesani, Federico   58
Ciabattoni, Agata   24
Corradini, Flavio   138
Cuartero, Fernando   178
Culmone, Rosario   138

De Nicola, R.   38
Decker, Gero   163
Díaz, Gregorio   178
Dumas, Marlon   163
Dustdar, Schahram   24

Fiadeiro, José Luiz   193
Fournet, Cédric   88

Gavanelli, Marco   58
Gilmore, Stephen   214
Gordon, Andrew D.   88

Hongli, Yang   273

Kazhamiakin, Raman   227
Kim, Il-Gon   242

Lamma, Evelina   58
Lanese, Ivan   38, 257

Laneve, C.   148
Lopes, Antónia   193
Loreti, M.   38

Martins, F.   38
Mazzara, Manuel   257
Melgratti, Hernán   123
Mello, Paola   58
Montali, Marco   58
Montanari, U.   38

Padovani, L.   148
Pesic, M.   1
Pistore, Marco   227
Platzer, Christian   24
Popescu, Razvan   107

Ravara, A.   38
Rosenberg, Florian   24

Sangiorgi, D.   38
Schreiner, Wolfgang   73
Storari, Sergio   58

Tobarra, M. Llanos   178
Torroni, Paolo   58
Tribastone, Mirco   214
Tuosto, Emilio   123

Valero, Valentín   178
van der Aalst, W.M.P.   1
Vasconcelos, V.   38
Vito, Leonardo   138

Xiangpeng, Zhao   273

Zaha, Johannes Maria   163
Zavattaro, G.   38
Zongyan, Qiu   273

Lecture Notes in Computer Science

For information about Vols. 1–4061

please contact your bookseller or Springer

Vol. 4185: R. Mizoguchi, Z. Shi, F. Giunchiglia (Eds.), The Semantic Web – ASWC 2006. XX, 778 pages. 2006.

Vol. 4184: M. Bravetti, M. Núñez, G. Zavattaro (Eds.), Web Services and Formal Methods. X, 289 pages. 2006.

Vol. 4180: M. Kohlhase, OMDoc – An Open Markup Format for Mathematical Documents [version 1.2]. XIX, 428 pages. 2006. (Sublibrary LNAI).

Vol. 4176: S.K. Katsikas, J. Lopez, M. Backes, S. Gritzalis, B. Preneel (Eds.), Information Security. XIV, 548 pages. 2006.

Vol. 4168: Y. Azar, T. Erlebach (Eds.), Algorithms – ESA 2006. XVIII, 843 pages. 2006.

Vol. 4163: H. Bersini, J. Carneiro (Eds.), Artificial Immune Systems. XII, 460 pages. 2006.

Vol. 4162: R. Královič, P. Urzyczyn (Eds.), Mathematical Foundations of Computer Science 2006. XV, 814 pages. 2006.

Vol. 4159: J. Ma, H. Jin, L.T. Yang, J.J.-P. Tsai (Eds.), Ubiquitous Intelligence and Computing. XXII, 1190 pages. 2006.

Vol. 4158: L.T. Yang, H. Jin, J. Ma, T. Ungerer (Eds.), Autonomic and Trusted Computing. XIV, 613 pages. 2006.

Vol. 4156: S. Amer-Yahia, Z. Bellahsène, E. Hunt, R. Unland, J.X. Yu (Eds.), Database and XML Technologies. IX, 123 pages. 2006.

Vol. 4155: O. Stock, M. Schaerf (Eds.), Reasoning, Action and Interaction in AI Theories and Systems. XVIII, 343 pages. 2006. (Sublibrary LNAI).

Vol. 4153: N. Zheng, X. Jiang, X. Lan (Eds.), Advances in Machine Vision, Image Processing, and Pattern Analysis. XIII, 506 pages. 2006.

Vol. 4152: Y. Manolopoulos, J. Pokorný, T. Sellis (Eds.), Advances in Databases and Information Systems. XV, 448 pages. 2006.

Vol. 4151: A. Iglesias, N. Takayama (Eds.), Mathematical Software – ICMS 2006. XVII, 452 pages. 2006.

Vol. 4150: M. Dorigo, L.M. Gambardella, M. Birattari, A. Martinoli, R. Poli, T. Stützle (Eds.), Ant Colony Optimization and Swarm Intelligence. XVI, 526 pages. 2006.

Vol. 4146: J.C. Rajapakse, L. Wong, R. Acharya (Eds.), Pattern Recognition in Bioinformatics. XIV, 186 pages. 2006. (Sublibrary LNBI).

Vol. 4144: T. Ball, R.B. Jones (Eds.), Computer Aided Verification. XV, 564 pages. 2006.

Vol. 4139: T. Salakoski, F. Ginter, S. Pyysalo, T. Pahikkala, Advances in Natural Language Processing. XVI, 771 pages. 2006. (Sublibrary LNAI).

Vol. 4138: X. Cheng, W. Li, T. Znati (Eds.), Wireless Algorithms, Systems, and Applications. XVI, 709 pages. 2006.

Vol. 4137: C. Baier, H. Hermanns (Eds.), CONCUR 2006 – Concurrency Theory. XIII, 525 pages. 2006.

Vol. 4136: R.A. Schmidt (Ed.), Relations and Kleene Algebra in Computer Science. XI, 433 pages. 2006.

Vol. 4135: C.S. Calude, M.J. Dinneen, G. Păun, G. Rozenberg, S. Stepney (Eds.), Unconventional Computation. X, 267 pages. 2006.

Vol. 4134: K. Yi (Ed.), Static Analysis. XIII, 443 pages. 2006.

Vol. 4133: J. Gratch, M. Young, R. Aylett, D. Ballin, P. Olivier (Eds.), Intelligent Virtual Agents. XIV, 472 pages. 2006. (Sublibrary LNAI).

Vol. 4130: U. Furbach, N. Shankar (Eds.), Automated Reasoning. XV, 680 pages. 2006. (Sublibrary LNAI).

Vol. 4129: D. McGookin, S. Brewster (Eds.), Haptic and Audio Interaction Design. XII, 167 pages. 2006.

Vol. 4128: W.E. Nagel, W.V. Walter, W. Lehner (Eds.), Euro-Par 2006 Parallel Processing. XXXIII, 1221 pages. 2006.

Vol. 4127: E. Damiani, P. Liu (Eds.), Data and Applications Security XX. X, 319 pages. 2006.

Vol. 4126: P. Barahona, F. Bry, E. Franconi, N. Henze, U. Sattler, Reasoning Web. X, 269 pages. 2006.

Vol. 4124: H. de Meer, J.P. G. Sterbenz (Eds.), Self-Organizing Systems. XIV, 261 pages. 2006.

Vol. 4121: A. Biere, C.P. Gomes (Eds.), Theory and Applications of Satisfiability Testing - SAT 2006. XII, 438 pages. 2006.

Vol. 4119: C. Dony, J.L. Knudsen, A. Romanovsky, A. Tripathi (Eds.), Advanced Topics in Exception Handling Components. X, 302 pages. 2006.

Vol. 4117: C. Dwork (Ed.), Advances in Cryptology - CRYPTO 2006. XIII, 621 pages. 2006.

Vol. 4116: R. De Prisco, M. Yung (Eds.), Security and Cryptography for Networks. XI, 366 pages. 2006.

Vol. 4115: D.-S. Huang, K. Li, G.W. Irwin (Eds.), Computational Intelligence and Bioinformatics, Part III. XXI, 803 pages. 2006. (Sublibrary LNBI).

Vol. 4114: D.-S. Huang, K. Li, G.W. Irwin (Eds.), Computational Intelligence, Part II. XXVII, 1337 pages. 2006. (Sublibrary LNAI).

Vol. 4113: D.-S. Huang, K. Li, G.W. Irwin (Eds.), Intelligent Computing, Part I. XXVII, 1331 pages. 2006.

Vol. 4112: D.Z. Chen, D. T. Lee (Eds.), Computing and Combinatorics. XIV, 528 pages. 2006.

Vol. 4111: F.S. de Boer, M.M. Bonsangue, S. Graf, W.-P. de Roever (Eds.), Formal Methods for Components and Objects. VIII, 447 pages. 2006.

Vol. 4110: J. Díaz, K. Jansen, J.D.P. Rolim, U. Zwick (Eds.), Approximation, Randomization, and Combinatorial Optimization. XII, 522 pages. 2006.

Vol. 4109: D.-Y. Yeung, J.T. Kwok, A. Fred, F. Roli, D. de Ridder (Eds.), Structural, Syntactic, and Statistical Pattern Recognition. XXI, 939 pages. 2006.

Vol. 4108: J.M. Borwein, W.M. Farmer (Eds.), Mathematical Knowledge Management. VIII, 295 pages. 2006. (Sublibrary LNAI).

Vol. 4106: T.R. Roth-Berghofer, M.H. Göker, H. A. Güvenir (Eds.), Advances in Case-Based Reasoning. XIV, 566 pages. 2006. (Sublibrary LNAI).

Vol. 4104: T. Kunz, S.S. Ravi (Eds.), Ad-Hoc, Mobile, and Wireless Networks. XII, 474 pages. 2006.

Vol. 4099: Q. Yang, G. Webb (Eds.), PRICAI 2006: Trends in Artificial Intelligence. XXVIII, 1263 pages. 2006. (Sublibrary LNAI).

Vol. 4098: F. Pfenning (Ed.), Term Rewriting and Applications. XIII, 415 pages. 2006.

Vol. 4097: X. Zhou, O. Sokolsky, L. Yan, E.-S. Jung, Z. Shao, Y. Mu, D.C. Lee, D. Kim, Y.-S. Jeong, C.-Z. Xu (Eds.), Emerging Directions in Embedded and Ubiquitous Computing. XXVII, 1034 pages. 2006.

Vol. 4096: E. Sha, S.-K. Han, C.-Z. Xu, M.H. Kim, L.T. Yang, B. Xiao (Eds.), Embedded and Ubiquitous Computing. XXIV, 1170 pages. 2006.

Vol. 4095: S. Nolfi, G. Baldassare, R. Calabretta, D. Marocco, D. Parisi, J.C. T. Hallam, O. Miglino, J.-A. Meyer (Eds.), From Animals to Animats 9. XV, 869 pages. 2006. (Sublibrary LNAI).

Vol. 4094: O. H. Ibarra, H.-C. Yen (Eds.), Implementation and Application of Automata. XIII, 291 pages. 2006.

Vol. 4093: X. Li, O.R. Zaïane, Z. Li (Eds.), Advanced Data Mining and Applications. XXI, 1110 pages. 2006. (Sublibrary LNAI).

Vol. 4092: J. Lang, F. Lin, J. Wang (Eds.), Knowledge Science, Engineering and Management. XV, 664 pages. 2006. (Sublibrary LNAI).

Vol. 4091: G.-Z. Yang, T. Jiang, D. Shen, L. Gu, J. Yang (Eds.), Medical Imaging and Augmented Reality. XIII, 399 pages. 2006.

Vol. 4090: S. Spaccapietra, K. Aberer, P. Cudré-Mauroux (Eds.), Journal on Data Semantics VI. XI, 211 pages. 2006.

Vol. 4089: W. Löwe, M. Südholt (Eds.), Software Composition. X, 339 pages. 2006.

Vol. 4088: Z.-Z. Shi, R. Sadananda (Eds.), Agent Computing and Multi-Agent Systems. XVII, 827 pages. 2006. (Sublibrary LNAI).

Vol. 4087: F. Schwenker, S. Marinai (Eds.), Artificial Neural Networks in Pattern Recognition. IX, 299 pages. 2006. (Sublibrary LNAI).

Vol. 4085: J. Misra, T. Nipkow, E. Sekerinski (Eds.), FM 2006: Formal Methods. XV, 620 pages. 2006.

Vol. 4084: M.A. Wimmer, H.J. Scholl, Å. Grönlund, K.V. Andersen (Eds.), Electronic Government. XV, 353 pages. 2006.

Vol. 4083: S. Fischer-Hübner, S. Furnell, C. Lambrinoudakis (Eds.), Trust and Privacy in Digital Business. XIII, 243 pages. 2006.

Vol. 4082: K. Bauknecht, B. Pröll, H. Werthner (Eds.), E-Commerce and Web Technologies. XIII, 243 pages. 2006.

Vol. 4081: A. M. Tjoa, J. Trujillo (Eds.), Data Warehousing and Knowledge Discovery. XVII, 578 pages. 2006.

Vol. 4080: S. Bressan, J. Küng, R. Wagner (Eds.), Database and Expert Systems Applications. XXI, 959 pages. 2006.

Vol. 4079: S. Etalle, M. Truszczyński (Eds.), Logic Programming. XIV, 474 pages. 2006.

Vol. 4077: M.-S. Kim, K. Shimada (Eds.), Geometric Modeling and Processing - GMP 2006. XVI, 696 pages. 2006.

Vol. 4076: F. Hess, S. Pauli, M. Pohst (Eds.), Algorithmic Number Theory. X, 599 pages. 2006.

Vol. 4075: U. Leser, F. Naumann, B. Eckman (Eds.), Data Integration in the Life Sciences. XI, 298 pages. 2006. (Sublibrary LNBI).

Vol. 4074: M. Burmester, A. Yasinsac (Eds.), Secure Mobile Ad-hoc Networks and Sensors. X, 193 pages. 2006.

Vol. 4073: A. Butz, B. Fisher, A. Krüger, P. Olivier (Eds.), Smart Graphics. XI, 263 pages. 2006.

Vol. 4072: M. Harders, G. Székely (Eds.), Biomedical Simulation. XI, 216 pages. 2006.

Vol. 4071: H. Sundaram, M. Naphade, J.R. Smith, Y. Rui (Eds.), Image and Video Retrieval. XII, 547 pages. 2006.

Vol. 4070: C. Priami, X. Hu, Y. Pan, T.Y. Lin (Eds.), Transactions on Computational Systems Biology V. IX, 129 pages. 2006. (Sublibrary LNBI).

Vol. 4069: F.J. Perales, R.B. Fisher (Eds.), Articulated Motion and Deformable Objects. XV, 526 pages. 2006.

Vol. 4068: H. Schärfe, P. Hitzler, P. Øhrstrøm (Eds.), Conceptual Structures: Inspiration and Application. XI, 455 pages. 2006. (Sublibrary LNAI).

Vol. 4067: D. Thomas (Ed.), ECOOP 2006 – Object-Oriented Programming. XIV, 527 pages. 2006.

Vol. 4066: A. Rensink, J. Warmer (Eds.), Model Driven Architecture – Foundations and Applications. XII, 392 pages. 2006.

Vol. 4065: P. Perner (Ed.), Advances in Data Mining. XI, 592 pages. 2006. (Sublibrary LNAI).

Vol. 4064: R. Büschkes, P. Laskov (Eds.), Detection of Intrusions and Malware & Vulnerability Assessment. X, 195 pages. 2006.

Vol. 4063: I. Gorton, G.T. Heineman, I. Crnkovic, H.W. Schmidt, J.A. Stafford, C.A. Szyperski, K. Wallnau (Eds.), Component-Based Software Engineering. XI, 394 pages. 2006.

Vol. 4062: G. Wang, J.F. Peters, A. Skowron, Y. Yao (Eds.), Rough Sets and Knowledge Technology. XX, 810 pages. 2006. (Sublibrary LNAI).